An Ethical Turn in Governance

An Ethical Turn in Governance

The Call for a New Development Narrative

Pearson A. Broome

LEXINGTON BOOKS
Lanham • Boulder • New York • London

Published by Lexington Books
An imprint of The Rowman & Littlefield Publishing Group, Inc.
4501 Forbes Boulevard, Suite 200, Lanham, Maryland 20706
www.rowman.com

6 Tinworth Street, London SE11 5AL, United Kingdom

British Library Cataloguing in Publication Information Available

Library of Congress Cataloging-in-Publication Data Available

ISBN 978-1-4985-9197-3 (cloth : alk. paper)
ISBN 978-1-4985-9198-0 (electronic)

*To my Heavenly Father who granted me the strength
and perseverance to complete this,
to my beloved mother and sister, and
in loving memory of my father.*

Contents

Contents

List of Figures and Tables

FIGURES

TABLES

TEXTBOX

Preface

What makes government effective and why should good governance and ethics be of concern are among the most important questions facing any society seeking a resolution to both. Governance is important because it determines whose needs are recognized and catered to and how public resources are allocated. It is a mechanism where state and non-state actors can interact to tackle societal issues. The outcomes include a set of checks and balances that helps to protect the welfare of the governed, their right to engage in decisions that affect them, and the collective experience of solving problems with fellow citizens. Particularly important elements of governance would include the political institutions of a society (collective decision-making, checks on politicians, and on powerful interest groups), state capacity (state ability to provide public goods), and regulation of *economic institutions* (how the state encourages or discourages economic activity by various actors). Likewise, how firms interact with these broad clusters of institutions in the context of corporate governance is intimately linked to economic growth and governance in general (Acemoglu, 2008:1; Crudas and Rutherford, 2010). Governance therefore involves the political, social, economic, and cultural orientation of institutions grounded in a dynamic conception of development.[1] Aside from polemics, the call for an infusion of ethics into the practice of governance is in response to the perceived failures of the macro coordination of market and government leaving many of our citizens nationally and regionally intensely disenchanted with the practice and prospects of government and governance. Regrettably, our inability to gainsay these inextricably linked ideas will present even more examples of countries replete with bad government policies, poor implementation, and ethical failures.

Herein lies the raison d'etre for this research. Throughout CARICOM the reoccurring image is one of a disintegrating civil society pushing leaders into an epistemological and ontological crisis in governance. The premise and direction of this research was fundamentally concerned with advocating for a conceptual turn to ethics in governance to enhance social progress and human emancipation in our societies. This book contextualizes the contemporary challenges to and the ramifications for CARICOM's governance and, by extension, development agenda. It invokes those concerned to recognize the threats to the region's sustainability and to [re]conceptualise the focus of governance within the region, this time around, with an emphasis on ethical considerations that should be systematically brought to bear upon public policy options and solutions.

NOTE

1. There is no singular definition of "good governance" although it has become one of the most widely used concepts in the contemporary political lexicon. More than democracy or rule by the people, however defined, it is popular democracy in its broadest sense, plus good political, financial and administrative management. It also assumes a high level of transparency and morality in public affairs, as well as a politically vibrant civil society that interacts continuously with state officials (Ryan, 2001: 74). The UN Development Program, in its "Strategy Paper on Governance" (1995), defines good governance as: the exercise of political, economic and administrative authority to manage a nation's affairs. It is a broad concept that encompasses the organizational structures and activities of central, regional and local government, the parliament and the judiciary. Importantly, the concept of governance also incorporates the institutions, organizations and individuals that comprise civil society, insofar as they actively participate in and influence the shaping of public policy that affects people's lives (Ryan 2001:75). As a concept, good governance is more fundamental to the question of how in a modern society democracy can be adapted to help countries resolve problems (OECD 1996). Appendix 1 presents a compendium of recent definitions from official and scholarly sources indicating the concept's complexity. While there are commonalities across these definitions—for example, governance deals with institutional process and the rules of the game for authoritative decision-making—they are also significant differences in specificity and normativity.

Acknowledgments

What started initially as a concept paper to be submitted to a journal has become a book. I would like to thank the editorial and production team at Lexington Books, Joseph, Bryndee, and Alison for accepting this project and seeing it through to its completion. Without their initial interest and support from the start, this book might have not seen the light of day. Sincere thanks and gratitude also goes to Andy Taitt for copy editing, proofing, and for being receptive and tolerant to my sometimes demanding interventions but still displaying a generous and healthy sense of humor. I am also grateful to the anonymous reviewers for their constructive comments, feedback, and recommendations of interesting texts to complement and enhance the arguments presented throughout this book. Finally, I wish to thank the authors and publishers several of whom were welcoming to the ideas and arguments put forward in the text by gratefully acknowledging my queries and requests and allowing me permission to reproduce copyright material in this book and on whose work I was able to build.

With several major libraries withering from the drastic cutbacks in funds and inaccessibility to their protected resources, the writing process benefited from the idea and ideal of open access publications allowing access to global knowledge. I am appreciative and indeed a celebrant of such an approach to the dissemination of knowledge.

To those who formed the fulcrum of my intellectual journey how can I express the immense sincere gratitude and support to you all without being invidious? Thank you!

Every effort has been made to trace copyright holders and to obtain their permission for the use of copyright material. If any have been inadvertently omitted, the author would be grateful to be notified at the earliest opportunity to make the necessary arrangements so that any corrections could be incorporated in future reprints or editions of this book.

Pearson A. Broome

Chapter 1

The Vulnerability of Governance in the Caribbean

Threats to Sustainability

INTRODUCTION: A REGION AT
THE POLITICAL CROSSROADS

Let me state from the outset this introductory chapter is unusually but necessarily lengthy. To justify an ethical turn to governance, it follows that the first task would be to identify and to conceptualize the politics, society, and economy of our region[1] by observing particularly, the threats to democracy and political stability from the inequality of opportunity that would make transparent the conditions within which the poor or excluded live. Multiple forces are at work within the region, some of its own making, others not, but the root cause of these challenges is the embeddedness of the region within capitalist modernization with its de-unionization, and rapid global competition precipitated and facilitated by actors and their actions within webs of relationships and responsibilities—often with disparities cultivated by conflicting responsibilities. As a consequence, I demonstrate in this chapter the need for injecting into society an ethical consciousness that would call *inter alia* for improving well-being, reducing inequality, empowering people to engage in their own development decision-making, realizing human rights and cultural freedoms, and minimizing corruption that must serve for reflection that lie at the nexus of the issues that this book seeks to address. This is because the present organization of knowledge and experience embodied in the major institutions of societies makes it extremely difficult and may even preclude the ability——to perceive, consider, and address the deeper challenges inherent in fashioning the development of an ethical understanding and action in governance. And as well for pragmatic purposes, the chapter details to a non-Caribbean reader broadly defined, what this region must contend with so that similar developing states may draw ameliorative lessons from this book. This chapter also presents the methodological praxis applied to interrogate the research problem before interweaving the objective justifications and the significance of this work to similar countries experiencing a range of corruptive factors at all social levels. The end result is that this chapter is summary panoptic, as well as synthesis, in ways that defies simple.

Once referenced as a quiet, pastoral region of beauty and warmth, endearing social behavior and rich cultural traditions in the creative and performing arts, modern institutional structures with representative democratic principles, state governance, and market economies (West Indies Commission, 1992; Sutton, 1999; Transparency International, 2005; *The Economist*, 2008a, 2008b) the Caribbean is currently on a shift away from public-spirited values toward those that stress materialistic work-oriented and private satisfaction, leisure, and the need for aesthetic self-fulfillment. There have been repeated denunciations and constant frustrated cries from representative voices to placate and resolve an entrenched culture of lawlessness with its disabling attitudes upon structures that have emerged on the societal landscape (*Guyana Chronicle*, 2009; Singh, 2012; UNDP, 2012; Caribbean360, 2018; BBC, 2019). These values are intergenerational but worryingly more pronounced in the younger generation. The fairness, probity, equity, justice, the rule of law, freedom of speech, and the rights of the individual, that once strengthened these democracies, are being eroded within a region in flux in which dangerous new fault lines have emerged (Singh, 2012).

Indeed, not a day goes by without extensive media coverage of some form of corruption, perceived or real, be it deafening cries from the public concerning the lack of productivity within the established government bureaucracy, increasing incidences of fraud and unethical behavior of public employees, or the reneging on promises to the electorate by holders of public office (Jessop, 2012; Prince, 2012; Caribbean 360, 2017; *Barbados Today*, 2017; Mishcon de Reya, 2017; Keefer and Vlaicu, 2017; Transparency International, 2018). In our inherited postcolonial Westminster style of governance, suspected transgressors if apprehended, are subjected to supposedly potent though ultimately innocuous, "commissions or omissions of enquiry," to ascertain more for form than for substance the reasons for the miscarriage of justice. Typically after such "trials," the recommendations therein are regarded as post-mortems and the cynicism emerges like a reflexive instinctive afterthought of their value and worth. In turn, the questions arise whether these various commissions of enquiry have led to the introduction of new laws, regulations, and codes of conduct to deal with the underlying unethical behavior of public officials and holders of public office with the intention of eviscerating or preventing further occurrences of the alleged acts of impropriety. And, perhaps most importantly, are such commissions of enquiry an effective use of public resources? Another even more disconcerting question after such exercises is whether the true intention of these commissions is to minimize the repetition of corruption and conflicts of interest by managing and effectively mitigating the deviant and recalcitrant behavior of individuals, employees, organizations, firms, and governments and/or are they just purposed by governments to serve merely as elaborate ruses aimed at distracting the public and delivering the inevitable outcomes of doing nothing? In such a context, it has become increasingly difficult to hold public servants accountable for their activities with Jones (1992b, cited in Minto-Coy and Berman, 2016: 46) noting the role of poor work ethics and the existence of weak institutions in encouraging administrative corruption. Jones also describes features of Jamaican (and Caribbean) society that give rise to conditions that facilitate corruption and poor governance, including a political culture underlined by low levels of trust and declines in the stock of social capital (cited in Minto-Coy and Berman, 2016: 46 see also Jones et al., 2016). Sutton has also noted the role of small size with corruption featuring in the form of nepotism and patronage (cited in Minto-Coy and Berman, 2016: 46; Obrien, 2015).

From the various pre-independence experiments, through the creation of the West Indies Federation, the Caribbean Free Trade Area (CARIFTA) and of more recent vintage and of immediate interest to this research, the establishment in 1973 of the Caribbean Community and Common Market (CARICOM), the introduction of the Caribbean Single Market and Economy (CSME), the establishment of the Organization of Eastern Caribbean States (OECS), the Caribbean Court of Justice (CCJ), and the Eastern Caribbean Central Bank (ECCB), the Caribbean has made strides in constructing a range of institutional arrangements aimed to engender a comprehensive mode of regional governance. This regional framework was the vehicle for gradually deepening a wider intergovernmental regional network to stabilize the political economy of these countries during challenging times. These efforts saw the further establishment of a range of complementary agencies such as the Caribbean Regional Negotiating Machinery (CRNM)—an agency of the Caribbean Forum (CARIFORUM) a sub-grouping of African, Caribbean, and Pacific States, and the Association of Caribbean States (ACS), the latter an attempt to create linkages between the Caribbean islands and their Central and South American neighbors bordering the Caribbean Sea. Both institutions were designed to play a vital technical role in managing the myriad bilateral and multilateral negotiations in which the region has recently found itself. Still, despite these attempts to augment regional unity to mitigate the deleterious effects of the global economy, observers of Caribbean political development do not see that this apparatus of formal regional and subregional organizations has distinguished itself as an effective set of structures. Neither on their own nor collectively do these institutions represent an optimal approach to managing West Indian affairs and interests in a world which has become increasingly unsympathetic (Payne and Bishop, 2010: 1; Girvan, 2011).

In 1996, in an effort to ameliorate this state of affairs, the CARICOM Secretariat established as a possible corrective measure, the Assembly of Caribbean Parliamentarians, to provide qualitative enhanced guidance to the development of regional norms for good governance. Shortly thereafter in 1998 the Charter of Civil Society was enacted to describe the duties of public servants, according to the major principles of the "Code of administrative procedure."[2] The charter sought, *inter alia*, to ensure continuing respect for internationally recognized civil, political, economic, social, and cultural rights; to uphold the right of the people to make political choices; to promote, foster, and maintain racial harmony and freedom of religion and to respect and strengthen the fundamental elements in civil society; and to implement all appropriate measures to ensure good governance that is just, open, and accountable. The charter document also provided for national committees to compile reports to advise the Conference of CARICOM Heads of Governments (through the secretary general) on measures adopted for, or progress achieved in compliance with the provisions of the charter. The committees are also expected to indicate and report on breaches of or non-compliance with the provisions of the charter by the state or by the social partners. The committees are to consist of representatives of the state, other social partners, and other persons of high moral character or recognized competence in their respective fields of endeavor (Ryan, 2001: 94–95; Edmunds, 2015), but with only a short text on the values and lines of conduct for public officials. The impact of both these mechanisms as regionally inspired instruments on enhancing good governance has been imperceptible. Neither has served to dispel the malaise that is, if anything, now greater than it was at the turn of the decade (Girvan, 2011). Trinidad and Tobago's Integrity in Public Life Act requires filings from public servants but this requirement is largely ignored with little consequences or penalty. It is with good reason then that Hall and Benn assert that the development of monitoring, control, review, and (importantly) enforcement systems has been underdeveloped (2003, cited in Minto-Coy et al., 2016: 46) with Maingot (2004), noting the existence of ill-formed institutions as a contributor to corruption in the region (cited in Minto-Coy et al., 2016: 46). As such, the number of measures undertaken to improve accountability and reduce corruption, including codes of ethics and anti-corruption legislation, have done little to improve practice on the ground (Minto-Coy and Berman, 2016: 46).

The political dysfunction that exists today also has as much to do with the system in which our leaders are asked to govern. After over fifty years of the adoption of a Westminster system of government, some scholars have argued the urgent need for an expanded and updated analysis of its history in the Caribbean. One notable project is a series of conferences by the University College of London, to consider how the political model inherited from Britain has been adapted to the conditions of the Caribbean, its impact on Caribbean democracy, and the challenges the model has faced over the period of independence (Smith, 2014; See also Girvan, 2011, 2015). The Organization of American States (OAS) has also questioned the quality of institutional arrangements for good governance in the inherited Westminster system practiced in most former British dependencies severely criticizing its *modus operandi* but particular drawing attention to its "excessive authority and overwhelming power constitutionally granted to the prime minister"; "administrative concentration of power due to the ineffective separation of powers between the executive and the legislature"; and consequently "the erosion of judicial independence due to infringement by the executive" (OAS, 2002). Further criticisms have been leveled at the outcomes of the electoral system based on the first-past-the-post voting procedural process that often does not accurately reflect election results in ethnically charged environments pregnant with conflict and often characterized by excessive partisanship and polarization. Though not rejecting the "Westminster system" outright, the prevailing view of the OAS was that there were serious and substantial reforms that could counter the excessive rules, regulations, policies, and officialdom to correct or at least alleviate imbalances and deficiencies in the current governance system (OAS, 2002; Girvan, 2015).

Besides these, other criticisms have been recorded. The region is left to cope with a political culture of continuing vapid political rhetoric characterized mainly by mudslinging, sensationalism, and a cornucopia of election campaign promises every five years, few of which are kept (Girvan, 2015: 100). Amid worsening social, economic, and political challenges there are no new governance initiatives of significance with successive governing leaders maintaining seeming contempt for structured consultations with constitutional, parliamentary opposition leaders (Nation News, 2016). Structured dialogue between a CARICOM head of government and the Opposition Leader is simply not a normal feature of what passes for good governance in our regional economic integration movement. Political instability and apathy are a given. Government and opposition alike do everything to try to prevent the other from succeeding. Amid this quite disappointing party political/ governance scenario, no CARICOM head of government seems seriously interested in, or willing to exercise any new, relevant initiative to avoid the further downward slide of a regional integration movement now in its forty-third year of existence (Girvan, 2011; Quinn, 2015; Singh, 2016). The parliament and the judiciary have become toys of the legislative branch. The ruling party becomes the executive arm of the executive branch of government with the cabinet and the party's executive being indistinguishable. Independent voting by parliamentary backbenchers is forbidden, as the parliamentarians owe their seats to the leader even in those countries, which use the constituency system (Smith, 2013; Ryan, 1999; Sutton, 1999; Ryan and Bissessar, 2002; Girvan, 2015). Nearly everywhere throughout the region there are rumblings—mainly from people, and not just political oppositions—against infrequent meetings of parliament; lack of information to and openness with the press and publics; severe censorship on the freedom of expression embedded in the silent specter of a culture of impunity; and the perennial debate of partisan control of state-owned as well as "private" media (Ramphal, 1991; Ryan and Bissessar, 2002; IFEX-ALC, 2012; Mills, 2014; Girvan, 2015; Bridglal, 2019).[3]

Governance and politics have become a brutish war of attrition that consumes everything including nation-building and economic development (Smith, 2014). This is evidenced in the Commonwealth of Dominica where the opposition levied charges of corruption against the government in connection with the sale of Dominican citizenship through the Citizenship by Investment Program (CBIP). A number of non-Dominicans traveling on Dominican diplomatic passports were arrested internationally (*World Tribune*, 2017a, 2017b). Protests quickly ensued, organized by the island's opposition parties and with demonstrators demanding the resignation of the prime minister, and degenerated into violence with thirty-two arrests and widespread loss and damage to businesses. Predictably, the protests prompted further acrimonious charge and countercharge over responsibility for the protests and the veracity of alleged claims concerning the revealed details of an attempt by opposition parties to "seize the seat of power of government." There was swift dismissal of this by the Opposition Leader as yet "another lie" by the prime minister to win the sympathy of Dominicans. The affair ended with a promise of the continued investigation by the police of the veracity of each claimant (*World Tribune*, 2017a, 2017b).

This political atmosphere characterized by bitterness and frustration rather than by tolerance, compromise, and value integration toward a system of politically progressive processes, has been honestly gained from the legacy of colonization that created a host of [un]intended consequences. It is important to [re]iterate that neither colonialism nor the struggle for political independence prepared a post-independence Caribbean to be egalitarian societies practicing good governance and true democracy. Indeed, both colonialism and the independence movement were improper preparations for real democracy and good ethics in governance, leading instead to a post-independence of mistrust and self-righteousness and the evolution of an elite political leadership intent on replacing foreign rule with self-rule. Invariably, and ironically, that elite emulated the colonial potentates they had successfully dislodged, perpetuating the very ills that had imprisoned their societies (Diescho, 2000;

see also Sutton, 1999; Hinds, 2008; Gill, 2012; Agbude and Etete, 2013; Jones et al., 2016). The political elite both helped shape and benefited from such practices, and consensually with the independence constitutionalists wanted no other form of government than the Westminster model, regarding it not as foreign derived but as autochthonous. In fact, major constitutional reviews of the approaches to constitutional order have taken place in comparatively few states. From these, major constitutional change has been cautious and incremental resulting in relatively modest proposals for reform that in nearly every case, has attempted to improve the system by adapting it to Caribbean realities. There has been little, if any questioning of fundamentals, and constitutional reforms have consequently been conservative with a small "c" directed at perfecting the system with its essence preserved intact (Sutton, 1999: 69; Girvan, 2015; Minto-Coy and Berman, 2016; Jones et al., 2016). Already, the critical difference between yesterday and today is the sense of "powerlessness" that has replaced the sense of "possibility" that came with independence (Ramphal, 1991; Broome, Hinds, et al., 2014).

The 2013 UWI/UNDP Democratic Governance Assessment project was conducted in Antigua and Barbuda and Barbados to generate comprehensive, comparable, country-specific, disaggregated, and accurate evidence-based indicators of the quality of governance in fundamental democratic principles and shared common values that should be enshrined in the heritage of any civilized society.[4] The report concluded unsurprisingly, that democratic governance is under threat of erosion in myriad ways and is perceived as inadequate. It further showed varying facets of the critical values essential for effective democratic governance in almost every disaggregated category surveyed with generally less than 40 percent of respondents viewing these markers of a flourishing democracy as "good," or "very good." Less than 50 percent of those surveyed generally considered the prevailing structures and systemic features in place for good governance as "average" (or were "neutral").

As if these results were not cause for alarm, another critically important revelation acknowledged within the report was the inability of political parties to repair the damage to every institutional facet of their existence if they are to derive and retain some element of legitimacy and authority. The survey found that political parties in both countries under review were weak in their management, choice of representatives, inclusion of all sectional interests, and their philosophical moorings. The report also highlighted that similar self-correcting mechanisms would also be necessary to repair the damaged image of the judicial system. Another finding of the report spoke to the importance of an urgent and committed approach to redressing the prolonged polarization between the power-brokers (businessmen and political leaders) and the vulnerable groups in the societies who believe their holistic personal development

Table 1.1 Corruption Perception Index 2016 for the CARICOM Grouping

2016 Rank	Country	2016 Score	2015 Score	2014 Score	2013 Score	Region
24	The Commonwealth of the Bahamas	66	N/A	71	71	Americas
31	Barbados	61	N/A	74	75	Americas
35	Saint Lucia	60	N/A	N/A	71	Americas
35	Saint Vincent and the Grenadines	60	N/A	67	62	Americas
38	Dominica	59	N/A	58	58	Americas
46	Grenada	56	N/A	N/A	N/A	Americas
64	Suriname	45	36	36	36	Americas
83	Jamaica	39	41	38	38	Americas
101	Trinidad and Tobago	35	39	38	38	Americas
108	Guyana	34	29	30	27	Americas
159	Haiti	20	17	19	19	Americas
*120	Dominican Republic	36	33	29	29	Americas

* Associate Status and Member of CARIFORUM.
Source: Corruption Perception Index 2016 for Caribbean Countries of the CARICOM Grouping: Data Adopted from Transparency International. Available at www.transparency.org/news/feature/americas.

is undermined and undervalued within a political, economic, and social climate inimical to their immediate needs. Another general sentiment expressed toward the functioning of democracy "recorded [a] strong sense of systemic powerlessness, resignation even, that Caribbean residents seem to feel towards the status-quo." The report was therefore instructive in recommending that "Democratic governance is in need of innovative thinking to correct its decline in the Caribbean if it is to foster sustainable development within our societies." It continued, "The issue ought not to be any longer of what is to be reformed? But rather, when will the reform begin." (Broome, Hinds, et al., 2014)

This diagnosis is not atypical of these two states for it concurs with that proffered by Transparency International in their annual 2016 report on perception of corruption in countries of the region. Of the 176 countries reviewed by the organization only 5 of the 15 countries of the CARICOM grouping made it into the top quartile of the least corrupt countries. The Commonwealth of the Bahamas at number 24 received the highest ranking while Haiti at number 159 was ranked the lowest (see table 1.1 for rankings).

STRUCTURAL ECONOMIC CONSTRAINTS ON GOVERNANCE

The quality of governance has also been threatened more recently by the reverberations from the global financial and economic crisis of 2008

(Girvan, 2011). Declining exports, induced harsh terms of trade [re]configurations, downturns in investment activity in critical economic growth sectors such as tourism, financial services, construction and bauxite, along with non-performing loans (NPLs) have all *inter alia* led to contracting GDP in nearly all countries of the CARICOM region (Wigglesworth, 2016). While it is widely accepted that most developing countries need to borrow to finance their economic development, a public debt/GDP ratio of over 50 to 60 percent is generally considered high and close to the debt tipping point. Beyond this, such indebtedness for an extended period of time exposes the financial system to the threat of debt default, and acts as a drag on economic growth (Girvan, 2011; Hurley, 2013; English, 2013; Wigglesworth, 2016). At the end of 2015, nine Caribbean states—Antigua and Barbuda, Barbados, Belize, Dominica, Grenada, Jamaica, St. Kitts and Nevis, St. Lucia, and St. Vincent and the Grenadines—had surpassed this stage and were considered in the distress range of between 60 to 90 percent (see figure 1.1).

Three years later in 2018, the Caribbean Development Bank painted a no less compelling picture of the worsening public debt burdening these states with Trinidad and Tobago and Suriname succumbing to similar travails as seen in figure 1.2.

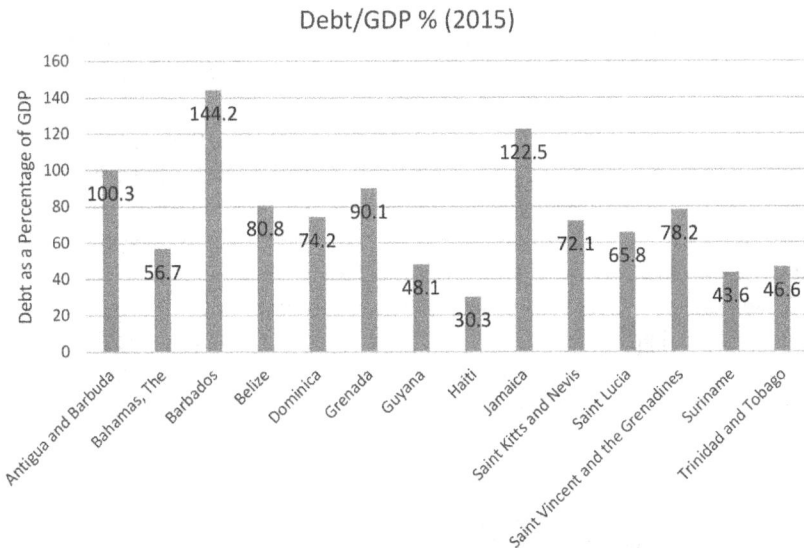

Figure 1.1 **DEBT/GDP Ratio by Percentage 2015.** *Source*: Caribbean Development Bank, (2019). GDP/Debt ratios for individual country economic reviews from Antigua and Barbuda to Trinidad and Tobago. Bridgetown: Caribbean Development Bank. Available at www.caribank.org/publications-and-resources.

Debt/GDP % (2018)

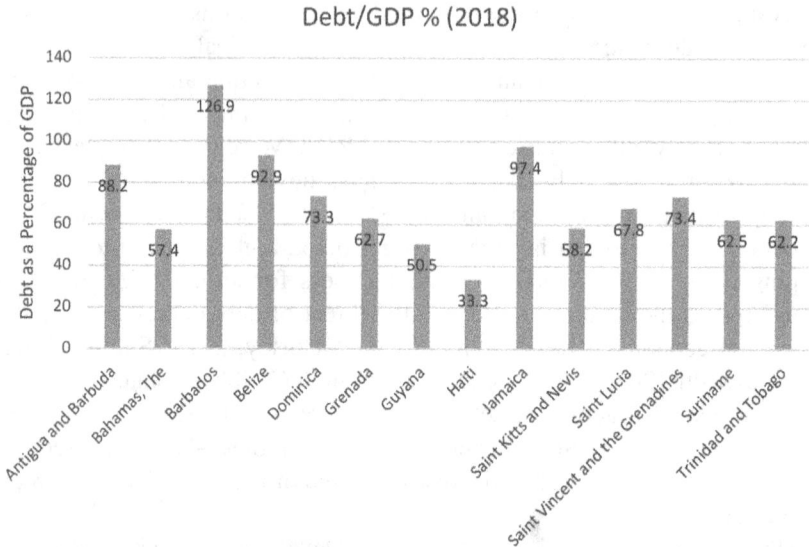

Figure 1.2 DEBT/GDP Ratio by Percentage 2018. *Source*: Caribbean Development Bank, (2018 A). Individual country economic reviews from Antigua and Barbuda to Trinidad and Tobago. Bridgetown: Caribbean Development Bank. Available at www.c aribank.org/publications-and-resources.

This bourgeoning debt scenario has made it more difficult and expensive for already struggling governments without coherent economic plans to borrow on the international capital markets to finance their large fiscal deficits (IMF, 2015; CDB, 2018b; ECLAC, 2018). Incidentally, the stagnant growth and unsustainable levels of public debt also reflect deep-rooted competitiveness problems being recorded by these countries, several of which already rank poorly on the World Economic Forum's Global Competitiveness Index (Rambarran, 2017; CDB, 2018b; ECLAC, 2018).

A lack of capital, whether natural, human, political, technical, or financial, has represented an enduring barrier to the implementation of critical decisions of governance. The rank and file, more so the poor and the vulnerable face uncertain years of austerity, government starved social welfare programs, and precarious employment accompanied by its usual corollary of increased criminal activity (Legarde, 2014; Beaton et al., 2017), induced by a wave of "structural adjustment" programs of varying intensity while simultaneously weakening the Caribbean state (Hall and Benn, 2004; Girvan, 2015; Levitt, 2018). Economic dependence on remittances as an important source of financial support to cover basic needs in education, health care, housing, and small businesses has displaced the nation-state's welfarism that shaped post-independence domestic policy and has become the fastest growing source of foreign currency earnings in every Caribbean country (Girvan, 2015: 102, 2011). According to the *Inter-American Development Bank Report* on Latin America and the Caribbean, in absolute terms remittance inflows to the Caribbean in 2012 equaled US$8.3 billion. In the case of Jamaica, for example, it represented a rise of 0.6 percent from the previous year to US$2.04 billion (IADB, 2012, cited in Broome, 2015). Remittances continue to play a central role in supporting national economies through providing governments across almost the entire region with additional foreign exchange, constituting more than 10 percent of the gross domestic product in Haiti, Guyana, and Jamaica (Jessop, 2013, cited in Broome, 2015).

LOOKING IN AND OUT:
THE CHALLENGES OF PUBLIC POLICY

There is also genuine concern that governments in the region have taken over more functions than their resources can cover, consequently overstraining the limited capacity of their state apparatus and impairing their overall ability for governance. Regrettably, governments seem to be all at sea over solutions to the point where despite the severe social economic and political challenges that have been inflicted on the region by narco-trafficking, some heads of government are still willing to throw all caution to the wind for a quick solution to the region's economic woes by advocating for the decriminalization of the marijuana trade, considered more lucrative according to one prime minister in real terms, than bananas (Bousquet, 2016). The logic in this is that in growing and distributing Caribbean varieties of the crop lies the hope of global sales with profits from exports to industrial economies. Thus continues the elusive search for viable and durable solutions to the pressing problems of meeting the most basic challenge of any government, namely, that of ensuring better living conditions for all its citizens.

Alternatively, a praxis of Elizabethan procrastination also always seems another viable solution with some governments preferring instead to: "Let's sit it out and wait because you are damned if you do and damned if you don't," also to be read as, "business as usual." This "ideology of mere survival" has served as the basic concept for the rationalization of state policies that extend into all spheres of public life. What is in doubt today are not just the economic and social policies but also the political institutions inherited from the past and the institutional framework through which governments govern. Liberal democracy is in grave danger within the region and will remain so unless drastic steps are taken to bolster and renew the democratic character and institutional capability of the political and social systems of the island states. Without such steps, the region will be lumped with other states that are negatively classified along the "good governance" continuum (Ryan, 2001: 74; Srebrnik, 2004) as failed states. The specter of evolving into failed societies is no longer a subject of imagination (Girvan, 2015). Already, Grenada, Belize, Jamaica, and Suriname have been put on warning, with Guyana at the more serious stage of elevated warning and Haiti in the category of high alert. Thus six states, more than a third of the countries within the regional grouping, are all considered at risk of becoming failed states if measures are not taken quickly to reduce this decline in sustainability (FFP, 2016). Environmental fragility, financial vulnerability, and a raft of complex global issues have unsettled the region and introduced constant anxiety that pervades citizens' lives, with an associated set of questions engaging our minds and hearts:

Who can we now trust?
Who can we look to for leadership?
How can we find meaning and purpose?
How do we make sense of all that is happening?
Is there a better way of thinking and acting?
What type of world do we want tomorrow?
How do we want to live our lives?
How do we want to relate to one another?

The way we respond to questions like these will have a profound effect on the world of tomorrow, and the legacy we leave for future generations (Howard, 2010: 507; Crudas and Rutherford, 2010).

Moreover, a much wider range of intractable issues has [re]surfaced influenced by global images that include the fight against discrimination based on gender, racial or ethnic origin, religion or belief, disability, age or sexual orientation; climate change; renewable energy; electoral fraud and naïve calls for integrity legislation; excessive delays in the administration of justice; safety and security; as well as the dilemmas in the administrative implementation of policies for public sector reform that inevitably affects all facets of society. Buoyed by the recent uprisings in Arab countries and the region's integration into the networked economy and embryonic information-based societies, there is evidence of regional citizens migrating to Syria to join the Islamic State of Iraq and Syria (ISIS), with the 2016 CARICOM IMPACS report suggesting that at least 200 men, women, and children from one CARICOM member state had already been trained in terrorist strategies and tactics. This, along with the potential spread of a radical ideology and the introduction of advanced military tactics and technology is considered a significant threat to this region for years to come, "particularly the current terrorism threat that takes into account the return of foreign terrorist fighters fomenting a nexus between terrorism and organized crime" (Caribbean News Now, 2017). This possibility of external challenges fomenting onto locally grown challenges has created the need for longer-term and more broadly formulated overall coherence of policy at the same time that increasing complexity of social order, increasing political pressures on government, and decreasing legitimacy of government make it more and more difficult for government to achieve these goals (Girvan, 2011). The symptoms of this ailment are apparent, numerous, and pervasive—widespread disrespect of others, murder, rape, larceny and robbery, petty and white-collar theft, and dishonesty, among others (Perkins, 2013: 6). Statistics from 13 CARICOM member states show there were 2,178 murders, 1,596 rapes, 10,227 robberies, and 2,488 illegal guns seized along with 32,364 rounds of ammunition. Between 2006 and 2016, 20,000 illegal firearms were removed from our streets—while still remaining are very difficult to trace polymer weapons, modular weapons, and 3D printed weapons (CARICOM IMPACS, 2016). A very similar diagnosis has been proffered by two later studies, the first of which, *Restoring Paradise in the Caribbean: Combatting Violence with Numbers*, based its findings on new crime victimization surveys carried out in five CARICOM countries, The Bahamas, Barbados, Jamaica, Suriname, and Trinidad and Tobago. The surveys concluded that violent crime rates in the five countries are among the highest in the world with the average rate of victimization by assault and threat (6.8%) higher than in any other region, including Latin America at (4.7%).

Guns were used about twice as often in robbery and three times as often in assault in the Caribbean as compared with the global average (Sutton and Ruprah, 2017). The most recent study by the International Monetary Fund further concurs that in several Caribbean countries, crime has risen sharply since 2004 and murder rates are now among the highest in the world with specifically violent crime being significantly higher than in any other region (with 6.8% of the population affected versus a world average of 4.5%) (see figure 1.3).

At the time of authoring this research, the final national and regional multistakeholder preparatory meetings for the International Conference on Small Island Developing States (SIDS) had taken place. A review of the agenda saw the roll out of the usual topics for discussion including:

> to seek a renewed political commitment by focusing on practical and pragmatic actions for further implementation of national policies;
>
> identifying new and emerging challenges and opportunities for the sustainable development of SIDS and the means for addressing them; and
>
> identifying priorities for the sustainable development of SIDS to be considered in the elaboration of the post-2015 UN development agenda. (United Nations General Assembly [UNGA], 2014)

Crime—partly fueled by this high rate of joblessness—is a major obstacle to growth in the Caribbean.

(growth rate, percent)

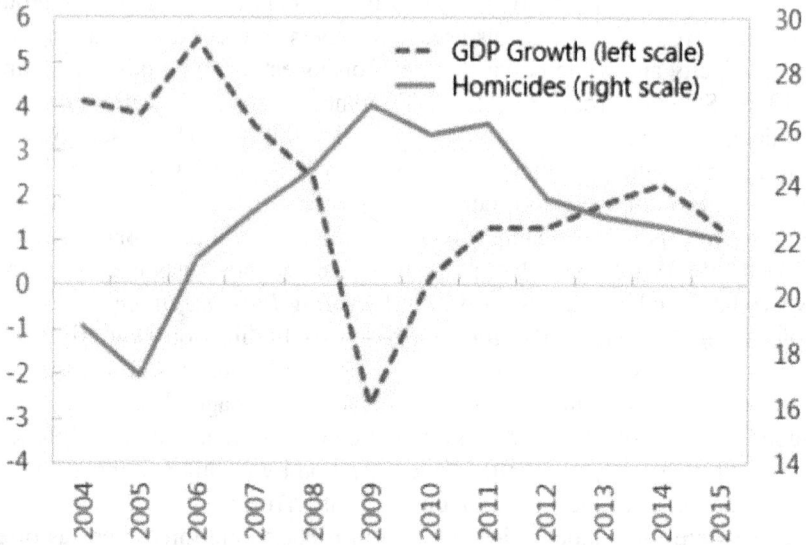

Figure 1.3 Crime Fueled by Joblessness in the Caribbean. *Source*: IMF Blog (2018) "Chart of the Week: Crime, Joblessness, and Youth in the Caribbean," in IMFBlog Insights and Analysis on Economics and Finance. Available at https://blogs.imf.org/category/cari bbean/.

The SIDS have also expressed their desire to highlight successful partnerships and areas of innovation in order to focus the world's attention on a group of countries that remain a special case for sustainable development in view of their unique and particular vulnerabilities (UNGA, 2014). This, like so many other previous regional and global initiatives—the *South Commission Report* (1990); calls by developing countries through the United Nations Conference on Trade and Development for a New International Economic Order (NIEO, 1969; Laszlo et al., 1978); the Independent Commission on International Development Issues (familiarly known as the Brandt Commission) 1977; the Brundtland Commission on Environment and Development (1984); and, right here in the Caribbean, the Special Conference of Heads of Government(1997/1998)—all to identify and address the political, social, and economic development concerns faced by these developing nation-states while proposing with little effect several action plans for their amelioration.

CURRENT AND FUTURE REGIONAL
PRIVATE SECTOR CHALLENGES

The world of business has also raised new and unprecedented governance challenges for the state. Barbados, Jamaica, and Trinidad and Tobago have seen the collapse of many high-profile financial institutions, in turn impacting their subsidiaries in the smaller economies of the OECS.[5] In each of the cited countries, though there were several pieces of legislation in place designed to enforce order and discipline, to regulate businesses, protect the public, and enhance transparency, disclosure, and accountability to ensure an efficiently functioning economy, the individuality of circumstances in each member state created disparities ranging from penalties for offences, effectiveness, and interpretation within the regulatory system. More adoption of good corporate governance measures within the nonfinancial sectors has been inadequate (Sookram, 2016; see also Cowell et al., 2007; The Jamaica Gleaner, 2015). Not only were small and medium-sized enterprises (SMEs) neglecting an ethical orientation; but also larger national firms and multinational corporations were being found guilty of systematically flaunting national laws and internationally accepted standards, indiscriminately avoiding observance of best practices knowing they could pay a fine, settle lawsuits, or even avoid prosecution (Cowell et al., 2007; Gleaner, 2011; Jessop, 2012; Caribbean 360, 2017; Jamaica Observer, 2018). Cases involving oil spills, defective automobiles, pharmaceuticals with dangerous side effects, and financial rogue traders resulting in harm to the environment and loss of life have been reported throughout the region. Failure in corporate governance is therefore attributed primarily to poor internal and external corporate governance practices and has raised questions concerning the roles of regulators, boards, executives, and auditors (Sookram, 2016; The Jamaica Gleaner, 2015). As a result, business malpractices then further exacerbate inequality in the distribution of wealth, inflicting egregious harm on individuals, communities, and the environment.

A functioning democracy for all must ensure the existence of an environment that warrants all sections within society are included in public consultation, policy formulation, and the decision-making process when solving problems. In practice, however, although several Caribbean countries boast of elective parliamentary systems, there is the often-expressed view that these democracies are being "held captive" by special interest groups and privileged individuals, particularly from among the business class, perpetuating unsustainable corrupt patron–client relationships. It is no wonder then that of the interest groups surveyed by the UWI/UNDP study (Broome, Hinds, et al., 2014) to determine the influence of specific groups—women, the church, businessmen, the poor, foreign aid organizations, minority groups, the youth,

Table 1.2   Survey Results of the UWI/UNDP Study 2014

Q. How effective are the following groups in influencing government decisions?	
Antigua and Barbuda	Barbados
Businessmen	Businessmen
Political Party Leaders	Political Party Leaders
The Church	The Church
Foreign Aid Organizations	Foreign Aid Organizations
Women	Journalists
Journalists	Women
NGOs	NGOs
Youth	Youth
Other religious groups	Other religious groups
The elderly	The elderly
Minority Groups	The disabled
The disabled	Minority Groups
The Poor	The Poor

Source: Broome, P., Hinds, K. et al (2014). *Statistical Report of the UWI/UNDP Democratic Governance Assessment exercise in small island developing states: The Case of Barbados and Antigua and Barbuda.* (mimeo)

the elderly, journalists, political party leaders, other religious groups, the disabled, and NGOs—on government's decision-making, respondents were unanimous on the dominant influence of businessmen on government's decision-making with the poor being at the extreme end of this spectrum as seen in (table 1.2).

These results suggest that a formal governance framework in each of the islands is required and that there is a need for an overarching Caribbean response on corporate governance issues. Regrettably, the recommended Caribbean Corporate Governance Code initiative advanced in 2003 to be implemented through the Caribbean Single Market and Economy (CSME), for various reasons never materialized (CTIR, 2005, cited in Sookram, 2016). Although various stakeholders may place demands on businesses to be ethical, these are frequently disconnected from the wider consequences of increasingly complex, multidimensional issues of governance and social life.

WHITHER DEMOCRACY THEN?

As outlined so far, the state as a governing apparatus has become moribund, morally bankrupt, and incapable of responding to demands with appropriate solutions all of which portend a bleak future for democratic government in the Caribbean. And so, social and economic inequalities remain substantial, and indeed appear to be widening still further. Redressing fundamental concerns such as poverty reduction seems much harder than anticipated in conditions arising in the context of multiple smoldering resentments due in large measure to governments' predilection to put special interests and those of large organizations ahead of ordinary people. The context embraces too high levels of degrading poverty, highly stratified and unequal social relations, morally bankrupt leadership at all levels, education without values, unjust systems of justice, and consumerist tastes embellished by global incursions (Perkins, 2013: 6; see also Graig, 2005; Kille, 2007; Campbell, 2010; Gill, 2012) as we move increasingly toward the new information or knowledge economy. Compounding this man-made disaster of epic proportions unfolding slowly but surely are increasingly unsettled populations demanding to be treated with respect, their freedom of speech and opinion secured, their initiative and responsibility rewarded. They are expecting their rulers to be fair and to refrain from capturing whole sectors of the national economy through rent-seeking and organizing privileges and developing patronage. Essentially, citizens within the Caribbean have been demanding a servant state and not a self-serving clique of state managers.

The health and stability of a modern democratic state depends not only on the viability of its political institutions and its capacity to implement policy, the hardware of the system, but on the attitudes and dispositions of the citizenry, their "affect" for the system and its decision-making procedures and their regard for key decision-makers. If the general citizenry feels that their symbolic and other identities are not mirrored in the system, or that they cannot affect outcomes by their actions, then that system is unlikely to attract the loyalty required for sustainability (Ryan, 2001: 96). As one political commentator aptly puts it:

> The integrity of a democratic political system depends on the desire of its citizens to participate in the political process in order to promote the public good and hold political authorities accountable; their willingness to show self-restraint and exercise personal responsibility in their economic demands, and in personal choices which affect their health and the environment; and their sense of justice and commitment to a fair distribution of resources. Without citizens who possess these qualities, the ability of liberal societies to function successfully progressively diminishes (Kimlicka, 1995: 175, cited in Ryan, 2001: 96).

Such are some of the manifestations of the crisis in governance in the Caribbean. The imagery that recurs in this portrait of governance within the region is one of the alienation of citizens and the breakdown of social discipline leading to disintegration of civil order in the presence of weak and debilitating leadership. The question of interest remains what initiatives will or can CARICOM Heads of Government now pursue to arrest the general decline in social behavior and moral decency.

With conditions like these, democracy, and by extension governance, goes into crisis as those most able to command resources will successfully emerge, and will even be immune from their environment. However, for the majority who looked to democracy as the provider of equality of opportunity (if ever it could guarantee such) this becomes a figment of the imagination. This is a seemingly virtuous circle except for the fact that it is the main driver of the systemic problems we face. The work of governing is therefore never done. In analyzing the effectiveness of government, there is the tendency to focus on the many policy choices that any government has to make in setting policy in a multitude of areas from the provision of education and health care to national security. In each of these sectors of national significance there are best practices, about which there is often wide consensus that have emerged from theory and comparative analysis across countries. Equally, however, there are many policy choices divergent from best practice that explain government's success and failure (Knill and Tosun, 2012; Stone, 2012; Kraft and Furlong, 2015; Wildavsky, 2018; Orr and Johnson, 2019; Johnson, 2019).

Regrettably, many of the solutions proposed by a post-independence scholarship for good governance in developing countries make up a repetitive litany of responses to [re]current crises, leading to an epistemological and ontological crisis over the source of the problems and the quality and type of solutions being proposed and implemented by policy planners. Interestingly enough, in all instances cited, much emphasis has been placed on structure-agency interpretations focusing on general laws, or institutional approaches embedded within the political systems and expressed through the application of political [solutions] such as changing or reforming the type of regime through experimenting with, or reforming political ideology (Hall and Benn, 2004, 2005; Meeks and Girvan, 2010; Lewis, 2010; Girvan, 2011, 2015; Minto-Coy and Berman, 2016; Bowles, 2018).[6] Causation in this context is unidirectional and the system of relations between the structures and agents is a closed (or self-referential) one existing within a broader system which is constituted by both structures and agents. Choices are understood to follow naturally from the patterns identified. Thus, for the diehard Marxist sentimentalists a call to arms is justified as their tired arguments would concur that it is utterly futile to expect to achieve any real sense of good governance in the future if the Caribbean continues to look to capitalism to solve its problems. And so, their usually anodyne and impracticable policy prescriptions are that the only way to solve these challenges to governance is to transcend capitalism itself. Blinkered still, they have failed to see that countries that attempted such a strategy failed. Alternatively, those pursuing conservative options of reform through developing and advancing their own particular forms of "political democracy," involving universal suffrage, regular elections, party competition, freedom of speech and assembly, as well as those attempting to formulate a new "Third Way" reconciling the free market with social democracy and social inclusion through appealing to the new public management ideals of the new "stakeholder society," have also underperformed. In all instances, underperformance is largely as a result of a confused ideological orientation, policy reversal, and weak institutional patterns (Schuler and Veltmeyer, 1988; Addo, 1988; Manley, 1988; Knight and Palmer, 1989; see Hall and Benn, 2005; Mills, 2014; Minto-Coy and Berman, 2016; Minto-Coy, 2016; Veltmeyer and Bowles, 2018).

The academic economists have sought solace in market-based privatization measures for restructuring these fragile and vulnerable societies out of the crisis. Under the guidance and dictates of international financial institutions and facing pressure to appease the unease of their populations, states have been busy dismantling or restructuring established systems of social welfare replacing them with new systems that prioritize budgetary prudence, private profit, and individual responsibility over social justice and community cohesion (see Esping-Andersen, 1995; Jordan, 1996, 1998; Pierson, 1998, cited in Martin, 2001: 191; Lewis, 2006, 2010; Meeks and Girvan, 2010; Conway, 2014; Nation News, 2016; Minto-Coy and Berman, 2016). Despite governments' claims to be greatly concerned about growing problems of "social exclusion" and citizenship rights, their over-riding imperative has been to secure national economic competitiveness and flexibility (Martin, 2001; Lewis, 2006). Prices tell the truth, GDP measures matter, markets are fairer, and therefore greater instruments of resource allocation (Wallis, 2010). Although there has been detailed observation and analysis of these transformations, it is now widely accepted that the teleologically bent neo-liberal experiments and solutions, based on seemingly value-free science and models (Proctor, 1999) for national development, often cast the success of good governance solely in economistic terms of enhancement of inanimate objects of convenience, such as an increase in the GNP/GDP brought on by the processes of rapid industrialization or technological advances. To be fair to this analysis, such approaches showed the economies of several member states recording significant economic and social transformation and growth with some 70 percent of them being characterized as middle-income countries. These are, of course, valuable and often crucially important accomplishments, but the region risks falling back into income poverty (UNDP, 2016; see also Lewis, 2006; Minto-Coy and Berman, 2016). In a world of uncertainty and change, however, current achievements are no guarantee of future survival even if the initial chosen set of principles, policies, and practices is good. No amount of careful planning can assure a government of continual relevance and effectiveness if there is insufficient institutional capacity for learning, innovation, and change in the face of ever new challenges in a volatile and unpredictable global environment (Neo and Chen,

2007: 1; Sen, 2000; Porter, 2000; Sachs, 2000; Lent, 2010; Grindle, 2010; Kliksberg, 2012). Caribbean governments have brought the comforts—but also the anxieties—of middle-class status to a growing majority of their peoples but around one-third of the population still lives in a poverty that is not declining (Levitt, 2018).

Moreover, consideration of the value of nonmaterialistic aspects of development and their impact on governance are still ignored because first, policy planners have simply not drawn the links between the nature of poverty, development, and weak governance (Singer, 2012). Second, policy planners also are learning that unlike the formulaic theoretical models proposed, democratic government does not necessarily function in a self-sustaining or self-correcting equilibrium fashion (Kung, 2012). A third concern is that economistic solutions are stymied because they often neglect the range of sociopolitical constellations within which economic forces engage and through which varied outcomes develop (Kliksberg, 2012; Weale, 2019; Orr and Johnson, 2019). These include economies shaped by powerful interests and/or mounting debts, as well as societies enthralled by and entrapped in rampant consumerism driven by global capitalism and now angered and indignant that they might have to forego their wants and desires. These tendencies if unchecked will undermine any solutions that could lead to the fundamental structural changes needed to take the region out of recession and will give rise to forces that eventually will lead to the undermining of democracy (Kung, 2012; UNDP, 2016). Responsibility must also be placed at the door of a fourth consideration, namely the onset of a period of confusion, muddled groping and a search for new paradigms in economics as well as political science, the two mother disciplines of development planning within the region. Notwithstanding the importance of each of the above, it seems that the single most important reason for the spreading disillusionment in governance is a "loss of hope," as Mary Kaldor once put it, in the erosion of the myth that development can create a just and humane society (Banuri, 1987: 8; Hutton, 2010; Richards, 2017; Levitt, 2018; Waeyenberge, 2018). For most if not all these countries, the national project has become a forgotten dream. Ancel Roget, president general of the Oilfields Workers Trade Union of Trinidad and Tobago said that, "Our beloved Trinidad and Tobago is in a state of crisis . . . Our post-colonial state has collapsed. (There is) a feeling of lost hope . . . This is not what our forefathers fought and died for" (Girvan, 2015: 104). Economic realities have turned national sovereignty into an illusion; a legal formality that is increasingly devoid of substance. Dr. Peter Phillips, Minister of Finance in Jamaica said: "We have not managed our sovereignty well and the first requirement of sovereignty is the ability to manage your own affairs and pay your way in the world and we haven't done that well" (Gov't United—Phillips, 2013 cited in Girvan, 2015: 104, 2011).

Thus, the tone of the times is doubtful, leading one prime minister to bluntly lament the fact that "CARICOM is in crisis, it is a crisis of our institutions, our societies, our economic models and our governance . . . [what] is happening in the Caribbean now . . . is traumatic. It has never happened before—never!" (Anthony, 2015) Or even more dire, as expressed by a leading academic, "I don't want to sound alarmist; but I don't think it would be an exaggeration to say that under a business as usual scenario, the Caribbean as we know it now will cease to exist by the middle of the present century" (Girvan, 2011: 1).

This research therefore poses two fundamental questions. Is political democracy, as it exists today, a viable form of government for the Caribbean and can these countries continue to function with the forms of political democracy which they evolved during the third to the last quarter of the twentieth century?

My thesis is that many of today's governance challenges are interdependent and no one can pretend that local, regional, or sector-wide solutions will suffice. These governance challenges are systemic and each choice made entails various other elements implicit in and related to the first. Consider how interwoven are economic growth, trade-related issues, environmental challenges, financial mechanisms, "too big to fail" banks, political regional and national constellations, social trust and respect of human rights, migration, corruption, and security threats (Girardin, 2012: 32; Posner, 2010). Similarly, one must note the many networks of shared responsibility with the emergence of new institutional arrangements such as social partnerships (as found in Barbados and Ireland). These are collaborative interorganizational, cross-sector mechanisms designed to deal with stubborn and vexing social issues (Rittel and Webber, 1973) and/or devise codes of practice to clarify the responsibilities of those exercising public power in the implementation of the policy process. These partnerships however have been fraught with difficulty as economic liberalization dismantles the social welfare state reflecting an increasing autonomization of the social, political, and economic spheres.

Another concern with these partnerships has been the disconnect between the rhetoric and the practice of their implementation, the presence of damaging politics and the absence of social corrections, the issue of trust or lack thereof between the actors involved, and the hesitating redefinition of the role of the public authority. Hence their formation without a simultaneous re-organization of the mechanisms of control and accountability can lead to the undermining of political legitimacy, and diffuse expectations and spread confusion between process and outcomes (Sootla, 1996: 5 cited in Vernieulen, 1998: 174; Sutton, 1999; Bouckert and Van de Wall, 2003; Benn, 2010; Girvan, 2015; Smith, 2017). Moreover, it alerts one to the fact that we must also look to the underlying attributes of the individuals and groups in our societies to determine new ways of governance. This systemic dimension frustrates policy planners because no linear causality or responsibility can be traced.

Such a brief analysis of social partnerships forces us then to ponder what role is there for ethics in such a process. Some would argue, none. Prima facie, yes, because the forging of a social partnership is conditional on the use of business contracts, negotiations, and trust between the various actors. To reach an agreement, the various actors must negotiate within a complex web of discussions to arrive at mutually beneficial exchanges with each other, and then must have confidence in the implementation of these agreements. A high degree of interpersonal trust and obligation is critical in the interest, in a broad sense, of each party to have win-win outcomes. Although this is desirable, differences among the partners may wane and may not drive all of them with the same degree of motivation at the same points in time. As such, at times breaches of the partnership will occur due to self-interest or other determinants of people's moral judgments and actions regarding some intractable or protracted issue of governance, or for reasons referred to earlier. The questions raised then are what were the factors that led to the breaches in the partnership? Does integrity matter? Why should the respective partners keep their promise to the agreement? In such a context, an ethical orientation to governance could be crucial toward improving the capacity of the respective actors to commit to development through the creation of an associative culture. The logic to this is that if stakeholders trust the collective initiative and expect that the community will benefit from investment in it, then that marks an actor's willingness to cooperate, further creating social ties that are essential for ownership and the success of the initiative. Governance in this instance requires the emergence of cooperative strategies linking social actors with differing and sometimes antagonistic demands that require institutional innovations able to produce "institutional compromises" (Lapeyre, 2004: 19; Kolthoff et al., 2007; Hofstede, 2012; Bowles, 2018; Howard, 2019).

A focus on ethics is therefore one of the institutional innovations that could be useful in questioning the decisions before an effective action, if and when faced with a dilemma that separates our subjective existence from constraining externality. This analysis of social partnerships is also useful insofar as it helps us to understand that beside the usual political-economy debate on the role of the state and/or the market, the language of governance must encompass an opening up of the intellectual discourse by considering an ethical response to the current crisis of governance which in turn impacts on the development of our societies. One would be hard-pressed to identify any sector that would not benefit from fresh thinking or in which we could not envisage a better way, whether it concerns international relations, the environment, health care, education, or welfare. This is not an easy task and for its full implementation will require fundamental changes in our thinking, policy prescriptions, and our basic assumptions about the economy (Crawford, 2004; Howard, 2019; Weale, 2019; Bowles, 2018).

Given these ends and the extent of the historical record it is noteworthy that in spite of these challenges posed to the conduct of public administration, little to no emphasis or consideration has been placed in intellectual debate or discussion by governments, experts, or stakeholders on the ethical dimensions of governance in development. What is the relation between public policy and ethics? A common answer to this question is that the government should uphold the "principle of neutrality" as far as possible and avoid taking sides in debates over values. Some would go further and say that public policy for governance should be made on objective grounds, supported by facts and data as the Weberian model of decision-making in public policy asserts. This approach is sometimes referred to as "management by numbers" (Yu, 2016: 197; Bluhm and Heineman, 2007; Schwenke, 2008; Boston et al., 2010, 2011; Howard, 2019; Weale, 2019). Not only is an ethical discussion absent from the annals of social science critique but, as I will also argue in subsequent chapters many of the governance challenges faced by contemporary Caribbean society and similar developing countries derive from a lack of attention to, and consideration of, the inextricable linkages to the deep-seated unobserved social costs that have been precipitated and reinforced by the impact of a natural-historical, long-term process of modernization[7] on human society (Wallis et al., 2009; Munck, 2018a). Nationalist political leaders sought to expand the role of the state as a means of transforming the lived conditions of their populations. As such, the promise and potential of modernization was used to dismantle the colonial paradigm through a [re]orientation of social and ideological reforms to engineer a program of national sovereignty and social rights for all citizens. This led to a spectrum of technocratic ideals that would see the design of state-led infrastructure projects, as well as the implementation of policies that would result in dramatic increases in macroeconomic performance (national income, output, savings, consumption, and investment) at the national level (Lewis, 1950, 1965, 1977; Bloom et al., 2014). As seen particularly in chapters 4 and 5, modernization did lead to improved conditions of change to modernity, but equally was also instrumental in producing deep unalloyed inequalities in power; crisis in representative and responsible government; the fetishization of consumption, production, and accumulation; weak and devalued stocks of social capital, generated by a broken political system and its manifestations; and by a bankrupt political economy forged from a sub-optimal performing industrialization process (Henry, 1987; Sutton, 1999; Sousa Santos, 2005; Taylor, 2012; Girvan, 2011, 2015). Thus in analyzing an ethical turn in governance we cannot by way of analysis advance its causes without understanding and recognizing the consequences of modernization in shaping our past, present, and perceived future. A challenge for policy planners when focusing on governance for development, then, is grasping the relationship and interplay between diverse social and public issues by developing an institutional framework to reflect such, in order to create an enabling environment for more effective strategic policies that are adaptive yet sustainable. The solution to any major problem therefore requires that its root causes be also tackled. Root cause analysis, as a technique of problem-solving, is when the analyst examines not just what is happening but also why it is happening (Mintrom, 2010; Knill and Tosun, 2012; Stone, 2012; Kraft and Furlong, 2015; Wildavsky, 2018; Howard, 2019).

> "In short we need a whole range of interpretation of the circumstances surrounding the stunting of the West Indian nation. We need a proper evaluation of where the West Indies has reached . . . we have to examine the record properly. The West Indian people simply have to take stock" (Best, 1990 cited in Alleyne and Sealey, 1992: IV). We must be continually deliberating the fine details of the human good, revisiting decisions previously made, and reconsidering what seemed to the last generation to be indisputable conclusions. Otherwise, we will lose the larger good we seek (Lovin, 2014: 12).

Considering the observations above, it was recognized that the Caribbean stands at a critical juncture in its evolution which compels it to adopt a creative, yet pragmatic, system of regional governance capable of advancing existing integration processes such as the CSME. The issue at stake was nothing less than the capacity of the region to deal with the plethora of multifaceted challenges it will continue to face (Payne and Bishop, 2010: 9; Jessop, 2009; Lewis, 2010; Meeks and Girvan, 2010; Girvan, 2011). Moreover, given the drawn-out status of the integration process and the compelling threats faced by the region, it was argued that "a decision on the subject be adopted with a due sense of urgency" (Lewis, 2006: 31 cited in Payne and Bishop, 2010: 9). The message could not have been put more clearly. Many of the foundations were already in place and only political will was required to make it happen (Payne and Bishop, 2010: 9).

I argue for a wholesale rethinking and reworking of the challenges of governance along the lines other than, but complementary to, the traditional approaches which emphasize institutions, actors, laws, and regulations. As such, I argue that any developmental approach must now be undergirded by or seek to treat as integral to its resolution the importance of a sharpened ethical consciousness embedded within an analysis of the material and structural factors of policy. This will ensure a more progressive strategy that sheds much valuable critical theoretical light on these multiple socio-spatial problems and inequalities, if we are to combat poverty and ensure sustainable development (Martin, 2001; Proctor, 1999; Shue, 2008; Kung, 2012; van den Hoven, 2017; Howard, 2019; Orr and Johnson, 2019). If these challenges were provoked by a manifest lack of thinking about ethics in governance, one therefore needs to ask: How can we elicit the opening up of this cognitive closure, so that we can have genuine ethical reflexivity? As such, one of the chief aims of this book is to lay out in an exploratory non-technical manner, rather than in a strictly empirical or normative way, the relevant thought-forms and vocabulary of an ethical discourse into why there is a need to incorporate this new way of thinking when discussing our democracies. Any honest dialogue about ethics and good governance requires the ability to communicate difficult issues and the courage to discuss oftentimes dissenting opinions, especially when we consider how fragile our democracies have become. This is because of the corrosive trends in our democratic institutions that see us unable to resolve many of our challenges posed by the unique vulnerabilities of our states and some of the thinking that reflects the civic responses to our flagging democratic societies.

AN ETHICAL TURN TO GOVERNANCE:
THE UNTRAVELED ROAD

As we reflect on the nature of government and what role can or should a democratic government play in shaping values, discussions concerning the ethical foundations of governance must not be the exclusive prerogative of moral philosophers or theologians. Neither should the knowledge of good and evil as a critical component of administrative thought be denied by any technocratic asepsis (Hodgkinson, 1996; Howard, 2019). The acknowledgment that there is or can be more than one perspective on important issues, and that each of these may have something to contribute to a deeper or fuller understanding of reality, is of universal relevance and deserves the attention of all those who wish to contribute to public life. For the sake of public trust and confidence, and good governance, a fuller and richer understanding of ethics is needed. The place of ethics needs to be integral in any scheme of analysis of good public management and administration, and it needs to be applied systematically (Crawford, 2004; Lever and Poama, 2019; Howard, 2019; Orr and Johnson, 2019). Ethics may not be a panacea for all of our ills—and I certainly do not purport such a conclusion—but it certainly deserves more honest and objective attention than it appears to receive at present. My propositions are that we simply must give to our human society the attributes of civilized states, and that this mandate has an essential and inescapable ethical dimension (Ramphal, 1988: 366). As creatures of the enlightenment—well, at least some of us—we are each moral agents in our own right, with responsibility for our beliefs, actions, and relationships. As Aristotle observed the ultimate purpose in studying ethics is not as it is in other inquiries, the attainment of theoretical knowledge; we are not conducting this inquiry to know what virtue is, but in order to become good, else there would be no advantage in studying it (Leibowitz, 2013). Likewise, this was precisely how Socrates envisioned his central mission in life, to remind people of the moral imperative to attend to their souls and create upstanding character and enlightened values within themselves: "For I do nothing but go about persuading you all, old and young alike, not to take thought for your persons or your properties, but first and chiefly to care about the greatest improvement of your soul. I tell you that virtue is not given by money, but that from virtue comes money and every other good of man, public as well as private" (Chaffee, 2012: 307; Bostock, 2000).

No doubt this charge will provoke a chorus of complaints from the academy within the social sciences as argued in chapter 3. This is a challenge. In the context of governance literature, anthropocentric concepts, and adjectives though ethical in nature—integrity and values, corporate social responsibility, social enterprise, "standards of integrity and conduct" essentially, to be fair, impartial, responsible, and trustworthy—are more likely to be used than the composite academic nomenclature "ethics." Likewise how organizations behave and give expression to their values, and to their nature and purpose, and how they affect the conduct of employees and the image of the organization, are to be honest, glanced at, and/or glossed over. Almost no reference to normative, prescriptive, or professional ethics is suggested or recommended as *sine qua non* in solutions or recommendations for facilitating mechanisms out of this governance morass.

Perhaps for many, conceptions of ethics in governance bring to mind religious conservatives telling people how to live and what they should do. And, in an age where scientific discoveries are increasingly rejecting traditional religious explanations as obsolete and giving way to social rationality, liberal notions predominate, eschewing any moral component of decision-making as naïve, as a religious imposition, plain hypocritical, and/or impractical, backed only by conscience (Elsetain et al., 1998; Williams, 2010; Kliksberg, 2012; Howard, 2019). In this regard, ethical discussions are generally disconnected from the design and development of governance strategies, with ethics sometimes even viewed as ineffective and an embarrassment to those who want to get a proper understanding of what is going on (Amunsden and Andrade, 2009: 6; Mintrom, 2010; van den Hoven, 2017; Orr and Johnson, 2019; Howard, 2019). Thus the language of ethics is all but ignored. This is then even more daunting when one considers that the several challenges confronting developing societies, such as the many ongoing government reforms and particularly those implemented within the framework of austerity/structural adjustment programs/policies, raise pressing ethical issues and challenges. It is as if the policies as designed, advanced, and implemented by various actors seem severely disconnected from the values, social norms, and mores that citizens purportedly hold. In this view, either the system is unresponsive to values or, if it responds, is unable to resolve conflicts among them.

Social scientists in the academy, particularly in developing countries such as the Caribbean, have often sidestepped, refused, or even overlooked the viable possibility of focusing on major research questions of ethics in governance (see for example some of the major anthologies on governance in the Caribbean, WIC, 1992; Braveboy-Wagner and Gayle, 1998; Hall and Benn, 2001, 2004, 2005; Ryan and Bissessar, 2002; Hall, 2003; Henke and Reno, 2003; Potter et al., 2004; Hall and Chuck-A-Sang, 2007; Minto-Coy and Berman, 2016; Ratter, 2018; Levitt, 2018).[8] If ethics is considered, it is decontextualized, blithely mentioned as an afterthought and/or narrowed to a sectoral approach. What usually follows from such research is a generic list of formulaic recommendations gleaned somewhere from an international organization's best practice portfolio and proffered to policy planners to be glibly followed. In those instances where scholars may have emphasized the role of individuals and organizations in the interpretation of ethics, little has been done to explain how the existing societal rules of the game that are socially constructed and routinely reproduced, are reflected in the ethical nature either of organizations or the behaviors of various actors. In a Schumpeterian-like way many modern economic, organization, and management scholars have therefore separated the study of the system of governance from explicit ethical analysis (Levitt, 2005; Pantin et al., 2005). This corpus of empirical study of scientific administration, human relations, and systems theory, as do analyses of bureaucracy and social psychology, forms a large and useful body of knowledge that seeks to clarify, organize, synthesize, and illuminate the existing knowledge about organization and administration in technologized or empiricized forms, and lays some claim to the honorific term *science*. Yet the general tendency is that the value elements that pervade administration tend to be elided, bracketed-out, suspended, ignored, or otherwise given short shrift by the scientists of administration (Hodgkinson, 1996). In its place is a vocabulary of economic efficiency that beckons these societies to manage the political process through a series of short-term solutions, without the need to articulate what we want over the long run or to reach even an interim agreement on our goals. This is sometimes referred to as a type of separation thesis (Nielsen and Massa, 2012: 135 see also Harris and Freeman, 2008; Shue, 2008; Hofstede, 2012; Thompson, 2018). The business of leadership is practice!

One can posit the view that this omission to deal frontally with an ethical turn in "good" governance arises from the subject itself being fraught with difficulty, primarily because the very nature of questions concerning values, norms and social mores, morality, right and wrong, or what is even good or bad is seen as undefinable, unquantifiable, and somewhat unscientific in this "postmodern" world. Or, that *homo economicus* (HE) is very straightforward and rational, making reasoned decisions according to rational preferences, and having a straitlaced and narrow set of character traits for conducting life in this simplified, world modeled according to cost–benefit analysis (CBA) that clearly lays out his objective best interests. He then makes the resulting "rational" decisions and holds consistent preferences in everything despite the richness and complexity of philosophical debate and uncertainty about the elements of human rationality—*rationalities*—that most models unthinkingly set aside in favor of a standard range of grossly simplifying assumptions (Christie and Astill, 2016; Hodgkinson, 1996). And so, while the relationship between theory and policy should be an interactive and recursive one, each informing the other to transcend the rupture between utopian normative political theory not grounded in real life, and predictive theory with no interest in ethics (Gasper, 2008: 5 Gasper, 2006, 2012; Lever and Poama, 2019; Weale, 2019; Howard, 2019), the theory is isolated from the practical needs and lessons of policy itself, becoming unlikely to provide a useful basis for the design of policy interventions. Similarly, policies that are not underpinned by empirically supported theoretical foundations are unlikely to prove especially effective (Martin, 2001: 199 see also Lafollette, 2013). This approach often paints a false and distorted picture of the impact and role of values on human behavior because in our day-to-day analysis of social, political, and economic behavior we often make judgments about, and assess the nature and impact of the values and norms operating in a society as a framework within which to understand these "behaviors." Yet we very rarely seek to focus attention in Caribbean social science theory and research on the realm of values, norms, personality traits, and primordial attachments that affect and constrain our political behavior and our public policy because this requires a wholistic approach to the analysis of society and human behavior which has largely been abandoned in the search for narrow disciplinary specializations (Stone, 1992: 2; Henke and Reno, 2003; Bluhm and Heineman, 2007; Boston et al., 2010).

The social sciences academy is equally culpable for its omission of the need for an ethical turn in the search for viable solutions and recommendations for good governance because rigid conflict between academic disciplines has led to their becoming so essentialized and isolated from each other that it has retreated from attempting interdisciplinary conceptual work. Instead it prefers to indifferently focus on narrow intellectual biases based frequently on a presupposition that there is agreement on the basic values of governance characterizing liberal democracies to placate this crisis in governance. Another component of the omission of requiring an ethical turn in governance is the pervasiveness of epistemic injustice in the theory and practice of governance. Epistemic injustice is a form of injustice rooted in knowledge premised on how we credit knowledge, how we get to "know" something, and so forth (Malavisi, 2014: 302, 2019). A field must be sufficiently distinctive and rewarding that enough people will listen and engage with it and continue to engage despite their limited time and the many competitors for their attention (Gasper, 2008: 7, 2006, 2012; Grindle, 2010). Fricker (2007), cited in (Malavisi, 2014, 2019), however, introduces us to two forms of epistemic injustice embedded within the academy: testimonial and hermeneutical. Testimonial injustice occurs when a reduced level of credibility is given to the words of some authors and disciplines within the academy, for example, ethics versus that of economics, whereas hermeneutical injustice describes of how power relations and privilege influence interpretations and understandings that are socially embedded in structures and agencies, as in for example, the power of global versus local institutions in brokering policy. Ethics, in this context, not only succumbs to a lessened intellectual rigor, but also presents a diluted, reductionist view (Malavisi, 2014: 302, 2019; Boulding, 1990; Hutton, 2010; Orr and Johnson, 2019; Howard, 2019; Weale, 2019). Furthermore, what constitutes ethics proper, as we will see in chapters 2 and 3 is often met with sharp disagreements. There is a need for greater interrogation of the assumptions on such values as freedom, and the debate over how freedom is shaped, safeguarded, expanded, or used, results in noisy political arguments (Bunting, 2010: 6). This is regretted because more than ever the current narrative of our societies requires a greater appreciation of what are the political values underlying and otherwise defining the kind of ethical behavior that should inform our thinking on the political considerations that might be brought to bear on governance. Indeed, Aristotle, in *The Nicomachean Ethics*, makes it clear from the start that he sees his enquiry as being concerned with the health of the polis. In defining the object of his text, he tells us that

> it would seem to belong to the most authoritative art and that which is most truly the master art. And politics appears to be of this nature, for it is this that ordains which of the sciences should be studied in a state . . . and since, again, it legislates as to what we are to do and what we are to abstain from, the end of this science must include those of the others, so that this end must be the good for man. (1980: 2 cited in Parker, 2003: 193)

In fact, Aristotle's desired state for human beings, *eudaimonia* (usually translated as "flourishing"), is very clearly a social diagnosis of the ways in which the characteristics of a person have some sort of fit with the characteristics of a given city-state. So polis and ethos are part of the same package: a good city is possible only with good characters, just as virtuous characters are likely to make for a flourishing city (Parker, 2003: 193). And so, this present research is a bid to [re]engage that noisy argument. It makes no claim to be comprehensive or definitive—only to provoke, I hope, the right questions. That is how one starts to get better answers (Bunting, 2010: 6; Lever and Poama, 2019).

This overview implores us to interrogate and evaluate existing intellectual biases on policies and policy-making practices to reveal their limitations, thus producing more appropriate and more effective forms of policy intervention (Martin, 2001: 198). This alone is risky business since ethics policies are very complex and technical. But our refusal to understand or incorporate them in our development has major consequences for policy-making, particularly the questions we ask, the methodologies we propose in resolving them, the values we embrace, and the weighting we give to different ethical principles. In pith, the invocation of ethics in academic discourse brings to the fore issues that are at the same time complex and sensitive and attempts to address them are time-consuming in the speedy careerist world of academia. The objective of this work, therefore, I hope will be to encourage and facilitate debate about the ethical principles that should inform our behavior, whether as citizens, voters, policy analysts, or decision-makers, as well as the normative considerations that should guide our choices over and above the substantive content of particular policies necessary for national and regional development. It is this shift in comprehension that I shall attempt to develop through this work in the hope that such an approach will be considered as a good starting point to further an honest dialogue about important and difficult issues.

I will also build the case that an ethically informed governance discourse is important in order to search for reasonable and coherent alternative perspectives to future development, in spite of the seemingly contradictory nature of key concepts and ideas inherent within any ethical discourse.

Methodological Praxis in Review

This book is conceptual in nature in that it seeks to argue the utility of the invocation of an ethical turn as a viable tool in mitigating and modifying the institutional and social behaviors that influence governance and development. It advances the view that at the root of the Caribbean's governance and developmental challenges are the perceptible influences of modernization as a technocratic creed and ideology with its implicit meanings and impact on governance within the Caribbean. The premise behind this logic is that it is in SIDS like the Caribbean that the forces of hegemonic and counter-hegemonic globalization collide most intensely and, therefore, excavating these disappearing and unacknowledged historical influences has become an ever more urgent task (Sousa Santos, 2005: XXIII). In addition the fortune and/or misfortune of each island is inextricably bound up with the future as a region because each shares a common history of imperialism, remote political and economic control, slavery, indentureship, cultural domination, discrimination by race and color, extreme fragmentation at community, national, and regional levels, a common language, a common outlook, and a common set of institutions. Despite some admitted island peculiarities, more of an exception rather than the rule, collectively the region faces similar problems of underdevelopment and economic dependence on developed countries, and so a resolution to the problems of governance can only be forged through the crucible of a common conceptual understanding (Demas, 1974: 5; see also, Schuyler and Veltmeyer, 1988; Girvan, 2011, 2015; Minto-Coy and Berman, 2016; Daniel, 2016; Goede, 2016; Nunez, 2016; Levitt, 2018; Munck, 2018b; Potter et al., 2019).

To competently understand and unravel the deeper multi-perspective challenges and their relationships that these circumstances portend for the region, the research very deliberately veered away from quantitative methods and employs a qualitative method of research depending on the extensive use of secondary data and employing content and descriptive analysis. This approach is utilized to reflect on both the practice and study of ethical governance from a global perspective of countries experiencing a range of corruptive factors at all social levels and to do so in a manner that is of value to those societies faced with these challenges on a daily basis. The central aim and objective of this approach is also to search through an overview of these common dilemmas for answers with good generalizable conclusions that can move toward a framework for continued theory development and empirical research in the future.

As with any interpretation or perspective applied to new regions or places, the novelty of new ideas, even when set against the omissions and weaknesses of old approaches, is not of itself sufficient to proclaim an advance in understanding. Ethical terminology may have become widespread within governance literature elsewhere but within the Caribbean academy many of the terms and concepts used and questions asked—such as what is the meaning of such central concepts as accountability and transparency, which put "integrity" in a context of managing competing values, such as democracy, lawfulness, effectiveness, and integrity—have yet to acquire commonly agreed definitions. Neither has the literature on political and administrative systems within the region expanded the meaning and the practical expression of the concept of ethics. Thus, when we evaluate some of our contending dilemmas in governance, how do we ensure efficient government versus

effective government? For, whereas efficient government is about more bal-
anced ratios between inputs, outputs, and outcomes, effective government
is about better solutions to problems and challenges (such as improving
health standards, fighting unemployment, reducing environmental pollution)
and ensuring higher quality levels of services for citizens. Good and ethical
government is about being good and achieving and maintaining societal standards such as democracy, trust, respect, integrity, and civility. This triad of
issues raises several other questions: can government be effective, efficient,
and good? Likewise, is doing good the same thing as doing things right? And,
can "good governance" accomplish both? (Demmke and Moilanen, 2011: 8;
Grindle, 2004, 2010; Girardin, 2012) As a consequence, an important causal
element of an ethical problem can be at the macro-institutional level (the
state) and not solely at the organizational and individual levels. Also one must
bear in mind that corrective measures to ameliorate some of our governance
challenges can lead to institutional logics that can be very different with correspondingly different ethical implications and, therefore understanding how
institutional and structural organizational issues influence ethical behaviors
can suggest different types of intervention strategies (Kolthoff et al., 2007;
Mintrom, 2010; Neilsen and Massa, 2013; Howard, 2019; Weale, 2019;
Lever and Poama, 2019; Orr and Johnson, 2019).[9]

In principle, intensive qualitative methods can be rigorous in their analysis and evaluation of the concerns and analytical horizons presented above.
There is also a case to be made for such an approach in that it offers cognitive
insights such as perception, analytical reasoning, synthetic reasoning, and
logical deduction, in the sense that such an approach can invoke carefully and
clearly articulated arguments each informing, while reflecting on and comple-
menting the other founded on detailed inquiry and detailed explanation. In
turn, this can enable the practitioner and scholar to elicit the identification
and causal role of the underlying mechanisms and structures (Martin, 2001:
197; Crawford, 2004; Etzioni, 2008; Howard, 2019; Orr and Johnson, 2019)
to justify systematic inquiry. In this research, my approach is to show how the
active researcher can elicit and work on complex data (statements) to eluci-
date their psychological significance. Inscribed in this very idea therefore is a
discussion which focuses on the ethics of individuals (the kinds of habits and
characters, mores, and norms, that are essential for the conduct of the good
society) remembering though that the challenge we face today in our societies
is the need to [re]configure a political response that must also acknowledge
the ethical responsibility of the society (Johnston, 2006; van den Hoven,
2017; Weale, 2019).

Of note, my intention here in this research is not to debate the often-dichot-
omous view which methodological approach is better be it quantitative versus
qualitative, for in any event, objectivity and truth are evasive. Both are created

and imposed in the minds of persons and so whichever approach is used, how we interpret and use the results as scientific information, read "objectivity," is still a question of subjective value to be negotiated by society. To the behavioralists, I am aware that the analysis drawn from the research will or can be contested with the common refrain that qualitative work is often semi-pejorative, with inherent personal biases and hence is dismissed as unscientific (Denzin and Lincoln, 1994: 4).[10] Fair enough. One is hard-pressed however to refute the stylized[11] trends discussed in these chapters on the grounds that they lack quantitative rigor to be considered destructive forces in our society. Nor do I agree with the claim that is so quick to emerge that such a stance is often the result of not being statistically savvy on the subject matter in order to make completely reliable analysis and conclusions. Tellingly, what is significant is the growing body of systematic empirical evidence that now backs up the maintained hypotheses in the literature on good governance and development. This is a conceptual work that argues through questioning and critiquing by careful scrutiny that something is broken in Caribbean society, causing the social fabric to be rent asunder. Whether it is by 1 percent or by 75 percent, it does not augur well for the future sustainable viability of these states and all attempts must be made to mend and strengthen. Further, I share the view of that section of the academic community that believes that, in hankering after academic respectability by arithmetically diagramming our discourse, the price exacted for operational precision may often be neglect of and failure to recognize the fundamental human problem of processing information in order to determine the consequences of phenomena (Hay et al., 2010) and for proposing solutions. And, as Guba and Lincoln (1994, cited in Christians, 2005: 158) argue, the issues in social science ultimately must be engaged at the worldview level. "Questions of method are secondary to questions of paradigm, which we define as the basic belief system or worldview that guides the investigation not only in choices of method but in ontologically and epistemologically fundamental ways. The current conventional view with its extrinsic ethics gives us a truncated and unsophisticated paradigm that needs to be ontologically transformed" (Christians, 2005: 158).

As such, this research is exploratory and recognizes that local political dynamics matter and that the dynamics of a reform process may themselves create new opportunities. It also underlines the need to understand country context, historical trajectories, the interests of key stakeholders, and the factors that are shaping them, and as such the value and the necessity of the qualitative approach are reinforced. Equally important, this approach is more cognitively accessible because it allows us to test our understanding of subjective reality—values and perceptions that influence governance——by posing questions that can be examined through the widest possible discussion with a view to reaching consensus. And so, if qualitative methodology emphasizes this distinction and strives to direct researchers' subjective processes toward making interpretation rigorous, then this research will make a valuable interpretive contribution to social science. Indeed, precisely because ethics involves the close interplay of theory, evidence, interpretation, and evaluation, it succeeds most where it is multidimensional and multi-perspectival (Crawford, 2004; Thunder, 2017; Howard, 2019; Orr and Johnson, 2019; Weale, 2019). Notably therefore, a qualitative approach more aptly enables practitioners and scholars to reflect more systematically on the limitations as well as possibilities of the mentioned criteria. But the differing realities of method instrumental to both the natural and social science research methods have not deterred this author on how the content in this work is to be treated. It has instead imposed greater caution and consciousness on the importance of the need for subtlety and nuance to inform the value and realities of this work. It is hoped that this research advances new perspectives on theorizing appropriate ethics for governance and development practice that could inform other developing countries with a view toward new policy [re]engineering.

Defining the Parameters

This book may be read in a number of ways and by a number of audiences so it is my task to identify some of those ways. There are some caveats to be noted upfront regarding this research. Being conceived as a multidisciplinary research project, it faced the usual disadvantages of such approaches. One is to exercise restraint from a tendency to digress in discipline-specific debates that may go awry. Certain very interesting themes that emerged during the literature review and interrogation of texts were not explored further because they were beyond its scope, although that body of work may yet see the light of day. Instead, only those themes that would contribute to the wider governance and development discourse in the region were explored.

In addition, my intention is neither to offer a ten-steps-to-success ethical handbook nor to reduce ethics to ideological precepts that harden into intractable barriers between human beings. Nor will this study focus on designing strategies, or compliance tools, or on producing integrity workshops and recommending manuals on "Managing Conflicts of Interests" as so commonly found in one-size-fits-all manuals from international organizations, though the research outcome could serve as a prelude to that task (see for example Transparency International, 2000; OECD, 2002, 2005; Gilman, 2005; CSPL, 2014; CARICAD, 2015; Institute for Global Ethics, 2016). My intention is also not to create a nostalgia project moving toward a conclusion which infers a return to some mythical golden age (Bunting, 2010; Lent, 2010) or to arrive at a consensus about agreed moral belief-systems. A democratic spirit has served to generate skepticism about authority and hierarchy in every sphere and judgments on values tremble before the incensed question of who can tell another how to live. Those who profess to have answers are ridiculed in a tone akin to those adopted by furious adolescents when probing at the assumptions of their parents. In the political arena, there is no faster way to insult opponents than to accuse them of trying to undertake the impossible task of improving the ethical basis of society. One can easily be charged with believing in that most odious concept of modern secular politics, a nanny state (Botton, 2010: 13). As such, this scholarship is a bit shy when discussing this ethical turn, understandably so, or of making too much of moral commitment in public discourse because society is very wary of high-sounding hypocrisy and conscious of the unavoidable plurality of convictions that will exist within an individual and indeed within a modern society (Williams, 2010: 9). There is nothing in ethical practice that quite matches "moralizing" ("sermonizing" or being judgmental about others' lack of morals), and that is one very good reason to retain our focus on ethics. In fact, "moralizing" suggests why moral discourse is unhelpful for our purposes: moral discourse is more judgmental and exclusionary than ethics discourse, which suits the purposes of those uncompromising policy makers who want to take "the high moral ground" and condemn, rather than converse with, their opponents for a lack of a "moral compass" (Urh, 2010: 8). This research does not intend to moralize or proselytize to anyone!

Finally this book is not just about the ethics of a governance in which democratic political executives are often tempted to use ethics as part of a credentialing package when seeking to increase public confidence and trust in government. All too often, texts, publications, initiatives, standards, labels, and codes that are concerned with the ethics of governance focus too narrowly on the institutional infrastructure in place (CARICAD, 2015). An example would be the office of ombudsman which is generally tasked with the responsibility *inter alia* to develop, recommend, and review the regulatory apparatus of central administration through the provision of formal and informal advisory opinions on their interpretation; and with overseeing the enforcement of ethics regulations at the agency level and referring possible violations to the respective regulatory authorities for consideration.

And so no grand meta-theory or ideology is proffered. Rather, the aim is for comprehension, clarification, and understanding in an analytical contribution that is addressed to an audience concerned with the relationship between development and social change and the impact that both portend for good governance. It aspires to serve as a roadmap for those seeking to understand the forces—both the external pressures and the internal failings—that have led us to the current crisis of governance. It offers as a policy response the pressing need for an ideological reformulation of governance along with the integration of the institutionalization of ethics into the discussion by those concerned with seeking appropriate public policy solutions toward mitigating the anguishing problems of Caribbean development.

Mapping out the Organizational Structure of Chapters

This research is organized into eight chapters, including this introduction. Chapter 2 is concerned with what is *ethics*. Consensus on what constitutes ethics proper is often met with sharp disagreements. Yet if we wish to gain any insight into the interconnected and interdependent relationship between ethics and governance and its implications for potential reform in the region, we need to define the parameters for how we think about ethics and its relevance to governance. Despite these considerable areas of vagueness, this initial research has privileged the definition of a vast analytical and interdisciplinary field, burdened with theoretical and empirical concepts, to provide a general impression defined along general lines.

Chapter 3 argues that the general omission of an ethical perspective as an integral component of analyses within the social sciences disciplines has created a perspectival lacuna that has fashioned the epistemological and ontological crisis of governance on the way forward. This is because of the exogenous tendency of the social sciences within the region to disconnect rather than integrate ethics within the social, political, economic, and cultural dynamics of governance, either on the grounds of relative unimportance and/ or because of their desire to demarcate their subfield from other specializations. And so, the chapter justifies the appeal to an ethical turn in governance as a viable methodological approach for [re]contextualizing the challenges of governance as a means of nullifying a long-standing academic rigidity in the region that has been precluding solutions. This in turn, the chapter argues, provides new perspectives and solutions to these protracted governance solutions that could win assent from people with quite divergent ideological pre-suppositions.

Chapters 4 and 5 are complementary. Chapter 4 examines the evolutionary development of the region. It reflects back to chapter 1 for emphasis and further expansion by advancing the argument that a significant reason for the current crisis of governance in the Caribbean is a fundamental inattentiveness and equally a disciplinary individualism within the academy. These oftentimes have so much fragmented the root from the proximate causes of the crisis, to the point where both policy planners and academics are now unable to make or see the causal connections, particularly the subtle interrelationships and the comprehensive nature of the problem under investigation. By incorporating this heuristic approach borrowed from public policy, the research advances the thesis that modernization and its various manifestations, without an ethical focus running through its role, impact, and systemic interrelatedness evolved through the institutions of capitalism, lies at the very foundation of the crisis. By distilling the primary features of modernization, the research acknowledges that the façade of modernization was achieved with advances in material progress for the region, but left in its wake, several innovations in the development praxis, producing disconcerting vulnerabilities emulating antidemocratic norms that have been ignored with dire consequences for the function of these states. From this synthesis of stylized facts and trends, chapter 5 continues to build on this thesis by correlating the requisites derived from chapter 4 with the policy implications (proximate causes) derived from the complex of modernization by explicating the inextricably link causal connections and how they have impacted the stability and functioning of these liberal democracies more specifically.

The aim of chapters 6 and 7 is to recognize that the conceptualization and institutionalization of an ethical turn in governance as a new policy orientation can be ambivalent and contradictory and fraught with difficulty. As such, both these chapters frontally address this fact by presenting the paradoxes such a turn could suggest since the ethical dilemmas presented by modernization do not easily yield immediate and workable solutions to the more complex problems, contradictions, and uncertainties of governance such as corruption, transparency, and accountability, largely due to the uncertain and indeterministic nature of the cultural, social, legal, political, and psychological mores of society. Both chapters acknowledge that this exposition could lead some to immediately rush to discard this ethical turn as ideologically and methodologically moot because of the wider debate of ethical relativism, but chapter 7 further argues for a constant conversation on these complex governance challenges since society is always evolving. It cautions those concerned that ethics like all social science disciplines is afflicted by the contradictions of ideological interpretations, and this should in no way detract from its importance as a method that seeks new insights into situations of political relevance. Rather its practical application and political possibilities should be embraced. The discussion concludes in chapter 8 which serves as a rejoinder by restating the case for the importance of ethics as a direct answer to new challenges, threats, and complexities posed by the crisis in governance in the Caribbean. The chapters are put into perspective through a discussion of the contribution of an ethical turn to the governance debate and an elaboration of some of the problems involved in doing so within the social sciences. But it goes further by asking the region to imagine the society they wish to see evolve and conceptually question what that reality will entail. Seen in this light therefore, an ethical turn in governance is not just about the inquiry into the nature of morality and its foundation, particularly the way in which human conduct is ordered, guided, and appraised in order to live together in well-functioning societies. It is also a distinctive way of thinking about the economy and its evolution of particular institutions and their role in shaping and regulating the socially, politically, and legally instituted forms of governance. The rise of this new form of governance could perhaps facilitate the increasing pervasiveness of a collective wisdom that will summon up a common will for self-organizing, toward governing without government. In this context, an ethical turn is used as a means for addressing the contemporary issues such as institutional development, capacity-building, decentralization of power and authority, relations between politicians and appointed officials, coordination, and the roles that heads of government play in promoting good governance (Agere, 2000: 5; Crawford, 2004; Crudas and Rutherford, 2010). But at the same time, it serves as a means to an end in that, in general, it contributes to economic growth, human development, and social justice. Our challenge now is to refine and update this thinking and to chart a practical path of convergence between the reality that exists in our system of governance today and the principles we strive to uphold and upon which our long-term prosperity undoubtedly depends.

CONCLUSION

The welcome implication gleaned from this research, I hope, is to acknowledge that good governance is wider and deeper than simply the good of the government and therefore that the call for an ethical turn in governance as a prospective activity examines the benefits, costs, risks, formulations, participation, and options for how ethical thinking can indeed have (more) impact, with reference to incorporation in policy and planning methods, professional codes and training, academic organization, and public debate and communication strategies (Mintrom, 2010; Crocker, 2011). The benefits, costs, and risks are typically hugely inequitably distributed, as is participation in formulating what are the benefits, costs, and risks and their relative importance (Kung, 2012). The crisis in governance should be a focus for us because it reflects a wider set of social and economic developments connected to the rise of an interdependent world and so we are struggling to come to terms with politics in the context of this globalized and rapidly changing world. How governance is pursued and practiced as we shall see in later chapters will determine what benefits are created to provide all humans with the opportunity to live full human lives. Thus understood, development is the ascent of all persons and societies in their total humanity (Goulet,1996; Sen, 2000; Nussbaum, 2011; Kung, 2012). And, "development consists of the removal of various types of unfreedoms that leave people with little choice and little opportunity of exercising their reasoned agency" (Sen, 2000: xii). An important task exists in laying new foundations, or, in more modest terms, in providing some building blocks that might be thought appropriate for foundation building. Essentially a core argument is about how ethics could inform governance and development, social change, and political order in developing countries. It is hoped that the following chapters make a timely and valuable contribution to the debates about this "third wave" of modernization and are able thereby to advance the development of alternative ideas about transforming our future.

NOTES

1. In this text, the Caribbean region will be conceptualized around the member states of The Caribbean Community (CARICOM) established in 1973 to promote foreign policy coordination, functional cooperation, economic integration, and collective security. Its fifteen member states are Antigua and Barbuda, The Commonwealth of the Bahamas, Barbados, Belize, Dominica, Grenada, Guyana, Haiti, Jamaica, Monserrat, St. Kitts and Nevis, Saint. Lucia, St. Vincent and the Grenadines, Suriname and Trinidad, and Tobago. Because of their shared colonial history the region is often studied as a bloc for whereas minor differences may prima facie be apparent, the micro and macro fundamentals of the region are similar: a shared history of European conquest and empire; a population mix of indigenous peoples, British, Portuguese, Africans Asians, Jews, and Arabs; political values from Western Europe transformed by Caribbean experience; a distinct cultural matrix fashioned by pre-Colombian Caribbean, Africa, Europe, and Asia with in-grown developments; European languages distinctively modified; and a similar productive and technological apparatus grappling with challenges of utilizing resources for continued development (see for example both Schuyler and Veltmeyer, 1988, and section 1 of Minto-Coy and Berman, 2016 for a comprehensive narrative of the Dutch and French Caribbean Sharing similar opportunities and threats to development). As a grouping of SIDS deep concerns exist as to their future viability as nation-states. As such, the grouping has as its central objective the CARICOM Single Market and Economy (CSME), a work in progress, which is the economic integration of all participating countries of the Caribbean Community through the free movement of goods and services; the right of Establishment—permitting the establishment of CARICOM-owned businesses in any member state without restrictions; a common external tariff for free movement of goods; the free movement of capital—through measures such as eliminating foreign exchange controls; a common trade policy; the free movement of labor—through measures such as removing all obstacles to intra-regional movement of skills, labor, and travel, harmonizing social services (education, health, etc.); providing for the transfer of social security benefits and establishing common standards and measures for accreditation and equivalency (source: www.CARICOM.org). Of note, while the conceptual focus is on this organizational grouping of developing countries, which in the grand scheme of global geopolitics may be narrow in focus, collectively however, they exemplify and are representative of an assemblage of ideas and issues on governance instantiated in current governmental practice, intrinsic and consistent with democratic government, broadly defined, that will be relevant to, and

resonate beyond this distinctive space to other developing countries and even those confronting poor residents of richer countries regardless of spatial and geographic orientation with a similarly shared sociohistorical culture. This stance stems from the fact that the problems and dilemmas faced by these countries are not theirs alone but a part of global tapestry of a shared common fate that cannot be exported, quarantined, or ignored with impunity but that they are connected to the larger universal and enduring truths of an ethical turn in governance.

2. In order to ensure morality in public affairs, member states of CARICOM agreed to establish a Code of administrative procedure governing the conduct of the holders of public office and all those who exercise power that affects or might affect the public interest, shall so order their affairs in accordance with national law that such ordering gives no cause for conflict to arise or to appear to arise between their private interests and their duties to the public, or to otherwise compromise their integrity (see Article XVII, Appendix II).

3. The "private or commercial" media within the region is no less immune from corruption than the opaque or government controlled ownership structures of state-sponsored media. Indeed, they too are also purveyors of it. Their *modus operandi* has been one of opportunistic convenience characterized by engineered silences through a mendacious cult of patronage rationalized by naked acolyte partisanship and a contempt for truth. More and more, unspoken of publicly anecdotal evidence suggests that sections of the regional press corps collaborate with and have been working through its infiltration by paid political party consultants through various forms of bribery such as cash for news, staged or fake news, gift giving, concealed advertisement (Transparency International, 2013: 1). Information access and dissemination by these strange bed-fellows is now a carefully and skillfully choreographed exhibition for the public using every contrivance at the medium's disposal—remarks and photos taken out of context, prepared questions and answer sessions for prime-ministerial monologues; denying, misplacing and/or misrepresenting convenient headlines placement in major dailies; the scoffing tone or cocked eyebrow of the reporter/analyst/expert during radio and television presentations; conducting and directing the party faithful to repetitively chorus the party slogans through populating "audience driven" public discourses; and the creation and use of social media platforms to support paid for political agendas.

4. The indicators were the following: Perceptions of Democracy—Strengths, Weaknesses, Opportunities and Threats; Democracy and what constitutes good governance; Citizenship Law and Rights; Government—Strengths, Weaknesses, Opportunities and Threats; Government—The Public Sector; Representative and Accountable Government; Legal and Judicial Institutions; The Police Force/Military; Civic and Political Engagement; Safety and Security; Access to Information and Democracy Beyond the State.

5. The OECS is a subset of the larger grouping of CARICOM states comprising the full Member States of Antigua and Barbuda, the Commonwealth of Dominica, Grenada, Montserrat, St Kitts and Nevis, Saint Lucia and St Vincent and the Grenadines, with the British Virgin Islands, Anguilla and Martinique as associate members of the OECS. The OECS came into being on June 18, 1981, and is an International Intergovernmental

Organization dedicated to economic harmonization and integration, protection of human and legal rights, and the encouragement of good governance among independent and nonindependent countries in the Eastern Caribbean (www.oecs.org).

6. Several regional studies, resolutions, declarations and decisions have been proposed by member states of CARICOM as development imperatives such as, the Brewster-Thomas study and other Integration studies by UWI economists in the 1960s; the Compton Bourne report in the 1980s; the CTAG Report of the early 2000s; the 2007 Single Development Vision; a Strategic Plan for Regional Development; a Regional Food Security Plan; the Jagdeo Initiative for Agriculture; a Regional Agri-Tourism Project; a twenty-seven Renewable Energy Project; The Report of the Regional Task Force on Crime and Security in 2001; a framework for promoting Climate Change Resilient Development approved in 2009; some regional nations seeking deeper involvement in the Venezuela-led Bolivarian integration process, the Bolivarian Alliance for the Peoples of Our America (*Alianza Bolivariana para los Pueblos de Nuestra America*, ALBA); while in 2010 Trinidad and Tobago was invited to join the inauguration of the OECS Economic Union (Jessop, 2009; Girvan, 2011).

7. The meaning I assign to modernization may not conform neatly to accepted usage. It is *not* without its objectors, but I shall try to be quite explicit about the connotations I give to it.

8. Even as far back as the post-independence era of the early 1960s to the early 1970s, the preeminent New World Group (NWG) that came to prominence then did not have a scholarly focus on ethics. Founded by Lloyd Best, the NWG was an eminent group of Caribbean, broadly defined, scholars among whom was a widespread sense that the emerging postcolonial order was in crisis. They attributed the root of this crisis to the colonial cast of mind particularly the epistemic dependency and flawed conceptualizations of the Caribbean's accepted models and practices in politics, economics and development. As such, independent thought was necessary in the economics, the politics, the society and the culture—all elements of an interconnected whole. And so, they [re]defined and [re]imaged the colonial legacy of imported formulations by presenting alternatives more aligned to the current realities of Caribbean society. At the core of their academic interrogation were central ideas that focused on West Indian integration and identity, imperialism, decolonization, racism, socialism, democracy, mass party, and economic development. (See Meeks and Girvan, 2010 especially chapters 1 through 5 for a comprehensive overview of the group's early thoughts.) In addition, for an abridged idea of the NWG's work see also Marshall, D. (2014) The new world group of dependency scholars: Reflections of a Caribbean avant-garde movement. In Desai and Potter (2014).

9. These inherent dilemmas of governance have also not been helped by the absence of a unifying democratic theoretical conceptual framework. A rich literature pioneered by the seminal publication of Kenneth Arrow's *Social Choice and Individual Values* in 1951, has demonstrated the logical impossibility for any decision-making system to be simultaneously fully inclusive and pluralistic, respectful of majoritarian preferences, and collectively rational, although these are all democratic values, which we may want our institutions to realize.

10. Because an interpretivist methodological approach focuses on validity and the structure of inferences through tracing the logical structure by identifying the substantive supporting arguments that are comprehensive, ubiquitous and causally important, it often raises the question of "falsifiability"—how can we tell when and if such content is right or wrong? How can we be sure that the beliefs and justifications for action that are articulated by public policy decision-makers are the actual reasons for their behavior, rather than public justifications or private rationalizations. No scholar can know for certain what someone else believes presumably because, interpretations can make "sense" and still be wrong. For this reason, while it may be one method of argument analysis of political argumentation, it is likely that the method could vary with the scope and types of arguments to be understood. That is, there can be misunderstandings, that may not articulate what the authors or the original text intended or believed either privately or intersubjectively. At the most fundamental level I am not sure that any social science theory or, much less a methodological theory of argument, belief, and culture, is falsifiable for positivist, rationalist, or even interpretivist approaches. To even suggest this is a promissory note to positivist science, for as this text will show, an ethical turn in governance is subject to interpretation, judgment and critique of a complex set of values explicitly and implicitly drawn from socio-economic, political, ideological and cultural realities and practices that are not amenable to natural science methodology. In any event, a natural science methodology is a paradigmatic approach to the organization of discourse around a scheme of common skills and exacting training. But even in this regard, such an approach relies on "political" discussion about itself through careful control of what is counted as competent, and what is counted as science, a deliberation which bedevils such research attempts at being "objective." Moreover, if one extrapolates on Jurgen Habermas "*Reconstruction and Interpretation in the Social Sciences* (1990: 21–42) the enlightenment's faith in reason has been profoundly shaken by its own logic and thus there is neither a higher nor a deeper reality to which we can appeal. Thus, establishing the causality of arguments and beliefs should not be the only aim of any research endeavor. Rather, aware of the contingencies and the content of ethics and governance, one can only try to get closer to the "data" through such a conceptual approach by procedural reason. That is, by thinking thoroughly historically and simultaneously by granting the role that one's own beliefs and context/culture are playing in the interpretive process that will be useful in helping us to understand useful outcomes that can be regularly explained by normative factors and may therefore tell a great deal about how and why actors do what they do (see for example both Rabinow and Sullivan (1979) and Patton (2015) for an insightful analysis and comprehensive overview of the interpretivist turn in the social sciences).

11. In the realm of the normative, "stylized facts are lightly theorized descriptions—theories of what is and what is worth noticing that offer an original 'interpretation,' 'reading,' or 'way of making sense' of a certain slice of the empirical world. They may shed new light on an empirical problem, help one understand some social process, and/or reveal what 'really' went on in a certain conjuncture" (Hirschman, 2016: 607). As such stylized facts are pervasive either implicitly or explicitly and serve as qualitative claims that the particular regularities identified are the ones most

important to study and or observe. They can take the form of rates of incidence or trends, whereby trends can be understood as non-robust dependence on time—that is, of a correlation between some variable and time, such as the implementation of a policy and its impact on the economy at a specific time in a specific period. Thus associations, incidence, and trends are all usefully understood as stylized facts. Used in this research for political scientists interested in policy-making, stylized facts offer an alternative entry point in the perennial quest to identify the influence of "ideas." Readers bring to these propositions their own values, biases and presumptions, their own epistemology, and their own wealth of experience, knowledge, and insight. This extends Kaldor's claim that stylized facts are necessary because they abstract away from the vagaries of measurement error and temporary perturbations. This abstraction is necessary to give canonical social science theories—meaning here both formal mathematical theory and models and more literary modes of theorizing—something about which to theorize, if, inclined to do so. Thus stylized facts are one part theory and two parts description, "medium" interpretations and/or facts with a dose of values. Stylized facts thus lie in the messy interstices between theory and description, minimal and maximal interpretation (Reed, 2011, cited in Hirshman, 2016), fact and value (Putnam, 2002; Gorski, 2013 cited in Hirshman, 2016). Moreover, stylized facts do not stay inside the bounds of academic discourse and are therefore useful for explication in public policy as the analytically ontological categories they abstract, usually, though not always, are defined in terms a non-specialist can understand that can be analytically separated and whose movements can be usefully observed thereby providing a bounded strategic realism for action (Hirshman, 2016)."

Chapter 2

What's in an Ethical Turn?

INTRODUCTION: WHY BE CONCERNED?

It is useful to acknowledge that societies are embodiments of institutions, practices, and structures recognized internally as legitimate. We are born into families, educated in school, and live out our adult lives in, by, and through a complex of organizations. Modern bureaucracy affects and embraces all levels of cooperative association from the purely familial up to the global influences of nation-states, multinational corporations, and international systems of administration. Each of us is a member not only of a national entity but also of a multiplicity of lesser organizations (Hodgkinson, 1996: 3). Without allegiance to a web of ordering relations, society becomes as a matter of fact, inconceivable. Communities are not only linguistic entities or permanent occupiers of a definitive portion of territory, they also require at least a minimal moral commitment to the common good. The common good is not "the complete morality of every participant" but a set of agreements among people who typically hold other less widely shared ethical beliefs (Bok, 1995: 99, cited in Christians, 2005: 154). Among disagreements and uncertainty, we look for criteria and wisdom in settling disputes and clarifying confusions through which the collective will is enforced. Through a common morality, we can approximate consensus on issues and settle disputes interactively.

This interdependence means that humans are social animals and their very existence and expression of that existence is dependent upon a supportive fabric of organization and administration that has a profound significance for the quality of human life. It follows then that if ethics is a humanism, it can never divorce itself from nor can it be ignored by the subject-matter and practice of governance because most of us hope for and expect ethical behavior and treatment from all institutions formal or informal, within our society

45

(Hodgkinson, 1996; Lever and Poama, 2019; Howard, 2019). And so, ethics is as old as creation and being ethical is a primordial movement in the beckoning force of life itself (Olthius, 1997: 141 cited in Christians, 2005: 150). Some of us pay close attention to the subject and seek to engage others in discussing (and practicing) it but, as with so many ostensibly well-understood concepts that provide continuing sources of disagreement, too much is left to assumption. Unsurprisingly, this is usually the case because so few of us really understand ethics as well as we think or as well as we should.

As much as ethics is integral to governance, its acceptance into systems of governance, however, means different things to different people according to their diverse sociopolitical, socioeconomic, ideological, and cultural backgrounds. When discussed, there is a widespread tendency to gloss over the fundamental nature of the subject—as if it is so widely and well understood as to obviate the need for frustrating, time-consuming exegesis (Foster, 2003: 1; Lever and Poama, 2019; Howard, 2019; Weale, 2019). Understandably, society is not entirely blameless in this state of affairs as regrettably consensus on what constitutes ethics proper is often met with sharp disagreements. It is a truism by now then, that the discipline of ethics is an intellectual and semantic minefield ripe with potential for misconstruing. In part, it has spiraled out of control and has become mired in the prevarication of concepts—the *ensemble* of rules, customs, norms, conventions, and interventions which mediate and support situational sensitivity, cultural relativism, and the challenges of universality/generalization which serve only to stymie even a conversation on the subject. Ethics is often held to be a hopelessly abstract and speculative field, one as impractical as it is incomprehensible, generally of interest only to scholars paid to think thoughts bearing little connection to reality outside of the ivory tower. It is not only limited to intellectual abstraction on the one hand, but the very term "ethics" also conjures up for many the spectre of strident declarations of right and wrong, of facile moral judgment, or, even worse, within the context of governance, of cloaking the realms of power in moral drapery, as charged by Marx in his dismissal of morality as ideology (Wood, 1993, cited in Proctor, 1999: 2 see also Perry, 1937; Van der Linden, 1984; Lukes, 1990; Rosen, 2000; Nwagboso, 2008; Lever and Poama, 2019; Howard, 2019; Weale, 2019). People, communities, and various nations have defined and/or conceptualized the ideas and ideals of ethics according to their social, political, economic, religious, and environmental beliefs. The standardized *Swahili Dictionary* (2004) defines the word *ethics* as a good trend in issues of justice, equity, and good teaching. In Islamic countries, ethical determination of right or moral is tied to such ideals as *ma'ruf* (approved), *khayr* (goodness), *haqq* (truth and right), *birr* (righteousness), *qist* (equity), *'adl* (equilibrium and justice), and *taqwa* (piety) whereas bad actions are described as *sayyi'at* (Beekun, 1996, cited in Al-Aidro et al., 2013: 2). These values are consistent with the religious foundations established by the Quran and the Sunna (Al-Aidro et al., 2013).

In societies more secular, the influence of religious beliefs may be less obvious. Instead, institutional experience based on observed and practiced social phenomena——precedent—and the role of organizations based on the rule of law often have led those societies to develop beliefs about what is of value for the common good, and to some extent, define what is right or wrong for the members of the organization and society. One example of this is the notion of reciprocity as reflected in "one good deed deserves another." Another is the notion of good intent as in "a man's word is his bond." Still yet, a third is the notion of appreciation of merit in others regardless of personal feelings as in "give the devil his due." All contain implied "shoulds" about how people interact and should behave toward one another in groups, organizations, and societies. These "shoulds" define collective effort because they are fundamental to trust and to team relationships that entail risk. The greater the potential risk, the more important ethical practices become (Copson, 2010). Some of its significant manifestations have been expressed in Socratic philosophy, the Aristotelian calculus of happiness, Kant's "categorical imperative," Benthamite utilitarianism, egoism theory, deontology theory, the divine command theory, virtue ethics theory, various religious precepts, and as recent as the late twentieth century in John Rawls's (1993) concept of the decent society. And so, because of these initial varied perspectives a disclaimer is necessary from the outset of this chapter because ethics cannot be done within this research or alone by this author.[1] Yet if we wish to gain any insight into the interconnectedness of ethics and governance and the implications of this interdependence for potential reform in the region, then we cannot but help with providing an expository approach of what ethics purports to be. This is particularly relevant for realizing the hope of strengthening and reappraising social science theory to be more responsive and applicable to the ontological and epistemological solutions of ethical and social problems as ends in themselves. This initial research therefore has privileged the definition of a vast analytical and interdisciplinary field, burdened with theoretical and empirical concepts, to provide a general impression defined along general lines.

WHAT ETHICS INVOLVES

In its purest semantic denotation, *ethics* is a word derived from two Greek words, ethos for habit, custom, and *ethikos* for character or disposition. At its simplest, *ethics* is a system of moral principles to help guide choice that affects how people make decisions and ultimately lead their lives (Schlick, 1939; Stiglitz, 2000; Bunting, 2009).

Issues of ethics and good governance have been evident since the writings of Plato and Aristotle.[2] For ancient Greek philosophers, citizenship had everything to do with active participation and involvement in government matters. In *The Republic*, Plato defended the necessity of government by stating that it enforced laws and resolved disagreements among citizens through deliberations in decisions about public policy. Similarly, Aristotle in his *Nicomachean Ethics*, built on this idea by maintaining that there is an intimate relationship between politics and ethics in that human beings are social and political animals and must live as such by participating actively in society through influencing public policy. Again, in the *Nicomachean Ethics* Aristotle understands and defines *politics* simply as the highest good attained by action; therefore, action is the final end if citizens or humans are to flourish, and human flourishing for him meant the good life or living well. Furthermore, the relationship between politics and ethics for which Aristotle argued is required from both politicians and citizens through leading a *virtuous* life as measured by the principle: "The ruler is always better when the ruled are better." This means that good governance changes ordinary people's lives for the better and governance is better when the people are better. Thus, on the one hand, public officers by occupying their important offices are required to make deliberations and perform actions that are directed toward the common good, so that all people may flourish. On the other hand, good citizenship is about holding public officials accountable for their decisions and actions, but to do this, citizens must know their rights and are morally obligated to participate in all democratic events, including voting. Citizens who abdicated their responsibility to hold politicians and government accountable were to blame for poor governance. This Aristotelian perspective suggests that good citizens have a moral obligation toward supporting the laws of the country (irrespective of whether they as individuals agree or disagree with those laws), which entails conducting their deliberations and actions in a manner that good citizens would do. Ethics are therefore needed to place government under greater scrutiny. By scrutinizing government deliberations and actions, citizens exercise their moral rights to participate as actively as possible in government matters.

Aristotle further postulates that practical wisdom informs how the individual character is formed and further argues that an individual can learn to be virtuous by habitually behaving or acting virtuously (Koenane and Mangena, 2014: 62; See also Bostock, 2003; Bluhm and Heineman, 2007; Boston et al., 2010, 2011). This practical wisdom or *Phronesis* according to Aristotle enables a person to be prudent in decision-making in his or her actions. In this way, some of our actions define our real selves; in other words, we are the landscape(s) of our actions because we are characterized by them. For Aristotle, behavior in and of itself is not enough as it creates a false separation between the doer and the deed where in fact the deed is not outside the character of the doer. Thus, actions are a manifestation or expression of character or moral agency, and moral goodness is accordingly a quality of a moral person whose character has cultivated the moral virtues, attitudes, and other values that define him or her (Keonane and Mangena, 2017: 66, see also Bostock, 2003). Since then, social psychology has appropriated or borrowed these Aristotelian ideas, aligning them into the principle of cognitive consistency which suggests that we have an inner drive to hold in harmony all our attitudes and behaviors such as obedience and conformity. Whereas the obverse, cognitive dissonance, holds that there is an inconsistency or conflict between our attitudes and our behaviors. Thus, although we may see ourselves as inherently good in certain circumstances, we are likely to behave less than honorably—badly—which has larger profound implications for the culture of ethical decision-making and how the state is governed (see Acharya et al., 2018).

Of course, Aristotle himself failed to live up to this ideal in his exclusion of slaves and women from the citizenry but the principle is still clear and necessary now in an enlightened society with universal access to education and information. Hence a better politics, and governance, are only possible when the community manifests sympathy. Citizens can then be bound by bonds of concern and not just of obligation. They would not just become friends in the "personal sense," but goodwill would tend to prevail and the courts would still have work to do. Such a society would also know social habits like respect, and would enjoy collective celebrations (Vernon, 2010). This integrative idea further found gravitas in one of the most important contributions to political/social philosophy—the theory of the social contract—arising later from seventeenth- and eighteenth-century philosophers such as Thomas Hobbes, John Locke, Jean Jacques Rousseau, and David Hume outlining government's moral obligations as well as the limits within which the government could exercise these (Bluhm, 1978). One of the main achievements of the social contract theorists was to impose political and moral obligations equally on the government as on citizens. In pith, social contract theory is about political authority (Lessnoff, 1998 cited in Keonane and Mangena, 2017), as well as its obligation, authority, and limits. Limitations were imposed on the government by putting in place checks and balances in the form of the separation of powers (*trias politica*) between the executive, the legislature, and the judiciary, the apparatus of democratic governance without which "the *raison d être* of democracy and governance would be a mirage" (Koenane and Mangena, 2017: 62; see also Bostock, 2003).

Only in the first half of the twentieth century were efforts made to construct an ethics purified of all forms of interdisciplinarity in what has come to be known as "metaethics." In the face of manifest needs for ethical guidance with regard to new forms of science and technology however, the metaethics project gave way in the second half of the twentieth century to what has come to be called applied ethics (Balsamo and Mitcham, 2010: 260; but see also Berger, 1974).

Ethics itself is constituted by systematic, critical reflection on human action with the aim of both increasing knowledge about and improving culturally or personally acceptable behavior (Balsamo and Mitcham, 2010: 259). Anyone who thinks about what he or she ought to do is, consciously or unconsciously, involved in ethics (Singer, 1993: V cited in Proctor, 1999: 2). Ricoeur (1991) also defines *ethics* as a teleological conceptual framework, with the aim of a social, collective, just way of living together in a "good life." Ethics is "the systematic and communal reflection on and analysis of moral experience," what "the good," "the right," and "the just" are. Advocates of a new normative belief or new behavioral norm, even one within the bounds of the dominant belief system, must persuade others that their position is superior on ethical grounds, or that ethical grounds are outweighed by or, conversely, outdo other considerations. In the role of resisting dominant (behavioral) norms or establishing new norms, ethical arguments can be used to denormalize (i.e., defamiliarize or make strange) the dominant norm and they may also delegitimize a dominant norm, showing how it is wrong and ought to be questioned. If successful, denormalization and delegitimization deconstruct the existing discourse (Crawford, 2004: 100). Ethics, then, is the science that enquires into morality and offers arguments to support critique of different moral practices or rules (Perry, 1937: 163; Howard, 2019; Lever and Poama, 2019). In addition, at the heart of ethics is a concern about something or someone other than ourselves and our own desires and self-interest.

In the cultural realm, ethics can be perceived as a legitimization process of this pluralism of conceptions of the "good life" (Ricoeur, 1991; Williams, 2010). This, then, leads to the questions: How do we know who is a good person? How do we know what is right action? How do we recognize a just community? These are the three questions which animate the science of ethics. Ethics explains or justifies that judgment by engaging in a process of moral reasoning through constant dialogue (Crawford, 2004; Perkins, 2013; Moore, 2013; Thunder, 2017; Gensler, 2018; Howard, 2019). Such thinking can be done monologically by the thinker thinking through things for herself, hopefully in response to what others say or have said in discussions and in writings; but it can also be done dialogically through extensive dialogue and interaction between people of different approaches, especially from different cultural backgrounds (Dower, 2019: 24; Crawford, 2004; Thunder, 2017; Gensler, 2018; Howard, 2019). There are several insights to be drawn from such a dialogue. First, is a decision of when to seek or avoid moral choices that an individual would require in order to take or reject a specific action. Second, narratives can be used to influence individuals' actions. A positive narrative appeals to moral precepts by asking questions such as: "What if that person were you?" or "What if everyone did that same thing?" A negative narrative changes beliefs by downplaying the harm of the action, or by blaming others for it (Tirole, 2018). An ethical argument can then offer a reconstruction by posing alternative prescriptions and suggestions for an alternative order that is conceivable, desirable, and possible. This may then have the effect of changing actors' conceptions of their interest, and may persuasively help in overturning the status quo once the powerful who once upheld the dominant norm can no longer impose the old norm or convince others to abide by it (Sen, 1987; Crawford, 2004; Thunder, 2017; Lever and Poama, 2019; Howard, 2019).

There is no algorithm to this process and success is never guaranteed. However, we have a better chance of finding satisfactory solutions to such questions if we are familiar with a range of practical moral problems, if we are concerned with other people's interests and the interests of society and if we have a good sense of the ways people reason about practical problems. In these instances, dialogue is the key element in an emancipatory strategy that liberates rather than imprisons us in such manipulation or antagonistic relations (Foster, 2003; Christians, 2005; Copson, 2010; La Follette, 2013; BBVA, 2012; Crawford, 2004; Thunder, 2017; Lever and Poama, 2019; Howard, 2019). As Roberts (1941: 282) notes:

> Men undertake this search because they believe that they can choose and that it will make a difference whether they adopt one set of principles or another, or none at all. If anything we do can make a difference, it must be that the future is not entirely decided or certain, that it may be any of a number of different possibilities, that what it shall be depends, at least in some details, upon the choices we make. We decide, that is to say, issues that, until we have chosen, remain undecided.

Ethical issues by their nature are also issues of conscience, and go beyond etiquette, to include matters that nearly every human society should and ought to consider significant. As such, ethics infuses debates on topics such as abortion, our rights and responsibilities, the language of right and wrong, moral decisions, human rights, and professional conduct which are more profound than a breach of a social *faux pas* (Perry, 2000; Thunder, 2017; Gensler, 2018; Lever and Poama, 2019; Howard, 2019).

WHAT ETHICS DOES

As important as understanding its nature, and what it is about, is also what it can do. Ethics concerns us with what to do and what not to do; who to admire and who to avoid; where to draw lines and where not to; what feelings to cultivate and which ones to repress. Our ethics is shown in our cluster of dispositions to encourage and to discourage various choices, characters, and feelings (Blackburn, 2013: 44). Because concepts of ethics have been derived from religions, philosophical constructs, and cultures, no one option in this regard is arguably wrong, or more wrong than right (see Balsamo and Mitcham, 2010). Rather, ethics/ethical practice is generally concerned with the continuous striving in efforts to ensure that people, and the institutions they shape, live up to the standards that are seen to be reasonable and solidly based (Perry, 1937; Girardin, 2012; Hofstede, 2012; Crawford, 2004; Thunder, 2017; Lever and Poama, 2019; Howard, 2019). Inquiring into the patterns of the empirical world, the theorist asks: What are the typical motives, goals, values of people who are politically engaged? Are these values universal, or do they vary from culture to culture? If they vary, what are the influences, both physical and social, that condition them? One should then seek to describe and classify the political systems through which men pursue their goals—the main forms of government, and their typical functions, structures, and processes. We must ask how the behavior of individuals and groups differs in the various systems. We seek to learn about the conditions which give rise to particular forms of government and to individual institutions. And we try to discover the causes of both evolutionary and revolutionary change. We should ask about the role of class structure, personality structure, economic organization, geography, climate, and historical experience in the determination and alteration of the political system (Bluhm, 1978: 5). Inherent in this pluralism of concepts is a diversity of ethical demands and responses that align themselves according to the professional, social, and cultural contexts in which they are formulated and used. Ethics therefore can provide a moral map, a framework that can be used to find our way through difficult issues (Roberts, 1941).

As a cognitive framework then, ethics can also pinpoint a disagreement through distilling ambiguous issues, thereby eliminating and/or clarifying key concepts and so enabling resolution on an [im]moral issue. Ethics is therefore not intended to give the right answers to questions; neither should it be strictly reduced to a process of obeying predetermined rules and codes such as the population being encouraged to abide by their organization, or working toward some kind of fragile democratic consensus following the organizational mission statements rather than their consciences (Schlick, 1939, Amunsden and Andrade, 2009; Crawford, 2004; Thunder, 2017; Lever and Poama, 2019; Howard, 2019). This is often a fallacy in understanding the role of ethics, one that in effect substitutes compliance and obedience for ethics (Schlick, 1939; Bauman, 1993; Gilman, 2005).

As a *leitmotif* to an earlier referenced notion of the social contract, although in political science we often talk about this "social contract," it is never formally written down. But which does not mean that it cannot nonetheless still be "broken," or be perceived to be broken with implications for the state. Thus the following extract sums up the Aristotelian notion of the social contract: "He who is unable to live in society or has no need to because he is sufficient for himself, must either be a beast or a god, he is no part of the state" (Saunders, 1995 cited in Koenane and Mangena, 2017: 62 see also Strang, 1999). And so, where there is the erosion of the social contract, there is a weakening of social cohesion, in ways which lead to more violence, more corruption, and more crime, and questions must be asked as to what is the culpability of those who have contributed to this evisceration of social capital. To what extent should they be held morally responsible for the consequences, especially when these consequences are the predictable—if not inevitable, or, at least highly likely—result of their actions (Stiglitz, 2000)? Ethics in this instance can be instrumental in identifying some of the range of ethical methods, conversations, and value systems that can be applied collectively, or individually, by persons to this particular problem. This allows for decisions to be made on what to do, and then how to react appropriately to the consequences (Schlick, 1939; Lafollette, 1991; Kung, 1997, 2009; Lafollette, 2013; Crawford, 2004; Thunder, 2017; Lever and Poama, 2019; Howard, 2019). Ethics then, is a process that utilizes our reasoning faculties, and reason is the capacity of the human being to identify his or her end and to choose the means to achieve it. Hence the invocation of reason helps us to judge the ethical contents not only of human actions and behaviors, but also of social institutions and norms (Argandona, 1991: 7; Berger, 2013; Crawford, 2004; Thunder, 2017; Lever and Poama, 2019; Howard, 2019). In fact, it is part of our practical reason, that is, the dimension of our human abilities that makes judgments and draws conclusions. This does not, of course, deny the place of moral sentiments, intuition, or imagination in ethics, but simply privileges the rational faculties (Perkins, 2013; Moore, 2013). In generalized terms, ethics has functioned as mediation and synthesis of: (1) human and cosmic reality, (2) individual and social orders, (3) reason and revelation, (4) science and human affairs, and (5) a pathway to insight (Balsamo and Mitcham, 2010: 261–262; Schlick, 1939; Berger, 1974, 2013; Crawford, 2004; Thunder, 2017; Lever and Poama, 2019; Orr and Johnson, 2019; Howard, 2019).

In order to sustain the virtue of a nation therefore, we need to be reminded of these contractual obligations as we consider how the individual connects with the public and the public with the political at multiple scales of evaluation (Pulman, 2010: 3) to themselves, to others, to the world, and to the transcendent (Howard, 2010: 507). That is to say, the circumstances of the world in which one finds oneself are relevant only insofar as they allow individual thinkers to clarify their absolute obligation to act as if their actions were to be a general law that applied to all others like themselves.

Here, ethics is also conceived as that still small voice within that insistently demands that you do the right thing, regardless of its consequences for oneself and for others. Conscience then, rather than being merely a private voice to be listened to or ignored, becomes a collectively adjudicated property (Parker, 2003: 194) of the constitutive practices of governance that involves, for example, the detailed interrogations of law, state, power, justice, equality, liberty, democracy, and human rights (Parker, 2003: 189; Campbell, 2010). This irreducible phenomenon, the relational reality, the in-between, the reciprocal bond, the interpersonal—cannot be decomposed into simpler elements without destroying it. Social relationships are preeminent. "The one primary word is the combination I-Thou" (Buber, 1958: 3 cited in Christians, 2005: 150). Given the primacy of relationships, unless we use our freedom to help others flourish, we deny our own well-being (Christians, 2005: 150; see also Sen, 1989, 1999a, 199b, 2000). Such an approach to understanding ethics is important because the world outside the national boundaries of a country changes due in no small measure to the onset and the subsequent disruption caused by modernization. As a process of transformation fueled by technological innovation it has accelerated change on all fronts—from traditional to modern forms of governance, production, and social life. New opportunities have emerged, while neighboring countries have either improved or declined, and international and regional legal structures and institutions [re]aligned. This perspective recognizes that we do not exist in isolation, either as individuals, people, nations, or institutions, and cannot ignore the impact of our actions on others. From the very beginning the process of modernization was not confined within separate national or "state" communities. The major economic trends and developments and the major political, social, and cultural movements which developed with the onset of modernization cut across national or political boundaries and have in many ways been international in scope and orientation (Huntingdon, 1971; Berger, 1974; Crawford, 2004; Eisenstadt, 2005, 2010; Weale, 2019; Howard, 2019). These external changes mean that the appropriate government policy choices change, priorities shift, and so do standards for performance. These complexities shatter any notion that good government is a static concept, and that government success depends on any individual decision (Dower, 2006; Neo and Chen, 2007; Boston et al., 2010; Kraft and Furlong, 2015). In this regard, major questions arise *inter alia* about governance in processes of decision-making (e.g., Chambers, 1997; Ellerman, 2005, cited in Desai, 2014) and about democratic responsibilities and their consequences for present-day [un]deserved advantages and disadvantages because of arguments that better alternatives are possible compared to what has happened, and that real choices exist for the future. In some instances, evidence of policy alternatives may lie in the experiences of other countries (Drèze and Sen, 1989 cited in Desai, 2014; see also Dower, 2006). Ethics then can be used as a stimulus to reflection by the practicing administrator, or it can be treated as an invitation to skeptical [re]examination of one's own presuppositions and administrative worldview (Hodgkinson, 1996: viii; Crawford, 2004; Thunder, 2017; Lever and Poama, 2019; Weale, 2019; Howard, 2019).

Taken within this context it is also important therefore that we understand the spatial nuances of the science of ethics and that there are many different ways of categorizing ethical perspectives. The most central division in international ethics has traditionally been that between cosmopolitan and communitarian approaches. These two ethical approaches conceptualize moral agency differently, with cosmopolitan perspectives focusing on the individual as the only genuine moral agent, while communitarian theory emphasizes the community—or often the nation-state—as central. They also define the source and scope of moral feeling differently, with the cosmopolitan perspectives emphasizing the universality of moral identity and responsibility, as well as relations between corporate bodies such as nation-states or business companies. As an enquiry it is often focused on the nature, extent, and justification of ethical values and norms that make up what may be called a "global ethic," generally understood as a common set of universal values and norms including some norms to do with trans-boundary responsibilities discerned by reason (see Pogge, 2000, 2002; Brown and Kleingeld, 2006 for an overview of cosmopolitanism). Communitarian approaches, however, focus on the particular communal sources of moral attachment that is, whatever the appropriate norms are for a given country or group's development, they are specific to that country or group and are not universal. From these divergent starting points, each approach provides a different account of the moral implications of international economic relations, with cosmopolitans emphasizing global responsibility for economic inequality, and communitarians focusing instead on the value of a community's economic autonomy and self-responsibility (Best, 2007: 109–110; see also Dower, 2006). While these distinctions may serve at times as useful heuristic devices for illustrative purposes, they may mire discussion in false dichotomies that often purposely and/or inadvertently ignore the mutual reciprocity occurring (Argandona, 1991: 7). To escape from this intellectual trap, this research acknowledges that relative autonomy of individuals may influence values and value changes in shaping and determining how core institutions themselves function and the content of their socialization; and, concurrently, that institutions may transmit values and norms and rules to the individual in the learning or socialization process that will determine how their behavior is conditioned. As such this synthesis represents the fulcrum on which our analysis will balance (Stone, 1992).

ETHICS AS A MEANS TO AN END
OR AN END IN ITSELF?

Twinned with good governance then, ethics is a multidimensional phenomenon that includes legality of government action, rationality in policy and decision-making, evolving a sense of responsibility, ensuring accountability, strengthening work commitment, creating excellence, facilitating a spirit of individual and organizational goals, developing responsiveness, showing compassion, protecting the national interest, safeguarding the spirit of justice, bringing transparency, and elevating integrity (Gaur, 2014: 490; Urh, 2010). In this regard, ethics can be used both as a means and as an end in itself. This is not only because both have moral significance as in an end in one context is a means in another (e.g., good health is an end in itself but also a condition of human flourishing); but also because ends and means invariably interact and involve each other (human flourishing is a factor in determining what counts as good health). In general, a practitioner's responsibilities—whether in designing institutions or formulating policies or giving advice—cannot be carried out without a simultaneous focus on ends and means. This principle has importance in many contexts—even in analyzing poverty, progress, and planning. Human beings are the agents, beneficiaries, and adjudicators of progress, but they also happen to be—directly or indirectly—the primary means of all production (Winston, 2015: 10). This dual role of human beings provides a rich ground for confusion of ends and means in planning and policy-making. Indeed, it can—and frequently does—take the form of focusing on production and prosperity as the essence of progress, treating people as the means through which that productive progress is brought about (rather than seeing the lives of people as the ultimate concern and treating production and prosperity merely as means to those lives) (Sen, 2003: 1). The theorist choosing to construct a political ethics must decide whether or not there are any rules, specifying either ends or means that carry an unqualified moral obligation to their performance, and the grounds of that obligation. It becomes an end in itself if it addresses all its major elements satisfactorily. This implies that society is generally satisfied with the procedures and processes of arriving at solutions to problems. It is good that a democratic form of government is in place, that people participate in decision-making processes, that services are delivered efficiently, that human rights are respected, and where the government is transparent, accountable, and productive, even if not agreeing on the methods and conclusions (Agere, 2000: 4). It also presupposes that democratic institutions and the incentives they put in place are necessarily stable and self-sustaining and that they have been so ingeniously designed that it ultimately pays to do the right thing. That is to say, our institutions are driven by principled leadership and citizens who share common judgments about the public purposes that institutions should serve guided by an inexorable logic of mutual self-interest redounding to the public good, and upholding the higher ends of justice, freedom, equity, and open access that we want our institutions to advance. However, as important as the project of incentive design has been for modern organizations, when it comes to politics there are limits to this approach. Incentive design works well in organizations because there are hierarchies that can impose rules. In politics, though, the rules of the game are continually rewritten by those playing it. It means then that our institutions, while powerful forces of organization and decision-making, are not guaranteed to work for the public good but rather depend on people acting in ways, sometimes against their immediate interests. Leaders and citizens have, in important respects, shared commitments to values that do not always advance their personal interests. In particular, people have been willing to accept decisions that disadvantage them when it is believed that these resulted from a legitimate process, such as a fair election (English, 2013: 14) Accordingly, the ancient question, "who will guard the guardians" admits of no permanent or static answer (English, 2013: 13).

It is in this respect that we can say that the region must be governed crucially according to an ideology and political culture that depends upon an ethical turn. The inclusion of an ethical approach into the discourse of governance should therefore entreat us to be capable of analyzing the consequences of political policies, of informing public debate on critical policy issues, and providing arguments for alternative policy interventions. It can also perform (Mullins, 2002) a pedagogical role, by teaching critical awareness of the moral content of choices, including as a pedagogy of the oppressed in case it is rejected as pedagogy by the oppressors (Goulet, 2000). This is so because every law that is passed and every development initiative implemented within the state makes a stand on whether something is right or wrong. A society of individuals with strong ethical criteria and behavior will provide the framework for a correct evolution of institutions. This means that ethics, while inspiring the ideas and values of the society, may help the social evolution process through producing a set of institutions and social norms that are both efficient and ethical, replacing the domination of circumstances and chance over individuals by the domination of individuals over chance and circumstances (Sen, 1989). Ethics provides criteria by which to judge the morality of social institutions and norms, and of behavior and actions. These (ethical) institutions will constrain the behavior and actions of men and women, driving them not only to efficiency, but toward morality. But ethics is also a criterion for judging institutional change: a change that breaks an ethical rule cannot be an ethical way to attain a better society (Argandona, 1991: 8, Sragens, 1973; Thompson, 1991; Crawford, 2004; Urh, 2010; Bunting,

2010; Sandel, 2010; Lent, 2010; Thompson, 2018; Thunder, 2017; Lever and Poama, 2019; Weale, 2019; Howard, 2019).

Within administrative reform, ethics is used as a means of addressing contemporary issues such as institutional development, capacity building, decentralization of power and authority, relations between politicians and appointed officials, co-ordination, and the roles that heads of government play in promoting good governance (Agere, 2000: 5). Ethics can also be regarded as a means to an end in that, in general, it contributes to economic growth, human development, and social justice programs of poverty alleviation and environmental protection and, in so doing facilitates the corrective interventional role of government (Agere, 2000: 4, see also, Singer, 2012; Thompson, 2013). In a similar vein, the inclusion and provision of streams of income to the displaced or underrepresented sectors of the population for them to build on often low productivity level activities within the informal sector, would imply an ethical imperative to rethink the criteria for the functioning of those markets within a wider ethical framework where, rather than being an end in itself, the function of the economy is to improve human well-being (INTAL Connection, 2017; Orr and Johnson, 2019). As a consequence, public policy makers should design a public policy that aims for the general happiness of the majority in society, while at the same time not threatening the basic human rights of the minority——the right to life, no confiscation of private property without compensation, and no deprivation of freedom. In addition, there should not exist a "permanent minority"—a single group of people that is always the minority and the "unhappy" losers in all or most public policy decisions. That is, on the whole, one may sometimes be the winner and sometimes be the loser in different policy decisions. According to Galston (2006: 544 cited in Yung and Yu, 2016), "[w]hile many individuals are capable of devotion to their fellow citizens and to the common good some of the time, and few are capable of that behavior most of the time, any political program predicated on the belief that most citizens are capable of it most of the time is bound to run aground." Public policy should, on the whole, balance out winners and losers at different times and generally target having the majority as the winners most (but at different) times; thus, in general, most, if not all, on average, are "happy" and have their welfare protected (Yung, 2016: 3).

Ethics also provides a framework for the development and change of institutions and norms, inasmuch as moral people with ethical ideas and values will organize the institutional change, even if spontaneously, toward ethical ends: the good of each individual and the good of others (Argandona, 1991: 8 Crawford, 2004; Thunder, 2017; Lever and Poama, 2019; Weale, 2019; Howard, 2019). Although these moral frameworks may seldom provide definitive or specific answers, they do call attention to candidates for fundamental ends in the light of which many current strategies and tactics might turn out to be morally questionable or even morally reprehensible. In this regard, an ethical approach provides lenses that enable us to see ourselves, our duties, and others in new and compelling ways by reinforcing our ethical motivations thereby [re]shaping both citizen and professional conduct. This means that the rules that govern the attainment of people's ends—the rules of ethics—are superior to their actions and also to the institutions that they create, purposeful or not. In this sense, ethics is a meta-institution in relation to social institutions and belongs to the realm of ideas and values (Argandona, 1991: 7; Hicks, 2008; Boston et al., 2010; Thompson, 2018; Crawford, 2004; Thunder, 2017; Lever and Poama, 2019; Weale, 2019; Howard, 2019; Orr and Johnson, 2019). Ethics controls the processes of governance and this research holds optimistically to this conclusion.

NOTES

1. Some may orate about the brevity of this chapter because it does not delve into some of the wide ranging and more intense theoretical arguments in an exegesis of ethics and governance. A comprehensive analysis of the application of ethical theories to governance would have been compelled to discuss those theories in much greater depth. I intend only to persuade the reader of the importance of an ethical perspective on the practice of governance and development.

2. There are at least five overlapping stages of the development of ethics that can be found in some of the ethical thought of all the major religious traditions and may be summarized as follows. (1) There is the Greek trajectory formation that broadly took shape in Greece in the centuries preceding the common era as an orientation toward understanding certain social norms as perfecting human nature by integrating humans into natural or cosmic orders. In this context the macrocosm of cosmic reality was thought to be mirrored in the human microcosm, as summarized in the phrase "as above, so below." From this perspective, study of the natural world was itself of ethical significance, insofar as the social order is itself viewed as the instantiation of a cosmic order. (2) Morality could also be understood, in a second interdisciplinary formation, as mediating between individuals and the social order. Greek philosophy, Hinduism, Taoism, and Confucianism all emerged in what Karl Jaspers (1949) identified as the Axial Age of human history—the period between 800 and 200 BCE—which gave rise to a set of basic ethical understandings of morality as distinct from but mediating cultural formations. (3) As articulated in Christian theology, ethics emerged in conjunction with Judeo-Christian-Islamic notions of divine revelation that articulated a revealed theology based on divine or supernatural infusions of knowledge from above variously understood as enclosing nature or opposing it. This kind of thinking is generally reflected later in the Catholic idea of the natural law applicable to all human beings. (4) In contradistinction, the fourth strand of the DNA of ethics as interdisciplinarity emerged in opposition to this idea of ethics as the handmaiden

to revelation. In this instantiation, a scientific turn is applied and infused as a parallel discourse of ethics especially as articulated in modern natural science. Moreover, during this period of the Enlightenment, ethics became an interdisciplinary mediation not so much between nature and society but serving as an interlocutor between the sociopolitical order and the pursuit of science in its distinctly modern form, which conceives non-human realities as devoid of moral significance except insofar as value is attributed to them by humans. As such, ethics is purposed as the protector of science and science should be aided by the state in maintaining its autonomy because of its derived benefits to society. An alternative perspective is that the dominance of science with its civilizational vagaries be reined in by ethics in order to protect humanity. (5) A fifth formation, is that morality can be conceived as a practice leading to some kind of enlightenment or revelation from below. This view of morality may be interpreted as having roots in the Axial Age, through the example of Buddhism, but is also illustrated in the belief that adherence to the scientific method leads to the production of true knowledge (Balsamo and Mitcham, 2010: 260–261).

Chapter 3

The Intellectual Bias against Ethics

We expect to have good governance. This begs the question, how? As indicated earlier there has been an epistemological and ontological crisis within academic disciplines over the way forward because of the exogenous tendency of Caribbean intellectuals to disconnect ethics from, rather than integrate it within, the social, political, economic, and cultural dynamics of governance. They reason that ethics is not their business, or that it is of relative unimportance and/or because of their desire to demarcate their subfield from other specializations. Perhaps unknowingly, they may be unaware that by adopting such a methodological stance they were also typically invoking a Weberian differentiation between value freedom and value relevance within the academy. Following Weber's argument that personal, cultural, moral, or political values cannot be eliminated methodologically and theoretically they recognize that in the discovery phase social scientists make their choice to investigate on the basis of the values they expect their research to advance (Root, 1993: 33 cited in Christians, 2005: 142). But Weber insisted also that social science be value-free in the presentation phase, and that findings ought not to express any judgments of a moral or political character but rather that professors hang up their values along with their coats as they enter their lecture halls. Given Weber's canonical status in the social sciences his distinction between political judgments and scientific neutrality within the social sciences has cast a long shadow on the global academy (Christians, 2005). This too is arguably a longstanding problem within the Caribbean social science academy that has contributed to this crisis, limiting the scope of the analysis in search of viable solutions to social change in the past as much as in the present (Berger, 1974, 2013). The crisis in governance should concern many disciplines and researchers with a domestic, regional, or global focus. This chapter will argue that the general omission by Caribbean intellectuals of an ethical perspective as an integral component of analyses within the disciplines of social sciences has created a perspectival lacuna that has led to the epistemological and ontological crisis of governance regarding the way forward. It thus justifies the appeal to an ethical turn in governance as a viable methodological approach for [re]contextualizing the challenges of governance in the direction of nullifying the academic rigidity in thought and/ or in practice that has been longstanding within the academy of the region and has precluded solutions. This in turn, the chapter argues, will suggest to the academy new perspectives and solutions to these wicked[1] and protracted governance solutions that will have a chance of winning assent from people with quite divergent ideological presuppositions.

It is worth remembering that in a relatively recent past the "Third Wave" of democratization has ushered in for many a new, more democratic dispensation wherein political science within the region has become encumbered with issues such as public *vs.* private interests, conflicts of interest, abuse of power, and corruption within the government. However, to prevent misconduct is as complex as the phenomenon of misconduct itself. It requires a high level of responsibility and commitment from citizens, political parties, parliamentarians, government executives, the judiciary, the media, business, non-governmental organizations, and religious and educational institutions because many of the challenges our societies face are interdependent. Fighting corruption, which provides a good example of cooperation across this wide array of social institutions, effectively requires that all social spheres pull together in a consistent and coordinated manner involving:

political ethics: laws, judiciary, institutions, and political will
social ethics: citizen associations, professional self-rule, media, and faith
    communities;
personal ethics: political leadership, and citizens as individuals or members of
    associations. (Girardin, 2012: 56, 101)

These challenges are systemic and attention to shared values among key players may help significantly in devising political processes for systemic decision-making and implementation (Kung, 2012). In the second place, a more thorough awareness of the nature of the development process may lead to a more rational pursuit of policies and strategies that aim at a pattern that satisfies a complex of objectives (Yeh, 1989: 68; Weale, 2019). In spite of this apparent reality, however, ethics is rarely a matter of concern in the ideological and policy debates regarding the role of the state in Caribbean governance. There is a paucity of concern within the canons of social science thought for cultivating an interface of ethics and governance. Much of our political argument and debate are concerned with how to make the public sector and central government function in the best way (Braveboy-Wagner and Gayle et al., 1998; Sutton, 2008; Minto-Coy and Berman, 2016), as in the types of regulatory institutions required for the region to achieve economic development, political accountability, poverty eradication, and other objectives considered essential elements of good governance. These debates have no doubt given rise to a better understanding of the responsibilities of the public sector, and how it should interact and interface with (elected) governments and with citizens, civil society, and foreign as well as domestic corporations and private business institutions. These debates have also been useful in enriching and expanding the range of conceptual frameworks we draw upon by exposing the limits of rationalist methodology and, through emphasizing the complexity and fragmentation of contemporary socioeconomic life, by highlighting the strategies that are used to construct and explain the realities we study (see, for example, Mills, 1970; Nunes, 1976; Khan, 1982; Thomas, 1988; Schuyler and Veltmeyer, 1988; Commonwealth Secretariat, 1997; Braveboy-Wagner and Gayle, 1998; Ryan and Bissessar, 2002; Hall and Benn, 2001, 2003, 2004, 2005; Hall, 2003; Potter et al., 2004; Sutton and Bissessar, 2006; Sutton, 2008; Payne and Bishop, 2010; Meeks and Girvan, 2010; Girvan, 2015; Minto-Coy and Berman, 2016; Marczak and Engelke, 2016; Veltmeyer and Bowles, 2018; Potter et al., 2019). But, despite their relevance to our present circumstance, only indirectly might a fleeting comment arise on professional ethics of civil servants, or to a lesser extent the professional and personal ethics of politicians and elected officeholders, with such issues hardly developed into a sustained and deliberate debate (Henke and Reno, 2003; Munroe, 2005; Minto-Coy and Berman, 2016). In fact, "ethics in governance" seems to many an oxymoron even though many politicians try to give their best for the common cause of a country or the international community. It is not uncommon therefore to find a poll which shows the electorate placing little trust in politics and politicians, or where politicians cannot eclipse the characterization as selfish and corrupt power-players, defending special interests instead of the common good of the population (Broome et al., 2014).

Yet, the skepticism over integrating ethics into politics systematically remains strong. Some leaders and citizens have confined ethics in politics to vision, declaratory slogans, programs, and intentions so that politics in this instance is philosophy, not practice (Girardin, 2012: 50; Guttman and Thompson, 2006; Kliksberg, 2012; Howard, 2019; Drydyk and Keleher, 2019). As one politician-turned-social commentator disdainfully notes:

"An ethical politician anywhere in the world, but most of all in Trinidad and Tobago, is an invisible entity. He or she simply does not exist . . . [S]kullduggery is the creed by which our politicians survive, and gutter-fighting is as natural to them as breathing or lying. No code of conduct, or for that matter, laws on campaign financing or procurement or integrity, will temper their thieving ways. The good Father must know the words "politics" and "ethics," while they rhyme, they are in fact antonyms, not synonyms" (Shah, 2014).

Or, to be more universally applicable to all lands and climes as a renaissance philosopher of administration once remarked that:

"if some of our rulers were to be confronted by a strict philosopher, or indeed anyone at all who openly and candidly might wish to them the awesome face of true virtue, teach them a good way of life and how a good prince should conduct himself, I am sure that as soon as he appeared they would loath him as if he were a serpent or mock at him as if he were dirt" (Hodgkinson, 1996: 4; Wildavsky, 2018).

What seems to be happening here is the use of the boundary to demarcate a particular understanding of the distinct domains that pertain to each discipline. Hence within the domain of ethics, the questions and problems that pertain to politics are made distant. *Ethics* derives from the Ancient Greek ethos, which describes the character or personal disposition of an individual and pertains mainly to the qualities of persons and their relationships constituted by what might be broadly called the *social*. On the other hand, *politics* is derived from polis, the city-state, and is concerned about structures and their ends and, within the domain of politics, ethics is therefore an irrelevant matter that can legitimately be bracketed with other kinds of conversations (Parker, 2003: 188). But why do I want to claim that this is a problem? For the ethicist, the world of the politician is merely vulgar power-seeking and it is difficult, if not impossible, to see any merit in political reasoning. Indeed, the sort of world that they seek to bring into being is one that would be profoundly unethical, one in which the accidents of success would masquerade as goodness (Parker, 2003: 191) and one where dishonor is more a tenable norm than honor (Hodgkinson, 1996). For the politician, the ethicist practices a pointless glass-bead game with no clear purpose. To make matters worse, such a game is possible only because politicians have tamed the world with their clarity of vision. To neglect the political arrangements that allow for solitary reflection, rather than (for example) the mass slaughter or starvation of moral philosophers, is an unforgivable act of hubris (Parker, 2003: 192). Likewise, Weber takes "for granted that there can be a language of science, a collection of truths, that excludes all value-judgments, rules, or directions for conduct" (Root, 1993: 205, cited in Christians, 2005: 143). Scientific knowledge exists for its own sake as morally neutral and neutrality is desirable "because questions of value are not rationally resolvable" and therefore neutrality within the social sciences is presumed to contribute "to political and personal autonomy" (Root, 1993: 229, cited in Christians, 2005: 143). In Weber's argument for value-free relevance in social science, he did not contradict the larger enlightenment ideal of scientific neutrality between competing conceptions of the good (Christians, 2005: 143).

And so, what has emerged within social sciences like political science is a *de facto* realist school with an emphasis on a Machiavellian-Hobbesian political realism, or "power politics," that encompasses a variety of theories and approaches. All share a belief that states (governments or ruling elites) are primarily motivated by the desire for economic power, privilege, and continuous rule (including military and territorial security), rather than by ideals or ethics (Amunsden and Andrade, 2009: 6; Boulding, 1990; Dror, 2002, 2008). Such realpolitik—politics driven exclusively by national or even vested interests—is deemed by many as the right and proper way of conducting politics, without the wishful thinking of ethics that ignores the reality of politics as a tough power game, with bargaining and double standards (Girardin, 2012: 32; Dror, 2002, 2008). The need for power is rooted in the *realpolitik* of organizational life. Without it the administrator is literally impotent. With it, accomplishment becomes possible. The more power an administrator has, the greater the ends that can be shaped, the greater the range of administrative possibility and hence, the greater the career advantage even if this means dominating, forcing, or manipulating the will of others (Hodgkinson, 1996: 71). Politics in this view has to resist such a "religious," "utopian," or "messianic" expectation which it cannot fulfil, and in fact often struggles to find a way to consistently justify moral restraints in the face of the ever-present nihilistic/Nietzsche challenge that what counts is not the so-called morals but rather power to do as one pleases (Girardin, 2012: 60; Ginsberg, 1951; Dror, 2002, 2008).[2] Advocates of political realism are of the view that the ends justify the means, might is right, and will dismiss any study of ethics as not pertinent to their work (Dror, 2002, 2008), preferring instead to rely on laws, that is, the constitutions and "the people." Political science refuses to be hunkered down by ethical correctness. Thus, while the idea of equality and social rationality rules the imagination that sustains our system of political culture, popular culture invites private codes and individual criteria. Politics then, by contrast, according to Machiavelli's advice to his Prince is not to dwell on such private matters. What is important, in being an effective politician is that the individual should see the whole situation realistically, and then act with whatever methods are most likely to achieve the desired goal. The methods must be appraised according to their likelihood of success and must be tempered with a cool-headed understanding of what human beings are like, both individually and collectively. If a prince wants to maintain his rule, he must be prepared not to be virtuous. He will find that some of the things that appear to be virtues will, if he practices them, ruin him, and some of the things that appear to be vices will bring him security and prosperity (Machiavelli, 1999: 50 cited in Parker, 2003: 191).

In public discourse, ethical values become blurred and are reduced to the private sphere, to the point of considering that democracy requires moral relativism, and that the existence of solid values must be rejected as fundamentalism (Kelsen, 1948; Stiglitz, 2000; Thompson, 2013). Those with such a view often forget that the contemporary concerns of "practical politics," problems of race, gender, exclusion, marginalization, and many other governmental functions are fundamentally moral issues invoking questions about justice, equitable distribution, and/or competing conceptions of equity or of competing conceptions of the common good or of the human good that must be struggled for and reconciled through ethical means. Governance at the end of the day must be concerned only with how (or whether) the politicians and rulers can be made to rule for the benefit of the people (the nation at large, economic and social benefits for all), of some special interest or for themselves.

THE LAW WILL NOT SUFFICE

In case of doubt, the political scientist and his practitioner counterpart, the politician, seek refuge in a default to the law transferring all ethical sentiment to their legal colleagues. It is perceived that governance is made even stronger through the presence of a legalistic framework that sets limits to secure peace and order. Legal institutions can act as significant counterweights to the state, with the judiciary in a unique position to support sustainable development by holding the other two branches of government accountable for their decisions and underpinning the credibility of the overall business and political environment. The World Bank argues that law plays a crucial role in promoting *economic* development by creating certainty and predictability by lowering transaction costs and by according greater access to capital and promoting respect for the rule of law by helping to establish a "level playing field" for the private sector. In its 2001 *Annual Report* the World Bank also argued that law plays a role in promoting *social* development by the harnessing of legal rights as a means of empowering the poor to take advantage of opportunities while protecting themselves against inequitable and arbitrary treatment. Thus the advantage of the legal reform agenda in governance is that it is a seemingly neutral means of improving countries' prospects for development (Collingwood, 2001; World Bank, 1994, 1997, 2001; World Bank, 2017). Leading legal scholars within the Bank have also suggested that the judicial system serves as a mechanism for conflict resolution through limiting the threat of arbitrary political interference, and providing laws to safeguard business interests and enforcement of contracts (World Bank, 2017).

This approach is best demonstrated and justified by public demands for tighter legal controls after any scandal. The result is that the infusion of an ethical approach to policy has been sacrificed on the altar of legal precision with the generation of manuals, handbooks, and addenda to the constitution (legal regulations) and institutional reforms developed to define the limitations and permissiveness of new responsibilities (Bunting, 2010; Demmke and Moilanen, 2011). Laws, policies, and institutional frameworks serve as guarantors and societal sureties to secure diversity of opinions and freedom of expression, beliefs, and rights to associations. A legal framework avoids discrimination or exclusion and minimizes polarization. The appeal to law is further justified because procedurally it is applicable to everyone, irrespective of gender, race, opinion, religious or political affiliation, or socioeconomic position because access to resources, education, influence, and information is equitably open without undue privileges, exemptions, bias, and preferential treatment (Demmke and Moilanen, 2011; English, 2013). However, in many instances the application of the rule of law varies, depending on who is involved. The government may be willing to enact a number of "good governance" reforms but there can be strong internal and external forces inhibiting enactment or, once enacted, enforcement. Multinational companies use bribes to achieve lucrative terms in privatization deals. In some circumstances, foreign companies persuade their own governments and donor-aid providers to pressure developing country governments into accepting unfavorable written legal contracts, using the withdrawal of aid as a threat. The danger is that in characterizing legal reform as a technocratic process, contentious, qualitative issues are overlooked in favor of less contentious issues that are easy to quantify and measure. Failing to confront the underlying political factors determining legal outcomes and securing government commitment to the reform agenda will clearly undermine the long-term sustainability of legal reform (Collingwood, 2001; Grindle, 2010). The upshot of this is that some citizens have come to believe that they can get away with wrongdoing (Thompson, 2018). This orientation drives individuals and businesses to "game the system," devoting extraordinary efforts to discovering and exploiting loopholes that run manifestly counter to the legitimate purposes of a law. Such behavior suggests an ironic confidence in the explicit rules and incentives created by our political institutions, as if they are all that ought to guide one's actions (English, 2013: 14). Pervasive gaming necessitates the development of extraordinarily complex and invasive legal processes that try to anticipate and prevent strategic exploitation of loopholes. The bad actions of a few thus lead to massive and costly systems of surveillance, further entrenching the idea that only the letter of the law matters. We come to be governed by complicated legal processes rather than meaningful principles.

By-passing laws fuels discouragement and resentment that may turn into political demands on behalf of racial, ethnic, religious, and regional identities, giving states an interest in containing and correcting any systematic inequity. Political systems may employ constitutions and laws to establish checks and balances through rules and institutions that will bind and limit power and provisions in case of abuse, excess, or infringement. Consultation enshrined in law or based on trust and civic commitment is the best wall against anarchy. Limitation of power is then no longer a matter of goodwill but of compulsory basic rules and legally binding provisions and regimes then achieve greater stability and predictability. In part, the overwhelming legalistic dominance in this narrative on governance undoubtedly stems from two problems noted earlier: the reasons behind ethics legislation are difficult to determine; and the reproach of double standards points to a deep discrepancy between principles and values on one side, and implementation, decisions, and risks on the other. In this regard, without agreement on ends and purposes, there is need for a more restrictive, legalistic frame of mind (Boulding, 1990; Vernon, 2010; Demmke and Moilanen, 2011). In addition, the legal fraternity is prone to argue against a separate focus on ethics because in any event there is considerable overlap between ethics and law, and much of the law embodies ethical principles such as respect for basic rights to life and property and the right of citizens to participate in political life. There is even integration of both the law and ethics in the combined legal ethics or legalism so, in their estimation, the law is as good as, or better than ethics at prescribing obligatory, prohibited, or permissible human behavior. Furthermore, the guarantee of law enforcement allows citizens to rely on the public administration of the state, with legality then one of the main characteristics, indeed the crucial pillar of the *etat de droit*. For this reason, the DNA of law is in the state's genesis and its legality rests on the communion of collective interests and desires that agrees that only through the congregation of efforts and wills can governance be achieved (Bilhim and Neves, 2005: 14; Thompson, 2018; World Bank, 2017). The law should suffice. Moreover, whereas an ethical framework may become self-defeating, generating negativity, if not cynicism, antagonism, and an adversarial reaction among those whose conduct the regulations seek to elevate, laws are taken as granted and seldom questioned from an ethical point of view. Finally, plain and simple the dominance of the legal profession in the governing executive and the legislatures throughout the Caribbean circumscribes any alternative debates to a narrow concourse of imagination (McKoy, 2012).

Regrettably, with respect to implementation, one controversial issue is that regulatory-based systems are not, however, fail-safe. Often the assumed premise is that the intrinsic value enshrined in legal terminology parallels that in the practice of human nature. Both assumptions are perfectly logical and understandable, but the correlation can be incongruent and faulty as both Anscombe (1958) and Fletcher (1966) credibly concur. Anscombe and Fletcher stress, like Aristotle, the character of lifestyle of the moral actor which they see as the chief determinant of the morality of an action, rather than conformity to a rule of right. Anscombe (1958, cited in Bluhm, 1978: 107) justifiably attacks this variety of rule-based ethics which she terms "consequentialism," on the grounds that according to this approach moral agents act responsibly when they measure their intention against the foreseeable consequences of an intended act. Thus, the justice or injustice of an act, and an understanding of what one ought to do, what it is one's duty to do are not determined by one's intrinsic good but by an estimate of consequences. This is the fundamental norm or rule of consequentialist ethics (Bluhm, 1978: 108). She further argues that based on this logic we have a standard which appears to allow us to avoid the hard question of whether a given act is intrinsically right or wrong (in conformity with or in violation of a moral absolute), and it also disregards the quality of the actor's intention. One looks only to outcomes, and thus the problem of moral action is reduced to the measurement of facts (Bluhm, 1978: 108). Anscombe further points out that the consequentialist has not really escaped but merely ignored the hard questions because they have adopted the standards of their society as their basic criterion of judgment (Bluhm, 1978: 108). Thus an individual applies implicit social standards to determine what one must decide are good and bad consequences. This is especially evident in decisions about "permissibility" in borderline cases. For in order to be imagining borderline cases at all, [one] has to assume some sort of law or standard according to which this is a borderline case. Where then does one get the standard from? In practice the answer invariably is from the standards current in one's society or one's circle (Bluhm, 1978: 108). Thus, Anscombe shows, that while the exponents of "law ethics" retain such legalist concepts as "moral obligation" and "moral ought," they have done away with the divine legislator which such concepts originally posited, and substituted the legislation of society's mere convention (Bluhm, 1978: 108).

In a similar vein Fletcher's attack on "law ethics," which he calls "legalism" is premised on the notion that just as legalism triumphed among the Jews after the exile, so too, in spite of the revolt of Jesus and Paul, it has managed to dominate Christianity constantly from very earliest days. In many real-life situations legalism demonstrates what Henry Miller calls "the immorality of morality" (Fletcher, 1966, cited in Bluhm, 1978: 110). For Fletcher then, as in the case of Anscombe, legalism grounded in Judaism and Catholicism spins elaborate systems of ethical rules, that operate as a total guide to all life situations and reduces one's ethical action to directives. Thus, solutions are preset, and you can look them up in a book. Protestantism too, while not constructing intricate systems offers no better alternative insisting instead on the rigid application of a few abstract moral rules, with the resulting attitude that "justice must be done, even though the world perishes" (Bluhm, 1978: 110). For Fletcher, the legalist is the man Mark Twain called "a good man in the worst sense of the word" (Fletcher, 1966: 17 cited in Bluhm, 1978: 110). And so, both Miller and Fletcher rejected contemporary systematic "rule-based ethics" or "law ethics" approaches with their historical origin in some form of the Mosaic Code and in the Christian legal-moral tradition, but which today are largely utilitarian in character (Bluhm, 1978: 107). Anscombe proposes that an adequate approach to ethics must have an adequate accompanying philosophy of psychology suffusing it in society (Bluhm, 1978: 108).

Extrapolating from history to the present provides us with ready examples to substantiate both scholars' arguments on the precision of the orthodoxy of procedural legalism as a society's sole guide for good governance because society, like the law, is variable. Our experience within the Caribbean with Anglo-American slavery, its dithering with various forms of modernization, and the more extant European examples with that of Nazi Germany will suffice. In these instances, these systems of governance were very "efficient and effective" in carrying out their atrocities because they were supported by a citizenry with "evil" intentions who were able to devise evil "laws" based on an "evil" consensus under governance administrations considered "transparent and accountable" to the "evil" citizenry (Yung, 2016: 10) wedded to particular concepts and ideologies. Thus, the kind of government and its policies are largely the product of the synergy that resulted from different actors in society (including media, civil society, political institutions, politicians, and bureaucracy) which ultimately rests on the quality of the citizens and the values they hold. Very often, public policies reflect and embody societal values. As indicated in chapter 2, in a way citizens "get" the kind of government and the policies that they "deserve." Good citizens with sensible values are the best guarantee of good government and good governance, ensuring the latter is in line with the former (Yung, 2016: 10; Grindle, 2010; Gensler, 2018).

Essentially, the central point is that there will be little impact from substituting the failure of the law to confront the intrinsically ethical nature of the reform process for a concomitant social process such as establishing behavioral norms. These norms include trust, tolerance, integrity, autonomy, and equality, where one is creating an enabling environment for business with pro-market policies by means of legal and anti-corruption reforms (Collingwood, 2001). Thus, having effective means including "sound procedures" in "governance" does not necessarily guarantee "good governance"; rather the outcome depends on whether something intrinsically valuable or valued as an end in itself is ultimately achieved (Yung, 2016: 10). Hence the cultivation of norms is necessary, as is being suggested, to ensure, enhance and protect peace, harmony, happiness, and the good life when confronted with the conflicting claims that we, as human beings, make against each other in the face of increasingly binding resource constraints. We may also say that human society derives norms from the need for survival of the species or because of the dominance of self-interest in the face of competition with other sentient beings (Bewaji, 2007). Fundamentally, an ethical turn forces us to recognize that the achievement of integrity in public administration is as much a behavioral challenge as a problem of institutional design and an unhealthy obsession with structural reform can often be used to mask the problems it seeks to prevent (Evans, 2012: 98; Hodgkinson, 1996; Crawford, 2004; Kolthoff et al., 2007). And so, addressing these issues will call for a much deeper evaluation of the society's role, philosophy, and governance as it seeks to determine what actions are right and why they are right, and to enjoin people in similar existential, sociological, physiological, and psychological circumstances to act accordingly rather than simply follow rule-based obligations (Bewaji, 2007; Grindle, 2010; Howard, 2019).

THE ECONOMIC IMPERATIVE:
HOMO ECONOMICUS SANS HOMO SOCIALISM

Not only has ethics been marginalized by the political scientists and the legal fraternity, but as well within the discipline of economics, further stifling the search for a new approach to governance. Ethics deals with values that are subjective and which cannot be assessed objectively, while economics deals with "facts" (Robbins, 1935) Many of our political-economic arguments have conceptualized *Homo economicus* as a rational man who attempts to pursue his selfish interests, with little regard for ethics. The rational agent, who maximizes his utility subject to the usual restrictions, is not undertaking ethically relevant actions. To put it another way: if the market takes care of the self-regulating economic relations, individual actions, which ethics regulates, are unimportant; whatever the conduct, the market will find a social optimum (Robbins, 1935; Andrews, 1991; Amunsden and Andrade, 2009; Astroulakis, 2010; Hutton, 2010; Crudas and Rutherford, 2010; Kliksberg, 2012). Arguments for drawing the line between ethics and the markets center on failures that limit efficient exchange between consenting adults. One such failure is the presence of externalities—where the actions of two parties' affect a non-consenting third party—as with pollution, child labor, and voting. Another is imperfect competition, where one party has extensive market power, leading to price gouging, with negative effects on consumers, and compelling contracts under duress. Imperfect markets also imply asymmetric information, where all parties do not have the information to make informed decisions. Markets may also lack morality due to internalities, arising from the failure of individuals to pursue their own self-interest. The main cause of this is a lack of self-control—people who smoke may not consider the negative effects on their own health, but rather their immediate gratification (Tirole, 2018).

This attitudinal approach harks back to Kant, who averred that a society of devils could be well governed if only their institutions provided the proper incentives (English, 2013: 13) and therefore it is important to focus on regulation to correct market failure. This hope in the ingenuous design of institutions suffuses throughout modern economic science which formally reduces human activity and social interaction to a self-regulating system of purposive-rational satisfaction of individual wants. Within this context, instrumental and strategic reasons are the organizing forces of behaviors that are abstracted from moral and ethical imperatives. As the classical economics of Smith, Ricardo, and Marx became the neoclassical economics of the twentieth century, the mathematization of the discipline seemed to promise the possibility of a truly value-free science. Since then, the legitimacy of economic ideas and institutions has rested not on any claim to moral soundness, but rather on the claim of neutral expertise. The irrelevance of moral imperatives appealingly offers the prospect of exact calculation of policy through, for example, rational choice theory (Taylor, 1982: 143).[3] By leaving out whatever cannot be calculated (Taylor, 1982: 143) this kind of exactness represents the semblance of validity (Christians, 2005: 144; Orr and Johnson, 2019). The representatives of institutions like the International Monetary Fund (IMF) have gone to great lengths to present themselves in such terms. Theirs is not the task of judging among various possible ends, and thus conceptions of the good life, they suggest; this is the purview of politics. Rather, they seek to determine the best means of achieving any given end by giving a country's leaders the economic tools necessary to pursue their own goals. The fund's legitimacy has thus rested in part on the separation of economics from ethics (Best, 2007: 108, Witztum, 2007; Atkinson, 2007, Astroulakis, 2010; Waeyenberge, 2018). The singular tragedy of the debate over globalization is that it is occurring at a time when universal markets value wealth more highly than wisdom. Instead of communities regulating and institutionalizing global markets, the market system tends to marginalize considerations of *justice* and to impose instead its own standards of instrumental *efficiency*. In the formalized model of rational market activity, individuals pursue their own wants with no community-wide reflection on the ultimate social consequences. The market system replaces *duty* with desire; it bestows the formal illusion of individual choice and responsibility at the same time as it imposes its own systemic imperatives that are altogether oblivious to moral and ethical concerns. Markets promise the most efficient production of plenty; at the same time, they invite us to entrust the future of the planet to the pursuit of profit (Day and Masciulli, 2007: X; Stiglitz, 2000; Keonane and Nye, 2000; Helleiner, 2001; Witztum, 2007; Atkinson, 2007; Rodrik, 2008; Astroulakis, 2010; Kung, 2012; Christie and Astill, 2016; Waeyenberge, 2018; Orr and Johnson, 2019). Thus we have many recycled dichotomous policy debates that revolve around welfare and freedom—increasing economic output through the possibilities presented by the ideal types of the planned economy or the *laissez-faire* and its derivatives (Sandel, 2010) in a world understood to be divided into "developed" and "underdeveloped" countries based on location along a range of indicators of material progress (Bloom et al., 2014: 22; Berberoglu, 2018; Levitt, 2018; Waeyenberge, 2018).

The economics canon within the region therefore reflects thematic variations in arguments concerned with the extent and by what means should governments redistribute income, whether between people or over the course of a person's lifetime; to what ends and to what extent and by what means should we seek to regulate economic activity, and/or where the state provides assistance of various kinds to citizens, should such support be conditional or unconditional? Thus, new subdisciplines began to emerge to inform understandings of political modernization and economic development with the field of development economics, for instance, becoming a critical one. This became a critical aspect of the formulation of policies of countries in the region organized to ensure and manage the transition to economic development and progress in a postcolonial economy.

The West Indian economist and Nobel Laureate W. Arthur Lewis pioneered these new developments. He considered colonialism to be an impediment to modernization and argued that the colonizing project bolstered the maintenance of a strict division of labor necessary to guarantee a supply of cheap raw agricultural and primary mineral commodities needed as inputs to capitalist industry in the colonial centers of Europe. This, he argued, prevented the accumulation of savings needed for investment and as long as the region continued on this trajectory development transition could not occur. For Lewis, colonialism denied the colonies an opportunity to embark on the path that led to the Industrial Revolution in Europe (Lewis, 1950, 1965, 1977; Levitt, 2018). He proposed a program of economic development premised upon national self-determination and independence from Europe and advocated a proactive role for the postcolonial state calling for the development of international organizations controlled and directed by a "development technocracy." Capital investments that were denied to the colonies under the colonial project were to be secured through fiscal and other incentives designed to attract foreign industries and foreign investors.

He argued for this form of "industrialization by invitation" as the necessary precondition for modernization (Lewis, 1950, 1965; 1977; St. Cyr, 1993; Levitt, 2018). This methodological approach further emphasized the need for "careful planning, organization, and allocation of resources" through a "detailed set of prescriptions, including goals, quantifiable targets, investment needs, design criteria, methodologies, and time sequences" (Bloom, Miescher and Manuh, 2014: 23, but also see Lewis, 1950, 1965, 1977; Pantin, 2005, and Lewis, 2013; Levitt, 2018). This interpretation led to the proliferation of policy papers written by technocrats from their own areas of specialization and expertise. These focused on immediate technically feasible or profitable short-run synergistic/symbiotic possibilities with the potentially broader social ramifications of such developments being relegated to a distant third (Pack, 1985; Peet, 1991; Farrell, 1993; Toye, 1993; Shaw, 1994 cited in Broome, 2003; Levitt, 2018). For these technocrats, there is an acknowledgment that some burden of the problem lies with external factors: enemies, rivals, obstacles, and capricious fate, facts of life, to live with and get around. However, they agree that the arrest of the Caribbean's development problems rested to a large extent with their ability to shape and reconfigure institutional processes and procedures (Farrell, 1993a: 201; see also Griffith, 1990 cited in Broome, 2003; see also Payne and Bishop, 2010; Girvan, 2011). And while these articles stand as exemplars of excellent social science, these new understandings of underdevelopment became tied to the narrow economic rationalities of production, consumption, and investment as fundamental conditions of modernization (Broome, 2003). Economic rationality became the motive force for development against the irrationality of colonial forms of mercantilism. The idea of a cultural transition from the "traditional" to the "modern" was replaced by the notion of progress in a process of modernization directed by policies of rational investments in industrialization, denied by colonial commandment (Bloom et al., 2014: 23; Manley, 1988; Pantin, 2005; Kiely, 2006, 2014; Petras and Veltmeyer, 2018; Potter et al., 2019).

Notwithstanding this new turn, development and modernization continued to be framed in such a way that ethical variables and issues were treated as ends in themselves and not solely or primarily as any other variable with exploratory or predictive capacity (Hutton, 2010; Neilsen and Massa, 2013). There is an implicit positivist assumption in a broad subset of these writings that the means for achieving social ends are separable from the ends themselves; and often, that moral considerations apply primarily to ends rather than to means (Henry, 1987; Rodrik, 2008; Milbank, 2010; Hutton, 2010; Kliksberg, 2012). As Hausman and McPherson (2017) note, there is a belief by both professional economists and lay followers of their work that the packaged abstract models of positive economics come with an indisputable built-in interpretation that provides unambiguous guidance to decision-makers. This difference has led to Sen lamenting that:

> the methodology of so-called "positive economics" has not only shunned normative analysis in economics, [but] it has also had the effect of ignoring a variety of complex ethical considerations which affect actual human behavior and which, from the point of view of the economists studying such behavior, are primarily matters of fact rather than of normative judgment. (Sen, 1987: 7; Goulet, 1994: 5 Williams, 2010; Maclean, 1998; Kliksberg, 2012; Weale, 2019; Orr and Johnson, 2019)

THE CONNECTING OVERFLOW TO MANAGEMENT

It is hard to characterize management science succinctly but it would be fair to suggest that rather like the *ceteris paribus* of economics, within management science only certain matters are defined as relevant and everything else becomes a form of background noise. The discipline of management science shares a broadly similar epistemic foundation as economics. As inextricably linked disciplines, economics studies how consumers, firms, and governments make decisions that together determine how resources are allocated and thus provides a broad understanding of economic activity within which all organizations function. Management science is concerned with understanding how managers behave and consider their role in the effective and efficient use and coordination of materials and labor within and between organizations and their environment in the pursuit of the organization's defined objectives. As intellectual disciplinary partners, scientific theories, models, and frameworks are used interchangeably to define and enhance the process of decision-making and as such only derivative facts and assumptions from these rather than values are definitive. The idea is that management science should be clear, read value free, and neutral in its orientation of analysis by giving its principal actors impartial advice and practical solutions from the latest findings and developments within the discipline to inform the process of decision-making. On trial are those administrators, managers, leaders, executives, officials, and functionaries who are generally preoccupied with organizational techniques, project analysis, technology, information systems, operational research, strategy, and solutions. They may regard any philosophical reflection at best as luxurious and distracting, or at worst a downright impediment to their central interest: efficiency and effectiveness. In their view, the underlying rationale in this general antagonism to an ethical turn may be that a centipede who indulges in too much self-analysis might have difficulty in walking. And so, it is neither uncharitable nor untrue to suggest

that there is a veil of anti-intellectualism that is endemic within this pragmatism. Whatever the reason, the fact remains that an ethical turn often has
to overcome distrust, dislike, suspicion, and on occasion contempt because
to them it is this intellectualizing that may prove detrimental to pragmatic
managerial efficiency and effectiveness once means are discriminated from
ends (Hodgkinson, 1996: 13; Cooper et al., 2006; Cowell et al., 2007). From
the systems standpoint and from the standpoint of scientific management,
organizations are morally neutral. The direct psychological implication of
organizational power, vis-à-vis its membership, is that individual sentiments,
affects, and interests are discounted. The organizational language game is
impersonal, even anti-personal.

As such, the academic institutions have trailed behind in seeing ethics
as constitutive and integral to the process of helping business and economics become more ethical through the introduction and development of new
programs. In those few instances offered at the University of the West
Indies they are directed to students in Masters of Business Administration
and Executive Masters of Business Administration (EMBA) programs but
throughput of graduates is low and in other instances there generally remains
(Rossouw and Stuckelberger, 2012: 27) ad hoc and unorganized course offerings. Though concerns about corruption and conflicts of interest seem to be
fairly widespread in the region, the development and application of ethics
to business have not been a priority with little research (see Alleyne et al.,
2013; and Cowell et al., 2007) being conducted from the point of view of
quantity, quality, and topic variety. Moreover, by implication, the utility of
business ethics course offerings at tertiary-level institutions in the region is
further questioned on the logic that by the time students reach this stage their
socialization process is complete and little or no useful purpose can be served
by exposing them to such limited and narrow training. In addition it is difficult to mitigate the impervious global business culture beamed through every
available information and communication technological device that peddles
powerful images of the impulse of CEOs to misbehave with impunity only
to reap the rewards of power, influence, and money (Cowell et al., 2007 and
Rossouw and Stuckelberger, 2012). A less often remarked feature is that texts
offering case studies in business ethics almost always frame such business
scenarios as a personalization of the issue concerned and are sterile when
compared to the circumstances of such influential images. This stress on the
agency of the individual—what would you do in this situation, give reasons
for your decisions, rather than, what is the nature of man or what is involved
in an organizational system based on the true nature of man—also seems to
obliterate consideration of the importance of structural constraints (see Danes
et al., 1995; Alleyne et al., 2013) aimed at improving an ethical dimension
of good governance. This is a crucial point, since it begins to expose the

ways in which business ethics has "de-socialized" these kinds of ideas. Yet given the highly interconnected economies that exist and the opportunities that emerging markets provide for investors, good corporate governance is fundamental to sustained development and cannot continue to be ignored (Cowell et al., 2007; Sookram, 2016; Jamaica Observer, 2018), nor be seen as leaching away meaning and purpose from the value analysis of the nature of the individual in the sociopolitical and cultural environment of his existence.

These glaring deficiencies exist not just in the academy alone. The Caribbean private sectors that inform the practice of business, apart from pursuing profit as if it were a "moral crusade," have endorsed Friedman's perspective as their categorical imperative with the accompanying view that ethics has little or no place in the business world (Friedman, 1970; see also Crudas and Rutherford, 2010). This image of management is not intended to demonize management as lacking in all ethics or virtue, but rather to compel firms to greater responsibility toward employees—which would require a significant shifting of classic industrial relations terminology to a point necessitating a reversal of the orchestrated swing in political power. Regrettably such a perspective appears to be wishful thinking as, inherently, management's current neoliberal economic and political orthodoxy has enabled capital to exploit global inequalities in labor conditions. Though we may ask our private sector leaders to have a certain charismatic or transformative zeal toward showing greater responsibility and sensitivity to local and regional labor, the interests of employees and the unemployed, unions, labor affiliations, and other such bodies, there is a real fear among management that such representation will inevitably see them free-falling in a "race to the bottom." To avert this, management in the interest of shareholders characteristically remain autonomous with the freedom intact to remain distant from the immediate emotional pull of interpersonal relations and the sentiments of labor and its organized representation, in order to advance a more compelling strategy for the greater organizational good and its viability in the long term. To achieve competitive success therefore, management must be able to exercise this freedom responsibly and should strive toward, and realistically heed, the particular qualities that advance the firm's cause on the basis of reason and calm rationality, drawing upon the best available models, education, strategies, and information—and not acting on whim, emotion, or impulse. As such, in the fiercely competitive world of contemporary capitalism, what matters most for businesses is ensuring four principal objectives involving loss of money and company reputation: (1) avoid breaking the criminal law in one's work-related activity; (2) avoid action that may result in civil law suits against the company; (3) avoid actions that are bad for the company image; and (4) discover ever more imaginative ways of making money from money (Friedman, 1970; Crudas and Rutherford, 2010).

In this regard, the values of autonomy, distance, rationality, self-control, and containment accord more favorably with the virtues of enlightened management than does ethical subjectivity with its associated widespread interpretations of personal, sentimental, or intimate relationships reserved for ethical and moral reasoning. Ethics therefore is seen as private and personal and should stay that way, out of business, because it clouds and compromises the open pursuit of profit (Friedman, 1970; Bhide and Stevenson, 1991; Crudas and Rutherford, 2010; Kung, 2012). In this respect, management may, if it cares to, genuflect to ethical concerns, but must be wary of the push against capitalism in a globalized environment that can be unscrupulous in its manifestations. In general therefore, what constitutes ethical practice by the private sector seems more like a clip-on contemporary approach to detailing codes of minimal conduct for the sector (Bishop and Preston, 2000), with an attitude perhaps of "Look, we've done the ethics, aren't we good!" which encourages the unfortunate idea that it is *somebody else's job* to "do the ethics" (Boddington, 2018: 54).

And so, perhaps unsurprisingly, a major weakness of the *Global Competitiveness Report* in any given year has been its failure or its oversight on how an understanding of ethics could fully apply to the relationships between macro-level social forces and micro- or individual-level changes and adaptations, as well as impact the motivational patterns, trends, and forces driving not only competitiveness but the rate of economic development (Stone, 1992: 8; Shue, 2008; Kliksberg, 2012). Although there can be good reasons to ensure that specific nominated individuals are assigned responsibility for certain issues, a code of ethics is a beginning not an end. So, the very idea of parceling ethics into a formal "code" is dangerous, because it leads to the attitude that ethics itself is just some separate part of life and other activities, rather than being more meaningfully looked at as a part and parcel of how we live individually and collectively, for it goes without saying then, that business as the engine of capitalism is inherently social and can only be successful in a society that is itself sustainable. It is thus increasingly the case that the business of business is that society be stable and sustainable.

What is needed, in fact, is analysis that moves beyond the iron cage of methodological myopia to encompass theoretical approaches that can be extended and deepened, accomplished through releasing and exploring assumptions in the interest of making the social science theory more powerful and applicable to the solution of ethical and social problems as ends in themselves (Neilsen and Massa, 2013: 145). In addition, by integrating rather than disconnecting our analysis from the mutual interface where ethics and institutional systems influence each other to impact social reality, we can advance our understanding toward improving the transparency of the motivations for studying particular institutional and ethical issues and problems beyond solely abstract theory building, theory testing, and convenience data sampling (Neilsen and Massa, 2013: 145; see also Maclean, 1998; Shue, 2008; Orr and Johnson, 2019; Howard, 2019).

DEVELOPMENT ETHICS

Unfortunately, as different theoretical and philosophical specialisms have proliferated within the regional social science academy there has been a disingenuous tendency to not acknowledge each other's thought and the meaningful contributions toward enhancing the scope for more effective solutions to governance. None more so than that of the omission of development ethics from social science epistemology. Less I be accused of the same common error in contemplating the ethical turn in governance, it would be remiss to ignore the epistemic challenges and the opportunities provided by the work being done in the field of development ethics. It can be defined as the ethics of global development and is the ethical reflection on the ends, means, and processes of beneficial social change (and maintenance) at the local, national, regional, and global levels (and their relations) (Crocker, 2014: 245; Drydyk and Keleher, 2019). As a "discipline," it sought to offer a corrective solution to the notion and meaning of development, serving as the conceptual cement for multiple diagnoses of problems with their policy implications. To do this it employed an explicit phenomenological approach that lays bare the value costs of various courses of action (Gasper, 2014) by presenting well-reasoned alternatives to mainstream habits regarding those choices. In particular, it clarified the values behind evaluative and prescriptive arguments from economics through querying its narrowness in using only values from the marketplace by introducing other relevant values thereby challenging an automatic superior status for economics arguments, in relation to, for example, human rights arguments (Gasper, 2014: 93; Drydyk and Keleher, 2019).

Books have proliferated asking what are the goals of development; what alternative strategies must be adopted, either in pursuing development or in repudiating it; how to rethink the Third World, its politics, and development itself; what are the Third World's options and its hopes for "another development"; and whether fifty years of World Bank and IMF global financial management has been enough to ameliorate the development challenges that we face (Goulet, 1996, 2000, 2006; Dower, 2006, 2019; Crocker, 2014; Drydyk and Keleher, 2019). However, these mainstream texts did not go far enough in seeking an organic unity by joining reflection to action and micro analysis to macro analysis in order to show the holism of development through the integration of the diverse disciplines. To distinguish from the conventional notion of development that gives prominence to economic or

technical achievements, which became the lynchpin of modernization thinking, development ethics instead emphasizes the notion of "authentic development" which emphasizes as a *sine qua non* the provision of a satisfactory
conceptual, institutional, and behavioral approach, the lodestone of—the
good life—the just society in a sound relation to nature.

Development ethics was prescient in criticizing explicitly the value
implications of competing development models, strategies, and programs
in the light of prevailing ideologies and political doctrines. It became the
new "discipline" which dealt *ex professo* with the normative dimensions of
development because it lay at the intersection of other major disciplines—
economics, planning, human geography, cross-cultural sociology, politics,
nutrition and demography, development studies, and development policy,
each of which brought its own concerns (Astroulakis, 2010; Gasper, 2014;
Dower, 2019). As far as the discipline was concerned no true interdisciplinary analysis could be achieved by a mere juxtaposition of partial view-
points. Even analytical and theoretical studies should be oriented toward the
transformation of social reality (Goulet, 2005). As such development ethics
generated a need for public reason by asking difficult ethical questions about
priorities and procedures, rights, and responsibilities, including such questions as: What is good or "real" development? What is the good life which
development policy should seek or ought to facilitate? What really are benefits? How are those benefits and corresponding costs to be shared, within the
present generation and between generations? Who decides and how? What
rights of individuals should be respected and guaranteed? When—for example, in the garment trade, the sex trade, the "heart trade," in-care services,
and the trade in human organs—should "free choice" in the market be seen
instead as the desperation behavior of people who have too little real choice?
(Gasper, 2011: 4, 2004, 2009, 2012, 2014; Nussbaum, 2011; Dower, 2019)
In this regard, development was not to be premised on an empty materialism meaning men and women *having and owning* more, but more so when
they were enabled "to *be* more," achieved through the collective bonds of
solidarity that exist (or ought to exist) among these populations and population groups (Goulet, 1996, 2000). Development ethicists recognize therefore
that they should attend not only to the cures of multidimensional poverty
but also to poverty's deep causes, such as inequality, and its consequences,
as well as instability and conflict. Moreover, they realize that often poverty
alleviation—because it can conflict with other good goals—should be linked
in a complementary way with other morally urgent objectives. In so doing,
development ethicists are pushing the frontiers of development and development ethics into new areas. It is not, however, that development ethics
should tackle every national and global issue (Crocker, 2000, 2009; Drydyk
and Keleher, 2019).

As one of the earliest pioneers of the discipline, Goulet from as early as the 1960s had articulated that the idea of development meant the economic, political, and cultural developmental changes that allow human beings, both as individual persons and as members of groups, "to move from one condition of life to one which is more human in some meaningful way." Goulet stressed the importance of distinguishing between different kinds of development such as "authentic human development," and those undesirable kinds which he sometimes called "false development" or "anti-development" or "mal-development," which assign supremacy to mere economic might hiding behind the mask of capitalist modernization espousing progress and civilization (Goulet, 1996). For him, development's ultimate goals ought to be not mere existence but about providing all people with the opportunity to be a full human in their totality toward obtaining the good life. However, despite his recognition of the differences in values of cultures and societies, Goulet (1995, 1996, 2000) consistently advocated three goals for development that were universalizable—in the sense that these goals lie behind the choices of whether to accept or reject development—namely life-sustenance, esteem (sense of self-worth), and freedom. The first concerns the meeting of basic needs; esteem is the feeling of self-respect and independence; and freedom is about "to be" and "to do." At the very least it signifies an expanded range of choices for societies and their members, together with the minimization of constraints (external, though not necessarily internal) in the pursuit of some perceived good (Goulet, 1995, 1996; Crocker, 2006; Gasper, 2004, 2006, 2008, 2009, 2012, 2014).

Although the discipline has done much toward the incorporation of ethics in contemporary development thinking, even here there has been vexing concerns of an epistemological and ontological nature. Development ethics continues to face the pressing tasks of understanding and ethically evaluating appropriate institutional responses to complex and contested phenomena such as globalization and development itself (Crocker, 2000, 2004, 2008). Charles Beitz (2001 cited in Crocker, 2004: 14, 2008) states the empirical aspects of the issue well: "There is a large, complex, and unresolved empirical question about the relative contributions of local and global factors to the wealth and poverty of societies" (Beitz, 2001: 113 cited in Crocker, 2004: 14, 2008). As such controversy exists among development ethicists with respect to which agents and structures are to blame for the present state of global destitution and unequal opportunity and where responsibility lies for societal change. Stemming from this concern is that of the agency and the kind of processes required to ameliorate these development failures (Crocker, 2004: 15; 2008). There is the view then that agent-centered approaches are more efficient and effective at the level of intervention when resolving moral and ethical conflicts. And so, various experts such as judges (and the constitutions they interpret), political leaders, donors and their technical experts, philosophers, or development ethicists, and, on the other hand, popular agencies of various kinds are able to give advice and take stands without falling into self-righteous moralizing and finger-wagging. Moreover, experts often excel at "know how," if not "know why" (Crocker, 2004: 14, 2008; Schwenke, 2019).

Against this, rule by experts or guardians can lead to new tyrannies or barbarisms, and many experts fail to facilitate ways in which "recipients" of development can be in charge of shaping and implementing their own development goals (Crocker, 2009: 50; Escobar, 1995). In this instance, process becomes important. To counteract such tyranny, emphasis is [re]oriented to enabling countries and their citizens access to genuine opportunities to be authors of their own lives and development paths rather than being merely considered and observed as passive recipients or beneficiaries of goods and services of the fruits of cunning development programs. The people have to be seen, in this perspective, as being actively involved—given the opportunity—in shaping their own destiny, through new forms of empowerment. A shift is therefore necessary from such an "agency-centered" development perspective to one that implies a deepening and broadening of democracy that includes but goes well beyond a universal franchise coupled with free and competitive elections, as important as they are. Neither must the process or object of deliberative democracy be hijacked by a brand of popular participation and democracy that is suspect insofar as it masks demagogic manipulative tendencies of majorities (or minorities) who might dominate others to the extent that people's beliefs and preferences are deformed by tradition (Crocker, 2004: 14; Escobar, 1995). Crucially important will be the engendering of venues—within both government and civil society—where citizens and their representatives can engage in deliberative give-and-take to solve common problems. Civil society is the realm of the most basic humanity, its ethic is defined by consensus, compromise, cooperation, and co-existence. It acts as an important "watchdog" and brake on a reckless government (Hope and Chikulo, 2000: 6; Goulet, 2000). Without civility, that is to say, without a great many unstated or vaguely articulated but still binding and operative limitations on such things as what is a permissible political argument, discussion is impossible and therefore government by discussion is impossible (Turner, 2003: 8; Thunder, 2019). Seen from this perspective the practice of deliberative democracy, grounded in the ideals of agency, dialogue, reason-giving, and reciprocity, has much to offer development ethics. The theory and practice of deliberative democracy emphasize social choice through public discussion that aims at solutions—that nearly everyone can accept—to common problems (Crocker, 2004, 2008; Escobar, 1995).

As the discipline evolved, the multiple meanings assigned to the term *development* mirrored the diverse political, economic, and social conditions found in varied urban and regional settings around the world and belied the fact that developmental processes themselves are dialectical, fraught with contradictions, conflicts, and unpredictable reversals (Goulet, 1988, 1996; Crocker, 2000). Further controversy surrounded the discipline in that development ethicists have also been divided on the status of the moral norms that they seek to justify and apply. Three positions have emerged: universalists, such as utilitarians and Kantians, argue that development goals and principles are valid for all societies. Particularists, especially communitarians and postmodern relativists, reply that universalism masks ethnocentrism and (Northern or Western) cultural imperialism. Pro-development particularists either reject the existence of universal principles or affirm only the *procedural* principle that each nation or society should draw solely on its own traditions and decide its own development ethic and path (Crocker, 2004: 11; see also Crocker, 2008; Elsetain et al., 1998; Gasper, 2006; Malavisi, 2014; Schwenke, 2019; Malavisi, 2019).

Another unsettled question with respect to the scope of development ethics concerns how wide a net development ethics should cast in the topics it addresses. It is controversial whether development ethicists, concerned with rich country responsibility and global distributive justice, should restrict themselves to official development assistance, or whether they also should treat such topics as international trade, capital flows, migration, environmental pacts, terrorism, civil conflict, state fragility, military intervention, humanitarian intervention, and responses to human rights violations committed by prior regimes. The chief argument against these extensions is that development ethics would thereby become too ambitious and diffuse, and could grow to be identical with all international or social ethics, leaving insufficient attention to alleviating poverty and powerlessness in various poor communities. Both sides agree that development ethicists should assess North–South (and South–South) relations and the numerous globalized forces that influence poverty and inequality in poor countries. What is unresolved, however, is whether development ethics should also address such topics as those listed when—or to the extent that—these topics have no causal relationship to absolute or relative poverty or powerlessness (Crocker, 2004: 10, 2008, 2000; Gearty, 2010; Schwenke, 2019; Dower, 2019).

An ongoing debate regarding distributive and redistributive justice has also been controversial among development ethicists. Of concern is how should development's benefits, burdens, and responsibilities be distributed within poor (and rich) countries and between rich and poor countries. The divide centers around the notion development ethicists hold of the "doctrine" of value neutrality or a narrow construing of the "mandate" or "comparative advantage," of their institutions, in contradistinction to policy planners who find themselves in the camps of the utilitarians prescribing simple aggregation and maximization of individual utilities. Rawlsians advocate income and wealth maximization for the least well-off (individuals or nations). Libertarians contend that a society should guarantee no form of equality apart from equal freedom from the interference of government and others (Crocker, 2004: 13; see also Crocker, 2008). Development ethicists are being challenged to debate with citizens and policy professionals the merits of substantive concepts of distributive and redistributive justice and the procedures for deciding this question on the grounds that development ethicists should move from value neutrality to challenge policymakers and citizens to forge, through fair processes, normatively appropriate ideals of economic and political justice. If affluent nations and individuals can relieve suffering and death without sacrificing anything of comparable moral worth, they are morally obliged to do so, for "equity" is not only instrumentally valuable but is also good or right in itself (Crocker, 2004, 2008; Goodin, 1995; Rawls, 2001; Schwenke, 2019).

Related to the debate on distributive and redistributive justice a controversy also exists in development ethics with respect to whether (good) societal development should have —as an ultimate goal—commitments other than to the present and future human good. Communitarian ethicists ascribe intrinsic value—equal or even superior to the good of individual human beings—to such human communities as family, nation, or cultural group. Others argue that non-human individuals and species, as well as ecological communities, have equal and even superior value to human individuals. Those committed to "eco-development" or "sustainable development" often fail to agree on what should be sustained as an end in itself and what should be maintained as an indispensable or merely helpful means. Nor do they agree on how to surmount conflicts among environmental and other competing values (Crocker, 2004: 13, 2008).

Regrettably, development ethicists became victims of the very same criticisms that they sought to resolve and so have been accused of being divorced from the reality of the poor. The existence of cultural paternalism among development scholars and practitioners rings true with regard to development ethicists as well, and prevents them from having a thorough understanding of the context and the suffering of others (Goulet, 1973; Crawford, 2004; Schwenke, 2019; Souffrant, 2019). Extreme poverty, squalor, endemic disease, and undeserved suffering are not good things. For those living under these conditions, feelings of helplessness and hopelessness prevail. Those who work for the betterment of people in such situations cannot thoroughly understand their plight merely by observation. This also resonates with the evident disconnect between development ethicists and development practitioners. This has been one of the obstacles to carrying out an interdisciplinary approach to development where more work needs to be done to bring different fields and people together.

It is also interesting to note that—with one exception (Penz et al., 2011)—the term "corruption" does not appear in the indices of major works in development ethics (Crocker, 2008; Deneulin, 2014; Dower, 2009; Gasper, 2004; Goulet, 1971, 1989; Nussbaum, 2000, 2011 cited in Crocker, 2014: 249) nor is it frontally addressed.[4] Why? Development ethicists, in wanting to avoid self-righteous finger-waving and a fixation on personal character, avoided addressing ethically deficient institutions and political policies and initially shied away from this issue trying instead (usually unsuccessfully) to dodge the question and change the topic (Crocker, 2014: 249). The perception of this discipline or sub-discipline (Gasper, 2012)—since there is still an identity crisis of determining placement within the academy—has become an ambiguous historical adventure born of tensions between *what* is sought and *how* it is obtained (Gasper, 2006, 2012) leaving very limited scope for its teaching and the grassroots discussion (Drydyk and Keleher, 2019). In spite of the best efforts, of practitioners, the discipline has been mired in unending and perplexed self-questioning with claims that it involves only an endless proliferation of different opinions and challenges to ethics and governance that arise in international development processes and that remain unresolved; and that it is superfluous and does not conform to a tidy self-enclosed field, or never makes an impact (UNESCO, 2000; Schwenke, 2019). There are few ongoing venues in development organizations or institutions in which the people who work on development policies, programs, and projects can discuss emerging ethical issues as they experience them. Moreover, the ways in which work is structured and directed in these organizations and institutions leaves little space and time for that discussion (Drydyk and Keleher, 2019: 11; Schwenke, 2019). In fact, much work on the same issues for investigation has not used the label development ethics. In addition a reading of much of this work saw issues of governance and the competing demands of various stakeholders in the development of appropriate governance mechanisms and the values and judgments that inform societal choices and political decision-making all together ignored or enveloped in procedural policy solutions resulting in proposed codes of practice (Crocker, 2011; Schwenke, 2019). Unmistakably, the emergence of development ethics has produced a form of scholarship which has been responsive to human needs by offering valuable insights into the study and practice of development. Rather than discarding all of, or ignoring development ethics because it became inflated and failed to meet all of its disciplinary expectations, scholars and practitioners within the region should consider it (at least) as an important supplement to traditional spheres of academic endeavor, because it offers us tools to analyze the ethical dimensions of particular kinds of relationships and practices in development. And, a focus on human relatedness and caring can be a starting point for the development of good governance because of its ability to contribute to building qualitatively enhancing social capital formation in poor countries struggling with a plethora of demands on their capacities while pursuing change in seeking a reasonable understanding of what good governance can deliver—and what it cannot.

ETHICS: THE EVOLUTION OF A SYNTHESIS

Given the individual divisiveness, disciplinary, and academic compartmentalization as well as conceptual inability within the social sciences throughout the Caribbean, it is no wonder then that several of our intractable challenges of governance remain unresolved. It is worth keeping in mind that these disciplines are not hard-edged contrasts in their orientation. Combinations of them occur to provide useful possible outcomes as fields of enquiry in teaching, research, writing, and public utterances. However, life's richness outstrips any single system of analysis and based on the disciplinary overview in the academy we would be hard pressed to identify any sector that would not benefit from fresh thinking or in which we could not envisage a better way, whether it concerns international relations, the environment, health care, education, welfare, business, and trade. None of the governance challenges we face can be truly resolved without an ethical turn, a reflexive turn which not only provides for an introspection of the individual's role in governance and development but must also focus on the macro and micro institutional framework of society. As a consequence, development ethicists may purport to offer a solution to the plight of various members of the human community on poverty alleviation, but they will agree that its actual implementation will require that all of the relevant institutions within the particular society in question be involved in its eradication (Gasper, 2004). As Sen (1999b: XIII) stresses in the preface to *Development as Freedom* and by extrapolation here to an approach for governance, it calls for an integrated analysis of economic, social, and political activities, involving a variety of institutions and many interactive agencies. Accordingly, we need a new way of thinking and acting, particularly one that acknowledges the key role institutional factors play at all levels in the economy, from the structure and functions of the firm, through the operation of markets, to the form of state intervention at multiple spatial levels (see Williamson, 1985; Hodgson, 1988; North, 1990).

Used here, *institutions* are defined both as formal mechanisms or institutional arrangements such as particular organizational forms such as states, firms, labor unions, political parties, and the formal (usually legally enforced) structures of rules and regulations and also as informal mechanisms or the institutional environment, which refers to both the systems of informal conventions, such as customs, behavioral norms, and to social routines transaction norms, and so on that constrain and control socioeconomic behavior. Both the institutional arrangements and the institutional environment cohere to determine what organizations or social milieu come into existence. For example, what political organizations emerge and how they function and evolve, is fundamentally influenced by the institutional environment. But equally, in the course of their operation, the institutional environment also reproduces and modifies the institutional arrangements. This reflexive iterative interaction can shape and influence the governance regime that will emerge across varying contexts. Thus state-led institutional change can take various forms, involving the reform of the legal regulatory environment of economic activity (e.g., changing the nature of competition law, employment law, etc.); major shifts in policy programs (such as changes in industrial policy, or monetary policy); and changing the legislative framework governing the form and operation of institutional arrangements and other economic organizations (such as corporations and labor unions). It can also take other forms such as reconfiguring the regulatory structures and apparatus of the state itself (e.g., setting up new regulatory institutions and changing the division of policy responsibilities between central and local government). Institutions matter once we are open to seeing that the subnational, national, regional, and global factors are causally and normatively connected with different weights and in different ways in different contexts pertaining to how they affect the national (and local) for good and ill especially with respect to the issues of poverty and powerlessness (see, Martin, 2000; Crocker, 2014: 246). Equally, consideration of institutions within ethics also encompasses consideration of the *cultural foundations* of the space economy such as the role of cultural processes in the formation of social structures and individual identities, consumption norms, and lifestyles, all of which may influence the formation and nature of informal conventions, constraints, and norms that impact on local and regional economic development as seen in figure 3.1 (Broome, 2003, see also Martin, 2000; Sen, 2000; World Bank, 2002; Frost, 2012).

The importance of institutions to ethics must be underscored with the issues of corruption, which influences governance by impeding the goal of economic growth for developing countries, and must become more explicitly and robustly involved in an ethical turn of analysis. Both IFEX-ALC (2012) and Crocker (2014) make note of the cultures of "impunity," which are among the causes and consequences of the enduring corruption that is part of our regional reality, whether expressed as disregard for either human life or human liberty. These cultures can alert us to the role institutions can play in shaping a society, in that before a country can move forward, it must often reckon with past wrongs, such as systematic violation of human rights, inequalities of various kinds, especially those of economic and political power, and other forms of social injustice. Overcoming power imbalances is

The Centrality of an embedded Ethical Institutional Framework to inform the Social Contract for Good
Governance and Development

Ethical   Actions   can   reinforce   an
institutional environment to help effect
institutional change for good governance
and development

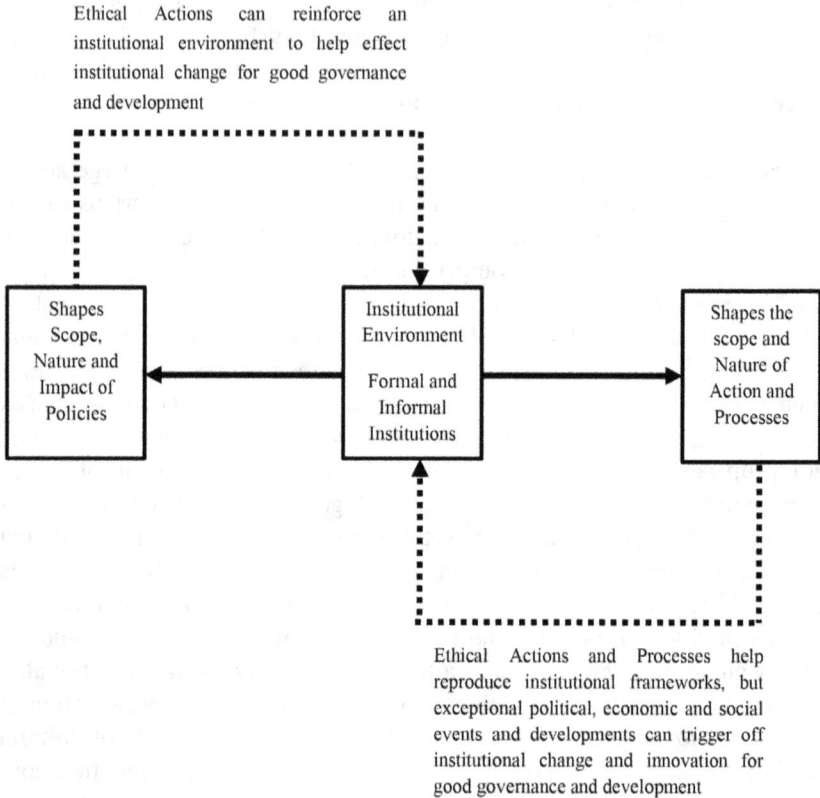

Ethical   Actions   and   Processes   help
reproduce institutional frameworks, but
exceptional political, economic and social
events and developments can trigger off
institutional change and innovation for
good governance and development

**Figure 3.1   The Centrality of an Embedded Ethical Institutional Framework to Inform
the Social Contract for Good Governance and Development.** *Source*: Broome, P.A.,
(2003). Information Technology and the Development Process: Caribbean Micro-States in
the Global Economy. Unpublished PhD. Dissertation. University of Cambridge.

frequently indispensable in righting past wrongs and removing their causes.
A nation or region emerging from a difficult past must decide not only why
and how it should reckon with that past, but also how it should balance
past-looking efforts with the creation of future-oriented policies and institutions (Crocker, 1999, 2002; Boulding, 1990; Crawford, 2004; De Greiff and
Duthie, 2009 cited in Crocker, 2014: 250). Among the means that nations
and international institutions have employed are "forgive and forget," truth
and reconciliation commissions, historical accounts, reparations, apolo-
gies, trial and punishment, museums, and artistic contributions. Finding the
right balance is crucial since too much or the wrong kind of attention to the
past can undermine efforts for a better future. Future dreams may turn into

nightmares if the past is neglected as past injustices may endure into the present and block or undermine efforts at good and democratic development (Spinner-Halev, 2012, cited in Crocker, 2014: 250). The best ways forward will include efforts to understand and transform the causes of past wrongs, especially when these causes persist in the present. Corruption, with its culture of impunity, is a past and enduring wrong that in and of itself constitutes an institutional norm. It is in this regard that the evolution or [re]orientation of individual and communal agency can be used either to commit further wrongs or—through citizen empowerment—mitigate appropriately against them to a more inclusive and deeper democracy (Crocker, 1999, 2002, 2008 cited in Crocker, 2014: 250; Ceva and Ferretti, 2019). The mere fact that institutions are such determinants of change and that values are implicitly constitutive in all of our institutions is precisely why there is a need for an ethical consciousness integral to influencing our patterns of interaction (Sen, 2000).

Moreover, because ethics bridges knowing and doing, it constitutes a site for multiple inter- and transdisciplinary engagements. Most commonly, however, although it is identified as a major branch of the discipline of philosophy alongside logic, epistemology, and metaphysics, upon closer examination ethics can be seen as *integrating* (my emphasis) a number of disciplines such as psychology and anthropology, as well as politics and economics, that may also be described as having emerged from it. Thus, ethics as an inherently interdisciplinary endeavor, can avoid the further development of multiple disciplines implicated in the creation of new hybrid research fields. It can do so through integration in a more synthetic unity, in a way that invokes a systematic and critical reflection on human action both to increase knowledge about and to improve culturally or personally acceptable behavior (Balsamo and Mitcham, 2010: 259; Howard, 2019; Lever and Poama, 2019). Regrettably, expecting a *rapprochement* within the longstanding social sciences by forging a relationship with the inclusion of ethics in governance has been a disappointment. Turn the other cheek in this instance, meant look the other way. Ethics, rather than being seen as a source of inspiration, instead carries a burdensome perception—a limitation (Vernon, 2010: 11) and as yet, its role in the processes of institutional transformation remains poorly theorized. Most studies still believe that ethics is too weak and too "nice" to be of real importance in what is regarded as the tough, dirty, and unprincipled world of politics. Some well-known sayings include: "morality has nothing to do with politics"; "ethics and politics are poor bedfellows;" "even worse, in political matters, ethical considerations can compound problems, worsen processes, derail policies; and are rarely part of solutions." "Morality in politics means naivety and naivety is dangerous: it underestimates difficulties and conflicts, it prefers not to believe in cruelty or wrath" (Girardin, 2012: 20; Lever and Poama, 2019).

Ethics is viewed as ineffective and an embarrassment to those who want to get a proper understanding of what is going on. As a result, ethics is often an "add-on," a sort of accessory and instrumentalized guarantee, not properly integrated or understood in its methods and objectives (Bunting, 2010: 5; Shue, 2008). Worst yet, an inclusion of values as part of the discourse on governance is usually considered as the cherry on the cake, an ornament of secondary importance that does not harm but neither does it help. Some skeptics refer to values as *window dressing*. Values are often seen as wishful thinking. And so, pragmatic politicians like to refer to values in fair weather but quickly revert to "interests" just as soon as the wind starts blowing. Cynics see values as a communication tool designed by spin doctors to camouflage political motives and conceal real decisions (Girardin, 2012: 83; Kung, 2012). In some cases, an appeal to values may hamper or even harm the political process and confuse or spoil decision-making, thus acknowledging in a sense that all human relations, meanings, and practices are grounded in power relations (Boulding, 1990; Williams, 2010; Mackie, 2013). For these reasons the idea of values points to a whole realm of concerns that somehow never get mentioned in scholarly discourse often due to their highly personal and political implications, and of course their assumed polarity with "facts" (Proctor, 1999: 3). The voices seeking to highlight the human consequences of economic activity or calling for moral restraint in the interests of "the common good," seem like ever fainter cries in a more and more inhospitable wilderness of governance (Williams, 2010).

Stoker argues that "viewing citizens as ethical actors is not the perspective of a hopeless idealist" (Stoker, 1992: 376). I think that this is not a vain hope, but if we are to make progress we have to think differently about the issues. Whereas "embedded ethicists" are now common in medical organizations, the fields of politics, economics, and social development remain resistant to ethical thinking and query its legitimacy and value-added to governance. Skepticism about the relevance of ethics to governance has been discounted, fed mainly by the experience of human failures and cynicism over the gaps between declaration and implementation, promise, and realization (Parsons, 1998; Girardin, 2012; Kilksberg, 2012; Drydyk and Keleher, 2019). And flatly put, today's development ethicists as indicated have shot themselves in the foot by getting considered as an academically insignificant discipline within the academy. This is because although it may have moved us further along toward seeing a new epistemological and ontological aperture, as well as a unique and distinct set of necessary tools and approaches for understanding and managing development challenges, as a disciplinary focus it did not grapple with the complexity of the phenomena as discussed in chapters 1 and 2.

And, this has not been helped by the invidiousness of labeling one discipline false and the other worthy of study—a common mistake that has long plagued the social sciences and in particular universities for encouraging such divisiveness as alluded to in chapter 1. Hausman and McPherson (2017) warn us of the dangers of working within a specialized discipline that employs and develops its own particular techniques and abstractions, on the one hand, and on the other judges the significance of that discipline's findings for the broader endeavor of seeking a better understanding of reality as a whole. They argued that the practitioners become blinkered by their immersion in the details of their work and unaware of their biased view of its importance. Accordingly, ethics without governance can become technocratic or managerialist in focus but will not address the question of ethos, a territory for human motivations and behavior beyond the reach of external regulation (Bunting, 2010: 5). Similarly, although one can see the importance of the application of administrative law and principles to the public sector, such rule-based mechanisms can become rigid, centralized, and obsessed with dictating how things should be done, that is, with regulating the process, controlling the inputs, while totally ignoring the end results. Moreover, the recourse to the law as a safe haven is not without its shortcoming because it is limited in its reach, not always effectively enforced and may be circumvented by the unscrupulous and the clever (Wray-Bliss, 2007: 506; Astroulakis, 2010).

In our case in the Caribbean over-specialization within disciplinary research has worked to our detriment, preventing us from inquiring into true insights of the forces that are already shaping the development of our societies. And so a caution must be issued over ethics splintering into many subdisciplines, where it is freighted with so many theoretical and normative presumptions that it displaces everything it was conceived to do and fails in its breadth to adapt to the requirements of modern times. Indeed, a positive interpretation of keeping watch over intra-disciplinary iterations is that each part of the discipline would proceed autonomously but in cooperation with the other and, in spite of the evolutionary trajectory, look within and through its own organic synergy to find solutions to challenging problems. This would require the ambitious pooling of disciplinary knowledge and expertise as a central way of organizing society (Breckler, 2005; Goulet, 2005b; Jones, 2009; De Rosa et al., 2018). Philosophical ethics, however useful as it may be, can over-theorize to the point of its divorce from an experiential base and so is ill-suited to be at the service of finding solutions and offering relevant advice to pressing issues of governance. This will remain the case unless purveyors of the discipline are forced by reality to renounce their pretentions to concern only with grand theorizing and merely enunciating grand ideals (Gasper, 2008: 9; Howard, 2019). This can sometimes create a challenge within and for the discipline, as the specialty areas acquire their own unique theories and methods and begin to look less and less like each other. Moreover another challenge is the struggle not only to keep up and communicate with colleagues within the discipline but also in making deep connections with other disciplines (Breckler, 2005; Goulet, 2005b; Jones, 2009; De Rosa et al., 2018). And so the ability of ethics to be applied—applied being used transitively—must increasingly become relevant in addressing society's challenges because it allows room for a multi-disciplinary discourse on human problems, and, more importantly for this research, it provides conducive epistemological and ontological grounds for the generation of more suitable conceptual frameworks that can assist in understanding and addressing contemporary ethical challenges of governance. One of the benefits of a common core trajectory is the interdisciplinary value of bringing together multiple disciplines, or of working at the intersections of disciplines, to, for example, critically analyze different cultures and traditions, synthesizing those observations, and recording clear opinions about them (Breckler, 2005; Goulet, 2005b; Jones, 2009; De Rosa et al., 2018).

It is my contention therefore that if we are to make progress in improving our governance we have to think differently about the issues and come to terms with the fact that, as Dynes and Walker put it, "something has been lost" and face up to the questions of how "we recover a sense of identity and purpose" and "what are the irreducible core of issues for consideration" (Dynes and Walker, 1995: 340; Hamelink, 1997; Strang, 1999; Goulet, 2005b). Therefore, although rational planning, judicious investment, new institutions, and the mobilization of the populace are necessary toward achieving governance, such measures by themselves can never be sufficient. More necessary will be an overall cultural revolution in the values our societies hold. We cannot fully exist without understanding this purpose, and finding the answer to this question therefore shapes our choices. In this regard we return to the social contractual theme and its importance as was expressed in chapter 2 and expanded on here.

This perspective recognizes we do not exist in isolation, either as people, nations, or institutions, and cannot ignore the impact of our actions on others. A person is an entity possessing relational capability—to themselves, to others, to the world, and to the transcendent. As a relational being we are members of one large human family, with much in common with even the most dispersed members of this family. From this sense of shared humanity we can then construct a way of relating to one another and to the world we inhabit. Although we recognize the complexities of the problem, we readily acknowledge that the local person, business, or nation should not act with disregard for other parts of the system. Although history is fraught with moments and stories of conflict, struggle, and inhumanity, large numbers of the current population have enjoyed, until recently, a relatively stable world where much was taken for granted and much was provided. The sense of community, belonging, and meaning that came from membership of trustworthy institutions is fresh in memory. These institutions, including family and extended family, local and national communities, and cultural and religious movements, provided the context in which we could live effective human lives and also provided the security and general confidence that we could live our lives with trust in the present and firm hope for the future (Howard, 2010: 507). Although each part of each system can be run ethically, failing to appreciate the wider interconnected systems can have a negative impact on someone else far removed as we shall see in subsequent chapters. Thus, as stated earlier, the weakness of the subdiscipline of development ethics was its wariness in linking the micro analysis of the individual role to that of the macro- and meso-levels of analysis. A "meta"[5] ethical perspective is incumbent on us because the increasing complexities, ambiguities, and interconnections of twenty-first-century life mean that we must embrace an ethical approach requiring us to adopt a new perspective from which to view our world, our institutions, our relationships, and ourselves, in the stream of timeless human values, recognizing our responsibility to the planet, our contemporaries, and the generations who come after us. But it goes further. If the empirical record of the region's history teaches us one thing, it should be that it no longer suffices to study the contents of the political system—parliament, government, the civil service, and public institutions brought on by random processes such as new technology. Neither is it enough to piously view "smarter" reforms as simply enough to solve our crisis. Rather, we must determine from the outset those "fundamental forces" at the micro levels of analysis of the economy that will determine what happens in the "superstructure" of politics. It would be equally wrong to decide by omission that wider—perhaps fundamental—interests determined by the individual have no role in our theoretical conception or empirical strategy. Such scholarship would suggest continuity of a patronizing society as if only some forces can determine what is good for the society (Orr and Johnson, 2019; Howard, 2019). Instead an ethical turn must prompt each individual to ask of him/herself: "what meaningful contribution can I make to my society," or as Nussbaum (2011: 74, 2004: 3) asks: how far should the chance of being born in one nation rather than another determine one's life chances? The fact that it is the randomness of where a child is born that determines his or her chances of surviving, getting an education, or living free of poverty cannot be accepted (Roser, 2019). And so, if our aim is to understand how it is that we got to the widespread malaise and institutional corruption of contemporary society, it is not adequate to think only what is to be done but equally how is it to be done (Nussbaum, 2011; Miller, 2011; Lepenies, 2014; Ceva and Ferretti, 2019; Roser, 2019). A read of Freire (1970) and Goulet (1988, 1996, 2006) is a reminder to current scholarship that much of development thinking is full of restorative and/or corrective measures but not always equally so of rehabilitative processes of how to do so and the resolutions are left as some kind of mystery.

It is important then to stress and amplify the contours, nuances, and reciprocal relations inherent in agency and empowerment as already noted, both of which have become important ideals in ethical reflection on governance and development. An ethical perspective should however distinguish and differentiate them by understanding agency as necessary but insufficient for what we should mean by empowerment (Drydyk, 2013 cited in Crocker, 2014: 247). Ethicists are indebted to Sen for his 1985 distinction between agency and well-being (Sen 1985, 1993, 1999; see also Crocker, 2014) which, although causally linked, are different. An agent is a person or group that acts on purpose without external or internal compulsion or makes a difference in the world. That agent is self-determining, the author of its own life instead of the object of another's coercion or the victim of the force of circumstance (Crocker, 2008: 153–163; Crocker and Robeyns, 2009; Leftwich, 2009, cited in Crocker, 2014: 247). An agent's life goes well therefore, when its "beings and doings" are those it has reason to value or the freedom to realize in life. Thus, being nourished, healthy, secure, and happy, as well as having real opportunities or freedoms for such, are examples of well-being achievement. And so, to exercise agency freedom (and have agency achievements), an agent requires at least minimal well-being so that the exercise of agency will increase well-being. It has become increasingly apparent however that agents can exercise their agency not only in ways that reduce and even end their own well-being or, that can harm or terminate the well-being of others. One way to understand the ideal of empowerment, then, is that empowered individuals and groups are agents who have the agency-power to work for their own well-being and that of others and do so by contesting and overcoming power inequities that limit their agency and well-being (Drydyk, 2013, cited in Crocker, 2014: 247; Drydyk, 2019). Thus for instance, a woman is not empowered if she is merely free to be employed outside the home, for the powers that be may subject her to jobs marked by harassment, discrimination, and decreased well-being (Koggel, 2013, cited in Crocker, 2014: 247 see also Sen, 1999B).[6] Women are empowered to the extent that individually and collectively they struggle against and (sometimes, at least) overcome the powers arrayed against their agency and well-being (Koggel, 2013, cited in Crocker, 2014: 247 see also Nussbaum, 2000).

It follows then that an ethical perspective must be concerned not only with promoting agency but also with empowerment that decides, challenges, contests, and seeks to overcome societal obstacles to a better life (Drydyk, 2013, cited in Crocker, 2014: 247). These phases include identification of need, deliberation about ends and means, monitoring, and evaluation. People have a right to exercise their agency and help determine and modify the policies

Table 3.1   Capabilities Approach and Its Explanations

1. Life.	To live to the end of a human life of normal length; not dying prematurely, or before one's life is reduced to be not worth living.
2. Bodily Health.	Ability to have good health including reproductive health; to be adequately nourished with adequate shelter.
3. Bodily Integrity.	Ability to move freely from place to place; security against violent assault, sexual assault, and domestic violence; having opportunities for sexual satisfaction and for choice in matters of reproduction.
4. Senses Imagination, and Thought.	Ability to use the senses, to imagine, think, and reason—and to do these things in a "truly human" way informed and cultivated by an adequate education, inclusive of literacy and basic mathematical and scientific training. Ability to use imagination and thought in connection with experiencing and producing works and events of one's own choice for example, religious, literary, and musical. Ability to use one's mind in ways protected by guarantees of freedom. Ability to have pleasurable experiences and to avoid non-beneficial pain.
5. Emotions.	Ability to have attachments to things and people outside ourselves. In general, to love, grieve, and experience longing, gratitude, and justified anger. Not having one's emotional development blighted by fear and anxiety.
6. Practical Reason.	Ability to conceptualize the good and engage in critical reflection about the planning of one's life, for example, protection for the liberty of conscience and religious observance.
7. Affiliation.	1. Ability to live with and toward others by engaging in various forms of social interaction. Ability to imagine the situation of another, through protecting institutions that constitute and nourish such forms of affiliation, and also protecting the freedom of assembly and political speech.
	2. Having the social bases of self-respect and non-humiliation by being treated as a dignified being whose worth is equal to that of others. This entails provisions of non-discrimination on the basis of race, sex, sexual orientation, ethnicity, caste, religion, national origin, and species.
8. Other Species.	Ability to live with concern for and in relation to the world of nature.
9. Play.	Ability to enjoy recreational activities.
10. Control over one's environment.	1. Ability to participate effectively in political choices that govern one's life; having the right of political participation, protections of free speech and association.
	2. Ability to hold property (both land and movable goods), and having property rights, the right to seek employment, and having the freedom from unwarranted search and seizure on an equal basis with others. In work, being able to work as a human, exercising practical reason and entering into meaningful relationships of mutual recognition with other workers.

Source: Modified and Adapted by author from: Nussbaum, M., (2011). *Creating Capabilities: The Human Development Approach*. Cambridge Massachusetts: Belknap Press.

under which they live, giving them the sense that they are respected agents "owning" their projects (Lever and Poama, 2019; Howard, 2019; Orr and Johnson, 2019). Therefore, agency is crucial in the expansion of valuable and substantive freedoms. That is, in order to be agents of their lives, both individually and collectively, Nussbaum (2011: 33–34, see also Nussbaum, 2000: 78–80) argues that a political order can only be considered as decent if essentially it secures for its citizens ten basic principles toward ensuring the notion of individual human dignity of empowerment. In summary, these aspects of agency in assessing what a person can do in line with his or her conception of the good life are summarized in table 3.1.

Without endorsing any one particular list of human capabilities, Sen argues that freedom to choose our capabilities in an informed and un-coerced way are ethical demands that are important and socially determinable.

One consequence of this approach then is that democracy, especially when it is inclusive and provides opportunity for the voices of the marginalized to be heard, reduces the danger of elite capture. Another real challenge for nation-states of the region rests with a flexible and iterative policy and decision-making apparatus that can respond to this diverse institutional context in ways that harness the multiple relationships that have become crucial for the performance of national economies. However, in the final analysis, decisions are made by individuals. Ultimately, therefore, it is the individual values as well as their social behaviors that are going to determine the quality of decisions made in business, in government, or in personal life. And, a transcendent ethical perspective that moves beyond the narrow paradigmatic limits within traditional disciplines capturing such issues to inform and enrich the discourse on governance, is therefore needed in the light of a growing public concern over a "confidence gap" with respect to the attitudes of citizens, the crisis of values, their attitudes toward public institutions, and society at large, particularly during these recessionary times of extensive austerity measures (Hicks, 2007). Given the importance of an integrated approach therefore, this research is not intentionally the transmission of specialized data as stated in chapter 1. In style and content it seeks to serve as a catalyst for recognition of the need for a critical consciousness of an ethical turn that invokes praxis and reflection on the challenges and opportunities of governance as a fundamental condition for social transformation.

NOTES

1. The term "wicked" in this context is not used in the sense of evil, but instead it refers to a policy issue that is highly resistant to resolution with implications for governance and society. The term's first use has been attributed to the seminal work

of Rittel and Webber (1973) and has remained within the intellectual discourse of public policy ever since. These "wicked issues" are also referred to as "intractable" or "vexed" policy problems and have attracted increasing focus because their formulation is contested, proposed solutions are controversial, the indicators and metrics of success are under constant review and discussion, the subject matter is complex, the parts of the world they are concerned with are dynamic and in constant flux, the technology involved is often new, the institutional context is populated by a great number of stakeholders with different views and values (van den Hoven, 2017: 11), and their changing requirements are often very difficult to recognize (see, Rittel and Webber, 1973; Knill and Tosun, 2012; Stone, 2012; Kraft and Furlong, 2015; Wildavsky, 2018; for "intractable problems" in public policy). Successfully solving or at least managing these problems generally require a re-assessment of some of the traditional ways of working and solving problems including the interrelationships among the full range of causal factors underlying them, as well as an understanding of the broader, more collaborative and innovative approaches to policy changes or adjustments (see in particular APSC, 2007, Head, 2008; Stone, 2012; Wildavsky, 2018).

2. When translated into their assumptions, arguments about the irrelevance of ethics or morality are powerful by those who contend that "morality is the product of power." Primarily, they believe that when individuals make ethical claims, such statements actually mask a variety of "real" interests that are not "moral" but are "selfish." Moreover, they also believe that these selfish interests or this "self-interested" behavior and arguments are motivated at root by material causes such as the desire for power or survival. Therefore, to act self-interestedly is to be rational, in the sense of utility maximizing, while action motivated by ethical concerns is irrational (Stoker, 1992; Crawford, 2004).

3. These arguments are actually a version of rational actor/choice theory. The basic assumptions are that people are a means to an end in that they devise strategies and engage in behaviors that move them efficiently toward achieving their goals. Secondly, such arguments suggest that people are utility maximizers and will choose the course of action with the greatest perceived benefits for them. A third assumption of this theory is that persons will calculate costs, risks, and benefits in an unbiased manner. A fourth assumption predicated on such theorizing is that preferences are known and are stable but there is no concern with the sources of preferences or interests and how these preferences change. Put differently, human behavior can be explained in terms of rational decision processes because individuals weigh costs, risks, and benefits of alternative actions, and will choose the course of action with the least costs and risks, and the greatest benefit, essentially utilitarianism, read another way (see Rostrom, 2005; Sabatier et al., 2007; Orr and Johnson, 2019).

4. At the time of writing, another edited collection on development ethics was published. *The Routledge Handbook of Development Ethics,* by Drydyk and Keleher (2019) is a major anthology on the development discourses and debates in development ethics, but it contains only one chapter on "Corruption" by Hellsten (2019) to address this idea. But even here, there is admission by the author that "from the point of view of development ethics, more specific research is needed on the different aspects of corruption and its prevalence in various forms and that [f]urther analysis

of the relationship between culture, political order and corruption would be useful because it would give policymakers and development administrators a better understanding of how different societies have developed and what their specific problems are in relation to corruption" (Hellsten, 2019: 364). Likewise, Souffrant (2019) in his *Global Development Ethics: A critique of global capitalism* by Rowman and Littlefield mentions the idea of corruption but has not explored its bearing on the construction of particular development approaches and doctrines.

5. "Meta" used here, with a common "m" does not denote the meta-ethical theorising that carries us into the realm of circular debates on moral realism and moral antirealism. Instead it is being used as a root to denote the need for a synthesis of principles of ethics that provide guidance to help us resolve ethical challenges within the academy as an approach to governance.

6. In his *Development as Freedom* (Sen, 1999: 104–107) also points out the analytical power of the capability approach to human development, through illustrating that there are approximately 60–100 million missing women in the world due to endemic gender discrimination in the form of sex selective abortion, and neglect for female health and nutrition, especially during early childhood, often resulting in severe capability deprivation and life threatening circumstances for women.

Chapter 4

Whence We've Come

The Systemic Dimensions of Modernization

The conscientious march through history in some measure induced by the passage of time is often blurred in human memory. There is then a danger that in denying ourselves an understanding of the past and imagining the future in isolation we wallow in the crisis of the present, seeing only the discrete elements of our current situation, often not recognizing the interrelatedness of past choices, attitudes, and values that are impacting on the present and thus shaping the future (Demas, 1975). In taking up the difficult theme of ethics and governance, there are three important questions we must keep firmly in mind. Since the act of governance is a process or movement, we must remember it is relevant to ask: where have we come from, where are we now, and where are we headed? This chapter considers the history and more general intellectual trends of modernization and the role they have played in public policy development and governance in the Caribbean. As indicated already in chapters 1 through 3, my thesis is that a significant reason for the current crisis of governance in the Caribbean is a fundamental inattentiveness to the evolution, role, impact, and systemic interrelatedness of the institutions of capitalist modernization, which sets in motion a dialectic of challenge and counterchallenge out of which changes—often fundamental—have occurred. This is obviously a value-laden and contentious claim but, as we shall see, the essential core of modernization is a syndrome of changes, closely linked to industrialization driven by the application of science and technology, that manifests itself *inter alia* in urbanization, changing occupational and bureaucratic structures, mass consumer societies, rising educational levels, and changing political capabilities and cultural change, with achievement motivation becoming the dominant individual level goal (Inglehart and Welzel, 2009: 1). Margetts (2015: 11) essentially categorizes this syndrome of changes occurring through modernization and its impact on public policy into three broad processes aimed at: economic efficiency and individual incentivization; integration, interconnectedness, standardization, and formulation; and specialization expertise, scientific advancement, and technological innovation. The praxis and theory of modernization however, has been controversial. It has been rejected as too linear, deterministic, and ethno-centric, sometimes accused of offering only an internal rather than external account for the backwardness of developing countries. Various social scientists have stressed the persistence of traditional values and institutions, low achievement motivation, population explosion, inefficient and corrupt bureaucracies, and the lack of productive investment. Others have negatively concluded that after its pursuit there is no guarantee that democracy and capitalist development would be the logical outcome (Grew, 1977; Phillips, 1998; Levitt, 2005; Veltmeyer and Bowles, 2018; Munck, 2018b; Potter et al., 2019).

It followed that the first step in addressing the Caribbean's desire to escape from the colonial condition, associated with plantation society and its underdevelopment, would be to conceptualize and set in motion its own reality of change and transformation based on indigenous ideas that did not rely on preconceived models derived from the experience of others (Lewis, 1968).[1] The plantation economy thesis became the dominant intellectual narrative indigenizing the evolution of Caribbean society, functioning as the conduit through which the region could interpret its past and present, and as a heuristic tool for deciphering areas of weakness to be transformed. This gave rise to certain institutional legacies within the region (Minto-Coy et al., 2016; Marshall, 2014). This psychological liberation advanced by George Beckford in his canonical tome *Persistent Poverty* (1972) was to be complemented and buttressed by the region's efforts to mitigate, if not ameliorate, its functional dependence. This arose, according to McIntyre's notion, not from the constraints of size or structure which still remain today as the default excuse for development lethargy, but from the debilitating policies pursued by the intellectual classes within these governments (Beckford and Girvan, 1989; Schuyler and Veltmeyer, 1988; Meeks and Girvan, 2010; Marshall, 2014; Levitt, 2018). And so it was within this intellectual milieu of foment that the Caribbean gained systemic insights into the pervasive effects of *inter alia* the structural dependency imposed by colonial powers and their associated agents, the transnational corporations that stymied their development and influenced all other economic activity and ultimately social inequality, persistent poverty, and vulnerability. Moreover, through this aperture of analysis scholars were legitimately better able to empirically appropriate, and justifiably so, the institutional rigidity of the social structures of class and race and their impact in contributing to a lack of institutional innovation so perpetuating a post-independence development climate of frustration and mediocre performance. Several scholars (Thomas, 1988; Addo, 1988; Levitt,

2005; Meeks and Girvan, 2010; Marshall, 2014; Minto-Coy, 2016) further explored the development constraints arising from the plantation thesis on the politics of governance and its derivative culture of excessive centralization and prime ministerial power as sources of the clientelist authoritarian state that prioritized order over development. This Caribbean enlightenment had forged the intellectual conditions in which the application of reason to practical issues could flourish through such "modern" institutions as the academy, the learned journal, and the conference. In turn, there was constituted both a "modern" audience for the dissemination of social and political ideas alongside a class of intellectuals that could live from writing about them (Hall, 1992 cited in Power, 2014: 157). In retrospect, the central thematic ideas have been insightful as a diagnostic and prescriptive analytical framework providing deeper understandings of the historical experiences and institutions as significant requirements to effect self-reliant growth, development, change, and transformation, but its epistemic focus on ethical considerations was mute.

Subsequent theories have emerged from the global academy of scholars including dependency school, world-systems approaches, neoliberalism, and globalization, each purporting in elaborate ways to debunk modernization while exalting their favored conceptual and analytical framework for understanding development (Conway, 2014; Conway and Heynen, 2014; Veltmeyer and Bowles, 2018; Klak, Potter et al., 2019). Each has also been mired in controversy, especially in their application, contextual relevance, and legitimization of claims to accurately reflect development and governance. Not only were these criticisms the principal challenges, but these too in their own hegemonic ways were perspectives on modernizing, as a way forward for developing countries. In the essential core of their formulation, without the specifics that informed their criticisms, was that something was fundamentally wrong with developing countries like the Caribbean, all the while holding implicitly, and some would argue explicitly, that the first world—North America, Europe, the former USSR—were models of progress, even perfection. Their denial as theoretical abstractions was that the Marxists/structuralists in their orientation and/or capitalists in others were pejoratively contingent imperialists. Another concern was how and what kind of corrective measures to propose for developing countries. This is not the purview of this chapter. Importantly in their formulation, they [re]imagined the globe as their *tabula rasa* on which they placed their imprints in new strategic areas by enabling, underwriting, and shaping the modernization of political and economic development (Scott, 2004: 196 see also Potter, 2014; Conway and Heynen, 2014; Klak, 2014; Veltmeyer and Bowles, 2018; Munck, 2018A; Potter et al., 2019) but without explicit reference to the ideas and ideals of ethics, which is the concern of this research.

Development ethics sought to forge an ethical path through much of this analysis but as seen in chapter 3, this as a theoretical and practical framework of analysis was fraught with difficulty (Goulet, 2000, 2005a; Keohane and Nye, 2000). The critiques and counter critiques would fill a sizable library and this author genuflects to these criticisms. Instead, this chapter proposes the view that the history of modernization as an institutionalization process is not only the modern idea as advanced in the 1950s and 1960s with the proliferation of texts but was on the way from the time of colonization and was reframed and refocused in response to the changing historical realities between developed and developing countries and the debate among the social scientists (Scott, 2004, see also Stiglitz, 2003). Just as the old colonialist imperialism fostered dependency and underdevelopment, modern (post-1980s) globalization has several salient features that are *de facto* neoliberal successors to these imperial mechanisms. They represent the following: (a) a program of binding individuals, institutions, and nations into a common set of market relationships; (b) a calculated strategy by the capitalist economies, corporations, and international financial institutional systems to encourage and stimulate capitalist growth for "winners"—core and emerging markets—but not "losers"—no comparative advantages, weak or failed states, the corruption weakened; and (c) a means of extracting surplus through the exploitation of cheap labor, high-quality manpower, and resources of the global South (Ghosh, 2001:158 cited in Conway and Heynen, 2014: 181; Lewis, 2010; Meeks and Girvan, 2010; Klak, 2014; Gilbert, 2014; Veltmeyer and Bowles, 2018; Potter et al., 2019). This research is not intended as a tautological debate on the entrails of modernization, or to discard other theoretical approaches that shed their own light on aspects of development. Rather, this research tries to analytically discern from among the variations on the common theme of modernization, the transformational trends that have occurred in the region and what they portend for governance. The reality is that the structural, institutional, ideational, economic, and geographical disruptions of one kind or another being routinely produced and challenging the cultural ethos of the region have been characteristically shaped and directly influenced from the Caribbean's inception into the world economy (Schuyler and Veltmeyer, 1988; Scott, 2004; Veltmeyer and Bowles, 2018).[2] The Caribbean region is the oldest outpost of European overseas colonial expansion. The emergence of "planetary" empires in the sixteenth and seventeenth centuries, the inauguration of an "oceanic" trans-Atlantic imperial orientation, begins with the Caribbean. And having had the earliest start in colonial history, Caribbean peoples are the first modernized peoples in world history, their cultures developed under unusual conditions. They were modernized by enslavement and forced transportation; by "seasoning" and coercion on time-conscious export-oriented enterprises; by the reshuffling, redefinition, and reduction of gender-based roles; by racial and status-based oppression; and by the need to reconstitute and maintain cultural forms of their own under implacable pressure. These were people wrenched from societies of a different sort, then thrust into remarkably industrial settings for their time and kept under circumstances of extreme repression. The argument here is that they have, as a result, a remarkably modern cast for their time into the twenty-first century (Mintz, 1993, cited in Scott, 2004: 191; Lewis, 1968; Schuyler, 1988; Knight and Palmer, 1989). Based on the preceding, although some may wish to reject modernization praxis as *passé*, this research takes as a given that it is still widely attractive continuing to be adopted, or imposed and accepted with enthusiasm by developing countries like the Caribbean through beamed images as a motivating force behind the entire process of development, in order to acquire a number of desirable things and to portray societies that are advanced (Phillips, 1998; Broome, 2003; Power, 2014; Petras and Veltmeyer, 2018). It offers a life strategy aimed at getting rich and looking rich. In fact, this author also contends that although recent celebrations marking fifty years of independence by some countries across the region have easily shifted attention away from the colonial legacy of modernization as articulated by independence-era leaders, modernization is still being rearticulated and re-coded in the name of nation-building expressed through public sector reform to improve delivery of public services, raise efficiency and effectiveness, and modernize public administration (Minto-Coy, 2016: 48); through constructing and reconstructing global capital, state institutions, and civil society so that they are permitted to continue the advance of capital investment and global trade (Sachs, 2012; Murray and Overton, 2014); and/or frequently being redeployed as Caribbean integration in programs of infrastructural development, cultural projects, and citizenship-making claims (Bloom et al., 2014 see also Fortner, 2011b).[3] And so for the Caribbean, the city-state of Singapore and more recently, the newly industrialized "Asian tigers" were particularly seen by leaders as lodestones of development (Addo, 1988; Broome, 2003; Potter, 2019) with success of their efforts convincing regional decision-makers to follow their example. Essentially, ideas and modes of analysis that seemed like a kind of breakthrough by the social sciences have turned out on introspection to be part of and surprisingly close to an old tradition: progress, with new gadgets on it (Grew, 1977; Inglehart and Welzel, 2005, 2009; Bloom et al., 2014; Potter et al., 2019).

This is not to say that the region's path to development is a deterministic one by default. As active agents the region, although this may not have been perceived at the time, has had real choices in fundamentally tackling grievances of governance and development through paradigm challenging approaches. When they felt they could do so, some countries of the region have rejected Western imperialism for intentionally different forms of autonomous development. These "new approaches to development" were ephemeral and created more far-reaching worsening development challenges than they could resolve (see for example Thomas, 1988; Schuyler, 1988; Manley, 1988; Addo, 1988).[4] The disappointment however has always been that in dealing with the intractable circumstances of governance engulfing the region, policy planners beguiled by insular disciplinary approaches have often defaulted to focusing on proximate causes[5] and/or solutions, rather than the root causes aimed at ameliorating the underlying existing conditions. Ironically, even these "new approaches" echoed common themes of Western development. Worsening conditions therefore demand that we reframe our analysis to expose and explain these prominent and pervasive root causes in modern society that affect our daily lives as part of our search for a solution to the epistemological and ontological crisis of governance engulfing the region. With this in mind, this chapter also explores the major political, economic, social, and ideational assumptions and the derivative practices that constitute perhaps the major core of the modernization process, and how they have informed the shaping of the regional landscape by eroding many of the key inherited post-independence institutional forms and arrangements. This has been done through inducing cultural changes incompatible with, and no longer capable of, providing a stable environment for good governance allowing for development as a logical institutional outcome. Capturing the complex facets of the socially dynamic issues within modernization and relating them to governance and development is all the more challenging because of the scope and rapidity of change that has occurred, and continues to occur, across all spheres of human endeavor. In both their extensionality and intentionality the transformations involved in modernity are more profound than most sorts of change characteristic of prior periods. On the extensional plane they have served to establish forms of social interconnection which span the globe; in intentional terms they have come to alter some of the most intimate and personal features of our day-to-day existence (Giddens, 1996: 4; Patterson and Macintyre, 2011; Eisenstadt, 2013). What we have come to know and define as the modernization,[6] industrialization complex nexus was translated within the collective psyche of developing countries to mean a better way of life, but it has left in its wake several development challenges that are posing grave concerns for the governance of developing societies.

Industrialization was often taken to be the first step in modernization. Several developing countries, the Caribbean included, emerged from a haunting past of the dire consequences of a disinterested colonialism and a lackluster post-independence performance which saw life continuing in poverty much like their forebears at the turn of the twentieth century. Modernization through industrialization, therefore, was seen by many formerly colonized developing countries as a political commitment to rapidly improving standards of living (Goulet, 2000). A crucial part of the "backwardness" with which these societies and cultures were perceived was the lack of thrift, discipline, and promptness, as well as traditional beliefs, indolence, and superstition that prevented people in such places as Africa, India, and China from mastering modern technology (Lerner, 1958; Lipset, 1960; Fortner, 2011b). This unprecedented project of developmental engineering in countries was justified on the basis of a supposed superiority of Western economic and political institutions with their science and technological apparatus and (initially at least) of Western values over non-Western (Banuri, 1987: 5; Manley, 1988; Munck, 2018b; Souffrant, 2019). The argument was that rapid development could be gained in developing countries through an infusion of financial and technological resources, through the transfer of institutional models and dynamic ideas from rich to poor countries such as import- and export-oriented industrialization (Lewis, 1950, 1965; Simmonds, 1985; Manley, 1988; see also Sachs, 2012; Munck, 2018b; Souffrant, 2019).

Rooted in the contrast between "traditional" and "modern" societies, modernization promised the existence of a common and essential pattern of "development" and defined progress in technology, military, and bureaucratic institutions, and the political and social structure. For the Caribbean that is geographically located within the continental periphery of culturally developed countries such as the United States and Canada, and that has become accustomed to accepting foreign developed cultures, overcoming psychic peripherality became the *sine qua non* to becoming properly modern assuming that through the instruction in and use of modern technologies the outlooks of people would be altered. To attain this, individuals in these societies would have to show "symptoms" of modernity in the form of *psychic empathy*, that is, the capacity to see oneself in the other fellow's situation. In the early days the most powerful catalysts for this objective would be the diffusion of mass communication technologies, particularly newspapers and radio, conduits for exposing people rooted in traditional structures to new opinions, attitudes, and ideas that created a greater empathy and association with others. This exposure also gave them new desires and aspirations leading them away from older social structures (Ekbladh, 2010: 173 cited in Fortner, 2011). The combination of economic development, industrialization, mass technologies, and education creates a society whose citizens are overall more assertive and politically aware.

Beginning with India in 1947, the former colonies of the British Empire emerged as independent nations and as in the Caribbean, by any purely rational calculus of future probabilities, the development enterprise of most countries was an exercise in "catching up" through a combination of policy, action, and understanding. The early days were characterized by an unalloyed confidence in social scientists to help Third World countries banish inherited problems and construct a new social reality from scratch. The self-assurance of the theorists was so unequivocal and the belief in their nostrums so widespread that voices of doubt and dissent regarding the sagacity, desirability, or feasibility of such a gigantic endeavor could readily be dismissed as irrational and misguided doubters if not as malicious mischief-makers. Accusations of failures could similarly be disregarded as resulting not from weaknesses in the practice of policy but in its implementation, because of the endurance of backward behavior, values and institutions in the countries concerned, or (at a later stage) from the inefficiency or veniality of politicians and bureaucrats (Mills, 1970; Banuri, 1987; Grew, 1977; Manley, 1988; Munck, 2018a, 2018b).

Urbanization, increased literacy, political and economic reform, scientific advance and technological progress, and inevitably wealth were often thought of as the universal incentives and outputs of the industrialization effort. It was believed that industrial wealth would buy power and skill and supply outward forms of affection and respect, rendering enlightenment and rectitude superfluous. Policy planners believed that a perfect combination of these incentives and outputs could solve the life-and-death problems of these societies (Lewis, 1950, 1965; Huntingdon, 1971; Montgomery, 1976; Knight and Palmer, 1989; Grugel, 1995; Margetts, 2010). This basic idea became the *raison d'etre* for the rationalization of state policies that covered all spheres of social life and development. Initially, such an approach to development was laudable but it became all too clear that the benefits of modernization did not extend evenly to all countries, in areas of class, colour, race, or creed (Minto-Coy, 2016; Daniel, 2016; Goede, 2016; Nunez, 2016; Granvorka, 2016; Veltmeyer and Bowles, 2018; Potter et al., 2019). The sociological realism of modernization eventually conflicted with political desirability, reiterating a core consequence of modernization praxis still valid today: industrialization produces pervasive social and cultural changes. Thus the rationale for my attention to modernization is that processes of social, political, economic, and environmental development brought both opportunities and threats for society, that affected the functioning of the liberal democratic state and hence the governance of these societies as will be seen in chapter 5.

In our pursuit of development and good government much effort was expended toward such managerial goals as efficiency, adequacy, institutional stability, and equating development with the "modern" mode of creating wealth through the systematic application of technology to boost productivity. Modernization then became synonymous with development an approach viewed as a straightforward economic problem, a simple matter of identifying and quantifying the composition of economic growth packages: raising agricultural output, diversifying manufactured products, building infrastructure, and increasing the provision of services. Growth objectives would be planned, resources mobilized to reach them, and the complex institutional apparatus for investing, managing, financing, and production, activated. This array of organized activities would yield "development," measured as higher national income, increased production, and greater output. Moreover, industrialization which first appeared in the West was often assumed to require Westernization of attitudes and values, evoking the cultural as well and becoming "the great ascent" toward which these newly independent countries would, and still continue to, aspire to *have* enough goods to *be* fully human (Goulet, 1996, see also Lewis, 1965; Huntingdon, 1971; Montgomery, 1976; Grugel, 1995; Inglehart, 1997; Inglehart and Welzel, 2005, 2009; Munck, 2018b).

Perhaps the best starting point for the analysis of the characteristics of modernization and the policies pursued in the political sphere of modernization meant that progress toward the "ideal type" political institutions, most notably those of the liberal democratic nation-state occurred through the intensification of the power of the central, legal, administrative, and political agencies of the state (Lipset, 1959; Mills, 1970; Huntingdon, 1971; Simmonds, 1985; Sutton, 1999; Sousa Santos, 2005; Inglehart, 1997; Inglehart and Welzel, 2005, 2009; Nhema and Zinyama, 2016). The strength of liberal democracy was only reinforced by the weakness of viable and sustainable alternatives and we were with the West! (Girvan, 2015: 97) Liberal democracies succeeded in separating the domains of economics and politics to a degree not seen in "predatory" illiberal authoritarian states. Post-independence politics, out of the need to entrench property rights and hold a well-defined bureaucratic hierarchy to account with the establishment of a democratic structure based on consent of the people with guarantees of freedom, justice, and equality, saw the emergence of embryonic liberal democracies as sufficient to assure the development of a flourishing democratic society (Moraes, 2006; see also Sutton, 1999; Ryan, 1999, 2001; Meeks and Girvan, 2010; Girvan, 2015; Mandle, 2016). The defining feature of public administration and politics became the Westminster-Whitehall (WW) system mutated from the United Kingdom as referenced in chapter 1 that privileges the party commanding a majority in the lower house of Parliament with legislative and executive power (Mills, 1997; Ryan, 2001; Minto-Coy, 2016). Essentially, ministers (and if necessary the whole Cabinet) take decisions that are implemented by a neutral civil service, in a simple chain of command where civil servants are accountable to ministers, who are accountable to Parliament, whose members are elected by and are accountable to the people, their constituents. The Whitehall model offered heuristic value by being the prescriptive content for the establishment of institutions such as the professional bureaucracy (predominantly the civil service/public sector). These institutions were ideally tasked by a professional class for implementing policies and in a policy advisory role governed by principles of meritocracy, generalism, impartiality, and anonymity in life-long career paths. The "ideal type" of bureaucratic regulation stresses the "rational," computative allocation in balancing budgets, and decision-making "rationally" worked out either according to the exigencies of any given situation, belittling allocation by elected representatives; or through processes of political or legislative decision; or by exigencies of the "impersonal" mechanisms of the market (Lipset, 1959; Eisenstadt, 1966; 1968, 2005; Mills, 1970, 1997; Sutton, 1999; Ryan, 1999, 2001). This approach was best characterized by technical efficiency in national planning benefiting from improved organizational development that included administrative choices such as preferences for public enterprises/statutory/parastatal institutions, over government agencies, or for an optimal location of new developmental ministries in the hierarchy of government (Demas, 1973; Sutton, 1999; Girvan, 2015). The "modernized" performance of citizens as clients was used as an indirect indicator of the success of good government, along with advice to strengthen electoral democracy and political stability through the establishment and expansion of stable mechanisms of transfer of power expressed through pluralistic political organizations, regular free and fair elections, and mechanisms for representative democracy through political representatives, voluntary associations, and professional organizations (Demas, 1973; Sutton, 1999; Hinds, 2008; Girvan, 2015). Electoral institutions would make those in power responsive to the public interest, freedoms of press and assembly would guide a rational public discourse. The independent judiciary—while retaining the British Privy Council just in case form trumped reality—would guarantee due process by the state, serving as a check and balance on the power of the executive and society by restraining abuses of power through transparent decision procedures. Although economic competition has often been regulated and viewed with suspicion, the larger framework of democratic competition was viewed as self-regulating and competent to police subsidiary social institutions. This view became ubiquitous in the quest to allay distinct fears and worries over majoritarian tyranny, demagoguery, and factional exploitation of political power, particularly for economic gain, through the safeguards devised like divisions of power, checks and balances, and regular elections (English, 2013: 2; Dahl, 2006). These were to be complemented by inculcating the "right" attitudes and behavior among the populace, some of whom included sophisticated Westernized elites all too eager to adopt the pro-capitalist, pro-liberal democratic strategy of modernization. Accordingly, given the specific circumstances of each country, legitimacy could be increased by expanded public liberties promulgated in rules promoting justice and fair competition applied impartially to all, and enshrined in constitutions, through the framing of modern liberal welfare and cultural policies, as well as through support for the specific goals propagated by representatives (Lipset, 1959; Huntingdon, 1971; Inglehart, 1997; Eisenstadt, 2005; Inglehart and Welzel, 2009). These institutions and their attendant "best practices" were assumed to coincide with those in Western countries, read Anglo/American democracy (Sader, 2005). They connoted continuity rather than rupture (see Girvan, 2015).[7]

Socially, modernization was characterized by social mobilization, the process by which major clusters of old social, economic, and psychological commitments were eroded and broken and people became available for new patterns of socialization and behavior (Eisenstadt, 1966, 1968, 2005). It draws strong influences from Durkheim's concern over the disruptive or dis-equilibrating consequences of industrialization. Durkheim proffered that as modern values and norms are diffused into the social life, the traditional orientations are threatened en route to being modern, therefore it is difficult to maintain the preservation of the organic unity of the society. Influential forces shaping these socio-psychological developments have been a concomitant global system of transnational and trans-political "practices that originate across state borders" with each characterized by a primary major institution: transnational corporations (TNCs); a transnational capitalist class (TCC) for political transnational practices; and the culture-ideology of consumerism for transnational cultural ideological practices (Sklair in Roberts and Hite, 2007: 242; Murray and Overton, 2014; Veltmeyer and Bowles, 2018; Potter et al., 2019). In this regard, one of the major derivatives this combination was the shaping and emergence of the mass consumer society. Among most of the economically successful, frugality had become an aberration, increasing affluence or a semblance of it saw the widespread sanctification of conspicuous consumption along with (Jackal, 1991: 68; Girardin, 2012) exposure to other aspects of the "modern life" through machinery, buildings, and consumer goods; literacy and the mass media; residential mobility; urbanization, with rural populations following public services to capital cities to the exclusion of rural communities; change from agricultural occupations; growth of per capita income; and so on. The occupational system witnessed the change from relatively uncomplicated manual, unskilled, and semi-skilled occupations to more perceived "middle-class" professions such as trade and manufacturing, business, legal, and medical services. With continued economic development, each of these categories subdivided into welfare, scientific, technological, and managerial and other services that emerged and increased as the various impersonal market systems for labor, money, or commodities, and more, underwent change articulated and facilitated by complex and proliferating bureaucracies at all levels of government (Eisenstadt, 1966, 1968; Huntingdon, 1971; Nohria and Berkley, 1994; Potter et al., 2004; Eisenstadt, 2005; Kiely, 2006, 2014; Hanna, 2010; Gilbert, 2014; Murray and Overton, 2014; ILO, 2019).

Here again, the increasing global flow of communications between societies also facilitated the impetus for the creation of new, and [re]orientation of established groups with their like in other countries, creating an international system of their own based on standardized global norms and mores (Castells, 2010; Rosenau and Singh, 2002; Sousa Santos, 2005; Fortner, 2011) as the normative consensus of the society was undermined. The diffusion of ICTs has also facilitated and precipitated the emergence of a semblance of the post-industrial society built upon a silicon infrastructure which has brought another wave of cultural change to the region. Human creativity becomes the most important production factor (Florida, 2002), with human effort no longer as much focused on producing material objects as on innovation, knowledge, and ideas. Routine tasks increasingly are taken over by computers and robots and, rather than cogs in a huge machine, workers in the knowledge sector exercise judgment and choice. Second, where mass literacy became widespread with industrialization, post-industrialization initiated a process of cognitive mobilization where modern service activities increasingly involve cognitive skills. Researchers, engineers, teachers, writers, lawyers, accountants, counselors, and analysts all belong to the "creative class," (Florida, 2002, 2019; Hanna, 2010; Graham, 2014) working with knowledge, in analytical tasks, using information technology. Service and knowledge workers deal with people and concepts in a world where innovation and exercise of individual judgment are essential, where creativity, imagination, and intellectual independence have become central, with a high degree of autonomy in work even within highly structured organizational hierarchies (Inglehart and Welzel, 2005: 28; Inglehart and Welzel, 2009; Eisenstadt, 2005; Potter et al., 2004; Hanna, 2010; Broome, 2014; Graham, 2014; Potter et al., 2019). While this provided the basis for expanding the global civil society, it also divided the people in developing countries, with the information-rich increasingly interacting with colleagues abroad, disentangling culture from the human condition in some cases, and leaving all-too-human problems unaddressed for others. The individual derives from this unhinging of local social norms and mores not merely a new livelihood and status but often identity and a sense of being and worth without which there is the threat of anomie, alienation, and despair. The solidarity that would be required for people to demand that their basic needs be a priority for government becomes weakened by unequal access (Fortner, 2011B:949 see also Castells, 2010; Rosenau and Singh, 2002; Hofmeister and Grabow, 2011; Hofstede, 2012, Broome, 2014; Levitt, 2018; Munck, 2018a, 2018b).

These social changes were twinned with the emergence of the secularization of culture or the rise of atheistic/agnostic evolutionary materialism, often imported from the Northern hemisphere, which de-emphasizes the ecclesiastical and in so doing leaving moral institutions behind. Consistent with this "post-Christian" society is that commitment to traditional Judeo-Christian values has been diffused, refracted, and weakened under the impress of secular humanism, liberalism, narcissistic, or hedonic materialism and heterogeneous pluralism or multiculturalism (Hodgkinson, 1996: 18). Also consistent with this secular asceticism, with its imperatives for self-reliance, hard work, frugality, and rational planning, and its clear definition of success and failure, was a ready-made prescription for building into the work ethic a new, but ribald self-interest, euphemistically referred to as "rugged individualism." It became the ideology that justified the "success ethic" for the upward-moving bourgeois class in their accumulation of wealth, and indeed their spiritual redemption for their inattentiveness to social inequalities that inevitably followed such accumulation (Jackal, 1991: 68, see also Eisenstadt, 1966, 1968; Elsetain et al., 1998; Inglehart and Baker, 2000; Eisenstadt, 2005, Copson, 2010; Taylor, 2012; Mullins, 2002). The Jamaica 2011 Census found an increase in those not affiliated with any religious denomination and slow growth and loss in numbers among denominations.

> The increasing secular perspective of many young people is important in this regard. Many are not comfortable with aspects of religious teaching that appear to reject reason while simply demanding faith. Such uncritical approaches to faith have proven less than satisfactory in today's knowledge society. This is further compounded by the disillusionment arising from the failings of many a religious leader, whose choices, actions and character cloud the message. Indeed, Christianity, in Jamaica as elsewhere, has, in fact, been the subject of much critique and even rejection. The upshot of that has often been the rejection/ejection of moral discourse from the public square as morality is seen as tied to Christianity, which has been somewhat discredited. (Perkins, 2013: 10)

The drive toward development was not to be a doctrinaire value-laden philosophical pursuit but a technical invocation of how to be most efficient in using resources, in mobilizing people to desire more goods and to labor to get them, and in fashioning institutional arrangements best suited to growth. To development's practitioners, such values were both not unimaginable and apparently self-evident and beyond dispute: modern citizens would build, manage, and operate factories harnessing technology to all human activities and enhance productivity (Montgomery, 1976: 2). The workforce had to be trained and people motivated to desire the fruits of modern production and to accept its discipline. They had to attend schools to gain and use relevant modern knowledge, foster changes in traditional cultural beliefs to encourage the attitude that economic well-being is, everywhere and for everyone, a good thing; they had to engage in health practices that would optimize their productivity and longevity or to produce more and better food (Montgomery, 1976:

2). Cows must now be defined as nutritional resources, not as sacred beings to be shielded from human consumption (Goulet, 1996). Broad similarities in the analyses of core values, such as freedom, justice, equality, creativity, or even power as experienced and defined in the West, were desirable (Goulet, 1996).

In the economic sphere, the transition to modernity for these states was mainly seen as an initial exercise through the conceptualization of the developmental state in a central role of *de facto* and *de jure* development agency. Depending on the country, concern with technological problems such as the feasibility of proposed industrial complexes and mineral exploitation schemes saw new techniques of production and the application of technological development to the primary extractive industries, which greatly affected the structure of the economic process being continually developed by specialized scientific institutions, and by the secondary (industrial, commercial) enterprises. This in turn also contributed to the emergence of tertiary (service) occupations and a small but growing and more complicated division of labor *within the* growing complexity of the general labor market structure. Likewise, there has been some transition from relatively small-scale units of production, such as family-owned firms, commercial and banking enterprises operating for relatively restricted, local markets, to a comingling of small factories (Lewis, 1965; Eisenstadt, 1966, 1968; Schuyler, 1988; Ramsaran, 1988; Beckford and Girvan, 1989; Banuri, 1987; Eisenstadt, 2005; Girvan, 2006).

While the "original transition" to modernity was mainly seen as a result of endogenous forces, the existence of this prototype to help promote development and modernization was also facilitated through the exogenous forces of the American, British, and Canadian firms entrenched in the principal economic sectors of bauxite mining, sugar, banking and finance, agriculture, tourism, and import trading. This prototype could help promote development and modernization through exogenous assistance and was marked by an ideological emulation which also required the pursuit of the "Washington Consensus" model. According to the mainstream rhetoric the way for a developing country to join the global economy and reap its rewards was to emulate the advanced economies, which all share certain key features (openness, private ownership, and corporate governance), and offer a relatively straightforward set of guideposts for the most fundamental reforms (Lapeyre, 2004: 7; Levitt, 2005; Ekbladh, 2010; Conway, 2014; Waeyenberge, 2018; Bowles, 2018) focusing on the following policies:

Controlling inflation through wage controls;
Privatization of publicly owned enterprises;
Privatization of public goods, resources and services (ranging from water, power, transportation to information dissemination and exchange, internet-use, communication).

Balancing state budgets through reducing government expenditure;

Changing perceptions of public and community good to individualism and individual responsibility.

Eliminating or reducing state subsidies on basic goods;

Generating foreign exchange through export-oriented industries rather than through support for import substitution;

Eliminating controls on foreign capital; and

Modernizing the production apparatus, the state and social institutions, reorienting them towards values and norms that are functional for economic growth. (Thomas, 1988; Ramsaran, 1988; Chang, and Grabel, 2004; Levitt, 2005; Nhema and Zinyama, 2016; Veltmeyer and Bowles, 2018; Levitt, 2018)

This research cannot overlook the importance of external influences on social change within a society or region. The process of modernization has not only been confined within separate national or "state" communities. Policy planners have also focused on other considerations. Major economic trends and developments have cut across national or political boundaries in the form of contemporary post-bureaucratic modes of reorganizing and disorganizing——flatter hierarchies, core/periphery distinctions, outsourcing, subcontracting, and offshore production (Osborne and Gaebler, 1992; Heckscher, 1994; Nohria and Berkley, 1994; Levitt, 2005; Inglehart and Welzel, 2009; Broome, 2014).

It was felt that through these policies all countries would be better able to develop their comparative advantages, enhance their long-term growth potential, and share in an increasingly prosperous world economy, if their policies were adapted to meet the requirements of the global economy. Developing countries and transition economies would access "the limitless accumulation of wealth" and achieve "an increasing homogenization of all human societies," by being able to import some prosperity from the rest of the world by joining the global economy—so goes the theory (Lapeyre, 2004: 7; Levitt, 2005; Gabay, 2012; Levitt, 2018). This period also constituted a watershed in the role played by the United Nations (UN) system in generating ideas and influencing strategies for development (Lapeyre, 2004: 3).

Those wishing to believe that the idea of modernization has long passed need only look at its continued expression and revitalization in the United Nations' universal twenty-one, now seventeen, millennium development goals by 2030. The interpretation of these goals indicates a modernization approach from a Eurocentric conception of development—new gadgets on the old model of progress based on the prejudices of old-fashioned optimism that involves a logic of ambitious social, cultural, and spatial engineering (Gabay, 2012; Munck, 2018a; Krageland, 2018; Potter et al., 2019). For policy planners in predominantly based agrarian societies emerging out of colonialism this direction to development was almost instinctive, uninhibited by the need to promote modernization. The rationalization for this pursuit lay in seeing as they imperiously gazed over their societies an image of themselves and their own assumptions mirrored, if not mired, in the industrial world. That industrial world often meant the unprecedented diffusion of an "American way of life," or variations thereof, with its physical infrastructure and culture based on the capitalist economy, or in some cases the alternative socialist experiment with similar developmental objectives (Yeh, 1989; Gabay, 2012; Power, 2014; Munck, 2018a). In a word, *modernization* was the pursuit of growth and development, of modern institutions, characterized by specialization and the division of labor, and desirable because they foster economic growth (Goulet, 1996, Chang, 2003; Chang and Grabel, 2004; Levitt, 2005).

Modernization therefore has served as the conduit through which the disappearance of many traditional patterns of expectation was engineered by a series of policy innovations such as growth with equity, and the provision of basic human needs in an attempt to transform rural societies (Wucherpfennig and Deutch, 2009). In dealing with these issues, however, planners often devoted little attention to the behavioral or social aspects induced by modernization and its impact on governance. How citizens participated in modernization, or the processes by which their acts of commitment were to be elicited, were taken for granted or left to chance. Practitioners have easily evaded values as relevant, and/or even as central issues. The political, social, and economic behavioral aspects of the modernization process and its impact on the democratic process became the black box of development planners. The conventional assumptions that economic gain alone could provide sufficient motives for change failed to accommodate the subtleties of these variations (Montgomery, 1976: 3; Addo, 1988; Escobar, 1995). It is no wonder then that the ethical implications of modernization were obscured, both by the reduction of local communities and traditions to a lesser status easily ignored in universal national laws, and by the necessary rationalization implied by the democratization needed for self-governing. Much of the literature developed a social science orientation and a universal model of modernization that did not account for the important structural variables like the role of the family or community relationships in determining the direction of individual motivation in adoption. Trueness to one's traditions, faith, values, and family ties were less necessary (or may even have been harmful) to the public trustworthiness needed in the homogenized public sphere (Schuyler, 1988; Escobar, 1995; Fortner, 2011; Kliksberg, 2012). Ethical questions on meaningful contribution, human agency, and empowering individuals and groups in their own well-being toward building a social, collective, just way of living "a good life" or seeking the kinds of prospects discussed in chapters

2 and 3, like the importance of human agency to freedom, were ignored. Such an ethical perspective thought of in this sense, implies choices derived from value judgments on the form and content of a better society, on the right of the existing society, to make such choices through general consensus and implement them through policies and strategies. The typology presented to developing countries continued to be driven by assumptions emerging from the individualistically inclined culture of the West devaluing national political and economic conditions at the expense of global, regional, and community dynamics (Schuyler, 1988; Stiglitz, 2003; Fortner, 2011; Kliksberg, 2012; Petras and Veltmeyer, 2018).

The implicit assumption in all these approaches was that the increased rationality of modernization would bring about greater freedom of expression, more democracy and growth propelled by innovations in science and technology, and forms of organization that displaced old and less efficient ways of doing things—a process that the economist Joseph Schumpeter famously described as "creative destruction"—and the political independence of the economy (English, 2013: 11). This account, although insightful, is idealized according to the dominant narrative of modern politics and economics and on reflection is naive. In reality, the success of modernization was limited by strong interests opposed to the dynamism it creates.

It became all too clear that the forces of modernization did not extend to all countries or social groups and was devoid of any structural, racial, or gendered analysis of poverty (Nusbaum, 2004, 2011; Gabay, 2012; Munck, 2018b). Fault lines have emerged between groups supporting liberal modernization and those that are frustrated by a reality that does not fill basic human needs. Modernization is then experienced by many as humiliating and a destructive loss of status grounded in tradition. Those who are unable to succeed according to the official standards of appreciation often feel deceived and tend to move toward enclaves of subcultures with clearly defined boundaries between "us" and "them," an idealization of the in-group and demonization of the out group (Pattyn, 2002; see also Stone, 1992; Przeworski, 1995; Helleiner, 2001; Levitt, 2018; Munck, 2018a; Souffrant, 2019; Roser, 2019). Nor has the assumption of "convergence" of modern societies been borne out by the reality of economic developments in the contemporary era (Inglehart and Welzel, 2009; Eisenstadt, 2010; Veltmeyer and Bowles, 2018) which in and of itself effectively precludes the pursuit of public policies aimed at social equality. Instead modernization for the majority of countries presented an intensifying interdependence of the transborder problems that have cut across national boundaries and are being felt by communities regardless of their geographical locations. Moreover, modernization has produced multiple simultaneous processes of development on the regional landscape, making it not uncommon to find co-existing features of agrarian, industrial, and post-industrial societies. With each stage of a linear dialectical process been truncated, the result is the inherent contradictory tensions of each being still present as society advances, leading to multiple modernities (for a comprehensive analysis see Eisenstadt, 2000, 2007, 2013; but also see Thomas, 1988; Castells, 2010, 2014; Munck, 2018b). The basic idea is that as most of the world becomes modern, the old dichotomy between traditional and modern societies is no longer valid with most societies for better or worse entangled into modernities (Eisenstadt, 2010: 43; Munck, 2018b). Thus inherent in these societies are parallel epochs of development. Compositely, this state of affairs has precipitated a crisis in governance outputs and outcomes.[8] What follows is a further analysis of the way that modernization and its proximate causes pose questions on the effective functioning of the liberal democracies of the region.

NOTES

1. I intentionally referenced G. K. Lewis's (1968) work *The Growth of the Modern West-Indies*. London: Monthly Review Press here because I am of the view that it can be seen as a precursor to the scholarship of the new world group. One can reasonably argue that the last chapter of this referenced work "The Challenge of Independence," on the need for a new type of public opinion, a new national spirit, and the need for invention of new institutions and new purposes engineered by Caribbean society from the common man to the Caribbean intellectual lays the terrain for the directional focus on which the new world group would travel. Beckford's (1972) work *Persistent Poverty* constitutes a continuum rather than a beginning as is so commonly perceived and believed by many of the new Caribbean scholars of the Caribbean's search for a transformational narrative out of its political, social and economic malaise.

2. These five "divisions" are not meant to deploy a precise historical narrative— this would be impossible given the different political trajectories of contemporary democracies.

3. A resurgence of the idea of modernization has reignited the belief that its implementation makes individual autonomy, gender equality, and democracy attainable.

4. Anti-colonial thought supported and influenced by the anti-capitalist Marxist/ Leninist ideologies of the Soviet Union influenced new movements in Jamaica, Guyana and Grenada. Ironically, their ultimate aim was also a form of modernization, cast this time in the image of the Soviet Union.

5. A major challenge facing policy planners and/or governments in considering corrective measures for a society undergoing uncharted transformations, is whether to concentrate upon ameliorating the immediate problems through framing policies that when applied produce a desired alteration in the present condition (proximate causes and solutions) at reasonable cost, or by contrast, inducing policies that will fundamentally alter the social and economic structures of society (root causes). Both are not mutually exclusive but a clear perception of the challenges faced and a

conceptualization of the types of policies and solutions we wish to propose to resolve them are crucial. Advocates for the former course will argue that a society cannot change the facts of its history and attempts to frame policy to reflect such is naively idealistic. Planners should instead focus on those immediate problems and apply solutions as the ultimate causes of phenomena cannot be the object of policy efforts. By contrast, advocates for addressing root causes consider such approaches socially conservative and superficial, merely reinforcing a prevailing tendency to maintain current policies and practices even when they have proven to be unsuccessful. Instead these analysts favour examining root and proximate causes of public problems through the values and belief assumptions behind the transformative changes.

6. Modernization theory became the foundation stone of this evolutionary prescription for development. This theoretical approach is not homogeneous, neither have variations on its common logical propositions been produced in a strictly sequential-temporal manner—numerous proponents disagreed on several key features. But in broad outline, theories of modernization have focused on deficiencies in the poorer countries and speculated on ways to overcome them. Traditional society was viewed in negatives: stagnant and unchanging, not innovative, not profit-making, not progressing, not growing (See Gilman, 2003 and Kiely, 2005, for a comprehensive account of the key authors of the intellectual ideas of modernization theory). W.W. Rostow's (1962) *Stages of Economic Growth: A Non-Communist Manifesto* is credited with giving modernization theory its most concrete and best known impetus in his well-known five stages of transition: traditional economies, adoption of modern technology, rapid capital accumulation and early industrialization, high industrialization with low standards of living, and the age of high consumption. And so modernization was seen as holding the key to a corrective change for development and governance its engine was capitalism. Innovation and technological growth became self-sustaining in Western Europe because they were embedded in the capitalist system. Entrepreneurs were in competition: profits were pursued by lowering costs and increasing revenues and re-investing in order to make more profits. This ceaseless accumulation and expansion spurred growth.

7. See Girvan (2015) for the prime ministerial sentiments expressed at the time of the granting of independence.

8. This text distinguishes between policy outputs (the formal actions that governments take to pursue their goals) and policy outcomes (the effects such actions have on society).

Chapter 5

Modernization and Its Institutional Manifestations on the Liberal Democratic State

Tocqueville gave a graphic description of the first general type of loss of legitimacy, referring mainly to countries that had moved from aristocratic monarchies to democratic republics: "Epochs sometimes occur in the life of a nation when the old customs of a people are changed, public morality is destroyed, religious belief shaken, and the spell of tradition broken" (Lipset, 1959: 87). The citizens then have "neither the instinctive patriotism of a monarchy nor the reflecting patriotism of a republic; they have stopped between the two in the midst of confusion and distress" (Lipset, 1959: 87). This description aptly continues to characterize the current crisis of governance in the Caribbean. At the heart of the problem also lies the inherent contradiction involved in the very phrase "governability of democracy." For, in some measure, governability and democracy are warring concepts. An excess of democracy means a deficit in governability and easy governability suggests faulty democracy (Crozier et al., 1975: 173).

While there is some praise for the performance of democratic government in these societies, there are also areas of critical weakness and potential breakdown. Modernization did induce valorized social change. The very fact that modernization entails continual changes in all major spheres of society means of necessity that it involves disorganization and dislocation—processes distinctively described by Joseph Schumpeter as creative destruction (Henry, 1987; Inglehart and Welzel, 2005; Patterson and Macintyre, 2011; English, 2013). In each CARICOM nation the demands on democratic government have grown, while government's capacity stagnates as the old institutional frameworks are sidestepped and marginalized by economic organizations, social groups, and states themselves searching for institutional configurations more congruent with the evolving national conditions. Identified common "governability" problems have been viewed as stemming from such

factors as the "changing democratic context," the rise of "anomic democracy," democratic "dysfunctions," the mismatch between expectations and
available resources, the "delegitimization" of authority, increasing dehuman-
izing of society "system overload," the "disaggregation" of interests, and an
increasing parochialism in international affairs (Crozier et al., 1975: 203; see
also Ryan, 2001; Girvan, 2011; Girvan, 2015; Minto-Coy et al., 2016). Other
entrenched explanations are self-evident. A lack of natural human, political,
technical, or financial capital has been an enduring barrier to implementing
existing agreements, and to embarking on new ones with agreements reached
often undermined and even "subverted altogether in the end" (Brewster,
2003b, cited in Payne and Bishop, 2010: 4).

   Chapter 4 identified the critical institutions and policies underpinning
the drive to modernize. As noted in earlier chapters, the epistemological
crisis of governance is equally the result of the disciplinary individualism
within the academy that has so often fragmented the root and proximate
causes and their solutions to the crisis, to the extent where policy planners
and academics themselves are now unable to identify causal connections,
particularly of the subtle interrelationships and the comprehensive nature
of the problem under investigation. My methodological approach in this
research is to be deliberate in using an extensive expository approach to
my analysis to ensure practitioners and scholars can systematically reflect
on the practices and processes of governance. Globally, as in the region,
modernization has fractured democratic governance resulting in twin
pathologies: of representation and of participation. The former is marked
by the gradual deterioration of effectiveness and efficiency in political
systems, with loss of legitimacy of governments, legislatures, and judicial
systems, and the demoralization of ideologies and political parties, leaving
citizens feeling less represented by those they have elected (Sousa Santos
and Avritzer, 2002). The latter is typified by a general increase in levels
of abstention because of the weakening of social organizations, corrosion
of the social structure and of culture, almost total lack of relevant political
debate, demoralization of politics to nothing more than dogmatism, lack of
interest in anything public, and increasing privatization of social relations
and the state itself. It is also further typified by a continuing global fad-
dishness where citizens abandon old loyalties, building allegiances shaped
by rapidly shifting ideas and hopes (Kim, 1999: 2; UNESCO, 2001) made
more acute by a crisis of values. Ironically, both pathologies have valorized
political apathy, an idea stressed by Schumpeter, for whom common citizens possessed neither ability nor interest in politics other than to choose
leaders to make decisions for them (Sousa Santos and Avritzer, 2002:
xxxvii). These same forces are also giving rise to bigness and complexity, overspecialization and circumlocution, inflexible inertia, obsolescence,

impersonal alienation, intra- and extra-organizational imperialism dysfunctions commonly associated with ever more complex social, political, and moral issues. Several authors confirm this illation, visible in the illusory nature of the threat to daily life. John Naisbitt highlights that we are in a "multiple-choice society," where alienation and dependency are striking societal characteristics. Marcuse talks about the "one-dimensional men" that can be translated to our time of consumption, where the recognition of the individual is made by a system of objects (Bilhim and Neves, 2005:10). Debord emphasizes an era of "generalized autism" (Debord, 1979: 43 cited in Bilhim and Neves, 2005: 10) and the still valid Feuerbach pronounces, "This is without doubt a time when the image is preferable than the thing, the copy instead of the original, the representation instead of the reality and the appearance instead of the being" (Feuerbach, 1904 cited in Bilhim and Neves, 2005: 10; Hodgkinson, 1996; Brooks, 2010).

Why then does all this matter to governance? The challenge for the region remains how well equipped are our political institutions to deal with the rising tensions between growing sovereignty (the control of governments by the governed) and decreasing sovereignty (the control of the governed by bureaucracy) and still yet by the quality of human experience and the social relations that facilitated by information and communication technologies, it makes possible. The trend toward superficiality and anomie is exacerbated by the intensified perception of modern citizens and their inability to modify or affect social, political, or organizational action. These issues ought to command our attention because in developing regions where the developmental project has been under way for some significant time there is, paradoxically, the emergence of undesired consequences from desired actions and vice versa, as will be further developed in chapters 6 and 7. There is a need therefore to reflect on the shifting underlying dynamics of culture, language, traditions, and identity without continuing to invest the concepts in the old institutions of the nation-state. Without this reflection, the nexus of causality becomes a challenge of how we rethink and/or redraw the possible solutions for the governance of our society. And so, in this chapter I examine the crises within the state as a function of this complex of modernization that is impacting the legitimacy of regional democratic political systems. Central to this discussion is further identifying the logical relationships stemming from the processes of modernization and their implications, to demonstrate that these challenges are part of a larger problem of political economic and social decay devoid of an obvious ethical ethos. It is against this backdrop of fragmentation and uncertainty (Kim, 1999; UNESCO, 2001; Girvan, 2015) for human well-being that I turn to a more expansive view of the changing forces impacting the liberal democratic state as a further justification for the infusion of the ethical turn in governance.

Wider lessons can be adapted. We can learn how a democracy is not merely a mechanism for electing governments, nor simply having the presence of a constitutional apparatus with the usual devices of separation of the powers of law making, law executing, and law adjudicating; the presence of special majorities for checks and balances in bicameral legislatures; and for voluntary organizations and national political systems as is well recognized and expected. Equally or more important, it ought to be a type of society that links individual behaviors, thinking about democracy in the republican tradition where values and institutions of social virtue and global justice can claim an importance within the state. If we fail to do so, prescriptive relevance becomes nothing more than a nonchalant reaction and the chance is missed for theoretical innovation to devise corrective formulae to resolve these fractured democracies for their future survival (Campbell, 2010).

THE CHANGING DIMENSION OF RESPONSIBILITY

As mentioned in chapter 4 the phenomenon of modernization, facilitated by global technological diffusion undergird the acceleration of global economic interdependence inducing changes in the institutional dimensions of these already fragile nations. These twinned forces are unleashing local antagonisms, [re]shaping the wider socioeconomic and political character of communities, societies, and nation-states in an explosion of complexity, contradictory forms of evolution and uncertainty substantially influencing the character of human interaction with the material environment (Kliksberg, 1999; Veltmeyer and Bowles, 2018; Levitt, 2018; Munck, 2018a, 2018b). Discussion of which came first may be moot as there is a mutual causation that makes it difficult to divorce either phenomenon. It would be possible to write an entire thesis on modernized globalization if we take into consideration that colonialism was a pre-existing form of modernization. My focus is not this, but rather to continue arguing that representative and responsible government is under threat in a myriad of ways by this nexus of modernization/globalization. Engendered by this nexus, the liberal assumption of political authority for some time now considered the cornerstone of modern political development, and the basis for the governance of nation-states, is being pulled apart by a crisis of ideas, beliefs, and values. Anyone looking on from a few steps back or off to the side should recognize that each measure proposed often generates conflicting proponents or beneficiaries. This has led to a crisis of implementation concerning the responsibility of the nation-state and its elected government and who is being represented. One could argue that in the good old days the grand narrative worked: representative and responsible government had its defects and inadequacies, but people felt—or perhaps were deluded—that they knew where things were. Society was, apparently, pretty predictable and reasonably certain (Parsons, 1998: 89; Keonane and Nye, 2000; Chang, 2010; Clegg, 2011). Today however, notions both of responsible and representative government are under threat.

Essentially the concept of responsible government involved the idea that the government of a country should be so arranged that citizens and their representatives would know where to fix blame, or hold to account because of the strong linkage between layers and levels of authority and responsibility. Thus, politicians with responsibility to the people made policy, and civil servants with responsibility to the politicians carried it out and were also responsible to the politicians for how they carried it out (Parsons, 1998: 88; Clegg, 2011). The state primarily had the duty to observe the legality of its acts and to respect citizens' rights and needs (Barata, 1998: 57). Today responsibility is thinning with a growing gap between the rhetoric of responsible government and its reality. Although citizens expect their national governments to be responsible, governments' ability to satisfy this role is increasingly challenged by the myriad expectations of citizens and their limited administrative apparatus to ensure efficiency, effectiveness, economy, and value (Parsons, 1998: 88). Attempting to provide these values for all, there has been experimentation with importing new bureaucratic practices such as new public management (NPM), encouraged and facilitated by international organizations such as the Organization of Economic Cooperation and Development (OECD), the World Bank, Inter-American Development Bank, Commonwealth Secretariat, and others imploring developing countries to adopt this "new best practice." The central hypothesis of this strategy is modernizing governance in a new kind of relationship between the state and the citizens at the macro level through "new" strategic public sector approaches to administrative governance including downsizing, privatization, outsourcing, subcontracting, the creation of public–private partnerships, and restructuring the state to make government more accountable, efficient, and hopefully, better. According to the new model, a market-oriented management approach by the state will, by increasing both efficiency and accountability, lead to greater cost-efficiency for governments (Osbourne and Gaebler, 1992; Hondeghem et al., 1998; Dimaggio, 2001; Sutton, 2008; Benn, 2009; Clegg, 2011; Minto-Coy and Berman, 2016; Minto-Coy, 2016; Bissessar, 2016; Soverall, 2016; Jones et al., 2016). It can be argued from this stance that responsibility will follow from the clearer statement of what is to be provided, who will provide it, and the pressure that results from consumer choice. At the micro level, responsibility would be delegated to the individual, who in this regard is expected to be independent, initiatory, enterprising, and prepared to take risks; responsible, communicative, oriented toward citizens; flexible, cooperative, confident, self-assured, able, and ready to learn; conscious of the quality as well as the costs; and committed, but willing to admit mistakes for the sake of progress. Staff have wider latitude for creativity, will become more independent and responsible in fulfilling their tasks, in turn assuring accountability to citizens who benefit from the provision of information on what their tax money accomplishes and on the real cost of administrational services, and can confidently expect the most efficient performance. The increased orientation of administration toward the citizens would enable them to rely on administration to take their wishes and needs into account in improved ways (Pracher, 1996: 154–155; Hondeghem et al., 1998; Ryan, 2001; Hicks, 2007; Sutton and Bissessar, 2006; Sutton, 2008; Bromell, 2010).

Philosophically, the invocation of NPM has however raised countless and complex ethical doubts. Often in the zeal to implement many of the reforms it was overlooked or ignored that the greater emphasis on institutional individualism, ushered in by the NPM project, released competitive intelligences of knowledge which fragmented and decentralized responsibility. This further delimited where ultimate accountability rested in government, leaving open the door for increasing corruption (Parsons, 1998) a context where rulers and citizens have ceased to know or care about the common good, preferring instead to seek their own private, especially, economic, interests. Frederickson (1997: 4) reminds us that absent laws, rules, social conventions, and/or social reciprocity will see rational persons and firms willfully act on the basis of self-interest. Further criticisms can be attributed to this strategic initiative. Paradoxically, the attempt to introduce market values into government increasingly brought an extension of the role of government in the creation of extensive regulatory mechanisms and agencies to manage the transition from state-owned to private-owned enterprises. One could say this was a manifestation of the increasing complexity of government, but in turn it produced several antagonisms (Pracher, 1996; Ryan and Bissessar, 2002; Clegg, 2011; Minto-Coy and Berman, 2016; Minto-Coy, 2016; Bissessar, 2016; Soverall, 2016; Jones et al., 2016). The newly created specialized departments and administrative units now responsible for producing results through the efficient allocation of resources "overloaded" government with many new responsibilities (Parsons, 1998; Grindle, 2004, 2010; Bromell, 2010). The range of such functions often required a level of structural differentiation and complexity that invariably, given their limited material and human resource capabilities, exceeded their ability to take advantage either of economies of scale or scope. Public administration specialists have also observed that though smallness may have the advantages of simplifying bureaucratic coordination, penetration of the society, and conflict resolution, small scale also constrains on bureaucratic capability and effectiveness, causing them to consistently underperform (Ryan, 2001: 83; Sutton, 2008;

Veenendaal and Corbett, 2015; Minto-Coy and Berman, 2016; Minto-Coy, 2016; Bissessar, 2016; Jones et al., 2016; Ratter, 2018). It is not uncommon in the Caribbean, and by extension other developing societies that have adopted the abridged Westminster style of government, to reshuffle and/or reconfigure the administrative arms of government at will. When organizations reinvent themselves, the responsibility of an agency/department/statutory corporation is now the responsibility of another acronym—now part of the private sector! Extrapolating from Ha Joon Chang's (2010) work, democratic responsibility is further compromised when the goals of an agency and its relative priorities are not made clear and/or when state-owned enterprises are monitored by multiple agencies resulting in their being not meaningfully supervised by any particular agency or in supervisory overkill that disrupts daily management. Instances exist of administrative leaders freed from the unnecessary and troublesome interference of upward accountability within the structures of government and subsequently able to take decisions on the use of resources and completion of works independently (Sutton, 2008; Clegg, 2011). The specialized departments, now responsible for their results and resources will—like the administrative leaders—be freed from unnecessary and troublesome interference and be able to take decisions on the use of resources and completion of works independently. The end result however is that checks and balances that guaranteed the delimitations of responsibility, so germane to the functioning of the liberal democratic state, have become blurred. The disconnections at all levels of the state have led to scapegoating rather than the acceptance of responsibility. Accountability and responsibility in liberal democracy work best when organizations are more grounded. Many, if not most of the problems associated with this *adhocracy* arise because the values of responsibility and accountability are in some degree spread over a wide range of institutions or are held in such a way as to preclude an obvious or natural consensus (Parsons, 1998; Dorbeck-Jung, 1998; Hondeghem, 1998; Clegg et al., 2011).

THE QUANTIFICATION OF GOVERNMENT

As responsibility and accountability became more indefinite and hierarchical than before, to ensure a degree of success in their development efforts, advocates of modernization took comfort in masking underperformance of economies often as a result of underlying bureaucratic pathologies, with arithmetical elegance or lack thereof. The degree of Westernization was to be the sign of progress or regress. One of the most striking tendencies of our time is the expansion of market-orientated reasoning into spheres of life traditionally governed by non-market norms (Sandel, 2010; Satz, 2010; Conway, 2014; Potter et al., 2019). The very issue of state reform has acquired strictly economic and managerialist connotations, no longer synonymous with democratization and the pursuit of good governance but becoming confused with the reduction of its regulatory functions, with an effort to meet the supposedly higher purpose of achieving fiscal adjustment (Sader, 2005: 449; Sutton, 2008; Gabay, 2012; Conway, 2014; Minto-Coy and Berman, 2016; Minto-Coy, 2016; Bissessar, 2016; Potter et al., 2019). The practice of politics has become a private activity, performed by professionals who belong to a political elite responsible for society's "management" through the state, increasingly understood as a "business company." As a correlate, prominent businessmen have become the model of "success" in their individualistic quest to solve their own problems (Sader, 2005: 453; Veenendaal and Corbett, 2015). At the heart of much of modern public management is the belief that the key to improving productivity, accountability, control, and efficiency is to improve measurability. Given the difficulties inherent in the value aspect of decision-making, it is no surprise that there is a tendency to over-concentrate on the factual and quantitative or managerial aspects of problem-solving. This is particularly noticeable in terms of the bias toward quantificationism and measurement. With responsibility for actions unclear, management has become more preoccupied with performance and calculating inputs and outputs (Parsons, 1998; Maguire, 1998; Gabay, 2012; Conway, 2014). Quantification has now become the sieve through which all policies are filtered and judged as either positive or negative according to their contribution to the balance of public accounts and to monetary stability. It connotes an orientation that is positivistic, technocratic, and instrumental focused on means rather than ends (Hodgkinson, 1996: 66). Political reforms presented to parliament can be assessed according to savings in state expenses (Sader, 2005: 449). A cynic might point out that by so doing policy makers can thereby distribute blame to those not in the policy loop but in management. Even if this were the case, over and beyond this, after the pie-charts, graphs, and histograms emphasizing disaggregated targets of country and global benchmarks have been presented, the shadowy figure of *Homo economicus*, with its rational orderings and strangely unencumbered and universalized approach to governance, begs the question, how to move the process of change along once we have been given the diagnosis (Hausman and Mcpherson, 2006). Time has shown that in our rush to develop, we have ignored difficult to measure goals such as human rights, and to what extent they can be justifiably suppressed, by reifying and separating them from social relations (Sader, 2005: 459) in the attempt to shoehorn the complex matter of human development into measurable log-frames and matrices (Gabay, 2012: 1252). It also conduces a policy process where outcomes can be a series of blind spots and distortions generated from partitioning and warping reality in patterned ways based on the naturalistic fallacy that wrongly presupposes policy outcomes can logically be derived only from facts (Hodgkinson, 1996: 67). It is in this regard that an ethical turn in governance must seek to redress such concerns. The incompatibility between the results and the public commitment to proceed to change must be engendered from within the complex comprehension of the human condition with its norms and procedures and underlying values of society.

WHITHER REPRESENTATIVE GOVERNMENT?

By diluting accountability and responsibility, adequate representation within our relatively nascent democracies is also structurally and philosophically challenged. One of the most troubling developments in the post-independence politics of many Caribbean states is the tendency of newly elected governments to assume that winners are entitled to all the spoils of office, in essence equating the state with their ruling parties and setting about monopolizing national resources, infiltrating all facets of economic life. As such, chairmen, members, and even chief executive officers of all statutory boards, commissions, and state enterprises are expected to resign or at least offer their resignations to make room for persons presumed loyal or sympathetic to them. The heads of organizations are in turn expected to extend the process by providing jobs and resources to persons known or assumed loyal to the party and to the prime minister who sees him/herself, anthropomorphically, as personifying the state (Ryan, 1996: 359–364 cited in Meeks and Lindahl, 2001: 77; Mills, 1970; Simmonds, 1985; Grant, 2003; Minto-coy and Berman, 2016). Representative government is compromised because it creates an implementation crisis, becoming at all levels ill-equipped for dealing with (and "managing") rapid change and flux. An institutionalized colonial legacy of balkanization inextricably mutated onto the process of modernization with its standardization of cultural norms and mores, has been compounded, leading unavoidably to pluralistic societies (not only of ethnicity but also of thought) with diverse cultures that challenge core values and the implications for governance. This introduces another feature to the crisis of governance: the problem of the relation between representation and cultural and social diversity (Manley, 1988; Ramadan, 2010; Glover, 2010; Margetts, 2010; Carens, 2012; Taylor, 2012; Girardin, 2012; Minto-Coy and Berman, 2016; Daniel, 2016; Goede, 2016; Nunez, 2016; Gaskin, 2020).

As the region moves toward enhanced consolidation in the regional integration of the CARICOM Single Market and Economy (CSME)[1] citizens of member states find themselves vying with each other as equal citizens for equitable treatment, but with different cultural and religious backgrounds and underlying political cultures. It raises a serious question of how a cosmopolitan and disparate society can hope to cultivate the solidarity and sense of mutual responsibility that a representative democracy requires for governance. Even if immigrants and their descendants have appropriate access to the legal status of citizenship, they can still be marginalized economically, socially, and politically (Girvan, 2011). If citizens of immigrant origin are excluded from the economic and educational opportunities that others enjoy, if they are viewed with suspicion and hostility by their fellow citizens, if their concerns are ignored and their voices not heard in political life, they are not really included in the political community. They may be citizens in a formal sense but they are not really citizens in a fuller more meaningful sense of the term. They are not likely to see themselves or be seen by others as genuine members of the community. In many important ways, they will not belong. This is clearly wrong from a democratic perspective. No one thinks that democratic equality requires citizens to be equal in every respect, but the democratic ideal of equal citizenship clearly entails more than the formality of equal legal rights. It requires a commitment to genuine equality of opportunity in economic life and in education, to freedom from domination in social and political life, and to an ethos of mutual respect, compromise, and fairness. In this regard, democratic states are supposed to provide all their members with democratic principles—such as rights to religious freedom and to live the life of one's choice while harming no one—requiring the substantive, not merely formal, inclusion of citizens of immigrant origin (Carens, 2012: 112; see also Nussbaum, 2004, 2011; Ramadan, 2010; Glover, 2010; Taylor, 2012; Girardin, 2012; Thunder, 2017). The slow process in our attempts at regional integration therefore cannot always be neatly diagnosed as the lack of political will or commitment (WIC, 1992; Sutton, 1999; Payne and Bishop, 2010; Girvan, 2015) but a crisis in the redistributive potentialities of a liberal democracy. As the number of actors involved in politics grows, and the ethnic and cultural diversity of social actors and the interests involved in political arrangements increase, the difficulty of representing specific agendas and identities becomes less convincing. The most socially vulnerable groups, the less favored social sectors, and ethnic minorities are unable to have their interests represented in the political system with the same ease as the majority or more economically prosperous sectors (Sousa Santos and Avritzer, 2002: XIVI; Carens, 2012; Thunder, 2017).

As if this were not a challenge in and of itself, the betrayal of representation is further exacerbated by the perennial ruse of governments reneging on their national responsibilities by taking policy issues into the international arena to the various constituencies of creditor and multilateral agencies as a strategy to escape domestic opposition (Lapeyre, 2004). Claiming "tied hands" from being party to international agreements may allow presentation of national policies that are unpalatable to some groups, and therefore politically difficult to implement (Thompson, 1990; Przeworski, 1995). With the image of national community confined to territorial and insular space, global actors have come to be understood as being outside the realm of democratic discourse. Their actions and behavior are not accountable to the will of the people. At the same time, it is these very global actors, more than anyone else, whose social power is constituted in the state, whose interests are represented as universal, and whose *class* privilege is protected by law. In this way, the image of democracy is preserved and supported by a governing elite playing musical chairs in the occupancy of elective office (Hintzen, 2001: 109; Munroe, 1999; Williams, 2011; Hofmeister and Grabow, 2011; Thunder, 2017) retaining the formal illusion of individual choice and responsibility. Moreover, many such choices will benefit some individuals or groups over others, giving substance to claims of democratic governance. At the same time, such procedural practices conceal the politics at stake by effectively ignoring the existence of structural inequalities circumscribing genuine representation. Representation through decision-making by the majority does not then guarantee that minority identities will be adequately represented in our national parliaments.

It is common knowledge that voting and non-voting citizens believe that many of their representatives are more responsive to special interests than to their own. There is also rising and outright dissatisfaction with policies adopted by legislatures on such problems as health care, containing the deficits, the environment and crime, and others that do not reflect a reasonable consensus of what citizens want (Broome, Hinds, et al., 2014). Added to this is the increasing professionalization of politics where politicians, to use the common Weberian distinction, live "off" rather than "for" politics (Veenendaal and Corbett, 2015: 541; Girvan, 2015). In turn, representatives accuse populations of unreasonable and unlimited demands on legislatures to fulfill often with very limited resources. In several jurisdictions (Antigua and Barbuda, St Kitts and Nevis, and St Lucia), heads of state have been replaced with persons deemed more sympathetic to the new political directorate (Obrien, 2015; AMG, 2014).

These challenges facing democratic governments are the products of past successes and of the changes from past trends. Substantial elements of the population rising into the middle classes have escalated their expectations and aspirations, resulting in more intense reaction when these are not met. Widespread material well-being has led to a substantial element of particularly the young and the "intellectual" professional classes, adopting new lifestyles and social-political values (Przeworski, 1995; Kung, 2012). Most recently, the temporary slowdown in economic growth has threatened the expectations created by previous growth, inducing the rise of one-issue NGOs; organizations or groups often formed as expressions of a new value awareness emerging from the cultural disarray and political disempowerment of national governments and public institutions (Kim, 1999: 10; UNESCO, 2001; Kung, 2012; Singer, 2012). But equally, the crisis of representation is being manifested in the presence of attenuated political parties and party systems unable to organize the electorate, simplify choices, select effective leaders, aggregate interests, and shape policy choices and priorities. Thus, the development and viability of political parties during post-independence, that went hand-in-hand with the expansion of the suffrage and the increased responsibility of governments to their citizens, making democratic government possible, is now under grave threat of administrative and ideational decay (Mills, 2013; Girvan, 2015; Hartnell, 2016).

THE CONFLICT OF RIGHTS AND REPRESENTATION AND THE RISE OF ANOMIC DEMOCRACIES

Another arena for discussion of the impact of modernization on the state and its effect on representation has been the evolution, proliferation, and diffusion of mass media and modern information technology and their impact on rights and representation. ICTs have facilitated easier access to knowledge, increasing society's informational autonomy with an excess of information via technologically enhanced manipulation of image and sound bites. Thus, rising levels of education, increasing cognitive and informational requirements in economic activities, and proliferation of knowledge via mass media make people intellectually more independent, diminishing cognitive constraints on human choice. Elaborating further, socioeconomic development diminishes objective constraints on human autonomy, creativity, and choice in three ways (Inglehart and Welzel, 2005: 29; Castells, 2005, 2010, 2014; Cardoso, 2005; Fortner, 2011). First, reduction of poverty diminishes material constraints on human choice and nourishes a sense of existential security (external security). Second, socioeconomic development tends to increase people's levels of formal education giving them greater access to information through the mass media in the same vein that the requirements of the emerging knowledge society mobilizes people's cognitive abilities. In this regard, it diminishes cognitive and informational constraints on human choice, fueling a sense of intellectual independence as it increases occupational specialization and social complexity, diversifying human interactions (Inglehart and Welzel, 2005: 24; see also Eisenstadt, 2005; Inglehart and Welzel, 2009; Schumann, 2015; Thompson, 2019). In these instances, growing diversity of human interactions liberates people: it frees them from ascriptive communal ties and closed social circles, bringing them to interact with others on a bargaining basis. Diversification of human interaction also frees people from fixed social roles and social ties, making them autonomous in defining their social roles for themselves and in shaping their social ties to other people. As Beck (2002, cited in Inglehart and Welzel, 2005) puts it, there is a shift from "communities of necessity" to "elective affinities" to others. Socialization and socializing become a matter of choice: people are free to connect and disconnect with whomever they want; and rigidly fixed roles for such categories as gender and class are eroding, giving people more room to express themselves as individuals (Inglehart and Welzel, 2005: 24).

The third effect of socioeconomic development is to diminish social constraints on human choice, nurturing a sense of social autonomy. Compositely therefore, the advances in ICTs have broadened human choice releasing emancipatory forces that have become the leading themes in all domains of life from politics to child care to gender relations to work motivations to religious orientations and civic engagement. Self-expression values and rising emphasis on freedom of choice emerge as increasingly favorable existential conditions that allow the universal desire for autonomy to take priority. Rising emphasis on human choice has immensely important consequences, generating pressures for more political liberties, and democratic institutions (Inglehart and Welzel, 2005: 47; Eisenstadt, 1966; Eisenstadt, 2005; Sousa Santos, 2005; Inglehart and Welzel, 2009; Hampshire, 2010; Glover, 2010; Hofmeister and Grabow, 2011; Castells, 2014; Keen, 2015; Thompson, 2019).

Admittedly, an obvious, invaluable strength of a democratic culture is that it allows relatively free pursuit of rights (Parsons, 1998). In theory, this was liberating for everyone. No longer tied to their allotted place in society, people could at last choose who they were and what they did (Gerhardt, 2010: 30) and through the pursuit of human rights, have won many freedoms. Rights have imposed constraints on the pursuit of collective goals. They function morally as safeguards of the position of individuals or particular groups where they can be invoked against the pursuit of collective goals in the face of social endeavors (Sumner, 2013: 289; Vernon, 2010). Thus the rhetoric of rights is very powerful and our societies are now replete with conflicts of rights and "new rights": young against old, ethnic minority against majority, nationals against foreigners, rich against poor, women against men, believers against non-believers, children against parents, employees against employers, consumers against producers, students against teachers, citizens against the police, and all against the state (Sumner, 2013, O'Brien, 2013; MRGI, 2007). The democratic spirit has become in spirit egalitarian, individualistic, populist, and impatient with the distinctions of class and rank. Authority has been challenged not only in government, but in trade unions, business enterprises, schools and universities, professional associations, churches, and civic groups, institutions that in the past played a major role in the indoctrination of the young in their rights and obligations as members of society, the family, the church, the school, and the army. The effectiveness of these institutions in socialization has declined severely, with the stress increasingly on the rights, interests, and needs of individuals and not on the rights, interests, and needs of the community. These attitudes have been particularly prevalent in the young, but have appeared in other age groups, especially those with professional, white-collar, and middle-class status. The success of the existing structures of authority in incorporating large elements of the population into the middle class, paradoxically, strengthens precisely those groups that are disposed to challenge the existing structures of authority (Crozier et al., 1975: 162; Eisenstadt, 2005; Gerhardt, 2010; Hofmeister and Grabow, 2011; Rego and Palacios, 2016).

It is therefore important to understand what these structures are, what their distinctive function in our political thinking is, how we might distinguish reasonable from unreasonable claims of rights, and how rights might fit into the larger framework of ethical governance. In promoting the collective social goals we deem to be valuable, like improving the general welfare of society through the pursuit of equality of opportunity and bettering the lot of the worst off, it might be unjustifiable to implement such measures because they exploit or victimize particular individuals or groups. These considerations become important because implicit in freedom and rights are other less appealing values such as the revival of chauvinisms, individualism, the proliferation of sometimes hazardous new religious movements, and the growing strength of various forms of fundamentalisms, particularly when they become all-pervasive (Kim, 1999: 10; UNESCO, 2001; Hampshire, 2010; Lent, 2010; Sumner, 2013). When everyone is claiming this or that by right, one person is pitted against another in a conflict of rights. It leads to people believing that the job of political, administrative, and religious leaders is to satisfy all their wants, fulfill life's aspirations, with no trade-offs or choices to be made.

Yet we know, unsurprisingly, that people want mutually incompatible things—better public services and lower taxes, children protected, but the state off their backs, more local control but no variation in services between areas (Oppenheim, 2010: 47). But without common purpose there is no basis for common priorities, and without priorities there are no grounds for distinguishing among competing private interests and claims. Conflicting goals and specialized interests crowd one another, with executives, cabinets, parliaments, and bureaucrats lacking the criteria to discriminate among them (Crozier et al., 1975: 161; Eisenstadt, 2005; Hofmeister and Grabow, 2011). This creates a culture of grievance in which people see the moral task as being, in essence, the securing of more rights against others who would otherwise take them away (Vernon, 2010: 11). At the same time, a pervasive spirit of democracy may pose an intrinsic threat and undermine all forms of association, weakening the social bonds which hold together family, enterprise, and community. Every social organization requires, in some measure, inequalities in authority and distinctions in function (Crozier, 1975: 8; Eisenstadt, 2005). Likewise, to the extent that the spread of the democratic temper corrodes all of these, it leads to uncertainty and confusion surrounding the existence and universal nature of these rights and values. Adding to this, when freedom is delinked from responsibility, principles such as "paying for consequences" are undermined (Girardin, 2012: 70). And, lest we forget the paradox inherent in freedom and rights: an individual's rights only make a difference to him or her if given by others (Parsons, 1998; Vernon, 2010). The system becomes one of anomic democracy in which democratic politics becomes more an arena for the assertion of conflicting interests than a process for the building of common purposes.

THE DECLINE OF THE WELFARE STATE AND THE RISE OF CONSUMERIST SOCIETIES

As with the other challenges of the modernization process, the crisis of representation and its consequences for governance has its groundings in the expansion and application of neoliberal policies. These policies emphasize the [re]orientation of government toward the marketization of service that has been found useful in the private sector and has become the un/official ideology of these democracies. The advocates of neoliberalism argue that the government should adopt the techniques of business administration and the *values* of business. The result has been the introduction of a raft of policies to dismantle the inefficient and highly bureaucratized welfare state, de-emphasizing the role of labor, introducing multiple-policy structural adjustment programs, and deregulating state enterprises, among others. The corollary to these policies has been reduction in formal jobs, the deterioration of public services, overdue wages, police violence, the commodification of culture expressed under the guise of entrepreneurship, and "social exclusion" with its deleterious emotional impact. The vast literature on the introduction of these policies bears no repetition here. The main concern here is that the danger of the eminent decline of the welfare state has precipitated its financialization, a further blow to its ability to represent the electorate given the overwhelming influence of financial and speculative capital on the institutions of governance—political parties, parliaments, electoral campaigns, political debates, political culture, and even trade unions despite protestations to the contrary (Sader, 2005: 450; Lewis, 2006; Sandel, 2010; Conway, 2014; Veltmeyer and Bowles, 2018; Potter et al., 2019).

Political parties have lost their ideological identity and elections no longer represent a confrontation of genuine alternatives, with electoral processes corrupted by the power of money and the commercialization of the voting process manifesting through vote-buying (Keefer and Vlaicu, 2017). As indicated in chapter 3, polarization of thought has become commonplace among economists, forgetting the discipline is an imperfect [social] science as they wrangle over the "correct" policies for fiscal adjustment. They, like the self-serving general media, engage citizens on clichéd omnibus dichotomous arguments—"the market" against "politics," "the market" against "the state," both claiming "rationality" in opposition to the "corporatism," "intolerance," and "incompetence" of politicians. Such distorted versions gradually diminish the quality of political debate and promote indifference toward politics, eventually contributing to the apathy and demobilization of the citizenry. Private capital is protected by the smokescreen which, in turn, leaves them more room and time for their profit maximizing and acquiring large sections of the state (Sader, 2005: 450; Parsons, 1998; Hood, 1998; Sutton, 1999; Sousa Santos and Avritzer, 2002; Mullins, 2002; Lewis, 2006; Girvan, 2015).

The commodification of culture, as expressed by the individual, provides the private sector with the commercial environment to maximize its gains. For this it employs the mass media to disseminate commercial and consumerist values dominated by imported Western, particularly American materials (Barney, 2004; Khiabany, 1999) that are often incompatible with the needs of developing communities. The very notion of "modernity" as a Western construct is permeated with implications for dependency as it serves as a propeller of social, cultural, economic, and political changes that converge with Western economic interests. Seeing this interplay within the modernization framework is crucial to an understanding of alternative forms of economy and socialization. For the fact can no longer be ignored that far from being an aid to development, the modern personality is oriented to escaping the backwardness of its country of origin either by personal consumption or by emigration. And, more often than not the defaulting concomitant reality is that the media and messages available to the "modern" citizen in developing countries are helping to produce a troubled local identity that neither belongs to its country of origin nor fits within the alien system (Stone, 1992; Khiabany, 1999; Sandel, 2010; Crudas and Rutherford, 2010; Carens, 2012). And so, the interaction of this double corrosion produced by neoliberal policies affects the value system and institutional structures of these open and vulnerable societies and has also been instrumental in much of the paralysis in representative government, characterized by "executive impotence," "party stalemate . . . party deadlock in the legislature," "lack of agreement on fundamental matters," "political inexperience and exploitation," and "demoralization and feeling of futility" (Stamps, 1958, in Carrow, 1998; Demmke and Moilanen,

2011). Moreover, decades of the application of hegemonic values propagated by the internationalization of modernization has significantly impacted the quality of social capital, that is, the attitudes and institutions at the very basis of social relations, with deeper implications for the quality of governance, as will be discussed in the following section.

DEVALUED SOCIAL CAPITAL = DEVALUED COMMUNITY

As noted, the caliber of social capital profoundly influences the working of the society. Unethical behavior comes at inordinate cost to organizations and societies. Works by Putnam (1993), Dimmaggio and Powell (2001), Ostrom (2003), Polyani (2011), Bourdieu (2011), and Granovetter (2017) give significant examples of the importance of social capital or of communities of congealed social relations to governance. A similar variation on a common theme of the importance of social capital to governance is expressed by Kliksberg (1999) and Woolcock (2010) who both note that the more social capital there is, the more long-term economic growth, less criminality, more public health, and more democratic governance there can be. Putnam (1993) has defined *social capital* as features of social organization, such as trust, norms, and networks, the history, attitudes, and motivations of the people that can improve the efficiency of society by facilitating coordinated actions. Social capital therefore is identified as one of the five types of capital necessary for development to take place, along with natural, physical, financial, and human capital. Kliksberg (1999) argued further that while development practitioners understand well the process outcomes from social capital, they are less experienced in providing a framework for and maintaining the mechanisms for generating cooperative behavior (See also Stolle, 2007; Bourdieu, 2011). How well this process is managed and understood however represents the master keys to technological progress, competitiveness, sustained growth, good government, and stable democracy (Kliksberg, 1999: 85). It will also determine what people will do spontaneously for each other, including the care meted out to its less fortunate members as well as the preservation and guardianship of common assets, or, as Woolcock (2010: 471) states, the idea of social capital in its most elementary form has such widespread resonance because it provides a name for an intuitive, transcultural recognition that we are inherently social beings. This has significant consequences for a host of other substantive issues we care about, through its providing a common frame of reference for conducting across disciplinary, methodological, ideological, and cultural lines conversations about these important issues that are vital—indeed necessary to the resolution of many of the issues themselves—but which otherwise occur too rarely. The sense of closeness to others in the community can be a major asset for that community. But equally these tacit behaviors must be complemented by codified structural institutions such as democratic institutions, constitutions, unrestricted universal suffrage; strong traditions of civic engagement; newspaper readership; and membership in choral societies and literary circles, civic clubs, and soccer clubs which are the hallmarks of a successful region (Putnam, 1993; Granovetter, 2017). Carrow (1998: 3), citing Kagan (1991), reconfirm this stance by noting that successful democracies must meet three conditions: "having a set of good institutions"; "a body of citizens who possess a good understanding of the principles of democracy, or who at least have developed a character consistent with the democratic way of life"; and to "a high quality of leadership, at least at critical moments." Elster (1989) identified in addition to the aforementioned the attributes of stable, regular, predictable patterns of behavior such as trust, feelings of personal well-being, achievement motive, improvement potential, and that of cooperative behavior. These embodied norms and networks of civic engagement are not only preconditions for economic development but the ingredients for the cement of society that holds effective government and social order together for promoting both national and regional consensus on the important issues confronting the community (Jones, 2003).

It is easier to erode than to create institutional or social capital. It is more difficult and time-consuming to build trust, confidence, norms of respect, responsible behavior, and motivated staff than it is to destroy confidence, motivation, and ethics, which can happen rapidly. Social capital can be eroded by a weak, corrupt, or divided government, whether democratically elected or not. A weak civil society unable to exercise accountability from below may also allow a democratically elected government to degenerate into abuse of power and privilege. Similarly, civil strife or insensitive external interference can easily destroy social capital. The exaggerated emphasis in many Third World countries on the transfer of physical and financial capital, as well as technical assistance, has had a disruptive impact on the existing social capital, as witnessed by the erosion of traditional norms and values in the wake of "modernization" (Frey, 1997; Trusted, 1998; Kliksberg, 1999; Stolle, 2007; Ryan, 2001; Madden, 2011).

When this social capital disintegrates, fragments, or is embryonic in its orientation, the social contract is weakened and modern society moves away from collectivity and community toward an insecure individualism. For an individual negotiating such insecurity, there is little to be gained from others by way of the commitments of time, concern, care, or solidarity that community involvement requires (Bauman, 1993, 2001; Madden, 2011). As a result, this individualization trend destroys social capital and the social cohesion of the society. Durkheim used the term anomie to describe this condition of individualization and autonomy occurring in society when rules on how people ought to behave toward one another were breaking down, a condition where norms no longer control the activities of the members of society. Changing conditions as well as adjustments in life lead to dissatisfaction, conflict, and deviance. Durkheim observed that periods of social disruption, for example, economic depression, brought about greater anomie (Demmke and Moilanen, 2011: 27) incurring negative fiscal and civic effects. First, public services deteriorate, as those no longer using the services become less willing to support them with their taxes (Frey, 1997; Demmke and Moilanen, 2011). It seems to make more sense for those who can to pursue an individualized life accruing and protecting the personal resources that enable one to live separate from others, no longer needing to consider or respond to the insecurities that plague them (Hampshire, 1978). There has been, argues Bauman (1993, 2001), (deploying Robert Reich's term), a "secession of the successful" in contemporary society: an individualized distancing from responsibility to and identification with community, and a systematic and deliberate storing-up and protecting of individualized wealth.

Second, as inequality deepens, rich and poor live increasingly separate lives. The affluent send their children to successful schools, leaving other schools to the children of families who have no alternative. A similar trend leads to the secession by the privileged from other public facilities. Thus communal spaces such as parks and buses cease to be places where citizens from different walks of life encounter one another and institutions that once gathered people together and served as informal schools of virtue become few and far between (Sandel, 2010: 8 see also Hampshire, 1978). Such subjects cannot see what staying in and with the community could offer that they have not already secured for themselves or still hope to secure through their own exploits, while they can think of quite a lot of assets which they might lose if they were to abide by the demands of communal solidarity. Society becomes merely a means or instrument toward individual ends. It is here that we must also note that there exists in society negative and moral social capital. Elster (1989) notes that within society exist varieties of human motivation such as envy, opportunism, or self-interest with guile, and codes of honor, or the ability to make credible threats and promises along with corruption, nepotism, and favoritism that aim at group-selective and discriminatory versions of human well-being (Carrow, 1998; Trusted, 1998). Sen (1999) makes a similar assertion noting that what is called "social capital," can have dichotomous features, since a strong sense of group affiliation can have a cementing role within that group, while encouraging rather harsh treatment of non-members, seen as "others" who do not "belong"(Sen, 1999a; Stiglitz, 2000; Fukuyama, 2000). The question, then, is whether these states can muster the resources to reverse the social and institutional decay that is manifest, and [re]build the social capital that is required to sustain good governance. UN Development Program's "Strategy Paper on Governance" (1995) warned that the fact that social capital can easily be eroded poses a considerable risk for interventions in this area. And, as already noted, this uncivic social capital has negative implications for democratic representation since the individual, like groups within society, often exercises important influence on the direction of public policy and ultimately on governance and development. My intention here therefore is to treat "social capital" as a general purpose asset, as a "contingent good," rather than an unconditional social good as a germane consideration for broadening our concern on good governance.

CRISIS IN LEADERSHIP AND/OR CRISIS IN CHARACTER AND THE IMPERSONAL ECONOMY?

No country can isolate itself from general change and as seen from the analysis to this point a confluence of institutional, political, social, and economic forces was unleashed on developing societies (Vernieulen, 1998), a confluence that can be attributed to disaffection with modernization in its various [re]incarnations. Its first incarnation as colonialism had intended to reshape and transform barbaric societies into the image of the colonial powers. From then until now, its application by respective purveyors has plastered over a range of structural dysfunctions[2] supporting and enforcing modernity often manifested and were exacerbated at their worst in periods of global economic crisis (Banuri, 1987; Mazrui, 2004). In developing societies like the Caribbean, the everyday life of vast sectors of the population is marred by acute unsatisfied needs and it is estimated that one-third of the economically active population is affected by severe problems of unemployment and underemployment (Legarde, 2014, UNDP Report, 2016). This state of affairs is incompatible with demands for egalitarianism and increased mass participation pressures, as the gap between promises kept and expectations has widened even more leading to repeated and frustrating clashes between the bureaucracy and various sectors of the general public over poorer and poorer government performances, and widespread feelings of political alienation. Cries of "systemic failure" and "state capture" resonate (Hicks, 2007: 14; Girvan, 2011; Roberts, 2011; Girardin, 2012). These are also linked to the "de-ideologization of politics" in the political space where there is no explicit formulation of any system values. Thus aspirant and incumbent political leaders do not see a pressing need to state their macro-vision for the region. These circumstances have led to a number of common societal features. For instance, power is seen as private property, not as responsibility and service and those in power seek to perpetuate their power. As such, CARICOM states have adopted a personalized political culture that relies heavily on the personal authority of Heads of Government exercised through the decision-making apparatus of the Conference of Heads of Government, the Bureau of the Conference, and the Quasi-Cabinet of Heads of Government. These have assigned thematic portfolios, with the latter two institutions also functioning as the primary regional implementation bodies—the regional executive. This political structure impedes other regional institutions such as the various ministerial organs and the CARICOM Secretariat from fully exercising their decision-making authority and also discourages the participation of non-political stakeholders. In brief, the heads, as guardians of sovereignty, use the decision-making process to preserve for themselves as much national autonomy and control as is possible.

In addition to the weaknesses in decision-making, CARICOM's legislative framework has failed to strengthen the regional governance framework with the Revised Treaty of Chaguaramas maximizing the sovereign control of heads, legitimizing the personalized political culture, and protecting each member state from regional interference in its affairs (Gilbert-Roberts, 2011; Payne and Bishop, 2010). The upshot is that the English-speaking Caribbean today, is left with the same overlapping mixture of poorly resourced and often competing institutions and the result has been indecision, insecurity, and friction between the CRNM, the CARICOM secretariat, and the heads of government, particularly where the ill-defined gray areas in their respective mandates have overlapped (Payne and Bishop, 2010: 10). Public wealth is appropriated by a class of bureaucrats and rulers. Public programs are distorted and do not meet real needs. Strategic sectors are captured by privileged groups and corruption is entrenched and builds a wall against newcomers and competition. In essence, political leadership becomes parochial rather than national and corruptly converts national resources into its project of primitive accumulation. Governments and administrations then hide behind thick layers of bureaucratic procedure and red tape. Policies are opened to limited questioning and debate but these attempts at dialogue or reform are frustrated by evasive strategies (Girardin, 2012: 41; Frey, 1997; Dukor, 2003; Graig, 2005; Issa and David, 2012; Agbude and Etete, 2013; Jones et al., 2016). Moreover, they downplay policy, management, and structural dimensions. Puzzled by complexity, frustrated, powerless, and disillusioned with poor achievement and promises endlessly postponed, citizens distrust laws, rules, institutions, compromise, and mediation (Girardin, 2012: 45; Hofstede, 2012; Jones et al., 2016).

A common response to this malaise, real and perceived, is to identify a "crisis at the top," and to bemoan their current leaders, looking to other leaders to steer them toward a better future. If we have a difficulty with our jobs, our lives, our government, or our world, the answer is often supposed to be better management, increasingly articulated as a universal solution to whatever problem presents itself. There has been an obsession with, and seduction by, leadership to serve several functions: simplifying and containing the complexity of organized life, while reassuring the anxious, atomized, organizational subject of the importance of individual action. Management then serves to protect us against chaos and inefficiency; and to guarantee organizations, people, and machines do what they claim to. Citizens are tempted to trust in charismatic leaders who present themselves as the "savior" or "reformer" of their country; management becomes both a civilizing process and new civic religion. Even non-believers in today's management often seem to believe that the answer is "better" management, rather than something entirely different (Parker, 2002: 2–3; see also Jackal, 1991; Massy and Boven's, 1998; Northouse, 2004; La Guerre and Bissessar, 2009; Issa and David, 2012; Hofstede, 2012; Mayanja, 2013; Jones et al., 2016). Criticism is limited to bad political management, an approach appealing in its simplicity and making a comeback today, at a time when politics is both seen as highly complex and opportunistic and is highly personalized by the media obsessed with political leaders (Girardin, 2012: 45).

Within this context, the role of the individual as an actor in the maintenance of good governance is often transferred directly to the political sphere. It is assumed that if leaders are honest, just, and respectful of the truth, countries will be managed honestly, justly, and with due respect for truth and democracy (La Guerre and Bissessar, 2009). Such simplistic notions of governance have led to the abdication of all responsibility by the need for accountability from the individual, with a callous refusal by citizens to even consider themselves as part of the crisis of governance. Although writing specifically about management and managerialism, Wray-Bliss (2013) drawing his inspiration from the work of Emmanuel Levinas on the dyadic relationship, provides us with the interesting observation, which also characterizes individual behavior in our society, that we lack a sense of the meaning of moral proximity in our social interactions at all levels. We are quite comfortable, indifferent even, in deposing ourselves of responsibility to each other, the state, and to others in other places (Brennan, 1998; Graig, 2005; Girardin, 2012).

Under these circumstances, the question of how to divide responsibility to evolve solutions toward remaking the world a better place poses a problem for ethics. In our face-to-face interactions, as in the physical distancing produced by methods of re-organization of capital, such as outsourcing, subcontracting, and offshore production, we lack an ability to see, think, and even care about the effects of our actions as contingent upon each other and of their impact on governance, both nationally and globally. If there is no sensitivity in taking responsibility for the other who is nearby, within reach or face to face, there will be even less for those whom we cannot see and do not know. Why care about the poor working conditions in overseas manufacturing and assembly plants for outsourced sweatshop labor that is physically and geographically distant (their conditions of labor are neither seen nor felt); or culturally distant, be they Chinese, Asian, African, South American—or Caribbean. What is more, such features of our global economy are nothing new having always been part of the long history of the economic and political expansion of modernization. "The kind of uncertainty, of dark premonitions and fears of the future that haunt men and women in the fluid, perpetually changing social environment . . . does not unite the sufferers: it splits them and sets them apart" (Bauman, 2001: 48, cited in Wray-Bliss, 2013; Crawford, 2004; Gilbert, 2014; Kiely, 2014; Veltmeyer and Bowles, 2018; Soufrrant, 2019; Potter et al., 2019).

Yes, of course, if piqued by pressure groups, there may be a registering of some concern. But, the important thing, less we forget, is that the company, its shareholders, institutional investors, and we ourselves, profit from such global relations, especially once we buy our designer labels at value for money and for some developing country governments, once such arrangements can serve as a conduit to reduce unemployment. Prevailing values of parochial and individual self-interest do not make the connections between I, us, and them, further involving the need for the application of an ethical turn in governance.

LOOKING OUTWARD: GOVERNANCE
BEYOND THE STATE

Given the preceding, this analysis would be remiss to ignore the manifestation of the nature of modernization that is expressly interwoven through the inverse antithetical dynamics of regionalization and globalization, and further combining to [re]shape the institutionalization of the structural conditions of the social, political, and economic landscape of the region. By refracting onto and undercutting the very basic social structures, traditions, class identities, and local contexts that it had created, and on which it had depended, these traditions and institutions have become the focus of reflexive interrogation and reconfiguration.

Progress and/or regression in individual countries and communities are closely linked with other countries and communities, and with the world. And so, a crisis in a single country can easily destabilize others and cause systemic damage. The complexity and deep interconnections of personal, corporate, and political self-interest, short-sightedness, and narrow vision that was precipitated in 2008 by the global financial crisis and which cascaded through the region, demonstrated this in stark reality, leaving the region well short of its development aspirations. Similarly, donor and development assistance provided to the region is influenced heavily by the principal donors who more or less dictate the "areas" or "themes" for action in the strategic plans (Girvan, 2011, 2015; Lewis, 2011; Malavisi, 2014, 2019; Bishop, 2016; Souffrant, 2019). In this regard, issues of governance are no longer confined to the national level but must consider the reality of an interdependence at varying spatial levels of actors and agency (Stiglitz, 2000; Sen, 2000; Helleiner, 2001; Crawford, 2004; Benn, 2009; Frost, 2012; Girvan, 2011; Lewis, 2011; Veltmeyer and Bowles, 2018; Munck, 2018a; 2018b; Souffrant, 2019; Potter, 2019), particularly, while being in the shadow of continental super-powers. The democratic ideals of these metropoles reinforce the democratic ideals of the Commonwealth Caribbean and anchor them to the core international relations interests of the region. To date, these have been to maintain and enhance the metropolitan connections as essential to survival and prosperity. They are likely to remain so in the foreseeable future (Sutton, 1999: 82).

   The Caribbean must therefore delicately respond to the challenges of global and regional changes (Ramphal, 1988: 170) characterized and defined by these international structures of governance with their rules, norms, procedures, and institutions influencing growing levels of global inequality due in large part to very unbalanced international negotiations. In both action and negotiation, CARICOM countries are imperceptible because they lack both bargaining power and expertise to shape the architecture for the functioning of the global economy (Munroe, 1999; Ryan, 2001; Payne and Bishop, 2010; Girvan, 2011). The region's vulnerability in expanding its policy options is made more acute within the international financial governance architecture such as the World Bank–IMF nexus and the satellite financial ranking agencies like Standard and Poor that serve to reduce the ability of national parliaments and regional groupings to control important areas of policy (Lapeyre, 2004, see also Munroe, 1999; Stiglitz, 2000; Ryan, 2001; Benn, 2009; Williams, 2011; Girvan, 2011; Nation Newspaper, 2017; Levitt, 2018). Moreover, this vulnerability is compounded by incremental and arbitrary shifts away from the order, stability, predictability, and rules that a greater multilateralism could offer to more favorable nationalist orientations (Ramphal, 1988: 187; Girvan, 2011; Boas, 2014; Conway, 2014). The result is the de-ideologizing of regional cooperation and integration in favor of a more rigid, individualistic, fragmented, and power-dominated international environment, leading toward greater uncertainty and exercise of power (Ramphal, 1988: 188; see also Hamelink, 1997; Lapeyre, 2004; Crawford, 2004; Polyani, 2011; Malavisi, 2014, 2019). The inevitability of this scenario is the further diminishing of CARICOM's capacity to influence international decision-making and significantly and effectively enlarge its global sovereignty, making the pursuit of domestic structural adjustment policy crucial to integration into the global economy, in the search for access to international financial flows as the source of opportunity for profits, economic growth, and better living conditions. At the same time, such policies portend a future of disruption, instability, and growing inequalities from the reduction and reversal of the same international financial flows for debt servicing (Lapeyre, 2004, see also Hamelink, 1997; Munroe, 1999; Stiglitz, 2000; Ryan, 2001; Gasper, 2008; Williams, 2011; Frost, 2012; Girvan, 2011, 2015; INTAL, 2017; Beaton et al., 2017). The World Bank claims that this free-market "shock therapy" stimulates growth and enables debt repayment, but instead of helping poor countries develop, structural adjustment has basically destroyed them. While developing countries enjoyed a per capita growth rate of more than 3 percent prior to the 1980s, structural adjustment cut growth in half, down to 1.7 percent (Hickel, 2012; Levitt, 2018). Likewise, the need arising from higher values of minimizing such social costs within economies, for ethical foundations and guidance is premised on the existence of networks of criminality and corruption that grow when public policies and regional or global cooperation agreements fail to establish the necessary regulations for these activities (INTAL, 2017). Within this context, without some deep restructuring of the international architecture aimed at improving global governance by incorporating the well-being of populations from the weakest regions, poor and weak countries will continue to be highly vulnerable with miniscule gains from globalization (Lapeyre, 2004: 23, Munroe, 1999; Ryan, 2001; Jessop, 2009; Frost, 2012; Kliksberg, 2012; Paris, 2015; Waeyenberge, 2018; Krageland, 2018; Levitt, 2018; Souffrant, 2019).

By abstracting from these complex, historically informed economic and political relationships, two immediate images of the international system emerge. In the first the structural model of development offered by advocates of modernization downplays the complex international economic interdependencies that reduce states' capacity to direct their own economic affairs while at the same time imposing its own systemic imperatives that are altogether oblivious to moral and ethical concerns (Stiglitz, 2000; Lapeyre, 2004; Best, 2007, Brown, 2008; Paris, 2015; Petras and Veltmeyer, 2018; Waeyenberge, 2018; Krageland, 2018; Levitt, 2018). In this model, the periphery is construed as a passive respondent to forces centered elsewhere with restricted options and room to maneuver. Power within the Bretton Woods institutions is presently apportioned according to members' shares, as in a corporation. Major decisions require 85 percent of the vote, and the United States, which holds about 16 percent of the shares (and controls the presidency), wields *de facto* veto power. Developing countries together hold less than 50 percent of the vote, which is shocking given that the institution supposedly exists to promote their welfare (Hickel, 2012; Waeyenberge, 2018; Krageland, 2018; Levitt, 2018). Such patterns of governance deny peripheral countries agency, allowing scope for a "victim mentality" to emerge while "fostering a morbid propensity to find fault with everyone but oneself" (Landes, 2002: 328 cited in Nhema and Zinyama, 2016: 155). The second image is one in which states are largely autonomous detached from their historical or structural place in the global economy and responsible for their own success or failure. This latter approach amortizes ownership and the right to self-determination as a double-edged sword and deems poor states to be primarily responsible for assuring their own paths of development, emphasizing their duty to improve their own lot through a measure of flexibility in return for the threat of blame in the case of failure (Stiglitz, 2000; Brown, 2008; Nhema and Zinyama, 2016; Waeyenberge, 2018; Krageland, 2018; Levitt, 2018).

Cognizant of these circumstances, an ethical turn in governance must envelop through regional consensus, a conceptualization of the good life and the possibilities of organizing both the initial and the final responsibility for determining such (Berger, 2013; Girvan, 2015; Munck, 2018b). The region will then determine whether it develops an ethical response to this predicament it faces by crafting a strategy that responds to the indivisible values and principles of a democratic imperative with policies both at home and abroad that strengthen rather than weaken freedom, independence, self-respect, and the right to pursue regional interest as the region sees best. Put otherwise— policies that return to the spirit of Chaguaramas (Ramphal, 1988: 185). With this approach CARICOM and similar small regional entities will reserve a right to an option to explore new possibilities and approaches with a capacity and will to exercise and advocate for a vision involving interdependence, solidarity, equity, and mutual cooperation in addressing transboundary and common practical social issues (Helleiner, 2001; Jessop, 2009; Twiss, 2011), several of which are closely related to the wider agenda of development and global governance needs. Some of these are a macro-strategy for long-term sustainable development, social justice, self-reliance, and a fairer international trading system with mechanisms for more equitable decision-making that can improve their contribution to sustainable development in the years ahead (Sen, 2000; Helleiner, 2001; Waeyenberge, 2018; Krageland, 2018; Levitt, 2018; Munck, 2018b). All of this has long been a matter of international debate in the UN and other global institutions (NIEO, 1969; Laszlo et al., 1978; *South Commission Report*, 1990; UNGA, 2014).

Alternatively, without recourse to explicit values and priorities, these societies may shoot themselves in the foot by succumbing to the lure of pragmatism for survival (Ramphal, 1988: 184) disintegrating into a myriad of small autocracies and losing their common ground. The immediate corollary to this circumstance is the natural state of regional fragmentation of their interests (Ramphal, 1988: 171; Jessop, 2009; Girvan, 2011). Ultimately, the challenge for the region remains once again its ability to initiate a new political and social dialogue on consensus building around the means and ends of governance. It is also a signal of the need for the region to look beyond structures of economic integration to the ethical basis of "community" in the Caribbean (WIC, 1991: 20; Girardin, 2012; Girvan, 2015; Waeyenberge, 2018; Krageland, 2018; Levitt, 2018; Munck, 2018). This shift in the way we think about governance would have many implications for the kind of strategies that may be deployed if we are to fully get to grips with the profound changes which have taken place to the theory and practice of responsible and representative government. This will inevitably require a willingness to take on controversial and pioneering issues. Controversial, because many will not be popular with some regional and major powers; and pioneering, because it must of needs look to the future if it is to succeed. The best that one can hope for is that policy advisers and their principals make their choices while being fully cognizant of them.

NOTES

1. The CSME is an enlarged market for the fifteen nation-states and fourteen million strong inhabitants of the Caribbean Community. The CSME offers a single space to facilitate, *inter alia*: more and better opportunities to produce and sell goods and services and to attract investment; greater economies of scale; increased competitiveness; full employment and improved standards of living for the people of the Caribbean Community. The ultimate goal of the CSME is to provide the foundation for growth and development through the creation of a single economic space for the production of competitive goods and services. The CSME is at the heart of CARICOM's economic integration. Like other areas of work in the CARICOM integration process, the implementation and operation of the Single Market and Economy is being undertaken by a number of stakeholders; principal among them are the CARICOM secretariat, member states, and community institutions.

2. The Caribbean and several countries of Latin America have always had to grapple with the colonial vestiges of a plantation economy with features that undermine substantive progress. In times of crisis its worst features are manifested. Attempts to reform this model of development have been fraught with severe difficulty. Whether by revolution or by progressive change, most changes have merely been cosmetic. My subject of focus is not on this, but I acknowledge its importance as a major structural dysfunction. For further reading on this see: Beckford (1972); Thomas (1988); Levitt and Witter (1996); Levitt (2000); Pantin (2005); Levitt (2005); Best and Levitt (2009).

Chapter 6

The Unintended Consequences and Paradoxes of Good Governance

INTRODUCTION: COMPETING ANSWERS

The continuous transformation taking place with market development has presented developing countries with a set of governance challenges, leading some commentators to reference neoliberalism as a form of "neo-modernization" (Waggaman, 1994; Kiely, 2005). These transformation processes involve introducing policies of privatization, [re]regulation, and deregulation, constituting a shift from "inward-oriented" strategies of development that promote national self-sufficiency to one of "outward-oriented" free trade and the transfer of resources out of local communities and regions with the goal of total integration into the world market. The processes share important commonalities with the trajectory of past modernization practices, which has far-reaching consequences for developing countries regarding not only how their economies are managed but also for politics, the organization of society, and the dynamics of a culture suffused with value systems from the North. These restraints have mired the form and *modus operandi* of representative government (Fischer 2009: 67) and the policy shifts in the process have had many significant consequences for good governance, including raising questions of participation, citizenship, inclusion, and equality. The common collective interest and the public good has been negotiated away by ideological, political, social, and economic power-plays, that privilege individual accumulation and self-interest among internal elites over communal obligation and societal responsibility for fellow human beings (Conway, 2014: 170).

For policy planners as much as for scholars of governance, in the work to provide practical direction and evaluate criteria for governance the time is ripe for dialogue on the political implications of an ethical turn in governance in which older issues of fairness and social cohesion must be considered

alongside more dominant concerns of competitiveness and economic efficiency. Prescriptions are then often in tension with each other because their
logics are incongruent with each other.

Not surprisingly, advocating good governance raises a host of questions about what needs to be done, when, and how. Among the issues to be
addressed is the overwhelming nature of the agenda, particularly its expanding length, and more importantly, that there is little guidance about what is
essential and what is not, what is priority and what should follow, what is
feasible and what is not. For instance, services that are fully responsive to the
needs and wants of some individuals may not be very efficient in terms of the
interests of the wider community (Grindle, 2011: 200). Besides these, ideas of
effective operational structures could be in breach of the law. Moving toward
good governance therefore requires accepting a more nuanced understanding
of the evolution of institutions and government capabilities; being explicit
about priorities and trade-offs for poverty reduction in a world in which all
good things cannot be pursued at once; approaching change from what works
rather than focusing solely on governance gaps; taking the role of government
in poverty alleviation seriously; and grounding action in contextual realities
of each country. There are no easy technical fixes to what is inevitably a long,
slow, reversible, and frustrating path toward better performing governments.
Trade-offs between valued principles are an ineluctable fact of any policy
designing process (Maclean, 1998; de Graaf and der Wal, 2010 see also
Kooiman, 2003; Dworkin, 2008; APSC, 2007; Head, 2008; Grindle, 2010;
Stone, 2012; Kraft and Furlong, 2015; Wildavsky, 2018). Making the distinction between governance-as-an-end and governance-as-a-means enables us
to recognize trade-offs that may otherwise escape our attention. It is in this
context that we must recognize the inadequacy of our discipline-specific and/
or binary ways of thinking in guiding action on the uncertain and in-determin-
istic nature of more complex problems, contradictions, and uncertainties of
governance. Incisive reflections on the concept of good governance may help
interpret these trade-offs, more so as the ethical dilemmas presented by modernization do not yield easy answers (Hezel, 1989; Gunatilleke et al., 1983;
Maclean, 1998; Staples, 2004) and the literature on political and administrative systems within the CARICOM region has not expanded the meaning
and the practical expression of the complexities of ethics in consonance with
governance.

A discussion linking modernization, governance, and ethics is therefore
timely, for it is a discussion of change, and a discussion on change requires
a consideration of ethics because change involves, and often does fall into
categories of, ethics, the study of good and bad, right and wrong, and just
and unjust (Schuler, 2008). The introduction of an ethical perspective into
the relationship between governance and development further exacerbates

the fissures over the value of incorporating contested principles such as accountability, transparency, participation, inclusion, and democracy into the analysis. The arguments for their incorporation into the broader governance structures are strong enough in principle to be justified. However, an over-arching message emerging from the existing analysis is the need for a strong dose of realism and caution regarding the superficial application of an ethical turn through an array of "plug and play" polices characterized by Carothers and Brechenmacher, 2014; Lessig, 2009; and Fenster, 2010 as the type of institutional reform agenda promoted by multilateral organizations such as the World Bank, IMF, or the World Trade Organization. Often biased toward the application of a best-practice model, these institutions presume that it is possible to determine a unique set of appropriate institutional arrangements *ex ante* and view convergence toward those arrangements as a corrective solution as inherently desirable for all lands and climes (Rodrik, 2008: 22; see also Schuyler and Veltmeyer, 1988; Waeyenberge, 2018; Kragelund, 2018; Levitt, 2018; Munck, 2018a, 2018b). Often such approaches create the intrinsic tensions that arise from the inconsistent or opposing imperatives of two (or more) conflicting things that are rarely acknowledged. For instance, we intrinsically value both governing with integrity and governing effectively and efficiently, but being good and doing well are not the same thing. Also, the very nature of regulations and top-down policies to enforce integrity can have untoward effects, especially with respect to the performance of public actors and agencies. Increasingly, the trending credo when promoting integrity in the public service often seems to be "the more, the merrier." This leads to another question for critical reflection: is good governance—defined as managing tensions between public values—possible, if managers are severely limited in their options for action? And, what are the minimum degrees of freedom required to hold an official accountable for good—or bad—governance? Political actions rarely have one cause and one effect. To what extent do the values and norms of governing good (having integrity) and governing well (being effective and efficient) conflict? What factors contribute to the conflict, and how do public actors deal with it? To be held accountable and to perform well, the institutions must be visible to the public but in the normal course of their bureaucratic operation, public organizations—sometimes with unethical or illegal intent—create institutional impediments that obstruct external observation (Fenster, 2010: 619).

When do we know an action is designed to be sinister or benign? Similarly, transparency is considered a desirable means in achieving a more responsive state that more effectively achieves democratically agreed upon ends. Its symbolic pull, its ability to grab the public's imagination, leads us to fetishize means at the cost of ends. Although the public must certainly know about the government's operations, it must also be made aware that obtaining that knowledge is not a costless transaction. And so, simplistic understandings of the state's operations and the potential of imposing equally simplistic understandings of transparency can lead to imperfect, costly measures to disclose information at the expense of less effective governance (Fenster, 2010: 623).

As noted, a democratic spirit has served to generate skepticism about governance in every sphere and I do not naively assume that an ethical perspective will solve all of our governance problems. But it is taken as a given that we should recognize that states, like other man-made institutions such as the corporation, are entirely artificial entities existing under the guise of the fictional, legal "person" and the only "reality" is that they consist of people who live and work or interact within them and of the social and physical environments that provide the context for governance (Longstaff, 1998). This may be to state the obvious but it helps to emphasize that good governance is ultimately about relationships and, as evidenced in chapters 2 and 3, ethics is also ultimately concerned about relationships. For example, to whom do I owe a duty of care: myself, my immediate family, my community, all humanity, or all creation?

Indeed therefore, the conceptualization and institutionalization of an ethical turn to governance discourses can be ambivalent, contradictory and, hence controversial, as this chapter and chapter 7 would attest particularly when we take into account the cultural, social, legal, political, and psychological background of society. The ethical problems posed by conflicts of interest are also often reinforced by philosophical contrivances of relativism, due to the multitude of positions that individuals may hold on key concepts of governance (Hodgkinson, 1996; Stiglitz, 2000; Johnston, 2006; Yung, 2016; Gensler, 2018; Weale, 2019; Howard, 2019). This in turn leads to important and undeniable tensions unresolvable to the point where democracy can undermine good governance, and with the reverse equally true. These tensions are at the heart of many practical and ethical challenges, such as the design of transitional governance structures, and constitute one of the major reasons why some policy planners and academics would wish to jettison the application of ethics as a plausible and viable corrective measure to the governance challenges the region faces. This chapter also argues that not all of the well-meaning and rational ideas introduced as a *sine qua non* for good governance will necessarily lead to the intended desired results, but can instead lead to surprising consequences that can undermine the texture of the social fabric of society (Margetts, 2010; Perri 6, 2010; Grindle, 2010; Yung, 2016; Weale, 2019; Howard, 2019). This chapter also cautions even the best-informed, best-intentioned policy planners and academics to critically [re] think their assumptions about governance and the ongoing transformative changes of modernization through the development, perhaps of an ethical "quotient," so to speak, of what works, what types of agencies are in play, and what types will have to evolve. And, how might the inclusion of people in these processes ultimately empower them to ethical conduct. It does so initially by drawing attention to some contradictions in the imperfect techno-cratic tools of the four principles of transparency, accountability, inclusion, and participation as a shared agenda. It introduces the arguments and the con-cerns that the demands of such ideals can animate as political and administra-tive symbols of open government, before embarking on an analysis of each with its own inherent inconsistency of logic. It also introduces the argument that naturally inspires the identification and interrogation in greater detail of other related institutional issues such as corruption, grandstanding, and relativism, and their implications, when addressing such divergent ends as consensual procedures and the toleration of dissent for democratic delibera-tion in an effort to make the state viable. And so, by interrogating these ideals this chapter seeks to address some of these ethical contradictions by tracing the conceptual origins, development, and diverse challenges of an ethical turn in governance, the tensions it arouses, and the variable, imperfect measures developed as areas of concern in response to the commands of governance and how they might be achieved.

CONCEPTUALIZING FIRST PRINCIPLES

Within the lexicon of the governance discourse, no text is complete without genuflecting to the ethical principles of accountability, transparency, partici-pation, and inclusion. In international politics and finance developing coun-tries have been instructed to abide by these good governance principles—with their strong appeal as inherently, unquestionably good things—as a condition for financial assistance from financial institutions such as the IMF and/or World Bank. Considered as basic ways of respecting human dignity and individual autonomy, many developing countries have rhetorically embraced these values and the international initiatives aimed at furthering them. And so, a powerful consensus has emerged in the international development community incorporating these principles at the macro and micro levels of government as if they have the quality of a magic elixir that aid providers sprinkle—at least rhetorically—on everything they do, in the hopes of giving their activities an appealing extra shine (Carothers and Brechenmacher, 2014: 13; Grindell, 2004, 2008, 2011). Including these ideals into the manifesto for good governance would supposedly infuse new energy into researchers and practitioners, enthralled by the ideas that their incorporation would effec-tively alleviate constraints on prosperity and equity——community develop-ment, basic needs, participation, sustainability, appropriate technology, and a host of other ideas. Indeed, the field of development and good governance can

be credited with much faddism of the magic bullet variety, overly susceptible
to the elasticity of use that grows in inclusiveness of these principles as they
become popular (Grindell, 2010: 1).

Despite the stated devotion to these principles, in practice however, policy
planners embedded within various institutional frameworks sometimes
treat them as boxes to be ticked rather than as genuinely significant or even
transformative elements to be pursued in substantive, sustained ways partly
because, despite their suggestive and appealing nature, these concepts are
sufficiently broad that agreeing on them in principle does not necessarily
translate into agreeing in practice (Carothers and Brechenmacher, 2014:12;
Hodgkinson, 1996; Johnston, 2006; Weale, 2019). References to these principles have also become so frequent and widespread that defining them often
proves difficult so that policy planners announce their intention to "promote
accountability" far more often than they know what it means to do so, and
certainly far more than they are committed to time, treasure, and political
fights it takes (Odugbemi and Lee, 2011: 3; Johnston, 2006; Weale, 2019).
Inconsistency surrounds the several approaches to its application, including
multi-stakeholder engagement or initiatives, civic empowerment and rights,
public engagement in policy making and government, institutions of accountability, demand for good governance/demand-side, and aid and domestic
accountability. Still other initiatives focus on strengthening non-state institutions of accountability such as civil society, while others focus on citizen
engagement in policy making and service delivery. Often observers lump
together accountability mechanisms within the state, such as ombudsmen
and parliamentary oversight, and those outside the state such as regular public opinion polling. Some focus on electoral systems and processes whereas
others concentrate on access to information and ICT (information and communication technology) for governance or e-governance. As a result many of
these labels imply substantive differences in meaning reinforcing uncertainty
of consensus in policy orientation and praxis (Odugbemi and Lee, 2011:4;
Hodgkinson, 1996; Johnston, 2006; Broome and Adugu, 2014; Weale, 2019).

Skeptics go even further and push back against this inclusive "good governance" orthodoxy, arguing that a number of governments have made significant developmental progress without embracing these principles (Carothers
and Brechenmacher, 2014:19; Chang, 2003, 2004; Grindle, 2010) and that
broad-based governance reform is neither necessary nor sufficient for growth.
It is not necessary because what works in practice is removing binding
constraints—in areas such as supply incentives, infrastructure bottlenecks,
or high cost of credit. Removing the constraints and their interactions with
other distortions will promote desirable governance arrangements. Import
liberalization supports integrating into the world economy when import-
competing interests are weak and the overvaluing of currency is unlikely,

but export subsidies or special economic zones work far better where those circumstances exist. Entrepreneurship is best stimulated by removing impediments to entry or subsidizing incumbents where the binding constraint is lack of competition or Schumpeterian rents (Rodrik, 2008). There is no neat correlation of historical and statistical relationships between those societies necessarily pursuing specific policy recommendations to achieve participatory, openness, and inclusion for economic growth and those that do not. Scholars therefore caution against attempts to impose generic institutional templates on wildly differing contexts, arguing instead for a capable and effective developmental state, a model prominent since the economic rise of the Asian Tigers in the early 1990s. South Korea, Taiwan, and Singapore especially, after which several Caribbean states wish to pattern themselves, rather than institutionalize Western-style democratic governance, rapidly grew their economies by centralizing state power, developing autonomous and effective bureaucracies, and actively intervening in the market process. In fact, scholars have argued that the success of these efforts specifically depended on limiting citizen participation in the political process and isolating state institutions from popular pressure and accountability mechanisms (Carothers and Brechenmacher, 2014: 19; see also Wade, 1990; Chang, 2002, 2003, 2004, 2010; Souffrant, 2019).

One Agenda or Several?

There is further disagreement over the extent to which these principles often grouped together in policy documents as mutually reinforcing for good governance actually constitute a unified agenda. In practice some natural links do exist among them, but these are only partial as the policy agenda driving the conceptualization of these principles is shaped by multiple agencies and interest groups, which is evidently a cause for concern (Carothers and Brechenmacher, 2014: 11; see Chang, 2003, 2004). It is this inconsistency in policy formulation that explains the plethora of approaches, labels, and ultimately the effectiveness, efficiency, and integration of these elements in implementing a good governance agenda. As such, some accountability consists of efforts to upgrade the technical capacity of selected agencies without attempting to improve participation or inclusion. In other cases efforts to incorporate transparency programs are narrowly designed to make government data more easily accessible to private sector and other stakeholder groups but not to consciously link these transparency mechanisms to accountability or participatory processes. Participatory development on the other hand often seeks to make participation itself the driver of change by helping citizens take charge of development in their communities but without fostering any particular ties to formal accountability mechanisms. And, both accountability and participatory development efforts sometimes fail to include marginalized groups and take their needs into account, though efforts in this respect have gradually improved. In addition, accountability programs often incorporate transparency as a constituent element while ignoring citizen participation in, perhaps press a particular government institution to be more responsive to public concerns (Carothers and Brechenmacher, 2014: 12; Grindle, 2010, 2012; Weale, 2019; Souffrant, 2019). So again the question, whose and what kind of agenda do we pursue?

An Intrinsic Case?

Besides the broader debate whether these principles are a unifying set of core values and whose version is being peddled, a similar tension arises over the efficacy of the intrinsic case for incorporating these same principles into governance. The intrinsic case for making accountability, transparency, participation, and inclusion major pillars of governance and development describes a relationship between governments and their citizens that honors and reinforces basic human dignity. Rights-based approaches to development take participation, accountability, and inclusion as inalienable rights integral both to development processes and to outcomes and thus representing an embodiment for the normative case. The optimists believe that evidence from both historical analysis and empirical studies indicates that inclusive or democratic governance is the key to generating and sustaining high levels of socioeconomic development (Carothers and Brechenmacher, 2014:15; Girardin, 2012; Weale, 2019; Souffrant, 2019). The same logic explains why a wide range of scholars have assembled significant research pointing to a positive correlation between various aspects of a country's governance—including transparent, accountable, and participative institutions—and its economic progress. North et al. (2008) and North et al. (2009) juxtapose "open access orders," characterized by political and economic competition, impersonal governance, and a shared commitment to equality and inclusion, with "limited access orders" in which elites engage in rent-seeking and pursue their personal interests. They argue that historically the former has been more successful at sustaining economic growth than the latter. As such, these four principles are good things in and of themselves that should be understood as intrinsic elements of development that a society is more developed when its people are treated in accordance with these values. A society is less developed absent these values because our political and economic institutions that have been powerful forces for public good can be hijacked by influences toward serving illegitimate and socially disastrous ends (English, 2013: 16; Ackerman, 2004; Rose-Ackerman, 2013; Yung, 2016). We can better understand the virtues of societies without petty corruption. Enthusiasts see these virtues as valuable priorities in and of themselves, regardless of whether they necessarily produce better socioeconomic outcomes and considered to be intrinsically good for building valued social capital within the state to promote progress, development, and governance. They have gained only partial ground.

Skepticism over the intrinsic case still persists. The concern is not over whether participation, accountability, transparency, and inclusion are good things. The fear rests with the idea of opening the door to what observers see as politically normative claims that will lead to even greater disagreements over the provision of basic public goods if they cannot be shown to yield better developmental outcomes. They are uncomfortable with the normative argument as a stand-alone rationale. This division exists within some of the practitioner sub-communities that have emerged around the four concepts: between those who view open data and access to information as an intrinsic human right and those who see it primarily as a tool for economic development, greater public sector efficiency, and anticorruption efforts (Carothers and Brechenmacher, 2014: 15; see also Broome, 2003; Crawford, 2004; Castells, 2014; Weale, 2019). Currently, emphasis worldwide is on developing information societies and knowledge-based economies, and critical to this transformation will be the ability to decisively measure and understand the impact of intangible capital on wealth creation. These ideals constitute intangible assets since they include all assets that are neither natural nor produced. To varying degrees, countries in the Caribbean have been focusing on elements that contribute to intangible assets, particularly education and governance. The central challenge therefore rests on the fundamental question of what is the point of incorporating these principles without attempting to address the systemic and structural fundamentals of development and governance processes, many of which were inherited from colonialism and fostered and reinforced by modernization? Although this may be the case, the related question raised is how are the values inherent in this developmental quartet measured and how are they used? This will be considered in the instrumental case for the incorporation of these ideas.

Instrumental Orientation?

As indicated, not only is the intrinsic case for the four concepts unsettled, but so too is the instrumental one. This is because the endemic conceptual imprecision of practitioners applying the four concepts results in incoherent and inconsistent policy interventions that cannot be neatly sorted into categories though they attempt to do so. Governance specialists view them primarily as tools to tackle specific failures in service delivery and to increase government efficiency and responsiveness remaining wary of appearing too political. As already indicated, democracy and human rights practitioners, for their part, reject technical applications that they believe risk stripping the concepts of their transformative political value and reducing them to mere formalities in program design and implementation (Carothers and Brechenmacher, 2014: 26; Girardin, 2012; Johnston, 2006; Crawford, 2004; Weale, 2019; Souffrant, 2019). Both approaches are used by policy planners as the default position, often in a moderated technical solution based on the argument that building the four principles into development assistance will produce better socioeconomic outcomes in aid-receiving countries. Thus the ever-changing complex and often indirect causal chains that connect work on the individual concepts to specific socioeconomic outcomes, along with often overlapping application and meaning of the terms, make it difficult to isolate any one of them to a specific element of development programming and to measure its specific impact on development outcomes. Moreover, development programming relating to the four principles often seeks to make program changes that target intermediate goals such as establishing a social audit process, strengthening the transparency of a particular ministry, or improving citizen input to a national planning process (Carothers and Brechenmacher, 2014: 17; Crawford, 2004; Johnston, 2006; Weale, 2019). Further, institutional innovations such as citizen advisory boards, civic journalism, participatory budgeting, public expenditure tracking, and social audits work to the extent that unauthorized, dispossessed, or otherwise quiescent principals make their needs and demands known to their elected and appointed agents. In these instances, their agents, as a result, better understand their constituency's preferences and work toward addressing them meaningfully and effectively. Anything outside the reigning technical frameworks is unlikely to be taken seriously, or be incorporated in actual programming (Odugbemi and Lee, 2011: 11). There is a caveat to such logic in translating technical inputs into the equation of developmental processes, as opposed to enveloping sociopolitical relations. Many studies show that such achievements in longer-term socioeconomic progress are much less common, or at least much harder to detect. The issue lies less with the political will than that the inability to translate these commitments into substantive political reform because of the difficulty of drawing generalizable lessons from highly context-specific interventions (Carothers and Brechenmacher, 2014; Fukuda-Parr and Shiva Kumar, 2003; Crawford, 2004; Souffrant, 2019; Weale, 2019; Potter et al., 2019). What works will depend on local constraints and opportunities, whereas best practices are by definition non-contextual and take no account of these complications. Insofar as they narrow rather than expand the menu of institutional choices available to reformers, they serve the cause of governance badly.

Where does this initial overview leave us? The broader point that these considerations raise is that there is no unique way of achieving desirable institutional outcomes that is not context-specific. Effective institutional outcomes do not map into unique institutional designs, neither does institutional function determine institutional form. From all accounts, effective governance, and by extension democracy, involves far more than institutional design and committed elites; it reflects the broader liberating forces inherent in human development and therefore demands of us an understanding of more nuanced approaches. The first step in any process of policy reform therefore must be a sound understanding of the broader and deeper pathological considerations of political economy (English, 2013: 9; Hodgkinson, 1996; Girardin, 2012; Crawford, 2004; Weale, 2019; Howard, 2019; Souffrant, 2019). In the absence of ethical commitments and a detailed knowledge of contentious issues refining the scope of politics, there is no reason to think that democratic institutions will support a form of government that is productive, sustainable, and redounds to the common good. How then are we to understand and cultivate the ethics and knowledge necessary for resisting the corruption of our institutions? (English, 2013: 33) Arguably, maldevelopment both causes and is caused by corruption, compounded often by the exclusion of the values of transparency, accountability, and participation in the continuing debate over their causal relationship to governance and economic development. Addressing these issues therefore requires theoretical work, policy analysis, ethical evaluation, and practical engagement in relating these issues to broader processes of socioeconomic change. Theoretical work includes conceptual, historical, and empirical argumentation with respect to the nature, types, causes, tenacity, and consequences of both governmental and non-governmental corruption. These political economy problems will not be solved overnight and any policy reform must come to grips with them and the perverse incentives that they create. Policy reform that does not heed the ethical turn to a political economy context might also lead to a distinctive see-saw pattern, with new policy distortions emerging to undo those that are being dealt with. For instance, if to remain in power a political party is forced to buy support with cheap credit to politically powerful groups, imposing central bank independence will often induce the use of other means to buy the same support. The seesaw effect does not mean that policy practice is impossible or always useless; rather in both academic and popular discourses (Acemoglu, 2008: 5; Johnston, 2006; Ceva and Ferretti, 2019; Hellsten, 2019) an emphasis must be placed on government's fundamental challenge in serving the public interest by balancing the pursuit of different, inevitably contradictory standards. Trade-offs between valued principles are thus an ineluctable fact of any designing process (de Graaf and der Wal, 2010: 5) because, although the principles of participation, accountability, transparency, and inclusion are instrumentally and intrinsically valuable to an ethical turn in governance, there are still very different understandings of and approaches to them in practice. Organizational goals may be, and usually are, pluralistic and un-enunciated goals may act to reduce or occlude clarity of goal accountability, and hence of organizational responsibility. A university may in good faith (let us make the best assumptions) declare teaching its chief priority where in fact it is really research and scholarly production—not necessarily the same thing. Moreover, some of the faculty will perceive the institution as a stepping stone. Compounding the problem is that in all such expressions of purpose the language of purpose conceals more than it reveals and is duplicitous often because the intellectual and emotional understanding of purpose is typically unevenly distributed throughout the power hierarchy of the organization (Hodgkinson, 1996: 167). In making moral distinctions to achieve participation, accountability, transparency, and inclusion, all of which arise automatically within democratic politics, there are no obvious and clear-cut solutions because purpose is deeply complicated by obfuscation, ambivalence, and ambiguity—quite apart from the omnipresence of contending interests and political forces. Instead they are generally cultivated from diverse ethical or ideological sources beyond the strict rule of self-interest (English, 2013; Hodgkinson, 1996; Crawford, 2004; Orr and Johnson, 2019; Howard, 2019; Weale, 2019; Souffrant, 2019). As such, in what follows, this chapter aims to spell out further elements of the debate over the four principles that are rooted in the larger, often fiercer discussion about the overall relationship between governance regimes and economic development. Stated differently, the emergence of genuine consensus on the validity and viability of an ethical approach to governance will depend greatly on how effectively its proponents deepen their understanding of crucial aspects of the democratic imperative, such as matters of form, function, and substance. This is because democracy reflects the preferences and opinions of citizens but cannot guarantee that these are good, feasible, or well-informed (English, 2013; Hodgkinson, 1996; Crawford, 2004; Johnston, 2006; Girardin, 2012; Orr and Johnson, 2019; Howard, 2019; Weale, 2019; Souffrant, 2019). It is within this context that a shared understanding of common ideas and ideals across all parts of the polity on these intricate institutional issues must be agreed on to redound to the good of governance.

TRANSLUCENT TRANSPARENCY

Transparent governance implies openness of the governance system through clear processes for providing citizens good access to public information. The aim is to liberate information, especially government data, so the public can better process and understand it, and to do so through policies that revitalize citizens' interests in politics, reflecting an ambition toward more engagement and collaboration within public institutions and politics in general. The most obvious areas for this new responsibility for disclosure are in data about the legislative process, and in making government data available for others to build upon (Lessig, 2009: 1; Fenster, 2010). To those committed to the expansion and strict enforcement of open government, the antidote to the wrong of excessive governmental secrecy is greater transparency. Without access to the government and its information the public can evaluate neither government's past nor current performance, nor deliberate over its future representatives or policies (Fenster, 2010: 619). High levels of transparency stimulate awareness of responsibilities and standards in public service through information sharing, which ultimately ensures accountability for the performance of individuals and organizations that handle resources and/or hold public office (UNDESA, 2005: 4; Johnston, 2006). Transparency has therefore become a watchword of liberal democracy and the market system in the modern globalized world. While the state has traditionally been an owner and withholder of information, sometimes inadvertently, willfully, or with good intent, citizens have become increasingly dissatisfied with situations in which they have the right but are denied access to and control of information relevant to them (Gotz and Maklund, 2014).

As a promising idea the word "transparency" brings with it a host of moral connotations: an IMF Survey pairs it with "candor" and "accountability," while a financial-sector commentator on the Asian crisis defined *transparency* as "easily understood or detected; obvious; guileless (free of deceit, cunning or craftiness); candid; open" (Fons 1999: 307 cited in Best, 2007: 16). Others explicitly contrast transparency with corruption, another term with complex and powerful moral overtones. The call for transparency thus makes a powerful moral argument for the universal value of such a policy approach (Best, 2007: 16) in a moral discourse that relies on a cosmopolitan ethics that uncritically appeals to the universality of its principles not recognizing their source in particular cultural norms. Appealing to the universal value of a single model of transparency, financial leaders effectively treat all alternative financial norms, regardless of their merits, as inherently opaque or even corrupt (Best, 2007: 16; Demmke and Moilanen, 2011; Girardin, 2012). These campaigns describe a fallen world in which the state is remote and apart from its citizenry, operating corruptly and out of the public's view. At the same time, these epithets of transparency promise a government that would be close, visible, trustworthy, and transparent (Fenster, 2010: 625).

In democratic societies there is a moral imperative, one might argue, for openness and transparency since a public official is the "servant" of a people with the right to know what government is doing. In this simple insight, "targeted transparency" as defined by Fung, Graham, and Weil (cited in Lessig, 2009: 4) represents a distinctive category of public policies that, at their most basic level, mandate disclosure of standardized, comparable, and disaggregated information on specific products or practices to a broad audience to achieve a public policy purpose. Citizens are demanding greater transparency and requiring disclosure from governments of significant conflicts of interest and information on the who, why, and how of decision-making. Transparency, despite its vagueness and connotation of vulnerability, has become a cherished value as we shall see. Its mobilization around the ideal of the visible state proceeds restlessly and endlessly, driven by the unsatisfactory nature of the corrupt present. At the same time, its progressive cast—its commitment to legal rules and institutions that can constrain the state and make it visible—attempts to address and manage popular discontent through a bureaucratic apparatus that has grown steadily since independence. The state's bureaucratic apparatus executes legal rules and regulations and is itself controlled by an evolving and expanding set of laws (Fenster, 2010: 631).Transparency is seen as essential in holding governments accountable and maintaining confidence in public institutions and greater transparency is key to upholding integrity in the public sector by reducing the risk of fraud, corruption, and mismanagement of public funds (Demmke and Moilanen, 2011: 14; Kung, 2012).

While we may applaud the benefits of more transparency, the constant call for detailed submission of personal data and information can question an individual's sense of integrity. The Wikileaks revelations and the subsequent Panama leaks which reverberated throughout the Caribbean revealed the importance of openness and transparency for good governance, but such revelations may also clash with other political and administrative principles with unintentional side effects. It is true the revelations identified comprehensive information on the impacts of financial crime arising from warped financial schemes in micro-states targeted by financial sophisticates because of their need for foreign "investment." However, such revelations have to be treated with extreme caution given that the economic survival of entire national economies is at stake. According to an old estimate the entire Latin America and the Caribbean (LAC) region alone accounts for US$0.7 trillion out of US$ 9.0 trillion that global high-net-worth individuals (HNWIs) store in these tax havens and offshore banks (Rabidas, 2016). Revenue lost to national authorities reduces the potential spending on public services such as education or health care, and in areas with job creation potential such as business support, transport infrastructure, and regional development. Furthermore, revenue losses attributable to the schemes revealed by the *Panama Papers* are likely to contribute to an increase in the inequitable distribution of tax revenues and income inequality both within and between countries (European Parliament, 2017: 8; see also Smith, 2016).

Herein lies the paradox. Should the laws and regulations of these offshore financial centers (OFCs) offer too much secrecy, particularly if these said

OFCs suffer reputations as havens for illegal funds, a force that may discourage legitimate investors? (McKee et al., 2000 cited in Rabidas, 2016) Conversely, should these centers prove too transparent to auditors and international watchdogs even for investors with legal assets (e.g., HNWIs) undermining their right to privacy and frightening them off? This is the immediate threat posed on the tight rope of privacy, secrecy, and legitimacy. The repeated demand for transparency policies can lead to more intrusion into privacy, opening the door for a range of new governance challenges leaving offshore banking centers continually poised at the knife-edge of marginal legitimacy (Rabidas, 2016, see also Patrick, 2016). There is also the fear that the inevitable success of any transparency movement, if pursued as a vendetta within and external to these countries with no sensitivity to the full complexity of the idea of perfect openness will lead not to reform (Lessig, 2009: 1), but to dire consequences for these vulnerable economies. There is therefore an error at the core of the unquestioned goodness of transparency demanding critical thinking on where and when transparency works or may lead to confusion or worse (Patrick, 2016).

The representational character of office creates another dilemma for the application of the principle of transparency. The ethical problems that public officials confront arise from two general features of public office—its representational and organizational character. Officials act for us, but they also act with others and in doing so assume rights and obligations that ordinary citizens do not have, or not to the same degree. The problem becomes more complex than this simple opposition suggests since constituents do not have a single will, and representatives have many different responsibilities (Urbanati and Warren, 2008 cited in Thompson, 2018: 3; see also Raes, 1998; Thompson, 2017; Coady, 2018). Acting on behalf of others, the duties of office may permit and even require officials to use force, lie, keep secrets, and break promises in ways that would be wrong in private life. There are a lot of things that colleagues might have good reason to say to one another in private that would nonetheless be very damaging if they went viral on social media:

Healthy brainstorming processes often involve tossing out bad or half-baked ideas in order to stimulate thought and elevate better ones.

A realistic survey of options may require a blunt assessment of the strengths and weaknesses of different members of the team or outside groups that would be insulting if publicized.

Policy decisions need to be made with political sustainability in mind, but part of making a politically sustainable policy decision is not to come out and say you made the decision with politics in mind.

Someone may want to describe an actual or potential problem in vivid terms to spur action, without wanting to provoke public panic or hysteria through public discussion.

If a previously embarked-upon course of action is not working, there may be a
need to quietly change course rather than publicly admit failure. (Vox, 2016;
see also Thompson, 2017, 2019)

These and worse violations of our shared moral principles create what is
known as "the problem of dirty hands" (Parrish, 2007; Thompson, 2017,
2018). It is commonly not viewed as immoral in the role of a fiduciary, to take
action or provide advice from which one might benefit; but it is immoral not
to disclose the conflict of interest so that those affected can take appropriate
precautions that may even be to one's detriment (Stiglitz, 2000: 2). In this
light, should a representative follow the will of constituents or the dictates
of conscience? To win and retain office (a democratically desirable end),
the representatives must sometimes act against their judgment about what
is right or what the general interest requires (a morally questionable means)
(Thompson, 2018: 3). But it is precisely such genuinely interesting issues and
mandates that make inevitable disclosure risky. The fundamental problem
with input disclosure is that it serves as deterrent to both misconduct and
frankness and honesty (Vox, 2016; Thompson, 2017; Coady, 2018).

To this day practical matters work against practical access, as in the case
of allegations of vote-buying in several countries of the region. Given the
universal indignation at the notion of politicians directly or indirectly brib-
ing electors, a criminal practice, and the numerous allegations, including
some from the highest offices, one would have expected at least one successful prosecution, if only to dissuade others (*Barbados Advocate*, 2018).
Journalists are interested in such matters and, unsurprisingly, everyone inside
the system knows claims of influence are, to some degree, true. It is the nature
of the system, as we all know. But it is impossible to know which particular contribution brought about or was inspired by a particular vote which is
benign or malign. Even if we had all the data in the world and a month of
Google coders, we would not be able to tell whether a particular contribution bent a result by securing a vote of an act that otherwise would not have
occurred. The most we could say—which is still very significant—is that the
contributions are corrupting the reputation of government. Where a representative of government acts in a way inconsistent with his/her principles or his/
her constituents but consistent with a significant contribution, that act at least
raises a question about the integrity of the decision. But beyond a question,
data, or photographs of an alleged vote-buyer say little else (Lessig, 2009).

And so, we return to the commission of enquiry scenario mentioned in
chapter 1. Do such institutions reveal whether a contribution caused a citizen
or a member of parliament to take a position, or a position caused the contribution; whether the prospect of a contribution will increase sensitivity to a
position? Does the contribution secure access or assure a better hearing? Do

aspirants compete for positions or covet committee assignments based on the expectation of contributions? The commission of enquiry as a political tool can generally attenuate issues of power or some inane political deed or misdeed, but does it resolve the question of values? The salience of money and the accompanying assumption of our political culture that at this time in our regional development everything is about money are so widely and deeply held that the first, and most likely the last, explanation of anything puzzling, is money. This unexamined assumption of causality and correlations sets the default against which anything different must fight, a default that will only be reinforced by these commissions of enquiry, confirming again and again the perception of what we believe (Lessig, 2009; Barbados Advocate, 2018; Thompson, 2017, 2019).

The organizational nature of public office creates another general set of problems for the ethics of transparency, in the form of difficulties in ascribing responsibility in the event of infractions caused by the structure of public office can undermine its efficacy. Where many different individuals acting as policy advisors and experts in an organization contribute to the decisions and policies, say, in framing foreign policy, it is difficult even in principle to identify who is responsible for the results (Thompson, 2018: 3; Stiglitz, 2000; Thompson, 2017; Coady, 2018). An administrator acting as leader rather than manager designs and creates roles for him/herself and for others; determines in part or in whole the organizational values and institutional ideology; and monitors and reconciles value disputes within the organization and negotiates with parties and levels of interest outside it. It is clear that moral, as opposed to legal or formal agency is inescapable (Hodgkinson, 1996: 175). In our quest to be transparent in this situation, the difficulty arises of to whom does one apply this ethical principle? It is here that organizational function intersects personal value experience, ethics, and morality. Two general approaches to this problem have been prominent: the collectivist approach of holding only the organization itself responsible as practiced in the Westminster system of government (collective responsibility); or the individual. In the first application of transparency to collective responsibility claims two principal advantages. If the organization is identified as the principal agent of indiscretion able to be held responsible without unfairly blaming individuals it follows that as an institutional actor it has the greatest capacity to provide compensation and undertake reforms. Legally both bodies—human and bodies—corporate are held "accountable" for their actions under the heading of "law" at local, national, or international levels through such legal redistributive devices as fines, imprisonment, and loss of license or credentials (Hodgkinson, 1996: 175). Conversely, and here we are concerned with the socio-psychological and philosophical implications of private decisions not with the legal aspects of agency, if the individual is identified then members of the organization may suffer the consequences of being ascribed responsibility and individual officials will have to respond. In addition, the excessive emphasis on structures leaves citizens with no way to connect their criticisms of the structures of politics with the actions of those who should be most responsible for changing those structures because often collective purpose carries with it an institutional override for the individual. Thus, on the one hand, examining the decisions and character of the individual can help identify the structural constraints on their action and point the way toward reform, while on the other, the trend toward a view of politics as structure could lead to a conception of politics devoid of human agency (Thompson, 2018: 7; Goodin, 1988; Etzioni, 2010; Thompson, 1991, 2017; Hodgkinson, 1996; Coady, 2018, Weale, 2019).

Likewise, scholars have warned of the frequent conflation of open data technologies with the politics of open government. Certain developments and technological advances, such as the distribution of e-services and e-government tools and the appearance of new Internet cultures, facilitated by ICTs in the context of citizens' everyday lives, have transformed our understanding of information cultures, their practices and impact on the meaning and practice of transparency. The Internet has largely blurred traditional definitions of who are information providers, content makers, producers, and consumers (Brun, 2008 cited in Gotz and Maklund, 2014: 211; Margetts, 2010; McIntyre, 2018). The issues of privacy and control, over information in particular, are strongly contested by both activists and governments. The proactive publication of information and the right to request access to documents may vary considerably between states, even those Caribbean countries that have proclaimed Freedom of Information Acts (FOIAs) because of cultural differences and divergent understandings of the role of government. The degree of transparency and openness of a state's information depends on its information culture, thus emphasizing that a government can "provide 'open data' on politically neutral topics even as it remains deeply opaque and unaccountable," with different governance contexts accounting for variations in the effectiveness of transparency initiatives. Moreover, beyond the bash-the-public-sector headlines, there are limits to the value of all this information (Chakrabortty, 2010). "More information," as Fung and his colleagues put it, "does not always produce markets that are more efficient" (Fung, Graham, and Weil, cited in Lessig, 2009:4) and "responses to information are inseparable from their interests, desires, resources, cognitive capacities, and social contexts." Because of these and other factors, people may ignore, misunderstand, or misuse information. Whether and how new information is used to further public objectives depends upon its incorporation into complex chains of comprehension, action, and response (Fung, Graham, and Weil, cited in Lessig, 2009: 4) made more difficult by a decline in the traditional media and the proliferation and diffusion of fragmentary social media platforms, disquieting the idea of objectivity in the media and the nature of our motivated thinking (Keen, 2007, 2012; Broome and Adugu, 2014; Adugu and Broome, 2017; McIntyre, 2018). To know whether a particular transparency rule works then, we need to trace just how the information will enter these "complex chains of comprehension." We need to see what comparisons the data will enable, and whether they reveal something real (Fung, Graham, and Weil, cited in Leesig, 2009: 4; Keen, 2007, 2012; McIntyre, 2018). Failing this, transparency then becomes translucent, most helpful to those already able and willing to use it—those with Internet connections and time to sift through data; those, as research has found, tend to be the same relatively well-off and highly educated people who are already well served by the public sector. Tobias Escher of Oxford University puts it as: "You end up giving more of a voice to those who already have pretty good representation" (Chakrabortty, 2010).

Finally, activists who support transparency must also consider in more detail the challenge that secrecy, as referenced earlier, poses to the idea of transparency. But tracking the connection between these two is a difficult empirical exercise because government's secrecy is at odds with the basic democratic principle of transparency. Shils (1956) demonstrated how perplexing and ultimately insoluble was the problem of liberal democracies premised on open discussion through more or less effectively functioning representative forms, having also to defend themselves and in the course of doing so, keep secrets (Turner, 2003: 6; Thompson, 2017; Coady, 2018). Making government more accessible to the public is vital to improving the quality of democracy for service to all. It is easy to think of instances where reasonable people would prefer that some government information be kept secret in the interest of public safety—police surveillance of known or suspected criminals; access to personnel records of government employees without good cause; genuine national security information; in the interest of the integrity of the electoral process the voter's ballot in a world where the strong can intimidate the weak through engendering a culture of fear or encrypted victimization if their preferences are known (Schudson, 2015); and if insidious personal dictatorships endangers us all by eroding the checks and balances that a healthy democracy requires such as intimidation of the media. Likewise in the realm of everyday social interaction, maintaining civility by tactfully withholding honest appraisals to protect privacy is a valid reason for secrecy (Schudson, 2015); as is the need for government decision-makers' trust in the confidentiality of their meetings and electronic communications if there is to be a free flow of conversation among them.

Secrecy is for the most part accepted as part of the package of realities that come with the act of governing. State secrets are not revealed when new governments take office not even with the most radical changes of government. The importance of transparency seems undisputed but many feel some degree of secrecy is needed since complete transparency would undermine effective functioning of governments (Turner, 2003: 7). The challenge lies in the ratio of secrecy and transparency we should seek in democratic politics, particularly when questions are raised about the violation of these conventions. While on paper the region might seem supportive of transparency, with respectable rankings with Reporters Without Borders (RSF) Press Freedom Index and laws like the Access to Information Act in Jamaica, it is not necessarily true that there is press freedom, and the real situation may be hidden by long self-censorship (Bridglal, 2019). Any discussion usually looks obliquely at what the central issues, and whether conventions have been honored or have been violated only in insignificant and harmless ways (Turner, 2003: 7; Mendes, 2013; Bridglal, 2019). And, if responsible government secrecy requires democratic oversight, does a select committee of the executive and/or legislative exercising "democratic" authority decide? There is authentic value in genuine intellectual inquiry into public issues such as the economy, alternative regimes of educational practice, and increasingly science and technology that deserves to be weighed against a public's right to know.

There is very often no such comprehension and the corresponding ability to judge what is being said and who is saying it, and consequently no possibility of genuine "discussion" (Turner, 2003: 12; McIntyre, 2018). How do we govern, or even devise, the conceptual parameters for acceptable behavior when there is a clash between a legitimate confidentiality of internal communications and a public right to information? And, concerns grow on impacts of challenges to authority, including that of public officials who operate behind closed doors. There is the danger to democracy of over-classification and enforced silences that exist only to save an individual, office, or policy from embarrassment and not to protect national interest, personal privacy, or decision-makers' legitimately confidential deliberations (Schudson, 2015; Keen, 2012; McIntyre, 2018). Most important now is the free flow of information, regarding governments' surety to their citizens on their accuracy in enacting policies to best minimize the transmission of the Covid-19 virus, based strictly on the best available scientific information and the application and use of geographical information systems that at the same time are not intrusive on civil liberties within the region. Further food for thought, does democratic commitment to transparency require that classified intelligence programs or closed-door political bargaining be abolished? Then there is a challenge that few scholars have taken up in that while fostering among their students both insight and oversight as public values, they have been rather embarrassed or too politically correct in avoiding moralism and sentiment of such.

The public responses to the Wikileaks disclosures assessed favorably, but few defended the idea of total transparency that inspired them. The detailed measures governing secrecy cannot themselves be subject to public discussion, without making them ineffective yet this does not make transparency an ultimate good that should be honored under all circumstances. If people in authority use the legal powers given them to classify as "secrets" things that ought properly to be part of genuine "government by discussion," and/or, if people acclaim and consent out of ignorance or on the basis only of what government allows them to hear, or are prevented from receiving conflicting information, attempts at transparency through public discourse quickly become a sham, for all that is discussed is that which governmental secret-keepers permit to be discussed (Turner, 2003: 7). And so, reforms for transparency are most likely to succeed in situations marked by a strong, vigilant, and vibrant civil society adopting a more critical attitude as a prerequisite for remaking and developing a country's democratic revitalization (Gotz and Maklund, 2014: 212).

PARADOXICAL TENSIONS IN ACCOUNTABILITY

Simultaneously, a microscopic focus must be levied at the paradoxical tensions associated with accountability as governments try to cope with the challenges and opportunities of improving governance capacity and trust through interactions of the state with the private sector and civil society. There is no way good governance can be discussed without introducing the ethical principle of accountability. *Accountability*, argues Cameron (2004: 59), "is an important element of governance," pointing to the importance of accountability in modern democracy and the role it plays in promoting good governance. What then is *accountability*, and what role does it play in modern democracy? (Miller, 2011) As referenced earlier in this chapter, there is no clear-cut definition of *accountability* per se which poses challenges particularly when explaining the differences in conceptual understandings shaped by idea complexes that can change over time and produce profoundly different, even conflicting interpretations of apparently identical social realities. Second, understandings are shaped by the participatory experiences of social actors and the two are integrally linked (Hintzen, 2001: 107). The World Bank argues that social accountability initiatives, besides facilitating better governance and improved public policies and services, can serve to "empower those social groups that are systematically underrepresented in formal political institutions" and to "ensure that less powerful societal groups also have the ability to express and act upon their choices" (Carothers and Brechenmacher, 2014: 15). Yet efforts to bolster the inclusion of marginalized groups often suffer from the problem of superficial application. For many mainstream donor organizations, inclusion emerged as a priority issue on the international aid agenda when women's activists argued that the economic, social, and political marginalization of women—their exclusion from education and political decision-making—perpetuated chronic poverty (Carothers and Brechenmacher, 2014: 14). The issue is how those working in development genuinely understand the business of "governance." If their view of governance is state-centric then there is no future to promoting government accountability to citizens in spite of the recent "accountability" turn in the rhetoric. If, however, they truly understand governance to be a textured, embedded, networked process in which citizens and government officials argue, bargain, and, sometimes agree (Susskind 2008 cited in Odugbemi and Lee, 2011), then the capacity of citizens to hold governments accountable will be seen as a fundamental part of the governance agenda, and promoting accountability of governments to their own citizens will have a secure future with potentially useful development outcomes. Sadly, the tradition of governance skewed toward development reform remains dominant in the same institutions, which often mouth but do not practice commitment to the accountability of governments to their citizens (Odugbemi and Lee, 2011: 5; Schwenke, 2019).

Relatedly, the same undeniable tensions can be said of the need for accountability voiced in repeated calls by the media and other public agencies for more standards and rules to discuss policies on administration. In this context, the role of the public service assumes importance with the dominant tradition being public sector governance, and New Public Management its paradigm. This has become particularly apparent in recent years in relation to attempts at administrative reform, where there has been resistance and slow progress even with the highest political priority. Little or no thought may be paid to the problematic issues, which may be counterproductive. An obsession with accountability through the imposition of standards and rules can reinforce a propensity for public officials to be extremely risk averse—to create more rules (of what not to do), and more codes (of minimal standards) (Hicks, 2007: 13; Thompson, 1987). Moreover, certain attempts to strengthen public sector accountability by increasing provider competition in service delivery may perpetuate patterns of marginalization, and poorly conceived participatory projects can exacerbate rather than alleviate the exclusion of disadvantaged groups (Carothers and Brechenmacher, 2014: 12; Parsons, 1998).

Paradoxically, the clear lines of accountability so prized by the liberal ideal are almost impossible to sustain in the context of small island states where individuals are called upon to play multiple roles, leading to persistent criticisms of nepotism and corruption. In small island states, senior and even middle-ranking public servants cannot be anonymous and find it difficult, if not impossible, to avoid playing an important part in the formulation and implementation of policy. At the highest levels, specific policies are often associated with particular officials and it is not uncommon to be victimized by politicians and indeed by society when there is a change of government or spectacular policy failure (Sutton, 1999: 75; see also 2006, 2008; Minto-Coy and Berman, 2016).

Equally important is that most of the discourse on accountability centers around making governments accountable to their citizens, while often ignoring the corresponding logic of making citizens or the private sphere accountable to government. Policies will seek to make improvements in governance through changes in law that impose constraints on elected officials and citizens, often shielding technocratic-guardians and special interests from scrutiny. Recognizing this, the question soon becomes: Who guards these technocrat-guardians? In addition, such instances further raise the question, ought not the region's policy planners similarly to insist that universities and the recent proliferation of medical schools, the main professional associations for the law, medicine, social scientists, subscribe to ethical codes through advancing tightened disclosure requirements such as listing their sources of income? These professional organizations, like the work in academic disciplines, are equally as likely to be pushed in one direction or another by internal and external influences. There is often a lot of money at stake in either business or politics, depending on what the "wisest" scholars claim to be the truth. Likewise, should an economist, judge, or a political scientist disclose his or her political and ideological affiliation? Does it matter whether they subscribe to Keynesian or classical economic theory, or, liberal and/or conservative ideals in shaping policies for governance considering how such ideological influences can affect the success and failure of government and society? And, while such legislation and standards may help *prima facie* to enhance notions of accountability within these organizations, should such legislation not be extended further to incorporate the kith and kin of the professionals within these organizations since it is not uncommon for familial relations of a major company or an institution to stand to benefit from his/her work? (Indiviglio, 2011) At times the government collaborates or negotiates with them in regulatory programs sometimes referred to as "new" or "new public" governance. In short, the formal logical structure of accountability is continuously modulated by complex, extraneous, and incommensurable forces. The influence exerted upon accountability is unquestionably important and can assume pathological proportions. It is a form of power that, not formally accountable to the organization and its purpose, evades authority and responsibility. It is subcutaneous and invisible upon organization charts but is always present, never entirely negligible, and fundamentally irreducible

(Hodgkinson, 1996: 73). If the state is to be visible and accountable, then so should all of its parts, including private individuals and entities interacting with or serving as adjuncts to the state. This is because in the populist understanding of transparency, and accountability, the private information in government possession or information that private actors produce or disclose while participating in or negotiating with government, becomes public information and should be available to the public (Fenster, 2010: 649). Unsurprisingly, these propositions have not prevailed. This issue pervades all national governments and, as Alasdair Roberts has explained, has caused a "conceptual muddle" over how "to determine where the boundaries of government lie" and how best to draft rules that can force disclosure upon private entities that "appear governmental." These conflicts between the gains of public-private collaboration, and the limits such collaboration places on the state's visibility, illustrate the inevitable and pervasive barriers to making the government thoroughly transparent and accountable (Fenster, 2010: 654).

Liberalization can also reduce political accountability. This problem is symptomatic of the broader problems raised by trying to implement market and institutional reforms simultaneously (Collingwood, 2001). While neo-liberalism accommodates the principle of providing state-supported social safety nets and insists on open democratic systems, certain reservations will always remain (Johnson, 2007: 164). Introduced at the wrong time, liberalization and macroeconomic reforms may actually weaken rather than strengthen the regulatory capacity and accountability of the state. Government's delegation of some degree of regulatory authority to private or hybrid public-private entities may increase the state's organizational complexity and may thereby decrease the state's visibility to the public. Further, if private entities that collaborate with the government thereby become subject to open government laws, they may be less willing to engage directly with government (Fenster, 2010: 650), their reluctance undermining the collaborative approach that new governance seeks to promote. In order to meet the public's expectations of the range and quality of services it must perform, the state must work with private entities, which may either make the state less transparent, or provoke treating private entities as state actors which will in turn then undercut the range and quality of services the state can offer. If the state must be visible, its efforts to provide effective regulation and services are likely to suffer (Fenster, 2010: 652). Deregulation can then undermine the state's ability to control corruption by weakening its capacity to monitor private, public, and corporate relations (Collingwood, 2001:18). In a system where the most efficient persons or firms receive the greatest returns, there is a clear prospect of a disproportionate skewing of society's surplus to the most efficient few (Johnson, 2007: 164). An additional hurdle is that developing country governments trying to achieve good governance conditionalities are forced to meet stricter demands for improved standards and economic performance while working with fewer resources and less influence (see also Smith, 2016). While the World Bank has consistently promoted privatization as a solution to governmental inefficiency and fiscal problems, it can nevertheless be damaging to developing countries if the preconditions are wrong (Collingwood, 2001: 18).

While references abound to the arbitrary and corrupt nature of the state, the private sector can be corrupt as well. Accountability is a key aspect of any form of service provision; democratic governments should be accountable to their populations, and they risk being voted out if they are not. Private companies, however, are not formally accountable to their customers and in a non-competitive environment do not face the possibility of being ousted by other, more efficient providers if the private sector is not sufficiently developed. Successful privatization must be undertaken in a transparent and well-regulated environment but private sector development is no easy task, and essential mechanisms must be in place in a country and in markets to support private growth and development (Collingwood, 2001: 18). However, as there is no guarantee that these resources will be used to benefit the wider society, this approach can be acceptable only if the behavior of such individuals is underpinned by strong ethical values. While competition will inevitably arise and reduce this surplus, the initial rewards will have already accrued (Johnson, 2007: 164; Weale, 2019). In the absence of these mechanisms, it is doubtful that privatizing public enterprises will lead to the development of a large private sector. For one thing, contracting out to private firms for service provision is not always possible in developing countries where a well-developed private sector is not present as contractors may not exist, or those that do may not be well-informed, efficient, or productive, making the contracting of public work damaging. Where a monopoly exists with no formal accountability mechanisms, private companies can be more damaging than governments (Collingwood, 2001). In an era of rapidly changing technology, pioneers will inevitably gain monopoly status and be expected to not only reap surplus, but to exercise dominance with the option to abuse a hegemonic position. The intervention of state agencies to control dominance is a poor solution because of the time lapse and the prospect of recurrence of abuses as new conditions arise. The best answer is adherence to sound ethical principles and ensuring that state intervention is available to ameliorate the impact of the few cases that do arise. This care and attention becomes necessary because of the pervasiveness of ethical lapses and their deleterious social and economic consequences (Johnson, 2007: 164).

Deregulation and privatization are then not such simple recipes for successful development since in many developing countries the government has not been able to create a competitive enabling environment suitable for such policies. This takes us back to the tension identified in the introduction to this chapter between good governance as a precondition for development and good governance as an objective of development. The Bank's policies vis-à-vis the private sector demonstrate the ambivalence of pro-market policies and without a guarantee that resources will benefit the wider society (Collingwood, 2001), this approach is only acceptable if the behavior of such individuals is underpinned by strong ethical values. Let us also not overlook the importance of defining the community the intended "public action" of accountability is to serve. This is because, as mentioned throughout this discourse, a variation in definition of contested principles of governance may see very different things carried out in the name of apparently common principles. Seemingly transformative concepts and approaches in reality often translate into superficial or limited applications. And so, although the default response is that all society ought to be held accountable, here again fundamental fissures over the value and application of this ideal further preclude an already deceptive reality. In the definition of the field, at one end would be a form of oligarchy or clientelism, where only a few well-connected individuals stand to gain directly and materially from being politically active will do so. Going to this extreme ensures a very high degree of personal commitment and investment among any participants. In addition, there is a more general range of "publics" in which participation is selective yet sufficiently representative of something to engender a meaningful sense of accountability. The "public" may be self-selected (anyone wishing to participate doing so), recruited selectively (usually quiescent groups such as the poor or religious and ethnic minorities), or recruited through a random selection process (as in citizen juries, deliberative experiments, or opinion polls). It may even be organized entities (either in civil society such as churches, or interest groups and lobbying professions, either as direct stakeholders or as agents of un- or underrepresented constituencies) (Odugbemi and Lee, 2011: 16). Likewise, the public can be categorized as the organization and culture of a political movement, a policy campaign, with rather different and varying demands. The categories are not hard-edged but the contrasts that they provide can be useful in specifying how inclusive or exclusive must be participation, in order to serve the ends of accountability in the key design element of mobilizing public will for good governance. This is not because public action is unwanted, but because the organization and culture of a political movement, a policy campaign, a development NGO, or a religious body are inevitably rather different and with varying demands (Schwenke, 2019).

One additional point to make on properly recognizing which "public" is or ought to be mobilized on a given issue, via a given social accountability mechanism, is that the term "citizen" too has important shades of distinction. As mentioned in chapter 5 not all citizens are equal and full members of a polity and great variance exists across national boundaries in the development of civil, political, and social rights. In this sense, citizenship is an important textured layer to our dimension of participatory inclusion or not. It is important to consider these features being careful not to rely on prefigured and valorized conceptions of "citizen" in defining a target population of participants: many of the most transformative social movements involve demands for greater inclusion and full citizenship. It is also important to keep varieties of citizenship in mind with there being many understandings of what citizenship entails at the individual level. Some may view their citizenship purely as a legal status—with accompanying rights (such as access to public services or legal counsel) and attendant privileges and obligations (such as jury duty, military service, or electoral office). Others may find in this thin conception of citizenship freedom from fear of political persecution, deportation, or other legally justified sanction. Yet others may view their citizenship as a civic, republican virtue or as an aspiration to an ideal human form (Odugbemi and Lee, 2011: 18).

Generically therefore, if accountability ought to be extended to everybody the complexity of the polity can undermine such logic, making this approach an impractical ideal. Universal accountability like participation is also impractical in the specific context of generating genuine inputs into social accountability mechanisms because such ubiquitous levels of citizen activism in heterogeneous publics would almost surely overwhelm institutional capacity and foster bargaining and coordination problems (Odugbemi and Lee, 2011: 16; Johnston, 2008).

And, Public Opinion?

Moreover, newly inscribed demands within the polity may envelop a discursive public opinion that can further determine who can be engaged and what ends to which they ought to be engaged. The role and value of public opinion cannot be disengaged from the praxis of accountability and participation. Public opinion is not blind prejudice, nor is it a mere aggregation of unthoughtful attitudes. It is the crystallization at the end debate and discussion of the relevant information available in the public arena, helping state actors better understand meaningfully and effectively address their constituency's preferences. Public opinion, thus understood, is at the heart of politics and governance. Shaped through access to information public information (Odugbemi and Lee, 2011; Johnston, 2006) can help citizens, through activism, to exert pressure on their governments for better spending on key basic services such as health and education. Public opinion is then closely connected to participation, and has become a prerequisite for accountable government. For if governance is not simply about force/command but is about arguing, bargaining, and, sometimes, coming to agreement, then two fundaments of good governance must be identified: first the majority opinion formed by the citizenry in specific contexts regarding a public issue or controversy, at the end of a process finding out, debating, and discussion; and second the institutions and processes that will determine the character of the public arena in a country. At least two interrelated questions about public opinion ought to begin any conversation on whether "genuine demand" for accountability can be generated. The first is whether public opinion can be coherent and competent enough to be an active, autonomous pressure for political responsiveness and good governance. The second is whether effective mechanisms are in place for the public to voice its will to and be heard by state actors (Odugbemi and Lee, 2011: 12; see also Hope and Chikulo, 2000; Johnston, 2006; Weale, 2019).

Currently, attempts at galvanizing public opinion into a political community of shared values by which citizens can directly hold governments accountable occur through the mechanism of the electoral process in representative democracies (Prezeworski et al., 1999: 3 cited in Odugbemi and Lee, 2011). This approach however is reliable neither in making leaders accountable on specific issues nor in securing improved delivery of public services nor in getting government's focus on the needs of the vast majority of citizens (Goetz and Jenkins, 2005; Odugbemi and Lee, 2011; Girardin, 2012; Thompson, 2019). An election involves a vast complicated jumble of issues and the elected rulers who survive an election can contrive to forget electors until another election comes around. Another approach is through the development of broad-based "democratic checks and controls" to sanction misrule, using arrangements such as the presence of civil society in participatory budgeting, citizen advisory boards, civic journalism, public expenditure tracking, and social audits that empower people (Odugbemi and Lee, 2011: 11; Thompson, 2019). Other forums for investigation and critique, such as think-tanks and universities, which articulate the cosmopolitan language of political reform and a better world, provide a similar function for issues of greater analytic complexity.

The simplicity of logic of transforming a shared public opinion into an approach focused enough to be an active, autonomous pressure for political responsiveness and good governance is not so easily translatable into mobilized publics and institutionalized mechanisms that work (Odugbemi and Lee, 2011:11). This discourse posits that the reason for this splintered state of affairs is that much of the analysis has overlooked the emergence of a global information society as a powerful democratizing force. When we evaluate the methodological approaches and assumptions on why democratic accountability as a form of activism is more discernible in some regions than in others, we find that many advocates of accountability have ignored a root cause. That root is the complex and rapidly evolving technological ecology in the use of mobile devices and ubiquitous computing within a maturing web ecosystem, along with its capacity to generate demands for focused participation and accountability, as well as the broad interrelated impact it has had on facilitating the interaction, engagement, and coordination of crowds toward the type of democracy desired.

By the same token, this research also argues that this state of affairs is compounded by absent institutional arrangements, which further diminish citizens' ability to become active, and opportunity for the public's will to be voiced in the issues of governance. The Internet has created new forms of individual power facilitated through the integration of social media and the use of a cluster of application technologies that build on the ideological and technological foundations of Web 2.0 (Joseph, 2012, cited in Broome and Adugu, 2014: 2; Thompson, 2019). Through social media, people or groups can create, organize, edit, comment on, combine, and share content, enabled by scalable communication technologies that have resulted in their becoming an integral part of modern society (Learner, 2013, cited in Broome and Adugu, 2014: 2). They include but are in no way limited to blogs, microblogs (e.g., Twitter and Tumblr), social networks (e.g., Facebook and LinkedIn), wikis (e.g., Wikipedia), and multimedia (e.g., Flickr, YouTube, and Pandora). Because they allow for interactive participation using the "wisdom" of crowds to collaboratively connect online (Learner, 2013, cited in Broome and Adugu, 2014: 2) they have also become conduits through which conventional sociopolitical movements can improve their global reach, facilitating and fomenting digital activism. Those who design media products are more important than ever to the flourishing of complex liberal democracies. These institutional and technological contrivances empower us in a myriad of ways. However, these very same humanly designed institutions and technologies also take away options and constrain our freedom to act, and they also structure our interactions in particular ways. Computer algorithms and computers allow us to process large volumes of data, but they also determine how we perceive the world when we run our computer models (van den Hoven, 2017: 11).

A reasonable discussion of social media and political change must therefore [re]image some of the analysis of how technological connectivity has changed in recent years and how social media and political change are mediated, moderated, and used by individuals of different backgrounds. Digital literacy must also leverage the application of civic literacy, including critical thinking, writing, and political literacy to express ideas, and reach a wider audience and engage with diverse people and ideas (see Lin, 2010; Liu, 2010, cited in Broome and Adugu, 2014: 14; Thompson, 2019). This is because digital literacy and cyber-activism tap into a community's distributed intelligence, consisting of several people, each offering individual skills, collaborating on a unified cause or project (Fischer and Konomi, 2007, cited in Broome and Adugu, 2014: 14; Keen, 2012; van den Hoven, 2017; McIntyre, 2018; Thompson, 2019).

The interplay of digital and civic literacies across distributed intelligences has implications for democratic participation, particularly how constituents will engage these new technologies using persuasive and pedagogical skills for political discussions (McClure, 1994; Farsagai, 2010, cited in Broome and Adugu, 2014: 14; Keen, 2012; McIntyre, 2018; Thompson, 2019). The press and related forms of social media have kept governments in check, by documenting abuses of power exposing corrupt bargains and alerting citizens to crooked dealings and dysfunctional institutions, thereby provoking outrage and reform. The larger public discourse that draws on these sources not only helps to spread basic ethical convictions but is also the conduit for developing a popular consensus on the standards that should govern new questions. Organizing this information for methodical analysis requires the less academically educated elements to be able to sift through and make sense of detailed content streams they have read, discussed, liked, and what they think is authoritative, all of which is informed by links forwarded to them on social media (Morozov, 2011: 10 cited in Broome and Adugu 2014: 2). Hofheinz (2011: 10 cited in Broome and Adugu, 2014: 15) refers to this as a "copy and paste" trend that can in fact have political consequences. Corrupt governments attempt to insulate themselves from critique by suppressing digital media, which leads to impoverished social discourses. Moreover, the skills needed to conduct insightful investigations in a world of increasing complexity are difficult to cultivate and often more lucratively compensated in other fields, because of the tendency of social media, due to the sheer volume of information available via the Internet and 24/7 news cycles to distract persons from important issues. In addition, those who finance the news, as well as those who consume it, have less and less patience for complicated stories (Keen, 2012; McIntyre, 2018; Thompson, 2019). The greatest challenge faced by journalists and/or reporters within the region, however, comes from those who are more interested in partisan politics than in uncovering the truth, tending to make them collaborators in the corrupting dynamics of democratic politics, rather than sources of independent judgment (English, 2013: 36; Keen, 2012; McIntyre, 2018; Thompson, 2019). This combination of factors makes social media platforms less efficient and productive as easily steerable tools in the goal of formulating complex, strategic political action (Tufekci, 2013, cited in Broome and Adugu, 2014: 15). Internet access is crucial but it does not ensure participation in a digital culture. Rather the degrees of access, literacy, engagement, intellectual maturity to know what to do, and knowing how to use social media skillfully will have to be considered according to how advanced are factors in a particular country. Thus, government, businesses, and individuals nurturing and investing in the capacity of social media, ensuring that an enabling environment is created to foster and encourage purposeful use of the Internet and of technology, maximizes and enhances chances of engaging a wider, diverse audience overall. For further clarity three examples will suffice.

No Messiah in the Crowd

Use of social media in the region for garnering a consistent and coherent public opinion is also circumscribed by two interrelated and mutually reinforcing factors, the missing messiah (leaderlessness) and the lack of an institutional outlet for change (Tufekci, 2013, cited in Broome and Adugu, 2014: 15). The plethora of social media platforms can create confusion by promoting and amplifying different grievances in different places particularly when there is no leader. In an analogue world there is generally a centralized leadership structure and clear lines of authority aiming to build consensus and set goals. The movement is therefore identifiable by a leader, the strong, passionate, articulate, visible face, and voice of the movement. In the digital world, social media has dispelled centralization with the result that the seriousness and sense of purpose are undermined by vague or convoluted information and causes that can be hijacked by a small band of passionate but misfit intellectuals and vagabonds (Sorkin, 2012, cited in Broome and Adugu, 2014: 15; Keen, 2012; McIntyre, 2018; Thompson, 2019). Social media acts as a conservative force by distracting people from "real" activism deluding them into thinking that they are effecting change when in reality they are not.

Throughout their history Caribbean populations have often responded to the charismatic leader to advance their cause. This in turn raises the question: Where there is no strategic thinking to develop a coherent and delimited set of policies to take the movement forward, how does one make difficult choices about tactics, strategy, or philosophical direction when everyone has an equal say? It is here that we see the Internet as a "tool without a handle" (Morozov, 2011, cited in Broome and Adugu 2014: 15) for though it can be seen to possess enormous liberating potential, harnessing this potential and translating it into political reality has proven far harder to accomplish (see also Etling et al., 2010, cited in Broome and Adugu, 2014: 15). Further, since activism can be a game of high-risk politics, who will be blamed or held liable for treason or civil disobedience if the movement is upended by the state? This is a question that should resonate within the mind of any social media user planning dissent.

When Apathy Collides with Pluralistic Ignorance

A scenario like the one presented above resettles the activist into a general state of apathy with the status quo or an inherent frustration institutionalized in pluralistic ignorance, both of which can detract from the use of social media for digital activism. "Pluralistic ignorance," refers to a group that might feel the same way but pretend to feel the opposite, and/or pretend they do not all feel the same way so as not to stand out or be the first to revolt. This pluralistic ignorance is a key factor in keeping unpopular regimes in power (Tufekci and Jones, 2011, cited in Broome and Adugu, 2014: 15) where many keep their true preferences private, or speak only with a few trusted people, fearing either that they are a minority or will meet with massive repression if they speak up. Both an inherent apathy and pluralistic ignorance are contributing causes to participation, or lack of, in using any form of medium.

The Cult of Anonymity

We must proceed with caution in drawing some of the obvious conclusions from these observations. It is a truism that severe restrictions on press freedom have encouraged a sophisticated censorship apparatus. Although involvement in discussions is a significant feature of active citizenship, the quality of online discussions is an important issue to take into consideration (Farsagai, 2010, cited in Broome and Adugu, 2014: 11). Bizarrely enough, at times there is an element of legitimacy to the complaints of policy planners who can contest the narrative-crafting and information-controlling capabilities of ordinary citizens, as well as the pernicious behavior of some activists behind the veil of anonymity. Within this new context of citizen journalism problems of accuracy and anonymity have surfaced: social media can facilitate interaction between users sharing content but the anonymity of the Internet that allows previously unheard individuals to express their dissent without fear of state victimization, can also be abused. Too often the privilege of anonymity can encourage "trolling," and the uncivil use of discussion fora to provoke, degrade, and distract others (Youmans and York, 2012: 319 cited in Broome and Adugu, 2014: 11), which has the potential to diminish the usefulness of these social media platforms as accountability tools (Cave, 2012, cited in Broome and Adugu, 2014: 11).

In extreme cases, small can also be easy to dominate, with numerous instances of populist leaders treating small countries as personal "fiefdoms" through control over most aspects of social life (see Crocombe, 2008: 643 cited in Veenendaal and Corbett, 2015: 541; Minto-Coy, 2016). Moreover, politics in small polities is, by definition, intensely personalized, possibly with electorates of a few hundred voters, often relatives or kin. Political actions stem from essentially personal relations rather than the indirect, administrative relationships and formal contacts of a larger society. In such circumstances, familial loyalties tend to override policy priorities and assessments of individual competence that accord with more utilitarian principles (Veenendaal and Corbett, 2015: 541; Minto-Coy et al., 2016).

In those instances where social media movements have been successful in serving as oppositional forces in focusing the voices of people, interest groups, or institutions, there still remain substantive questions regarding what should be advocated, what is best for the people. The peoples' own ideas are problematical because of the range of individual ideas and questionable representation by highly politicized interest groups with opaque agendas; or a contextual ethic that abjures rules and implied principles altogether. Moreover, after the service of advocacy, there are generally no institutional arrangements such as formalized mechanisms of representation or of decision-making (Tufekci, 2013, cited in Broome and Adugu, 2014: 15) such as the authority of the legislature to promulgate decisive corrective changes through laws and the state budget. For the most part then, trade unions and or interest groups may at times have the ability to galvanize the concerns and to "speak on behalf of users" but with suboptimal action. How, then, do we reckon a role for public opinion in generating bottom-up demand for political accountability? Accountability framed within this context also brings into direct focus the dilemmas encountered in trying to stymie claims, real or perceived, of corruption.

THE PATHOLOGY OF CORRUPTION

As with accountability and transparency, the often-repeated allegations and actual charges of corruption are of concern within these societies. In fact they are inextricably linked in the pathologies both generate. Yet as seen in chapter 3, the predominant way in which corruption is treated in mainstream literature contains nothing on the specific approach of ethics to corruption even though demands for responsible interpretation and application depend on the cultivation of the virtues that support good administrative judgment. These paradoxes are explored in a rich, varied, and rapidly growing literature on governance. Corruption used here refers to breaches of ethics that, due to their context and severity, warrant intervention of the criminal justice system (Gunatilleke et al., 1983; Hodgkinson, 1996; Robben, 1998; Amunsden and Andrade, 2009; Campbell, 2010; Demmke and Moilanen, 2011; Minto-Coy et al., 2016; Ceva and Ferretti, 2019; Hellsten, 2019). But here again, the inherent contradictions exist not only in the definition of what constitutes the idea of corruption, but also that the forms of corruption are diverse in terms of who are the actors, initiators, and profiteers, how it is, and to what extent it is practiced. Also, the causes of corruption are complex and diverse, and have been sought in both individual ethics and civic cultures, in history and tradition, the economic system, in the institutional arrangements such as the policies of a particular country and its bureaucratic traditions, and in the political system (Amunsden and Andrade, 2009: 36 see also Collier, 2005; Ceva and Ferretti, 2019; Hellsten, 2019). The consequences are anathema to economic development and include little to no capital formation to develop entrepreneurship, misallocation of scarce resources, where the rational behavior of market actors in respect to incentives and rents explains corruption outcomes (Bracking, 2007: 10; Hellsten, 2019) and the constraining of good governance and development through the abuse of public trust and stifling the emergence of civil society. As will emerge in this chapter, both the institutions and mechanisms that are used to communicate change and to insist on compliance with such change often threaten the very qualities that support responsible judgment. While all acts of corruption are unethical, not all unethical acts are considered corruption as seen in our discussion on transparency and its inherent contradictions. The challenge is that this absence of specificity results in corruption meaning different things to different people, illustrating as it does so the weaknesses in conception, delivery, resources, and context—perhaps the nature of the beast. Upon careful examination, there are inherent political dynamics in modern democracies that have proven uniquely pernicious. On the one hand these countries are imbued with a *pays legal*, a legal structure which is the focus of attention for multilateral donors and Western states, and on the other hand, a *pays réel* where real power is wielded. In extreme cases this duplication can lead to the existence of a hidden structure that surrounds the systemic mode of everyday life and is resident in political institutions to the extent that these gave the hidden or *pays réel* realm of politics the term "shadow state" (Bracking, 2007: 9; see also Reno, 2000; Hodgkinson, 1996; Hellsten, 2019; Ceva and Ferretti, 2019). That is to say, the challenge of institutional corruption is an immanent feature of our political system. We therefore need to understand their underlying logic and aggravating factors if we are to hope to counteract their corrupting tendencies (Quah, 2010; Ceva and Ferretti, 2019; Hellsten, 2019).

To begin, a central concern is that even though there may not be a serious problem of corruption, it is almost expected that corruption is a norm. But oftentimes the problem is not the actual practice of corruption, rather it is a problem of perception—its constant suggestions of a sin that is present sometimes but not always, hence the difficulty of finding solutions (Giengob, 2000; Hellsten, 2019). Another concern at first glance is that institutional corruption may appear to have increased, but has it? Or has a chance artifact of organizational drift occurred, and is it something that minimal vigilance can guard against? A third is the presence of weak constraints on politicians, making it possible for them to pursue policies to enrich themselves. Such policies are supported by political environments where it is possible, and/or even necessary, for them to use clientelistic policies that pander to powerful constituencies both to remain in power and, worryingly so, to ensure the preservation of a state. Moreover, although the explicit discussion of institutional corruption generally centers around those accounts that see corruption as a phenomenon of individual failings, it can be problematic if there is a tendency to assume only that institutions become consequently corrupt, as opposed to being corrupt from the beginning——what might be called its structural insinuations. In fact, corruption is often embodied in the very purpose and design of the institution. In these instances, the processes of institutional corruption become pathological, making it increasingly difficult to distinguish between legitimate and illegitimate actions and purposes (Hodgkinson, 1996; Crawford, 2004; English, 2013; Yung, 2016; Thompson, 2017; Weale, 2019; Hellsten, 2019). Textbox 6.1 summarizes some of the many social practices to which "corruption" refers.

TEXTBOX 6.1   A COMPENDIUM OF UNRESOLVED PARADOXES AND THE PATHOLOGIES THEY GENERATE AS A SYSTEM OF INTERLOCKING VICIOUS CYCLES

Paradox of Obligation: If public servants are free to choose, but at the same time are obliged to act only as authorities choose for them, then, for all practical purposes, they are not free. Alternatively, if public servants are free to choose, then their actions may violate obligations to authority, making their exercise of free choice irresponsible.

Pathologies Generated

Bureaucratic Opportunism: The sacrifice of principles to do what is expedient and accommodating to self-interest. Refers to these small acts, or rent-taking actions, by civil servants. Bribery, influencing, and gift giving are sometimes seen as different forms of petty corruption. Public administrators, particularly those with direct encounters with members of the public, who accept bribes for expediting documents or, in the case of the police, not charging a suspect.

Reification of Obligations and Authority: The unreflexive use of principles to produce decisions that are compelled by principles rather than freely made (Roberts, 2002: 659; Bracking, 2007: 5–6).

Influencing: Forcing a decision in one's favour. Political lobbying is a form of influencing and is legitimate, but secretive contacts or suspicion of favouritism or influence that are suspected to be disproportionate to public interest may be considered as corrupt.

Revolving doors: The movement of individuals between the public and private sectors —known as the revolving door—may lead to conflict of interest situations, increasing the risks of corruption. Given their decision-making power, access to key information and influence, former ministers and members of the government can be an important asset for private companies (Roberts, 2002: 659; Bracking, 2007: 5–6).

Paradox of Agency: If individuals acknowledge personal authorship, as expressed through their own exercise of moral agency, then they deny their ultimate answerability to others. On the other hand, if they assert ultimate answerability to others, they deny their own moral agency.

Pathologies Generated

Buck Passing: The declaration of one's innocence by denying personal authorship or sufficient authority and resources to achieve an institution's goals.

Scapegoating: Blaming an individual in order to shield an institution's complicity and to protect its members' illusion of their collective innocence.

Atrophy of Individual Moral Agency: The assertion of moral innocence by claiming victim status and thus discouraging the exercise of personal authorship and responsibility.

Avoidance of Individual Responsibility: The relaxation of standards to perpetuate the illusion of victim innocence and the lack of confrontation and candor necessary for instilling a sense of personal answerability (Roberts, 2002: 659; Bracking, 2007: 5–6).

Rent Seeking: Private payments to public officials, and the "capture" of their area of jurisdiction, in order to affect laws, rules, decrees, regulations or capture resources, for example, contracts. The interests of firms who need to pay and the public in general are side-lined.

Improper use of authority (for noble causes): Use of illegal/improper methods to achieve organizational goals (within the police for example illegal methods of investigation and disproportionate violence)

The Pathology of superficiality and its attendant features are endemic in institutions and is characterised by:

Unread, or merely scanned serious reports on controversial organization issues, despite the labour that may have gone into their production. (The report or consultant study may often be used not to solve a problem but to defer it or to "buy time").

Problems demanding action may repeatedly be deferred through other executive engagements and priorities until events force a decision point.

Only the briefest time is available for any kind of serious value-fact-probability-consequence analysis and none at all for any philosophical reflection. Reliance for critical intelligence is placed on informal contacts with peers inside and outside the organization, or with cultivated sources in the informal organization network—essentially gossip.

Problems are not dealt with in their full right but on an ad hoc or "fire-fighting" basis. Impending confrontations are deferred or sidestepped. Time itself becomes both friend and enemy but is always in short supply.

Lesser formalistic delaying routines such as, executive inaccessibility behind ranks of subordinates and protective secretarial cover, Inaccessibility by travel, by conference, by conventions, by being "tied up," or simply by non-response to calls, and correspondence—all used to decelerate or retard conflict resolution or in the effort to derail, deflect, and deter criticism and opposition (Hodgkinson, 1996: 192–193).

Paradox of Accountability: If public servants are solely accountable for the achievement of purposes mandated by political authority, then as instruments of that authority they hold no personal responsibility for the products of their actions. If, however, public servants participate in determining public purposes, then their accountability to higher authority is undermined.

Pathologies Generated

Atrophy of Personal Responsibility: Denying public servants the responsibility to establish public purposes prevents them from accepting the consequences of their actions and acknowledging the moral consequences of their manipulative control of others in the interests of "effective management."

Atrophy of Political Authority: Granting public servants the responsibility to establish public purposes makes public servants answerable only to themselves and enables them to covertly manipulate political processes that determine public purposes (Roberts, 2002: 659).

Private time misconduct: conduct in one's private time which harms the public's trust in administration/government.

Grandstanding/Infeasible Obligations: Democracies are ruled by the politics of appearance, and nothing is more important for a politician's career than the appearance of having "done something." This naturally leads to the commissioning of large and unsustainable capital projects indebting the state and overloading the state's agenda, to politicians making promises they cannot fulfil, passing laws they do not understand, taking credit before it is due, often neglecting helpful policies that might decrease their power to claim credit or extract donations, and obfuscating their responsibility when policies fail (English, 2013: 24).

Ignoring Cultures of Impunity. State's inability to reconcile its history with the present circumstances. If not discussed past injustices such as inequalities of various kinds, especially inequalities of economic and political power and racialized social structures may endure to the present, undermining efforts at good governance.

Transnational economic sectors: The manipulation and domination by a political and economic elite of a global environment of open economies with free flow of capital and global inter-linkages, creating in some cases "dubious" offshore financial centres of unaccountable privilege and excessive wealth outside the purview of the formal institutions of state. The state often lacks the constraints on counteracting agencies charged with policing and enforcement of the laws, and attempts at eliminating such economic sectors will decimate the life-blood of some economies. Less favourable international agreements. Less transparency in international agreements (Crocker, 2014: 25; Bracking, 2007).

Sources: Adapted and revised from: Bracking, S. (Ed.) (2007). *Corruption and Development: The Anti-Corruption Campaigns*. Basingstoke: Palgrave Macmillan.

Crocker, D., (2014). Development and Global Ethics: Five Foci for the future. In *Journal of Global Ethics*. Vol. 10, No. 3, pp. 245–253.

English, W. (2013). *Institutional Corruption and the Crisis of Liberal Democracy*. In Edmond J. Safra Working Papers, No. 15, Massachusetts: Harvard University Edmond J Safra Centre for Ethics available at https://papers.ssrn.com/sol3/papers.cfm?abstract_id=2281305.

Hodgkinson, C., (1996). *Administrative Philosophy*. London: Pergamon.

Roberts, N. C. (2002). Keeping public officials accountable through dialogue: resolving the accountability paradox. In *Public Administration Review*, Vol.62, No.6, (November/December) pp. 658–669.

And, unlike petty corruption, the sheer complexity of modern institutions often means they will be governed by economies of influence that are dynamic and that render opaque the ability for transparent and accountable government. That is to say, the logic of democratic politics generates centripetal forces that systematically threaten to corrupt our political institutions. Whether due to devious and premeditated conspiracies or to an artifact of seemingly innocuous [mis]placed incentives that aggregate to bad outcomes, the overriding concern remains the same. Rose-Ackerman (2014: 798) cautions us to be equally as mindful of insidious forms of corruption, such as low-level corruption that goes undetected or is simply overlooked without recognizing the eventual pathological implications it can have for the effective operations of the state, as of systemic corruption, on the other, that implicates an entire bureaucratic hierarchy, electoral system, or governmental structure from top to bottom (Rose-Ackerman, 2013). In this instance, Rose-Ackerman (2013) defines *low-level corruption* as occurring within a framework where basic laws and regulations are in place, and officials and private individuals seize upon opportunities to benefit personally. Several generic situations qualify: first, scarce public benefit assigned to official discretion to assign to applicants with the highest willingness to pay and the fewest scruples; second, low-level officials with imperfectly monitored discretion to select only qualified applicants may collect bribes from qualified and unqualified, with incentives for payoffs depending on the ability of superiors to monitor allocations and on the options for the qualified, as in approaching another, potentially honest official; and third, the bureaucratic process itself may be a source of delay, creating incentives for corruption arise as applicants try to get to the head of the queue. Low-level corruption can lead to the inefficient and unfair distribution of scarce benefits, undermine the purposes of public programs, encourage officials to create red tape, increase the cost of doing business, and lower state legitimacy (Thompson, 2017; Coady, 2018; Ceva and Ferreti, 2019; Hellsten, 2019; Weale, 2019).

But I turn to the more foundational corrupt practice of rent-seeking because of its more deeply destructive impact on state functioning—bringing the state to the edge of outright failure and undermining its future. To cite but one example, this practice describes acquiring wealth through the unwarranted use of political power, rather than by generating wealth through productive activity. Such activity is the result of vague and restrictive laws, high tax and customs rates, and controls on domestic prices and foreign exchange that produce opportunities for private gain. It is especially likely when citizens do not view the state as legitimate or deserving of respect. Civil service systems that do not reward officials for honesty and competence also fuel rent-seeking networks (Hope and Chikulo, 2000: 4; Rose-Ackerman, 2013). Caiden summarizes that the availability of personal gain via public corruption recruits skilled personnel into an otherwise unattractive, unrewarding bureaucracy, motivates an otherwise lackadaisical administrative system into the timely actions necessary for economic development (Caiden, 1993: 3 cited in Bracking 2007: 10), and must be understood as opportunistic (rent-seeking) behavior that is related to the scope and extent of government regulation of private exchange (Hope and Chikulo, 2000: 6; Ceva and Ferretti, 2019; Hellsten, 2019).

Companies that lobby for subsidies, protections for trade and unregulated tax loopholes, and removal of barriers to competition increase their revenues through generating economic "rents" without enhancing the overall wealth or welfare of the society. Moreover, these activities handicap competitors who might have otherwise innovated better ways of doing things, and provided more social benefits at lower costs. Rent-seeking both redistributes wealth from the many to the wasteful and inefficient few, deterring new enterprises from entering the market offering better solutions to social problems; and serves as a powerful insulation for businesses from accountability, transparency, and competition. The proliferation of licensing requirements and other barriers to entry is one specific way for existing business interests to keep competition at bay (English, 2013:17) under the rationale of "protecting infant industrial capacity" and or the framing of "industrial policy." It follows from the need to carve out and append a myriad of benefits for special interests, often in ways that obscure who are the beneficiaries. Once a bill with an attractive title and political support gets going, additional supporters are brought on board by attaching clauses that benefit their donors, and existing supporters use the bill's momentum as an opportunity to append additional favors for their own donors (Hellsten, 2019).

Interestingly enough, this problem of special interests exploiting political power is also evident in the fraught area of "more legitimate" regulatory policy. Governments are rightly tasked with creating frameworks that enable markets to operate for the greatest good through the introduction of forms of external or internal commitments aimed at enhancing the domestic investment environment: fiscal rules, central bank independence, tariff bindings at the WTO, regional trade agreements, and IMF or World Bank conditionality. Or consider the establishment of free-trade zones (FTZs) where firms are allowed to operate under different fiscal regimes and less burdensome labor laws. Once again, the same logic inherent within the "vice" of rent-seeking ironically explains a wide range of legislation that has lined the pockets of a few at the expense of everyone else, while massive subsidies or loan guarantees for ill-conceived "green energy" projects destined for bankruptcy may now be considered effective as growth policies. This includes enforcing property rights and contracts through a judicial system, as well as crafting policies that address market failures such as negative externalities (pollution) or information asymmetries (insider trading) and the provision of multiple different concessions to economic winners. However well-intended might be the design of regulatory policies, they can be hijacked to serve the interests of the regulated in ways that harm rather than protect the public. Rather than inhibit this corrupt alliance between politicians and rent-seeking special interests, democratic institutions facilitate it. In an unsurprising move the civil service devolution and downsizing strategies that often result from marketization have not been as new public management logic suggests the panacea for reducing rent-seeking opportunities and instead have created a particular threat to the security and reproduction of elites (Szeftel, 2000, cited in Bracking, 2007: 11; Hellsten, 2019). Thus, rent seeking undermines the political process. Those who can reap the rewards have the greatest incentives to mobilize political resources through turning out campaign contributions (English, 2013: 20). When political power becomes a means to economic power, businesses will try to, and do, influence politics and the more some businesses choose to seek political favors, the more that all will have to, if only to defend themselves. The result is a system that comes to look more and more like a corrupt state, in which one must be politically connected to be economically successful. The more important point is the real danger of the next decade or so witnessing a resurgence of forms of industrial policies under different guises. One solution would be to take rents off the political bargaining table by developing a broad social commitment to limit government's ability to pick economic winners and losers. The aim would be to put the liberalism back in liberal democracy, disciplining the scope of politics with a more rigorous standard of the public interest and a broad deference to economic competition (Hellsten, 2019).

There are, however, serious difficulties to facilitating such changes. Every lobbying group concocts a reason why benefits to their clients promote the public interest and deconstructing these appeals, examining the weaknesses of their premises and their frequent misuse of statistics requires nuance and attention to detail. Such a call would require a massive ideological shift in public opinion, and in practice would run up against two problems of political judgment: Does the nation-state in question have the ability and available expertise to judiciously discern these challenges? Thus, the complexity of issues makes it difficult to prevent certain sorts of rent-seeking, as appropriate criteria of legitimacy are not obvious but rather need to be worked out (English, 2013; Thompson, 2017; Hellsten, 2019; Ceva and Ferretti, 2019).

Grandstanding as Corruption: Infeasible Obligations

Another form of endemic but often undiagnosed corruption is the perpetual attenuating circumstance of grandstanding, which morphs into the accumulation of insurmountable unsustainable national debts or infeasible obligations. Because it is less thought of as a form of endemic corruption, corrective measures are often not proposed as punitive but as par for the course in the management of any national economy. Agenda setting in public policy in democracies magnifies our human weakness for focusing on the immediate at the expense of the long term (English, 2013: 28; Hellsten, 2019). Democracies are ruled by the politics of appearance, and nothing is more important for a politician's career than the appearance of having "done something." This naturally inflates the rhetoric of political campaigns and leads politicians to promise and attempt more than the state is capable of, thus overloading the state as referenced in chapter 5, while neglecting helpful policies that might reduce politicians' power to claim credit or extract donations. Increasingly then, politicians make promises they cannot fulfil, pass laws they do not understand, take credit before it is due, and obfuscate their responsibility when policies fail (English, 2013: 24; Grindle, 2010; Hellsten,

2019). Grandstanding then, is one manifestation of this phenomenon, but the more serious structural problem that it introduces into democratic politics is the unsustainable accumulation of future liabilities in order to pay for present benefits. In short, it is the problem of unsustainable spending made possible by the issuance of debt.

Before examining this problem in detail, it is crucial to note that there is nothing wrong per se with debt, an essential and not inherently flawed tool of modern government. Debt makes economic sense when it finances investments that will yield returns greater than the costs of servicing the debt. Debt provides an invaluable means of insulating government expenditures from temporary economic shocks, particularly during recessions and at very low interest rate if managed well (English, 2013: 29). The most important economic reality currently defining regional politics, however, is that the greatest liabilities are not financing investments that yield higher returns, but supporting transfer payments guaranteed by entitlement programs like the provision of social services such as education and health care. The growth of the debt is also due in part, to stagnant or shrinking export revenues brought about by the removal of trade preferences under World Trade Organization rules (Girvan, 2015: 103; IMF, 2013; Rustomjee, 2017). In the absence of sustained economic growth, spending at these levels is unsustainable and, like all unsustainable trends, will come to an end.

The expansion of government benefits today with the promise to pay tomorrow is democratic in the fullest sense of the term, expressing widely shared preferences of the majority of citizens. However, contrary to the view of myopic voters and politicians, debt is not free money and the short-sighted psychology that gives rise to unsustainable spending must ultimately be called to account by the mathematics of a balance sheet. Debt is a future tax, to be collected either directly or via inflation or not repaid, with generally more dire consequences (English, 2013: 30). There is the real threat of many countries within the regional grouping being caught in a vicious spiral threatening their survival as viable economies, functional polities, and cohesive societies (Girvan, 2015: 103; IMF, 2013; Rustomjee, 2017).

A second problem that infeasible obligations pose for democratic politics is making negotiating out of fiscal crises extremely difficult (English, 2015). A noted regional policy advocate and scholar had warned that:

> You are not going to find the money domestically when the state is already heavily indebted. Neither can you borrow abroad commercially, for you are no longer credit-worthy. At the same time, concessional funding is hard to secure because most Caribbean countries are not among the world's poorest. When you can no longer service the debt, you have no recourse but to the IMF or invoking IMF styled programmes. That means budget cuts; further depletion of resources

to fight crime, build up your human and physical capital, and pay your teachers and policemen adequately. More professionals leave. You are into IMF trustee-ship. (Girvan, 2015:103)

Citizens who have come to expect certain benefits from the state therefore fight fiercely to keep them. The bargaining game involved in winding down expenditures is nasty, brutish, and long, with every constituency asking another to concede more, and veto multiple players such as trade unions who can threaten to block any final deal (Smikle, 1997; Alleyne, 2017a, 2017b, 2018; Ceva and Ferretti, 2019; Hellsten, 2019). Winding down unsustainable entitlement spending requires making moral distinctions between those in genuine need and those receiving excessive benefits. However, if there is an absent common ethical framework, and in the face of differing degrees of self-interest, it is difficult to find a popular consensus on prioritizing beneficiaries. That question is both contentious and complex and the difficult work of cutting benefits that people have come to expect is rarely done under the normal conditions of democratic politics, even when the problem is clear. Rather, these issues are addressed only when the fiscal balance sheet has reached crisis stage and bond markets take away the ability to finance expenditures through additional borrowing. This generally occurs during recessions, at which point the requisite austerity strikes a double blow to a country's economy. The problem is that, in addition to having facilitated such debts, democratic politics makes it exceedingly difficult to scale back spending in the manner necessary to avoid painful, fiscal crises. The democratic desire for expanded government benefits, coupled with the ability to postpone the true costs of such benefits, provides a recipe for unsustainable spending (English, 2013: 30).

Throughout the region, short-term political expediency driven by the pressures of competitive electoral systems has led to a vicious cycle of indebtedness. Dr Omar Davies, the former Finance Minister of Jamaica, said that:

(Our) $1.7-trillion debt indicates that we have been taking decisions which were not sustainable, and we were borrowing to meet those obligations . . . .To me, it is a personal embarrassment that there are issues which we should have seen or felt but, for whatever reason or little bad patch or tribalist thing, we can't make a move, or even in circumstances within our own party we can't make a move because we feel we goin' lose some votes, when we are taking positions which are not sustainable. (Blame Us and Let's Move on Says Davies, 2013 cited in Girvan 2015: 104)

Grandstanding also ultimately ratchets up state power through rent seeking, as policy planners continue to reward supporters with narrow benefits and write blank checks to agencies and prosecutors. Politicians promise more than they can deliver, and in their rush to appear to have done something, enact wasteful and unjust policies. Moreover, as with rent-seeking, complexity only makes the problem worse, as this expansion of power is characterized by a lack of rationality and responsibility. Also, and ironically, the dysfunctional bureaucracies created in the process can themselves become handmaidens of grandstanding. They are denounced for their capriciousness, and politicians can score points with constituents by personally "intervening" in the seemingly irrational decisions agencies ultimately make. The process of writing thoughtful, detailed, and comprehensive legislation is difficult, time-consuming, and contentious, so it is no surprise then that legislators pass vague laws that allow them to grandstand while leaving it to regulators or prosecutors to decide what is actually legal. In such circumstances, where it is difficult to evaluate individual contributions to policies, or the long-term consequences of those policies, it is difficult to hold politicians to account: the electoral cycle has changed the "blameless initiators." This further undermines the central features of transparency and accountability within a democracy, which was always that it would make those in power responsive to the public interest by allowing voters to remove malicious or incompetent public officials (English, 2013: 26; Hellsten, 2019). Passing the buck, avoiding individual responsibility, atrophying of individual moral agency, and scapegoating as seen in Textbox 1 becomes the norm and creates a dangerous lack of accountability that corrupts the practice of government. Not only should public policy makers balance out winners and losers in public policy so there would be no "permanent losers," they should also strike a balance between immediate, short-term "happiness" and future, long-term "happiness," between that of the present generation and that of future generations (Yung, 2016: 3). The epistemic challenges to making this feedback mechanism work are significant, within the time horizon of most election cycles.

As indicated earlier, neither the legal order, the formal structure of public authority, nor the political order, the political groups constituting the political authority, can be understood alone, and must be seen in relation to the value system and way of life of a society, and only in relation to all of the institutions and all of the groups which compose that society (Bluhm, 1978: 112). Likewise we neglect another form of encrypted corruption by not focusing on the cultures of "impunity," wrought on our societies by a history of development, which is among the causes and consequences of the endemic institutional corruption that must become a focus for the future (Crocker, 1999, 2002; De Greiff and Duthie, 2009 cited in Crocker, 2014: 250; Hellsten, 2019; Ceva and Ferretti, 2019). The best ways forward must include, as indicated in chapter 5 innovative efforts to understand and transform the causes of past wrongs. Inequalities of various kinds, especially inequalities of economic and political power, are often among the principal causes of past injustices; overcoming power imbalances is frequently indispensable in righting past wrongs and removing their causes. Individual, communal, and national agency can be used either to commit wrongs or—through citizen empowerment—to defend against and to reckon appropriately with them. It is within this context that the region can and should exercise its empowered agency to resist passivity, overcome those powers that maintain an unfair playing field, and find new ways to keep hope alive. Failure to do this will continue to result in the presence of quasi-authoritarian societies, as well as insufficiently democratic societies which become the nurturing ground for terrorist movements such as ISIS as the human rights of minorities (or majorities) frequently are violated. Reckoning with a society's past wrongs can and should be part of transitions to a more inclusive and deeper democracy (Crocker, 1999, 2002, 2008 cited in Crocker, 2014: 250). Embedded institutional corruption, with its culture of impunity, is a past and enduring wrong that transitional justice must combat through an ethical turn if there is to be any transition to a more just and democratic society (Freedom House, 2014, cited in Crocker, 2014: 250; Hellsten, 2019).

Yet there is the naïve suggestion that designing the "right" institutional arrangements whether through organizations or by implementing "integrity legislation" through constitutional change or, as in extreme extant cases in Ghana of commissioning firing squads for those found guilty of corruption is all one needs to curb the challenges of corruption and accountability en route to establishing democracy and by default good governance. The logical thought from this simplistic view is a policy emphasis on legislative fiat by which political office bearers and civil servants declare their interests and assets and society will be magically imbued with ethical principles. This mode of thinking is grounded in the first-best mindset which mimics institutional performance by, say, counting the number of days it takes to register a firm, or to settle a commercial dispute in courts in different countries—without no attention to the binding constraint or the potential interactions with institutional features elsewhere in the system. Often such advocates forget to reflect on the complexity of the idea of corruption and to ask whether such declarations serve the purpose to be addressed whether it be deviant official behavior, malfeasance, and misfeasance without asking the central question of to what extent do the ethical principles that govern political office and by extension society differ from those that govern moral life more generally (Hampshire, 1978; Thompson 1987; Robben, 1998; Ceva and Ferretti, 2019; Hellsten, 2019; Orr and Johnson, 2019; Weale, 2019). As one scholar has pointed out, normative statements about corruption require a point of view, a standard of "goodness," and a model of how corruption works in particular instances (Geingob, 2000: 5).

Reference to corruption presupposes the previous existence of something better which has degenerated now into something less desirable. This is not always necessarily the case as when we reflect on our development, very little in the past could serve as a useful barometer of incorrupt practices or good governance (Diescho, 2000: 36; Hellsten, 2019). Moreover, within societies where deep suspicions and distrust toward each other have been cultivated, does the declaration of one's interests and assets radically alter perceptions of corruption in the eyes of an electorate that generally believes that their gains have been stolen even though their gains have been hard earned? Further, does legislative fiat of integrity legislation or the application of Lord Nolan's principles[1] also apply to the business interests increasingly in alliance with public officials in public–private partnerships and able to extort incentives from policy makers in exchange for favorable decisions as seen in rent-seeking? Governance reforms have resulted in a significant influx of private sector philosophy, money, and indeed personnel into government service, manifested in the public sphere in the problem of "revolving doors"—individuals with what might be viewed as a contingent interest—encompassing several new risks to democracy. Taken together with the growing—and partly consequent—professionalization of politicians, and the advent of market-friendly management and organization in the public sector marked changes are suggested as the way in which government should function (Sutton and Bissessar, 2006; Sutton, 2008; Minto-Coy, 2016; Bissessar, 2016; Soverall, 2016; Hellsten, 2019; Thompson, 2017).

As with lobbying, the revolving door as an issue is not regulated within the region as par for the course. Those who serve special interests well while in public service often get rewarded with lucrative positions after public service. Some governments may be aware of the conflict of interest to which that gives rise, and may seek to mitigate the ethical issues which inevitably arise by insisting that those who leave government service must wait a period of time before entering into the employ of those where there might be a conflict of interest, or still yet, that they restrict the kinds of activities in which they engage. Other governments, including several within the Caribbean, will see this scenario as innocuous and so it is common practice throughout the region for former members of the national, regional, and international civil services to crisscross bureaucracies trading their advice within the context of "ensuring that the best advice is provided," because "the region lacks sufficient competently trained human resources in technical and other specialized expert areas" and as such calling on this cadre of personnel is mere service to the community. Certainly, without such rules (but even with them), it would be unethical to give such advice which favors those interests, without disclosing both the consequences for those groups and what might be viewed as the contingent interest of the advisor. To be sure, the firms or agencies [re]hiring these "devoted" public services claim that they do so not as a reward for past services but on the basis of demonstrated acumen while in public service. It should be obvious that it is virtually impossible to draw the line between the two (Stiglitz, 2000: 4; Bromell, 2010; English, 2013; Thompson, 2018, 2017).

The application of ethical principles may, for example, require public officials to disclose information about themselves that would violate their privacy if they were ordinary citizens; they may be prohibited from using their office for personal profit in ways that would be acceptable in private occupations: they may be held responsible for consequences over which they had little or no control, and for which they would be excused if they were in private life (Thompson, 2018: 3, 2017). In essence, laws by themselves cannot overcome the problem of corruption, neither is more legislation necessarily the way to improve implementation (Kung, 2012; Hellsten, 2019) and might shift corruption to a different level. Consider, for instance, that a person caught breaking the law, maybe arrested, charged, or convicted depending on the police, the prosecutor, and the judge. Do we then need structures to police the police, the prosecutor, and the judges? (Geingob, 2000: 7; Hodgkinson, 1996) This is only at the national level. We run the risk of focusing too much upon dramatic actions of a local political nature ferried by narrow political and sectional interests that attract the attention of the media. By doing so, we also forget that in a global environment of open economies with free flow of capital and global interlinkages, corruption does not recognize national boundaries and increasingly morphs into the formal economies, as indicated earlier, in the development of offshore financial centers which are the lifeblood in some instances of these economies. In these instances, where does responsibility lie? How is punishment apportioned? Is integrity legislation still valid in a political economy dominated by unaccountable privilege and excessive wealth enjoyed by an economic and political elite outside the purview of the formal institutions of state? One reason for the failure to counter this kind of corruption in some countries has been a lack of constraints on counteracting agencies charged with policing and enforcement of the laws and on the bureaucrats who work in those agencies (Geingob, 2000: 7; Hodgkinson, 1996; Johnston, 2006; Thompson, 2017; Coady, 2018; Ceva and Ferretti, 2019; Hellsten, 2019). More generally, though, no framework can provide an exhaustive set of good incentives for the future. What works in one corruption type may fail to work in another and may even result in more corruption since power constellations and corruption types vary significantly, and strategies to combat corruption must vary accordingly. To borrow a phrase from legal theory, all political institutions rest on "incomplete contracts" whose success requires that leaders and citizens uphold the spirit of an institution despite temptations to undermine it for personal gain. These temptations exist because there are always ambiguities in constitutions and laws that can be exploited. Laws with nice titles, but substance not thought through, grant unwarranted power to those who define and enforce them. The final arbiters of enforcement—prosecutors—face their own perverse incentives for professional advancement and careers are sometimes made not by discerning the spirit and legitimate purpose of a law, but by pursuing the maximum number of convictions that the letter of the law will allow. Prosecutors thus participate in their own form of grandstanding which further corrupts the ideal of a society governed by fair laws. On top of that, the spirit and legitimate purposes of institutions can themselves be contested, requiring legitimate exceptions to be made to otherwise clear rules (English, 2013: 13; Hodgkinson, 1996; Parsons, 1998; Coady, 2018; Toonen and Doorn, 2017; Ceva and Ferretti, 2019; Weale, 2019; Hellsten, 2019).

There is no doubt that formal institutions of coercion and accountability undergird the complex cultural equilibrium of good governance and therefore a commitment to an ethical turn must remain a *sine qua non* of successful modern societies. Citizens capable of productive self-governance are not simply born, but rather are the result of extensive moral cultivation wrought through civic education. The first step in any process of policy reform toward good governance must therefore be a sound understanding of the political economy context, particularly the rise of the distortionary practices. Problems that did not arise from a single decision are not easily solved by any single decision. Without a doubt, the expansion and creation of new bureaucracy(ies) will be needed to monitor the requirements of governance, a tall order in light of the increasing complexity of tasks governments are called upon to fulfill and honor both within the public and the private sectors further increasing their workloads as already indicated. Urgency and pressures of time as well as the delegation of responsibility will determine the level of priority of implementation, the Achilles heel of every political administration. Not to be forgotten, the ability to implement is affected by increased administrative costs, financial or otherwise, particularly for those struggling political administrations in any society already burdened by the stresses of delivering multiple public services. The cost-benefit arguments that dominate such issues leave the disputants hopelessly in disagreement. Acting ethically and being a role model under these circumstances represent a big challenge and inevitably the result is more compliance with tighter accountability mechanisms, and perhaps a preoccupation with toeing the line, which diverts attention from the practice of statecraft (Hicks, 2007: 13; Girardin, 2012; Toonen and Doorn, 2017; Grindle, 2010; Hellsten, 2019). Moreover the proclamation of more ethical policies does not guarantee nor act as a bulwark against further unethical conduct, particularly if the standards are set and assessed internally, leaving those on the "outside" no real basis on which to judge for themselves the merits or otherwise of a particular case. This not only raises the challenges associated with the conflict of interest, but also those of enforcement (Hicks, 2007: 13; Amunsden and Andrade, 2009; Demmke and Moilanen, 2011; Girardin, 2012; Toonen and Doorn, 2017; Coady, 2018; Orr and Johnson, 2019; Hellsten, 2019; Ceva and Ferretti, 2019).

As such there is the need to understand the more complex forms of governance, which are often contradictory in their demands and effects on the practices of good governance. As indicated in chapter 2, ethics then has a strong element of social responsibility (Geingob, 2000: 8; Crawford, 2004; Toonen and Doorn, 2017; Weale, 2019; Orr and Johnson, 2019; Souffrant, 2019). It remains one of the challenges to creating an environment conducive to preventing and combatting unethical conduct on the part of those who hold public office, particularly when they are buttressed by great institutional rigidities and by powerful special interests and their ideologies. Moreover, if we are to resist the corrupting processes of rent-seeking, grandstanding, and unsustainable spending, an ethical turn must assess the moral merit, effectiveness, and durability of different sorts of strategies in attacking and reducing corruption in the search for a new less individualistic ethic of the common good. This is why it is imperative to have a holistic and integrated approach that recognizes the importance of working toward reconciling and promoting ethical values. As referenced in chapter 2, an ethical evaluation as a cognitive framework enables the individual with the ability to understand and determine the rights of citizens and the duties of states with respect to the various forms of ethical dilemmas posed by governance. Public policy must therefore be inclusive of the citizen, the policy planner, and/or legislator elected to an ethically sensitive office, who can conscientiously grasp and appreciate the range of values that is at stake in a policy choice and employ a systematic method of ethical decision-making about identifying ways to improve laws, incentives, and institutions.

NOTE

1. Lord Nolan's principles seven principles promulgated in 1995 are: selflessness, integrity, objectivity, openness, accountability, honesty and leadership. Available at https://www.gov.uk/government/publications/the-7-principles-of-public-life/the-7-principles-of-public-life--2.

Chapter 7

The Paradox of Democracy

When Democracy Can Undermine Good Governance

Much of the discussion of the good governance agenda has underlined the emphasis on various forms of corruption, accountability, transparency, and participation and their impact on democracy. Despite these valuable insights into the trade-offs in values that can come with the incorporation of these concepts, there are dilemmas in the substructure of democracy that often surface and that are not directly addressed by them. Therefore, the issue of an ethical turn as a corrective approach to bad governance cannot be tackled without tackling its political roots, which often lie in the efficiency criteria of the liberal-democratic models in use in the region. It is simply that such an insistence on those criteria does not allow us to perceive the possibility that democratic forms are not enough in themselves, to ensure democratic substance.

This form of overconfidence lies at the root of the second widely shared belief, namely an enthusiastic but inchoate trust in "democracy." On the one hand, proponents widely assume that there is a "democratic answer" to every problem (and that it is the right answer!); but in practice it is seldom clear what this means (English, 2013: 14). We have come to understand democracy as a political system that supplies regular constitutional opportunities for changing the governing officials, as well as a mechanism for resolving social and political decision-making among conflicting interest groups that permits the largest possible popular participation. In large measure abstracted from the works of Joseph Schumpeter and Max Weber, this definition implies a number of specific conditions: (a) a "political formula," a system of beliefs, legitimizing the democratic system and specifying the institutions—parties, a free press, and so forth—which are legitimized, that is, accepted as proper by all; (b) one set of political leaders in office; and (c) one or more sets of leaders, out of office, who act as a legitimate opposition attempting to gain or regain office

(Lipset, 1959: 71; Bluhm, 1978; Dworkin, 2008). This array of forces cannot mean just voting because as referenced in chapters 5 and 6 there is always the question of how the rules of voting and what is voted on are decided. Moreover, the processes of bargaining, issue bundling, and compromise in legislatures admit to no clear-cut solutions (English, 2013: 15) because the general principles of democracy can be embodied differently, depending on the context. Thus, while democracy is the system in which "sovereign power lies with the people," the methods of its exercise can vary according to the specific social and economic system of development peculiar to each country. Those methods also tend to change depending on political, demographic, economic, and social change (Boutros Ghali, 2002). Further, there is a corpus of literature in political science that shows it is possible to arrive at situations in which whatever policy is proposed, a majority of people will always prefer something else, particularly if parameters are not clearly defined in policy design (Hodgkinson, 1996; Parsons, 1998; Crawford, 2004; Grindle, 2010; Kraft and Furlong, 2015; Orr and Johnson, 2019; Howard, 2019).

What we call democracy can be in fact a messy process of contradictions. Its main virtue is that it fosters public debate with a tendency toward making politicians responsive to popular concerns. However, "democracy" provides no magical decision algorithm that always guarantees good outcomes. By idealizing democracy we distract ourselves from the tough political decisions and trade-offs that have to be made and, as discussed in chapter 6 we are likely to lose sight of the values that must constrain democratic bargaining if it is to respect the rights and liberties of both minorities and majorities (English, 2013: 15; Dahl, 1983; Dahl et al., 2003; Crawford, 2004; Gasper, 2014; Dahl, 2006; 2015; Orr and Johnson, 2019; Potter et al., 2019). One of the central aims of this chapter therefore is to bring to light some of these inherent contradictions of democracy, though not to present a detailed examination of the historical record within since the relative degree or social content of democracy is not the real focus of this chapter.[1]

Some concerns over the structural characteristics necessary to a democratic political system do merit brief discussion. Indeed, they present some particular dangers. For instance, there is a demand for state accountability, but less so for accountability from businesses and citizens. There is a call for strengthening of property rights, but not for agrarian reform that would facilitate land redistribution to enable ownership of property. And there is failure to acknowledge that although desirable, pluralism without representation favors the most organized and powerful groups, eventually reinforcing the practice of elite capture. In practice, therefore, one must be wary of the Janus face of democracy and its institutional applications increasingly corrupted by vulnerabilities immanent to the democratic process (English, 2013; Margetts, 2010; Perri 6, 2010; Orr and Johnson, 2019).

First, in attempting to legitimize the democratization of our institutions by incorporating large elements of the population in safeguarding good governance, the success of the existing structures of authority can also, paradoxically, challenge the existing structures of authority. For instance, a university where teaching appointments are subject to approval by students may be a more democratic university but is not likely to be a better university if claims of expertise, seniority, experience, and special talents are undermined by the claims of democracy as a way of constituting authority and which, in the long run, will only serve to frustrate the purposes of those institutions (Huntingdon, 1975: 114; Przeworski, 1995). Likewise there is the profound contradiction implicit in simultaneous calls by some advocates for, on the one hand a completely libertarian polity and a highly emasculated executive authority and, on the other for the immediate solution of the economic and social problems of unemployment, and maldistribution of wealth and income. Such a call is prescient because it is a glaring illustration of "you cannot have your cake and eat it." Both experience and *a priori* reasoning would suggest that in developing countries a very rapid and thorough going attempt at transformation of economic and social structures is to a large extent inconsistent with the full maintenance of the well-known liberal democratic values and the emasculation of the power of the executive. The real problem in the Caribbean, as in a majority of developing countries, is to strike the right balance between the need for social discipline (benevolently and not repressively administered) in the interests of nation-building and development and the need to maintain to the fullest extent the classical political and civil freedoms of Western liberalism. Probably in the end a balance will be struck between the legitimate desire for participation and the need for social discipline and authority; between the healthy desire for rapid social and economic change and greater rationality in pursuing such change; and between verbal about the need for change and recognition of the need for organization and hard work. In addition, those in authority will give more weight to the opinions and views of dissenting minorities and will establish better channels of communication between themselves and the objects of authority (Demas, 1973: 59; Crawford, 2004; Grindle, 2010; Yung, 2016; Howard, 2019; Thunder, 2017).

The arenas where democratic procedures are appropriate must therefore be carefully considered, more so because another inherent contradiction of the democratic principle is brought into question. For its effective operation democracy usually requires some measure of apathy and non-involvement on the part of some individuals and groups lest the political system be overloaded with demands that extend its functions and undermine its authority. It begs the question therefore, how is more self-restraint on the part of all groups exercised for the good of all (Crozier, 1975: 114; Dahl, 1983; Dahl et al., 2003; Turner, 2003; Dahl, 2015). The contemporary challenge of cultural diversity, however, has raised the stakes and made easy solutions impossible. One of the most urgent and vexing issues on the democratic agenda at present, more than just the moral obligation to treat ethnic differences with fairness, is how to politically recognize explicit cultural groups. Communitarianism as the basis for ethnic plurality rejects melting pot homogeneity and replaces it with the politics of recognition, where due recognition is not just a courtesy we owe people, it is a vital human need. This foundational issue of the character of cultural identity must be resolved for cultural pluralism to come into its own. And so the region must come to grips with its ethnically balkanized past and grapple with the weighty issues as in what sense should the specific cultural features of different races, the physically disabled, or children publicly matter? Should not public institutions ensure only that democratic citizens share an equal right to political liberties and due process without regard to race, gender, or religion? The basic issue is whether democracies when major institutions fail to account for the identities of their members are discriminating against their citizens in an unethical manner (Taylor et al., 1994: 3 cited in Christians, 2005: 153 see also Minto-Coy, 2016; Daniel, 2016; Goede, 2016; Nunez, 2016; Granvorka, 2016; Gaskin, 2020), for beneath the rhetoric of participatory and representative democracy is a fundamental philosophical dispute that Taylor calls the "the politics of recognition." As he puts it, non-recognition or misrecognition can be a form of oppression, inflicting harm and imprisoning some in a false, distorted, and reduced mode of being (Taylor et al., 1994: 3 cited in Christians, 2005: 153) because democracy amplifies the limits and weaknesses of human nature, including our ignorance, short-sightedness, and partisan self-interest. Moreover, democracy empowers the organized, can be a vehicle of corruption if its characteristic dangers are not constrained by a moral commitment to rights, freedoms, and responsibilities that are not open to political bargaining. The ability to defend these commitments requires a certain level of factual knowledge among the population at large, something that must be continually cultivated as society evolves (English, 2013: 32; Howard, 2019; Hellsten, 2019).

Given this then, it seems clear there is a crucial element missing from a naïve functionalist justification of democracy as *sine qua non* for good governance. The intrinsic autonomy demanded of democracy must be more than a capacity for individual freedom, or even a capacity to "exercise civil and political rights"; it must be embedded within and informed and constrained by an ethical conscience expressed in commensurate values and accompanying unfettered practice. What is crucial then is "deep democratization"—not only electoral or constitutional democracy, but enabling and encouraging citizens to understand that the value of democracy includes its intrinsic importance in human life, its instrumental role in generating political incentives, and its constructive function in forming values (and in understanding the force and feasibility of claims of needs, rights, and duties). Those are immediate choices on which the case for democracy in the contemporary world depends (Sen, 1999a). Thus, to combat partiality and create a legitimate political order, we must build into the very institutional or structural logic of democratic practice a procedural optimism, and do as necessary in any case for democracy as a universal value meant to forge a substantive tie between individual affluence and the goals and incentives of democratic representatives and one in which all needs are expressed, understood, and addressed.

DIALOGUING OUR WAY THROUGH ETHICAL DILEMMAS

Developing the ethical convictions that lead people to do good even when it is costly is no doubt easier said than done. Contemporary liberal democracies are being defined, not by amorality, but by various partial moralities derived from sources as diverse as religion, family, sports, media, literature, philosophy, and the arts. We increasingly live in a technocratic age that views moral formation as contentious and unscientific, and is more inclined to see incentives as the primary means to shape behavior. Some liberal ethical convictions are widely and persuasively cultivated, while others that should follow are neglected. We take for granted that slavery is unconscionable; that women should be educated, allowed to vote, and not be beaten; and that diversities of lifestyle, opinion, and religious belief should be tolerated if they cause no grave harm. Underlying many of these convictions is the basic principle that there are moral limits to what one can demand from or do to others regardless of the benefits one might reap (English, 2013: 33; see also Biggar, 2010; Girardin, 2012; Thunder, 2017).

The ethical convictions at the heart of liberalism that appear reasonable, obvious, and natural as referenced in chapter 6, are historically anomalous and not shared in many corners of the globe today. Tempting as it is to see the civilizing process that produced these convictions as inevitable, history suggests their frightening contingency and malleability. Partisan debate, either conservative moralizing or technocratic optimism, often, and unfortunately, tends toward extremes. Many contemporary liberals are reluctant to affirm the importance of a common ethical framework, given toleration of diverse conceptions of good as a hallmark of classical liberalism. Yet they are mistaken to deny an underlying ethical core to liberalism: conservatives have underappreciated how substantial this core is and technocrats have grossly underestimated the extent to which our social institutions are grounded on behavior motivated by liberal convictions. Even, the term "liberal" has taken on many meanings, but really it indicates a respect for the liberty, tolerance, and equality of others, along with rights to fair treatment that reasonably follow. In the liberal empirical outlook the important issue is not what opinions are held, but how they are held: undogmatically, subject to modification by new evidence. Liberalism also holds that certain rights and liberties of person, property, and conscience are so fundamental they should not be subject to bargaining or sacrificed for utilitarian ends. Above all, liberalism demands that laws, regulations, and public expenditures be governed by strict criteria of public good, and condemns the use of political power for private gain. Although some consensus has been achieved, there are still extensive controversies about the details of such rights, subject to legitimate and ongoing debate (English, 2013: 33 see also, Lipset, 1960; Bluhm, 1978; Sandel, 1984; North et al., 2008, 2009; Biggar, 2010; Dahl et al., 2003; Crawford, 2004; Girardin, 2012; Dahl, 2015; Thunder, 2017; Weale, 2019; Orr and Johnson, 2019; Howard, 2019). And, as discussed previously, although these ideals evoke powerful notions of citizen empowerment, in practice policy makers often do not share the same interpretation of these concepts.

Participation, for example, generally refers to input by citizens into governmental processes, such as planning, designing, implementation, or policy that varies widely in type, duration, and intensity—and can be formal or informal, sporadic or continuous, limited or far-reaching, local or national. Participatory measures can be part of broader accountability efforts relating to public financial management and service delivery, forming an integral element of attempts by citizens to exercise some discipline over the state. The term is also used to describe broader consultations and public input into decision-making processes that remain firmly in the hands of governments or other stakeholders. These efforts are often directly linked to powerful claims that such participatory practices would advance capacity-building, local ownership, and citizen empowerment. But numerous critics have detailed how seemingly transformative concepts and approaches in reality often translate into superficial applications that fall short of their transformative aspirations, resulting instead in superficial forms of public consultation that offer no substantive input into development decisions, or change the balance of power between citizens and states (Carothers and Brechenmacher, 2014; Hodgkinson, 1996; Turner, 2003; Crawford, 2004; Grindle, 2010; Gasper, 2014; Schwenke, 2019; Potter et al., 2019).

From this variation in definitions and practices, very different policies can be carried out in the name of apparently common principles. At a more institutional level, a further question is prompted. Where different stakeholders in the governance debate have differing perspectives and aspirations for good governance, whose views will matter? Thus, in various ways, questions immediately arise as to whose and what kind of ethics should a society follow in [re]constructing and designing the institutional arrangements and in fostering an institutional environment to better govern society (Dworkin, 2008; Crawford, 2004; Thunder, 2017; van den Hoven, 2017; Howard, 2019; Weale, 2019; Lever and Poama, 2019; Orr and Johnson, 2019). These questions are even more relevant now in a world within which we are all connected via the Internet requiring that the traditional conceptions of morality, responsibility, and human agency be less restrictive and particularistic (van den Hoven, 2017: 27). This is because our actions are amplified and extended through global infrastructures, mechanisms of connectivity, and therefore have effects across time and place, connecting the fates of people across the world in a network of interdependencies (van den Hoven, 2017: 28). The quality of life of people at one place is a function of a network of institutions, infrastructures, and technologies. In a world with these characteristics it is very difficult to figure out where responsibilities lie, which regulations, governance schemes, and institutional frameworks are adequate, and which mix of economic incentives, education policies, and innovation strategies will help to bring about the desired collective behavior (van den Hoven, 2017: 11). Those who attempt to solve the problems soon feel overburdened by a range of conflicting value commitments and multiple constraints since their fundamental assumptions have become problematic (van den Hoven, 2017: 27).

The invocation of these dilemmas raises the unavoidable discussion of relativism, which must be addressed if we are to agree that an ethical narrative will offer a better medium through which good governance can be realized. As discussed in chapters 2 and 3 ethics is acknowledged as a discipline fraught with the situational or the relative because there is no universality or generalization of ideas. Often, its epistemic circularity[2] tends to suggest that ethics is somehow impossible and/or an implausible ideal to concede to if we wish to think of an ethical narrative as a new aperture for the study of governance. Thus its appeal would suggest from the outset and conform to earlier criticisms that ethics is a moot hypothesis or is at an end (Caputo, 2013). And, *prima facie*, this view of ethics, which lends to its immediate rejection by those who would suggest it is implausible to reason with ethics, is drawn increasingly from the dominance of imported ideas and in confluence with those of an evolving culture of relativism expressed in such statements as "What anyone believes is true for that person" (Wood, 2004; Blackburn, 2013; Gensler, 2018). Relativism has been, in its various guises, both one of the most popular and most reviled philosophical doctrines of our time. Defenders see it as a harbinger of tolerance and the only ethical and epistemic stance worthy of the open-minded and tolerant. Relativism, both philosophical and political, recognizes that only relative values are accessible to human knowledge and human will, and insists that no one individual or group has a monopoly of the knowledge of the absolute good. Hans Kelsen

(1948: 906–908) conceives of the two concepts of absolutism and relativism as fundamental in both philosophy and politics. Because relativism denies the possibility of absolute knowledge and values, it is tolerant; it upholds freedom of thought and speech and protects above all, the rights of minorities and opposition views. Thus there is a parallelism—both logically and historically—between philosophical relativism and democracy. In contrast, detractors such as Morris Ginsberg (1951: 4–5) dismiss it for its alleged incoherence and uncritical intellectual permissiveness for removing the problem of values from the sphere of reason leaving politics, like ethics, to be put to widely varying uses. For if moral judgments express nothing but individual or group desires or preferences, the content of morals will vary with the interpretation of these desires or preferences. If moral ends are not open to rational investigation, the function of reason becomes restricted to the issue of means: if reason cannot harmonize conflicting ends on a just and equitable basis, conflict and violence take its place and inevitably lay the foundation for the philosophical absolutism that buttresses totalitarianism and autocracy. Thus debates about relativism permeate the whole spectrum of philosophical subdisciplines. From ethics to epistemology, science to religion, political theory to ontology, theories of meaning and even in logic, philosophy has felt the need to respond to this heady and seemingly subversive idea (Baghramian and Carter, 2017; see also, Ginsberg, 1951; Brinkman, 1999; Chokr, 2007; Trigg, 2007; Dower, 2006, 2019; Gensler, 2018).

The appeal to relativism therefore becomes a threat to the use of an ethical approach to governance, particularly when we think of the implementation of standards of choice and conduct. Rather reductionist, relativism is the view that truth and falsity, right and wrong, standards of reasoning, and procedures of justification are products of differing conventions and frameworks of assessment, and that their authority is confined to the context giving to their rise. More precisely, "relativism" covers views which maintain that—at a high level of abstraction—at least some classes of things have the properties they have (e.g., beautiful, morally good, epistemically justified) not simpliciter but, only relative to a given framework of assessment (e.g., local cultural norms, individual standards), and correspondingly, that the truth of claims attributing these properties holds only once the relevant framework of assessment is specified or supplied. Relativists characteristically insist, furthermore, that if something is only relatively so, then there can be no framework-independent vantage point from which to establish whether the thing in question is so (Baghramian and Carter, 2017; Trigg, 2007; Gensler, 2018).

Likewise, a similar variant in cultural relativism looks beyond morals, ethics, and values and addresses judgments of time and space and volume, differences in perception and cognition, and conduct (Herskovits, 1973: 52, cited in Rosado, 1996). Its appeal commits one to the objective rightness of all the moral beliefs and practices that have ever existed, but in the context of a specific culture as it denies that there is any such thing as "absolute" truth. It also holds that all truth is relative to the person who believes it. One's attraction to relativism is also premised on the *en vogue* culture of political correctness because to many it expresses and supports the expected attitudes of open-mindedness and tolerance, and rejecting this fundamental commits one to arrogant dogmatism and narrow-mindedness (Kelsen, 1948; Ginsberg, 1951; Rosado, 1996; Gensler, 2018).

The direct psychological implication of this on the public sphere is that individual sentiments, affects, and interests are discounted. The problem with tolerance as a fail-safe default value to some insidious forms of relativism however, is that once no contentious philosophical issues are involved, it is as harmless as choosing between an Indian or Chinese restaurant (Trigg, 2007: 2). Through an appeal to multiculturalism, in recognition of different cultures with their varying practices and beliefs relativism can appear to offer a foundation for tolerance and respect. No culture, or set of beliefs is then allowed to set itself up as a judge on others and all cultures have to be respected and accepted equally. In other words, we do not live in one common world (Trigg, 2007: 2; Thunder, 2017; Gensler, 2018; Howard, 2019). These politically correct social conventions of convenience are beguiling in their simplistic notions of acceptance but quickly dissipate when relativism is held to the fire of divergent opinions that abhor tolerance, further exposing its inability to defend itself as a value of self-perpetuation (Turner, 2003). And so when difficult questions and situations present queries to our democracies on tolerating threats to peace within the state—whether these are ideational, cast as deviant subcultures, interests that reject the liberal rules of the game, can one person attack another for their personal habits, appearance, sexual predilections, or parentage—are the responses to such discussions appropriate, given the existence of competing conceptions of equity or of the common good or of human good? (Turner, 2003: 4; Trigg, 2007; Sandel, 1984) As unsettling as the thought may be, sadly but generally, there is self-removal from, or public silence on such discussions because of these contentious issues and inconvenient truths in the region. Why is this? In practical standard operating procedures it equates to the Lasswellian distributive and redistributive allocation of scarce resources within the state apparatus. Relativism then is called out for its universalist pretensions as it cannot demand that we ought to be tolerant, an appeal to a non-relative standard, and societies that are intolerant and prone to oppression of others, cannot be criticized, regardless of whether such action is right or wrong (Trigg, 2007; Turner, 2003; Gensler, 2018). Conceived in this way, tolerance then cannot be a *carte blanche* virtue to all manners and matters of difference. Neither should the idea be gullibly construed as instrumental for concretizing the often suspect liberal convictions in the pursuit by insidious dictatorial leaders or quasi-authoritarian states of a perceived utility for ideological diversity in order to suppress or express diverse sources of governance within that society (Thunder, 2017: 19; Gensler, 2018).

Since the opposite of "relative" is "absolute," the opposite of "relativism" should be "absolutism," a word that usually connotes "authoritarianism" or "dogmatism" (Wood, 2004: 27; see also Kelsen, 1948; Ginsberg, 1951). Besides this, relativism's appeal to the human condition tends to lend uncritical support to dominant cultural views and practices. Those who want to question or criticize traditional creeds and values at least have to admit that they might be wrong. But since relativism holds that everyone's belief is already true (for them), it implies that there is never really any need for anyone to change their views about anything. Cultural relativism also implies that on any moral question within a culture, an opinion is always necessarily wrong whenever it goes against the still widely held traditional beliefs. Those individuals who raise moral questions about accepted practices are always in the wrong, and any movement for moral reform within a culture, even if eventually successful, must have been in the wrong at the outset. It is therefore always absolutely wrong to try to reform any culture's accepted moral beliefs and practices (Rosado, 1996; Wood, 2004; Trigg, 2007; Anderson, 2009; Gensler, 2018).

It is within this context that these stubborn issues must be brought to the fore for discussion, recognizing that the moral problems that cultural relativism is trying to address are real ones. In most cultures ethical questions are the subject of debate and it is not always obvious what to do (or even think) when confronted by practices that offend our moral sense and contradict our deepest convictions. Some actions toward others are quite evidently the results of traditional superstitions and unjust distribution as was earlier referenced in chapters 5 and 6. On the other hand, actions often have different meanings within cultures, and we are quite aware that we lack the capacity to understand and evaluate the practices of those societies. If we do nothing in the face of evident moral evil, we completely forfeit our integrity; but if we act on the basis of convictions held from our admittedly incomplete perspective, then we run the risk of arrogantly setting ourselves up as infallible moral judges of people who may know more than we do about what is being judged (Wood, 2004: 25; Brinkman, 1999; Dreier, 2006; Mackie, 2013; Gensler, 2018; Hellsten, 2019; Schwenke, 2019; Howard, 2019).

The maturation of modernization in an age of globalization is seeing traditional cultures and inherent moral norms from other parts of the world becoming homogenized closer to modern Western culture in ways we approve. The big issue of gender equity remains particularly relevant, as does the continued advocacy for an end to discrimination against women and young girls in many societies of the developing world once given "justification" through an appeal to the arguments of "moral" and cultural relativism. Should we applaud this process as a moral victory in empowering women through education and ending discrimination or should we deplore and oppose these changes that amount to the evisceration of that culture's priceless heritage? (Serageldin, 1998) Moreover, how are we to determine what are the ethical beliefs of the prevailing culture? Does this require an overwhelming consensus among the culture's members, or is it a matter of simple majority vote? Or does cultural relativism imply that the longest surviving and ethnically traditional moral opinion is always the right one? The invocation of the idea of relativism is therefore popular because it is an easy intellectual defense mechanism to invoke. As an idea, it claims to have the answers to questions like what is justice, and has filled the gap left by the deterioration of faith in the truth of religion and the inability of science to provide quick and easy answers to the most pressing and the most difficult questions (Trigg, 2007; Gensler, 2018).

Scientific method has provided answers to some types of questions far more readily than to others. It can explain how to aim and fire a cannon with precision but not the much more difficult question of justifying the firing of the cannon. These abstract moral problems when is killing a human being justified were the issues that relativism sought to resolve (Anderson, 2009; see also Wood, 2004) readily providing the answer that whatever you believe is true for you irrespective of anyone else. In effect, relativism marginalizes everybody's standpoint except one's own. In relation to humbug, relativism tries to protect me from manipulation by my being cool, blocking the beliefs others are trying to impose on me against my knowledge and will by cutting me off from any pretense at serious communication with them. In relation to what I seriously believe, however, relativism also cuts me off from serious communication with others and thereby serves as a self-protective mechanism in another way (Wood, 2004; Dreier, 2006; Chokr, 2007; Trigg, 2007; Blackburn, 2013; Gensler, 2018).

Thus, when I begin a discussion on an issue I may suddenly discover powerful arguments and theories I never considered before, that challenge the opinions I have always taken for granted. This can be very disturbing, leading to a sense of insecurity. Because relativism is absolutely neutral, it comes to my rescue making my opinions all "true for me" enabling me to remain above the fray and taking the high ground away from those who lobby for their particular version of the absolute truth, revealing they have an axe to grind, a chip on their shoulder. A relativist never has to bother with the frustrating details of any philosophical dispute because relativism explains ahead of time why the dispute will never get resolved, and why my view is perfectly all right. One can agree that inquiry, reasoning, and argument, read expressivism,[3] are fine, if someone happens to feel like paying attention to them, but I can rest assured that they need never seriously threaten my own beliefs (which remain true for me however the arguments come out). In this way relativism will encourage the one kind of tolerance for which one has the most desperate need: tolerance toward my own intellectual cowardice, laziness, and incompetence. And when it protects me against all those whose powerful arguments might threaten my comfortable little world of convictions, relativism also makes me think I am tolerant toward others, since it releases me from the need to experience their alternative views as a threat to mine, and hence from the need to resist their arguments or to argue back (Wood, 2004: 35–36; Dreier, 2006; Blackburn, 2013; Gensler, 2018). It simply demands the acceptance of whatever standards people happen to have, and if they are intolerant and prone to the oppression of others, they cannot be criticized because relativism cannot discriminate between "good" and "bad" beliefs (Trigg, 2007: 2). I can just live and let live. Ironically, the very social complexities, mutabilities, and controversies that make relativism attractive also render it useless, unclear, and implausible as an account of ethical truth (Chokr, 2007; Ginsberg, 1951, 2018).

My concern in this book is not to rehearse the contextual nuanced debates on the pernicious influence of relativism and its meaning and application within the discipline of ethics. Critics may readily jettison the ethical turn as a probable justification when considering it as a guide toward enabling us to find answers to some of our most intractable governance issues. Such an attempt would lead to the search for an elusive perfect solution that would in reality lead to no agreement and hence no progress—though inevitably I have had to touch on some of the more controversial issues. Instead I am suggesting that there is a need to retain the idea of relativism and its various dimensions moral, situational, or cultural, within any ethical debate. As in governance/government where checks and balances are required for the effective and efficient democratic functioning as discussed in chapter 2, so too must the idea of relativism be retained for this purpose. As with Aristotle, there is a need to embrace a more transcendent form of principled relativism that recognizes the importance of "principles or maxims or general rules" that appeals to a higher truth about right or wrong and that are independent of what anyone may think or feel in illuminating decision making (Gensler, 2018: 205). But there must also must be a recognition that given the multiformity of empirical circumstance, no general rule is adequate for decision-making (Bluhm, 1978: 111; Crawford, 2004; Girardin, 2012; Howard, 2019; Weale, 2019).

One must constantly employ reason to fit the rule to the situation, in a prudential way, like Aristotle's man of "practical reason" (Bluhm, 1978: 111).[4] Here I want to discuss this view further to justify my initial idea for an ethical turn in governance. Much of the discussion of relativism and its variations are logically dichotomous based on the idea of the non-application or application of the universalization of values. Thus I am right and the other is wrong about something (see Baghramian and Carter, 2017, for a comprehensive overview). Further the problem of the use of relativism as an idea that is true in any discipline is that its presenters tend to view reality exclusively from its own narrow perspective. Failing this, one must endure tautologous dogmatism with the continuous use of normative vocabulary, and with the stipulation that it is to be understood as relativized to particular moral codes, under the pretense of having found a simple, general, tidy, and unambiguous answer to questions, and where any answer of that description is almost certainly wrong, falling easy prey to the fallacy of circularity (Blackburn, 2013; Caputo, 2013; Gensler, 2018). In yet other instances, the discussion is mere semantic and technocratic wrangling over the [in]appropriate use or not of adverbs and adjectives. Objective reality, science, metaphysical truth, and advocacy are confused, resulting in ludicrous if not self-indulgent argument, validating a *cause celebre* for nihilism (Ginsberg, 1951; Dreier, 2006; Boghossian, 2011; Gensler, 2018; Howard, 2019; Weale, 2019).

Part of the problem with relativism lies with the vexed charge of determining the focus of authority. The promotion of ideas and ideals of virtue, and ethical behavior and morality, was once bound up with the legacy of institutional religion the intertwining of particular institutions and the long shadow they still cast over society. As the monopolization of these institutions declines and changes in some quarters, what emerges is a vacuum of "qualified and certified" authority since "faith" unlike "science" is not public reason with publicly established rules of evidence that can command agreement. Science then gains a monopoly on reason and truth because it is thought able, at least in principle, to explain everything. Conversely, individuals can search for a meaning in their personal lives, which is seen as the province of religion. Religion then retains no function on the public stage, and can be simply tolerated as a private source of comfort (Trigg, 2007: 4; Turner, 2003).

One further response to this overall explanation of intractable moral diversity is that the truths in ethics are culture-bound and we should celebrate the diversity of pluralism. This might mean the mere existence of different beliefs alongside each other, but it can also mean that all beliefs have to be accepted equally, and none has a right to claim pre-eminence, to be treated as simply true. Diversity of belief is seen as something to be welcomed. What is true for one religion is not for another, which may seem obvious, and there is no asking who is right as there is no objective reality against which such beliefs can be measured. The problem is that such a statement appears to claim the same truth relativism often seems to, it is true that there is no truth, only what we believe (Trigg, 2007: 2; Acharya et al., 2018; Gensler, 2018; Howard, 2019). Who dares now to talk on such subjects with confidence?

I want to move beyond these forms of discussion and argue for relativism as a philosophical construct whose use as a basic premise within the discipline of ethics cannot be ignored, in spite of valid arguments highlighting its weaknesses. It implores us to constantly test our understanding of objective reality by framing hypotheses that can be examined experimentally with empirical data. In other instances, although a metaphysical value is not testable as a hypothesis with empirical data, whenever our understanding of objective reality is threatened by ethnocentric trends in values that force changes in life, invoking discussion of principled relativism can encourage thinking that tests our understanding of subjective reality—values—through questions to be widely examined with a view to reaching consensus, or close to (Sandel, 2006, 2010). Or, as Williamson emphasizes, one absolute value upon which the Christian, the scientist, and the citizen can unite is unconditional allegiance to the truth (Williamson, 1947). Without truth as an aim, all intellectual endeavor, and all belief, whether in religion, science, morality, or elsewhere, become pointless and there can be no progress, and no growth of knowledge, since no belief is better or worse than any other (Trigg, 2007).

As La Follete (1991) rightfully acknowledges we must recognize that there are ways in which ethical principles and behavior vary legitimately from culture to culture and from individual to individual. The challenge, however, is to maintain a dialogue that strives for a rational yet relativistic ethic that emphasizes the exercise of cultivated moral judgment rather than rote application of extant moral rules (see also Sterba, 2013; Gensler, 2019; Howard, 2019). In Jurgen Habermas's (1993: 66) terms, discourse in the public sphere must be oriented "toward mutual understanding" while allowing participants "the communicative freedom to take positions" on claims to final validity (see also Habermas, 1990, cited in Christians, 2005: 154). As stated in chapter 1, how to interpret and use information is a question of subjective value to be negotiated by society. And so, it bears repeating here in inquiring into the patterns of the empirical world, that an ethical turn will serve to ask what are the typical motives, goals, and values of people who are politically engaged. Are these values universal, or do they vary from culture to culture? If they vary, what are the influences, both physical and social, that condition them? It will also seek to describe and classify the political systems through which people pursue their goals—the main forms of government, and their typical functions, structures, and processes. In addition, it would ask how the behavior of individuals and groups differs in the various systems. An ethical perspective would seek to learn about the conditions that give rise to particular forms of government and to individual institutions. Such an approach would try to discover the causes of both evolutionary and revolutionary change by asking about the role of class structure, personality structure, economic organization, geography, climate, and historical experience that determine and alter the political system. Thus we may "learn the hard way" that some actions generate unacceptable consequences or we may reflect upon our own and others' "theories" or patterns of behavior and decide they are inconsistent. The resulting views are "tested"; we act as we think we should and evaluate the consequences of those actions on ourselves and on others thereby correcting our mistakes in light of the test of time (Lafollette, 1991: 154; Crawford, 2004; Norman, 2010; Margetts, 2010; Perri 6, 2010; Weale, 2019; Souffrant, 2019; Howard, 2019).

There is something to be said regarding the issue of time and its interaction with relativism, good governance, and the ethical turn that must also concern us. It is worth remembering that relative to a fairly recent past, the "Third Wave" of democratization of the 1990s has ushered in for many a new, more democratic dispensation. Grindle (2004) therefore advises us to think about the advantages of thinking in time because much of the research and advocacy that has contributed to the good governance agenda is ahistorical. She advises that in our haste to demand good governance and pursue its agenda we often forget that the practice of good governance emerged slowly and haltingly in today's developed countries and was often the work of generations. Undertaking more analysis of the emergence and consolidation of the ingredients of good governance, and the sequences in which they were undertaken can provide insightful clues into the sequences of changes that are essential, and those less so, and point to alternative paths to better performance by government.

She distinguishes her main idea from that of Ha-Joon Chang (2001 cited in Grindle, 2004: 531) who explored the development of different institutions of good governance and industrial development in the history of now developed countries. Ha-Joon Chang found that many factors currently considered pre-conditions for development, such as the demand for institutionalized democracies, professional bureaucracies, rules for corporate governance, modern financial institutions—particularly those of accountability and transparency—and extensive social welfare services were actually consequences and not the causes of development. Grindle's invoking of the factor of time in assessing the relevance of an institutional reform agenda as a signpost for the development of effective governance strategies is given gravitas by the works of Dani Rodrik and others (2003 cited in Grindle, 2004: 531) who argue that growth is often unleashed by a relatively few policy changes and that institutional innovations can follow rather than be a precondition to reform. Thus, as governments become more proficient at getting the institutions "right" through institutional development, their overall organizational capacity for more advanced features of governance improves. She cautions us, though, that while today's agenda need not be shaped by the historical emergence of institutions in now developed countries, or that some institutional innovation cannot be ignored in the development process, they still provide a platform for questioning the "essentialism" of current good governance reforms. As Chang (Grindle, 2004: 531) concludes, "Given that institutions are costly to establish and run, demanding [that developing countries] adopt institutions that are not strictly necessary can have serious opportunity cost implications . . . .Even when we agree that certain institutions are 'necessary,' we have to be careful in specifying their exact shapes" (see also Chang 2003, 2004). More so because, as indicated elsewhere, although current international conditions would suggest, or even force, developing countries to pursue best-practice approaches to government reform initiatives, the more general lesson is that all good things are not necessarily prerequisites to laudable goals such as growth and poverty reduction.

Consulting history can also provide insight into the time dimension of change and promote greater tolerance for less-than-ideal characteristics even in the midst of improvements over time. Most developing countries are young and under pressure to create conditions that took developed countries decades and even centuries to achieve. Fistfights, duels, and use of firearms were regular characteristics of the institutional development of the U.S. Congress well into the nineteenth century, spoils were a central fact of life in U.S. politics well into the twentieth century; a devastating civil war occurred long after the country was "stable"; and that its early experience was hedged about by compromises to hold the fledgling republic together, including tolerance for the morally obnoxious condition of slavery (Ellis, cited in Grindle, 2004: 533, 2010). This is certainly not meant to justify violence, spoils, civil war, or slavery, but to be a reminder that the consolidation of good governance can take a long time, even while economic growth occurs and poverty is reduced. Knowing more about the emergence of good governance over time can provide additional insight into cause and effect relationships, historical sequences that suggest ways to discriminate between the essential and the merely desirable, and between changes that can be instrumented in the short term and those that take longer to emerge and produce benefits. More generally, thinking in time can be important in distinguishing between being developed and getting developed (Grindle, 2004: 533, 2010).

Here my point is that moral and ethical concepts change and evolve as social life changes and as do the governance of public sector behaviors, legalism, equality, and democracy that are now being emphasized as the main principles to be incorporated into governance. These social values are influenced and shaped by a myriad of sources as Yung (2016: 5) highlights. One source of emerging social values rests in human psyche and physique, and what is essential for the continuing well-functioning of human society (as discussed above) tends to be universal since they are essential for human flourishing in any society. Without them human beings will not flourish and their society may disintegrate. Then there are social values that evolve from the social, economic, political, and technological conditions under which a particular society exists, which may be relative and vary with changing societal conditions. And so, as the societal conditions change, this category of social values also changes (Yung, 2016: 5; see also, Trusted, 1998; Sen, 1999a, 1999b; 2000; Grindle, 2010; Nausbaum, 2011; Mackie, 2013; Howard, 2019; Weale, 2019). Moreover, these practices and principles of public administration ethics were not always *en vogue* to determine the ideal of good governance, neither were their etymologies constant because cultures and societies are constantly interacting with values and ideas interpenetrating one another and constantly redefining meaning.

Furthermore, as discussed in chapters 3 through 6 global changes have brought new and complicated situations, and consequent challenges to the work of civil servants. Public work has become less regulated and more entrepreneurial. With the Internet revolutionizing communication, there is more obvious social value placed on instantaneity, simultaneity, and interactivity in major aspects of human and social life, such as human communication and social networking, ways of conducting business and education, and the way of viewing knowledge and information. These three categories of social values are not discrete but overlap, with blurred rather than clear-cut boundaries (Yung, 2016:5; Quinn, 2013; Broome, 2015; van den, Hoven, 2017; Howard, 2019). The high degrees of communication and information exchange, connectivity, interdependence, and international mobility facilitated by these socio-technical systems mean that issues of governance can no longer be relativized to the individual nation-state. The global nature of the problems such as corruption, financial crises, climate change, including issues of social justice require collective action on the part of governments and other organizations (van den Hoven, 2017:17; Crawford, 2004; Hellsten, 2019; Souffrant, 2019). These and many other changes mean that the duties and responsibilities of public servants will have to be re-defined to some degree in the future.

The above analysis of social values is in line with Wei's (2009 cited in Yung, 2016) distinction between "core social values" and "non-core social values." According to Wei (2009 cited in Yung, 2016:6), the "core social values" are those reflecting basic "social relations" that are and need to be "durably stable," thus preventing social disintegration. Wei's "core social values" correspond to categories (1) and (2) discussed above and thus tend to be universal, "independent of change of social relations," and "proactive, deeply affecting basic social relations" (Ibid.). The "non-core social values" are "reactive," (Ibid.) responding to change of social relations (which in turn rests on societal changes and circumstances), corresponding to category (3) discussed above which is relative in nature. Thus, social values may be universal or relative in nature, depending on the characteristics of the social value in question. Not only does time alter the definition of *ethical principles* but in so doing it can also alter the problem to be tackled and the policy response and options to be decided (Yung, 2016:6). At the societal level, there may be disagreements among members over the meaning and prioritization of conflicting values or over how a balance should be struck across values at odds with each other. With the passage of time and with changing societal conditions, such consensus or prioritization of conflicting values may vary in comparison with the past (Grindle, 2010; Margetts, 2010; Perri 6, 2010; Hellsten, 2019).

These are substantive values. Even if, as argued in chapter 2, we cannot provide an algorithmic explanation why some features are relevant or especially weighty, we should morally and rationally evaluate our actions and not just tailor moral principles to our own selfish interests (Lafollette, 1991). Rather, despite these limitations, the principle of universality of values should be retained because it properly emphasizes the need to reason about values and their application to governance (Lafollette, 1991; Serageldin, 1998; Trusted, 1998; Sen, 1999a; Crawford, 2004; Sandel, 2010; Lafollette, 2013; Howard, 2019; Weale, 2019; Souffrant, 2019). Faced with these challenges, the first possibility for dealing with relativism is simply to embrace it by recognizing that there is no solution, that relativism is true, and so conflict is endemic to life. The second possibility is to argue in hope of arriving at a moral consensus. Arnold Brecht (1959) has hypothesized for the inclusion of a procedural consensus, whose existence when discussing such social issues might be checked with the methods of social science research. In Freire's terms, the goal is conscientization, that is, a critical consciousness that directs the ongoing flow of praxis and reflection in everyday life. Research therefore is not the transmission of specialized data but, in style and content, a catalyst for critical consciousness (Christians, 2005: 156). If one finds through discussion and persuasion, ultimate values "open," one must work out a rubric for filling them in, for building or creating them, since they are not considered as given and discoverable. In this regard, one must decide whether variations in empirical circumstance affect obligations or the manner of applying obligatory rules. There is also the need to order political values in a hierarchy, and the need to work out principles for situations that involve value conflicts, in which to pursue one good involves the destruction of another. And so, one must at all times work within the limits set by psychological and physical "givens" of the empirical world with the hope that a consensus can be reached. Very often, the consensus represents the views of the majority of those concerned at a particular moment (Hodgkinson, 1996; Crawford, 2004; Margetts, 2010; Perri 6, 2010; Souffrant, 2019; Van den Hoven, 2017).

To further diffuse the intellectually problematic notion of ethical relativism Wiredu (1998, cited in Souffrant 2019: 151) determines that human society approximates a public good promoted and is nurtured by a fundamental principle without which human society would be intolerable. Wiredu (1998, cited in Souffrant 2019: 151) facilitates our understanding of such circumstances by applying the principle of sympathetic impartiality that something is a good act if the actor contemplates the value of its impact on others. This is so because people, though they are the product of culture, are beings with potential minds. These minds are realized through communication with other human beings capable of "reflective perception, abstraction, deduction, and induction," equipping them with such mental abilities regardless of their specific locations. This in turn enables them to share a common basic apprehension of their nature which permits them all to interact with their respective environments. As such, Wiredu (1998, cited in Souffrant 2019: 151) is convinced that all human societies practice the principle of sympathetic impartiality regardless of cultures and that they adapt the principle to the various local requirements. Human society then can be conceived as a public good promoted and nurtured by a fundamental principle without which it would be intolerable and that values such as honesty, truth, and the like, are universally constant in any culture. The changes at times noticed in their local expressions are variations in the meaning the concepts have for particular cultures but the appearance of alternative moralities is simply articulations of composites of universal morality in peculiar customs (Souffrant, 2019: 151). Successful communication therefore will depend on impartiality that becomes essential to the harmonization of human interests in the society while the sympathy is what the moral motivation evinces (Ujomo and Olatunji, 2015: 172). Obviously, this understanding of concepts, ideas, and symbols within our consciousness does not imply a ready application or instantiation. In some instances a "round-square" is well understood that is, substantively, but ostensibly lacks any application. In another impression, it may be the case that one grasps the criteria of application tacitly without being able to articulate it. These conceptual (that there be something) and epistemic (that something or other is true) universals support the position that there are universals and sympathetic impartiality motivates the universality that moral rules embody (Souffrant, 2019: 151; see also, Ujomo and Olatunji, 2015).

Finally, those who may still wish to exaggerate the idea of relativism in order to reject ethics in informing a new narrative in search of an epistemic and ontological application to good governance must also reject the academy of social sciences in their search for solutions to the causes of things. For each discipline, be it economics, sociology, political science, or geography has its area/s of relativism when understanding, evaluating, and recommending corrective policies to some aspect of society. As such, almost every ostensible "nonspatial" policy has spatially varying consequences and implications because development in human societies involves value-laden choices. Different ways of thinking about development bring greatly different outcomes requiring thinking openly, carefully, and fairly about the priorities and principles that guide these choices, which groups are favored, neglected, or sacrificed, even about the choices involved in the related ways of thinking (Hodgkinson, 1996; Crawford, 2004; Gasper, 2015; Weale, 2019; Howard, 2019).

Moreover, national (and indeed international and supranational) policies often reflect the economic and political power of specific socioeconomic groups and areas, resulting in policy outcomes tending to favor those groups and areas. In other cases, even where such hidden spatial biases are not present, national, international, and supranational policies often work to intensify geographical inequalities in economic development and social welfare by ignoring regional and local differences in socioeconomic structures and conditions (Martin, 2001). Combined with the study of real cases, no theory can therefore generate specific strategies, tactics, and skills to be used independently of specific contexts (i.e., for all times and places) (Foster, 1993: 125, cited in Martin, 2001: 204; Howard, 2019). In this instance, ethical theories and precepts are important not because they solve all moral dilemmas but because they help us notice salient features of moral problems and help us understand those problems in context. They help us see problems we had not seen, to understand problems we had not understood, and thereby empower us to make informed moral judgments which we could not have made without an appreciation of moral theories (Lafollette, 1991; Crawford, 2004; Girardin, 2012; Margetts, 2010; van den Hoven, 2017; Weale, 2019; Howard, 2019; Lever and Poama, 2019).

Some might argue that such language speaks to the heart, and not just the head. Chorusing with Stiglitz, one can support the view that decisions about public policies inevitably need to speak both to the heart and the head and that it is important to think deep and hard about the moral dimensions of our economic decisions. For instance, questions about the appropriate balance between markets and administrative regulation draw upon ideas of personal freedom and responsibility. In addition, one can, and indeed should, combine this kind of moral analysis with a hard-headed analysis of the consequences and risks associated with alternative policies. The lack of a moral demand to do so has all too often allowed ideology to have sway—an ideology that dishonestly claims more favorable and more certain benefits than the evidence would support, an ideology that suppresses meaningful democratic discussions of alternative courses of action and that ignores, or at least puts insufficient weight on the adverse consequences to the poor (Stiglitz, 2000: 16; Copson, 2010; Kung, 2012; Weale, 2019).

And so, if we understand ethics in this way it is incumbent on us not to surrender the intellectual independence it provokes. Neither does it mean that ethics becomes subservient or a threat to particular political interests under-mining their own integrity (self-refutation). What it does mean, is that for an ethical turn in governance to be persuasive it has to be relevant and practical. Above all, it has to be backed up by persuasive empirical investigation as well as clear and logical argument particularly with respect to the key issues in terms of which choices of ideas—social equity and inclusion, social justice, citizenship, democracy—should be judged and the ways in which "geog-raphy" and "place" matter for the conduct and content of policy discourse (Martin, 2001: 200; Caputo, 2013).

The essential duty of governance is to effectively and equitably implement and manage the social contract, as stated in chapter 2. To achieve this, it will be necessary to employ the usual mix of argument, intuition, and experience (Boghossian, 2011) in the ongoing dialectical investigation of the truth (Bell, 2014). As particularly referenced in chapter 6 and this one, the discussion requires reflection, and perhaps patience, with the process of reasoning as trade-offs between universalism and particularism, space and place, essential-ism and individualism or difference, the natural and the socially constructed, ethical thought and moral practice, and between is and ought (Smith, 1999: 275; see also Elsetain et al., 1998; Crawford, 2004; Berger, 2013). It may not be easy.

There are no ready-made principles. It would be dysfunctional for cultures to be so fully defined as to leave little room for maneuver, adaptation and growth, and no set of social rules can be totally clear and able to handle all new situations. The need for new interpretations will arise, and these will be debatable. This contributes to heterogeneity. The idea of monolithic, given cultures, fixed beyond the reach of reason, is partly a legacy of colonialism, which downplayed the role of reasoned debate in Southern/"other" cultures. Cultures are fluid—not fixed and always evolving especially in the modern era. In sum, an ethical turn is not straightforwardly given from intuitions or community codes (Gasper, 2006: 5).

Importantly then there will also be the need to avoid the "antinomian" approach to ethical situations entering into the decision-making situation armed with no principles or maxims whatever, relying in every "existential moment" or "unique" situation, upon the situation itself, there and then, to provide its ethical solution. The antinomian either becomes a libertine, or a "Gnostic"—one who claims a special insight into situations, a super-conscience (Brecht, 1959 cited in Bluhm, 1978: 111).To mitigate such a circumstance we must identify good enough estimations, not play with phi-losophy for philosophy's sake; and we have to deal with the limitations of any system of ideas when applied, and usually to negotiate and compromise with other idea-systems (Gasper, 2015: 15). For the one thing that every theory of well-being agrees on is that suffering is undesirable (Phillips 2006, in Gasper,

2015; Kung, 2012). This may take the form of rational debate characterized by a strong belief in the power of reason to resolve moral differences, recognizing that in a democracy values are always open to negotiation and (re) interpretation of their nature and meaning (Mackie, 2013; Bell, 2014).

The emphasis on increasing rationality in development analysis and decision making does not imply a completely harmonious technocratic style of development. Choice will always be a political process; debate and conflict over choices have a legitimate place in any acceptable style of development. In addition, policy choice and public policy advocacy is a form of contest among political parties and social movements linked in politically competing ideologies—liberal, libertarian, conservative, social democrat, environmental, feminist, socialist, and so on, ideologies understood as webs of belief linking goals, instruments, and conceptions of social and political order through which individuals and groups construct an understanding of the political and policy world combined with claims about how to act given that understanding (Weale, 2019: 52; Schwenke, 2019). The outcome may be a coherent style imposed by a single dominant group, or a semi-coherent style emerging from compromise among groups with basically compatible objectives, or even an impasse where no group is able to dominate and the positions are too far apart for a developmentally viable compromise (Yeh, 1989: 70).What is non-negotiable is participation of the oppressed in direct cultural formation. If an important social issue needs resolution, the marginalized groups must be active participants (Freire, 1970). In any event, globalization extends radically to all citizens of this planet the possibility to construct their individual cultural identities through voluntary action, according to their preferences and intimate motivations. Now, citizens are not always obligated, as in the past and in many places in the present, to respect an identity that traps them in a concentration camp from which there is no escape—the identity that is imposed on them through the language, nation, church, and customs of the place where they were born (Vargas-Llosa cited in McCloskey, 2007: 4; see also Kung, 1998, 2009, 2012).

There are extensive controversies about the details of such rights as liberty, autonomy, and equality of others, and rights of person, property, and fair treatment that reasonably follow but it is noteworthy how much consensus has been achieved. Within this context, it is no longer necessary to decide whether we should support a local value ("custom") that is abhorrent to us or the dominant ideology. Rather, a primary objective must be to move beyond cultural relativism or a faulty form of situationism that relies on "doctrinaire by-the-book theory" or the "ethical code" solution to problems of corruption in society and government as too confining and narrow (Bluhm, 1978: 112; Ceva and Ferretti, 2019; Hellsten, 2019), toward building global consensus on values in areas that affect sustainability, either positively or negatively, and tolerance for cultural diversity in areas that seem not to affect it. In other words, local context matters in the formation and practice of policy and we need critical ways of thinking about how ecological, economic, social, cultural, and political conditions get produced, and of evaluating the justice and injustice of those differences. Thus, we must demonstrate the crucial "difference that place makes" in the construction, implementation, and impact of policy (Martin, 2001: 203; Kung, 2012) and educate both ourselves and those currently in power, while informing and empowering the marginalized in making decisions for a sustainable future.

In this chapter and in chapter 6, an emphasis was placed on addressing the conceptual dilemmas in considering an ethical turn in governance. The concern here is that in the introduction and application of ethical codes to these issues we must be mindful that their public discussions does not tend toward homogenization and generalization of rules, categories, policies, or procedures in a copy-and-paste approach (best-practice is the euphemism) leading to conflict of ideas (Girardin, 2012; Carothers and Brechenmacher, 2014; Ceva and Ferretti, 2019; Hellsten, 2019; Howard, 2019). Reformers when designing specific interventions need to be aware of the functional dependencies and organizational linkages among the components of an ethical infrastructure, particularly because there remain unanswered questions about which institutions matter most and which kinds of interventions are most likely to promote development in individual countries and regions (Hodgkinson, 1996; Grindle, 2004; van den Hoven, 2017; Weale, 2019; Orr and Johnson, 2019; Lever and Poama, 2019).

And so, although values held by a society may change with time, the pace of change might be quite slow. The values that are quite resilient to change will limit the choice of policy solutions to problems, very often making only incremental policy changes politically feasible. This is what is called "path dependency" in public policy and refers to the phenomenon that past policy, resting on past societal values, makes certain "competing policy options unattractive because of high potential political or economic costs" (Peters and Pierre 2006: 7 cited in Yung, 2016: 10). On the other hand, unchanged or only slightly changed societal values give rise to inertia, involving high political cost in the form of strong opposition to radical policy changes. From these arises the trend that past policy limits the pace, nature, and scope of future changes, with societal values and their comparatively slow pace of change serving as its backdrop.

The actual operationalization of social values into public policy allows variations that may be an issue of disagreement (Yung, 2016: 10; see also Peacock, 1998). It therefore begs the question of the need for "good enough governance" rather than unrealistic expectations of maximum governance that is the implied mantra of so many advocates for governmental reform

(Levy, 2014). "Good enough governance," as a concept, suggests that not all governance deficits need to (or can) be tackled at once, and that institution- and capacity-building are products of time and that governance achievements can also be reversed. Good enough governance means that interventions thought to contribute to economic and political development need to be assessed in the light of historical evidence sequence, and timing, questioned, prioritized, and made relevant to the conditions of individual countries and selected carefully for their contributions to particular ends such as poverty reduction and democracy (Levy, 2014).

Good enough governance directs our attention to considerations of the minimal conditions of governance necessary for development and has provided a platform for questioning the long list of institutional changes and capacity-building initiatives currently deemed important for development (Grindle, 2011: 200). As stated this is beset by ambiguities, challenges, and the potential for failure. However, it is one promising way of addressing these circumstances because it will depend strongly on the need for greater realism regarding the types of reforms achievable in a given country context, tackling only the most crucial blockages to socioeconomic progress rather than attempting to achieve the standard templates or reform sequences that result in unrealistic governance expectations (Levy, 2014). These templates have emerged and have been expanded based on the research, experience, and advocacy of international financial institutions, multilateral and bilateral donors, and international nongovernmental organizations. All of these have demanded simultaneous commitment to democratic government, universal human rights, sustainable development, empowerment of the poor, free trade, participatory development, and other "desirable" conditions (Grindle, 2004: 527). Assessing the historical experiences of developing countries that have achieved good enough governance can also help sort out changes that are essential from those that are less so and the factors that contributed to decent conditions of governance. From yet another perspective, what governance imperfections were tolerated—or were even instrumental? (Grindle, 2004: 533, 2010) A conceptual agenda must therefore recognize different political and institutional pathways that can lead countries to sustainable development by proponents for an ethical turn deepening their conceptual understanding across all parts of the society.

NOTES

1. The very idea of democracy has been fraught with philosophical and political controversy about its nature and value from its initial *Anthenian* conceptualization to the present day and so carries no singular unified definition. Although authors and

organizations may at times agree in their general normative positions about what democracy is, and/or ought to be, they more often than not vary on the exact implications that these positions have for the implementation of public policies. Controversy also surrounds the substantive variations across distinct policy areas and issues, even in cases where those areas and issues are contiguous or otherwise connected. This absence of a unifying view of democracy can also be accredited to a natural consequence of what Rawls calls the "burdens of judgment" (Rawls 1996: 54). This is an expression meant to capture the difficulties society confronts in prioritising competing moral values and principles, the hard selection and weighing of complex evidential matters, or decisions about the least implausible instantiations of vague normative concepts.

2. An epistemically circular argument defends the plausibility that there is no way to know or to be justified in believing that our basic sources of belief—such as perception, introspection, intuitive reason, memory and reasoning—are reliable except by relying on the premises that are themselves based on the source.

3. The tradition of expressivism holds that the key to ethics lies in the practical stances that we need to take up, to express, and to discuss and negotiate. It also emphasises that ethics is fundamentally about practice and the choices and actions made and taken. Our ethic is shown in our cluster of dispositions to encourage and to discourage choices, characters and feelings. A sincere moral opinion is the expression of one of these dispositions. Because practice is so important, these dispositions need discussion, to be queried, and sometimes qualified and replaced (Blackburn, 2013:44)

4. Two types of "reason" are distinguished in the Aristotelian tradition, while Plato had spoken only of one. There is the reason that "contemplates the kinds of things whose originative causes are invariable" and there is the reason that regards "variable things." Contemplation is the higher, of the two activities, because it is the activity of pure reason. The objects of the contemplative reason comprise what we would today call the objects of scientific, mathematical, and metaphysical inquiry. It is a self-sufficient activity, because reason is a divine thing, because its objects are the best knowable objects, and because its pleasures are the purest and most enduring. Its purpose can be achieved in perfect isolation, apart from all human society. The end of the contemplative reason is understanding only, theory. In contrast, practical reason is moral action, the good for man. Practical reason works out broad criteria of moral choice lying in a mean . . . determined by a rational principle, and guides the particular choices of the moral agent. The object of this exegesis is moral virtue, which is a "state of character" concerned with choice, involves our whole composite nature, the passions as well as reason. It is the excellence of that which is specifically human in us. Practical wisdom is a true and reasoned state of capacity to act with regard to the things that are good or bad for man. Thus the rational activity of man will have two kinds of excellence, intellectual and moral excellence and requires society for its development (Schlick, 1939; Kelsen, 1948; Bluhm, 1978; Bostock, 2003).

Chapter 8

Conclusion

Governing without Government?

I return briefly to issues raised earlier in this research. The successful attainment of a more acceptable pace of governance and development calls for wider conception of the governance process as an interrelated system of societal change in a complex of forces. Consolidating and sustaining democracy is not a mechanistic process of simply designing the "right" constitution or installing elites committed to democratic norms. It must also reflect on systemic problems that necessitate examination of the entire system (Lederach, 1997: 26). At this juncture it is important that citizens of our democracies [re]examine their basic premises and their *modus operandi*, a process that can contribute to promoting the central purposes of democratic government. I have sought to develop an interpretation of the current era that challenges the usual views of the crisis of governance and to justify with this research the need for an ethical turn in good governance. Before exploring some of the central points of the discussion, the book started with defining the context for the rationalization of such an academic turn, which is that the Caribbean, like other developing regions, is again in a situation of crisis of governance. This has been precipitated by modernization with its ongoing institutional processes that have evolved out of complex forces of political intervention, cultural development, technological innovation, and path-dependence at multiple spatial levels. This is a fact and cannot be wished away.

Although the particulars may vary from place to place, the broad issues described here are generally applicable to the region because of the involved relationships that lie deep at the heart of a common trajectory of development. These changes are even more profound in societies still grappling with poverty, inequality, and the onslaught of social values often determined by external forces that decisively affect the everyday life of citizens, and ultimately the governance of these societies. Compositely therefore, there has been a

223

general societal disruption with inconsistencies that cannot be easily worked out and tensions that will not be quickly resolved. This tension between what has been and what will be is at the root of the ethical dilemmas we have discussed. Nor is there any real hope that tomorrow will bring a sudden halt to the process that has been amplified by the globalization of information and communication technology.

My argument is that Caribbean scholars and policy makers have sought to prevent impending crises of governance through solutions from mainstream social sciences, without recognizing serious shortcomings in the analysis, and corrective measures these disciplines propose. There has generally been a tendency to ignore or obfuscate the need for building conceptual bridges to an ethical factor in dialogue on governance. Again, my argument is that ethics may be alluded to, though often not taken seriously, neither is it explicitly developed. There has never been a clarion call for the institutionalization of ethical policies nor for initiating a serious public discourse on ethics. Thus, I have emphasized the need for discussion by showing, through the constant shifts in politics, economics, and social life, that modernization in its various forms including colonialism as a form of modernization, has continued to unleash the contradictory forces of modernity on our societies, undermining the familiar structures of governance and creating significant and recurring crises for the liberal democratic state.

I have also argued that modernization has not only placed the organizational structures under severe strain but by introducing new strains of intellectualism focusing on the marketization, consumerization, and managerialism of the state, it has put pressure on the social norms and democratic principles, essential to the success of democratic institutions. Moreover, it is imparting new qualities to governmental institutions, civil society, and economic relations and threatening to reduce all to the "cash nexus" and a near universal disaffection with democracy. I contend therefore that we are finding that the quality of social capital which should transmute into the renewal of the good society is neither reflected in public policies conducive to effective democratic government nor is it expended in the daily interactions of individual citizens. Moreover, delinking one challenge from the other and its local impact from the global is futile. Each is a trigger for the other because of the dissipative, open-ended structures that define the ecosystem of governance. The corollary to this is that it has left society after society with premonitions of a dark future if not addressed. As a consequence, in thinking of renewing governance we must shift the nature of the discussion from the mechanical causal sense to the comprehensive, understood to involve considerable indeterminacy, uncertainty, and multi-causality.

The importance of ethics is also a direct answer to new challenges and complexities posed by the crisis in governance. Hard questions must be asked and answered on what our conceptualization and reality of governance entail. *Governance* presumably refers to the ability of governments to give effective direction to the economies, societies, and political communities. But, could it also be argued that a traditional characteristic of democracies is that we do not ask governments to direct economies, societies, and political communities, at least not to the extent that non-democratic societies do? Might it then be argued that to raise the question of governability in relation to democracies is to ask whether the power of government should be increased, rather than restored? Is it not misleading to imply that governments in past democracies had those powers which are now demanded for them? Should we not occasionally remember that one purpose of democracy is to enable people to operate in what might be called a market environment rather than an environment largely determined by directives from government and political institutions? (Dahrendorf, 1975: 188)

Good governance, like the democratic project, is not an event. No single nation can claim to have perfected good governance. All nations, either through their own institutions and laws, or jointly through international bodies such as the United Nations and other regional organizations, strive to bring about the better world that guarantees all citizens good living. Good governance is an ideal sought after as a nation meanders through history, claiming both successes and failures with the experience stretching beyond individual contribution. It is indeed a cathedral perpetually under construction (Diescho, 2000: 39). The fundamental point to be grasped is that Caribbean political independence can be justified only if used to create something new—a better society with an identity of its own. If we do not use our independence for this, we will have changed our status from outposts of the British Political Empire to outposts of the North American Economic Empire. There is no reason why other developing countries could not adapt "The West Indian Way" or "The West Indian Model" to their own situation. For this the new Caribbean society must rest on an indigenous and not an imported ideological basis. If we are to create a distinctive society in the Caribbean, we must formulate the intellectual and moral bases of this society in the light of our own situation, our history, and our own possibilities and aspirations. Caribbean society must look inward for ideological inspiration devising ways to reduce the negative metropolitan impact and turn the opportunities from metropolitan contact to its advantage (Demas, 1970: 5, 1973).

New problems will demand new perspectives, new mental assumptions about the underlying fundamentals of life. A new sense of urgency will be needed, for one of the crippling handicaps of West Indian life has been the deceptive sense of security engendered by colonial rule. The real problem of independence is whether the West Indian society can respond creatively to that challenge or if it will react negatively, seeking in typical colonial fashion to find alibis for inaction, or even to deliberately evade responsibility. Equally, a new sense of personal responsibility, of personal involvement, must grow up, for much of what passes for a new national spirit is frequently a sterile anti-colonial prejudice (Lewis, 1968: 388–389). In other words, the region must be cautiously selective in its contacts with the metropolis—no less in economics, than in ideology, culture, and values (Demas, 1970: 5, 1973; Girvan, 2011, 2015).

Seen in this light, an ethical turn in governance is not just about the inquiry into the nature of morality and its foundation, particularly the way in which human conduct is ordered, guided, and appraised, in order to live together in well-functioning societies. It is also a distinctive way of thinking about the economy and its evolution and about particular institutions and their role in shaping and regulating the socially, politically, and legally instituted forms of governance. A crucial question in sustained and sustainable growth and development is how can a governance system remain relevant and effective, continually changing, innovating, and adapting to new and emerging needs in the ever-evolving environment of an era of rapid globalization and technological change (Crawford, 2004; Neo and Chen, 2007; Frost, 2012; Thunder, 2017; von den Hoven, 2017; Orr and Johnson, 2019). The rise of this new form of governance could perhaps facilitate an increasing collective wisdom that will summon up a common will for self-organizing, toward governing without government (Rhodes, 1996; Landes, 2000; Fairbanks, 2000; Lindsay, 2000, Harrison, 2000; Grindle, 2004; Crudas and Rutherford, 2010; Berger, 2013). In this context, an ethical turn could see governing structures authoritatively allocating resources and exercising control and coordination in public policymaking. Our challenge now is to refine this thinking and to chart a practical path between the reality of our political economic system and the principles we strive to uphold, upon which our long-term prosperity undoubtedly depends. We must be continually deliberating the fine details of human good, revisiting decisions and reconsidering what seemed to be indisputable conclusions. And so the prescription of means to a given end ought to be carried on with an awareness of how the many ends of man are related to one another. Otherwise we will lose that larger good we seek (Lovin, 2014: 12; Orr and Johnson, 2019; Johnson, 2019).

In the final analysis, the call for an ethical turn to enhance the benefits of governance is no utopian ideal. It is easy to argue that since ethics throws seemingly abstract and contradictory issues to the fore, it is unequally suited to provide any more guidance than the other social sciences. And of course, such views and their solutions can be legitimately debated. This being said however, I have no intention here of settling questions with definitive and dogmatic replies. Rather, this research recognizes this complexity and has argued it is a question of putting forth points of view that stimulate individual thinking toward collective debate. A serious communication effort is needed around the idea of ethics. The crisis of conventional social science thinking has opened up an opportunity—in the search for a broader and more integral view of governance—for the incorporation of an ethical dimension as an important contribution that can affect the practical aspects of and inspire some change in the fight against poverty, and for the development of social integration, the strengthening of values in the fields of community action, solidarity and participation, and more (Singer, 2012; Howard, 2019; Orr and Johnson, 2019). This will involve changing attitudes, habits, and virtues while reforming institutions and systems within the society (Landes, 2000; Fairbanks, 2000; Lindsay, 2000; Harrison, 2000; Hofstede, 2012).

In these discussions we therefore need to ask ourselves questions such as how do we want to live and in what kind of society; what is the role of social values in public policymaking in our democracy? Is it sufficient to say that we have no control over technology; that government costs too much; that government is not doing enough so let's change it? These questions provide a conduit through which we begin to think about ethics and will help inform further discussions. And so, I return to ethics as I end. If some do not take ethics seriously, it is an indictment of them, not ethics; like conscience, the more it is demeaned, the more it protrudes (Bowman, 1996).

Appendix I

Table A.1   Compendium of Definitions of *Governance* and *Good Governance*

What is Governance?	What is Good Governance?
Governance is the exercise of economic, political, and administrative authority to manage a country's affairs at all levels. It comprises the mechanisms, processes, and institutions through which citizens and groups articulate their interests, exercise their legal rights, meet their obligations, and mediate their differences (UNDP, 1997:X;1998; 2006; 2012; 2016).	The UNDP over the years has identified eight core values and principles of democratic governance that are important means of achieving and maintaining development goals. These are: participation; equity, non-discrimination and inclusiveness; gender equality; rules-based; transparency; and accountability and responsiveness. They are congruent with key human rights principles set out in a variety of United Nations declarations (UNDP, 2011:279).
The term *governance* implies the existence of a political process. "Governance" involves building consensus, or obtaining the consent or acquiescence necessary to carry out a program, in an arena where many different interests are at play. The wide applicability of the term has been used routinely over the course of many centuries to refer to the exercise of authority within a given sphere. It has often been employed as a synonym for the efficient management of a broad range of organizations and activities from the most local to the supranational. Considering problems of "governance" is relevant in strengthening civic cultures, promoting voluntary action, and thus improving the societal bases for democracy. It is also increasingly important in considering how the international community can construct the institutions required to promote order and justice in the context of globalization (Hewitt de Alcantara, 1998:105–106).	Processes through which there is incorporation of more creative and less technical understanding of reform, more dialogue about institutional and programmatic change, more concern with the public sphere (state and civil society) and how to strengthen it, more integration of economic policy and institutional reform, more attention to both national and international factors that affect governance (Hewitt de Alcantara,1998:112–113).

A state which understands the connection between economic and social policy and promotes both human development and the conditions that encourage economic growth. The kinds of policies governments adopt, and whose interests those policies serve, are also critical factors. Politics must therefore determine whether governments rule for the public good and importantly the state must determine the effective and efficient allocation of scarce resources between competing interests including those of poor people. Importantly also is that human rights conventions affirm that all people are entitled to participate in government, either directly or through freely chosen representatives and these rights must be accompanied and supported by the fundamental freedoms of speech and association, and equal and universal suffrage in periodic and genuine elections (DFID, 2001:11; 2011).	Seven key governance capabilities: to operate political systems that provide opportunities for all people; to influence government policy and practice; to provide macroeconomic stability; to promote the growth necessary to reduce poverty; to implement pro-poor policy; to guarantee the equitable and universal provision of effective basic services; to ensure personal safety and security; to manage national security arrangements accountably; to develop honest and accountable government (DFID, 2001:9; 2011).
Governance can be seen as the traditions and institutions by which authority in a country is exercised for the common good. This encompasses: (1) the process by which governments are selected, monitored and replaced; (2) the capacity of the government to effectively formulate and implement sound policies and public services, and (3) the respect of citizens and the state for the institutions that govern economic and social interactions among them (Kaufmann, Kraay, and Mastruzzi, 2003:2).	Can be measured along six dimensions—voice and external accountability; political stability and lack of violence, crime, and terrorism; government effectiveness; lack of regulatory burden; rule of law; and control of corruption (Kaufmann, Kraay, and Mastruzzi, 2003:3–4).

(Continued)

Table A.1 Compendium of Definitions of *Governance* and *Good Governance* (*Continued*)

What is Governance?	*What is Good Governance?*
Governance is defined as the formation and stewardship of the formal and informal rules that regulate the public realm, the arena in which state as well as economic and societal actors interact to make decisions. *Governance* refers to the "voluntarist" intervention at the level of the regime to protect, amend, or just sustain specific rules that are important for how the political system functions and the political process operates. Because political processes are embedded in historical and cultural contexts, governance is a structurally contingent activity in the sense that "agency" is not completely free but to varying extents shaped by structural or institutional factors that are specific in time and space (Hyden, Court, and Mease, 2004:2).	Can be measured along six dimensions: (1) civil society, (2) political society, (3) the executive, (4) bureaucracy, (5) economic society, and (6) judiciary, each arena corresponding to a functional aspect of politics. Civil society socializes individuals to believe in certain things that form the basis for articulating ideas and interests. Political society adopts and aggregates these "inputs" from civil society. Government, the executive function, makes key decisions for society at large, provides policy with an authoritative stamp, and sets the stage for policy implementation. The bureaucracy makes and implements policies. *Economic society* refers to how relations between state and market are structured to obtain a satisfactory equilibrium between concerns for efficiency and distribution. The judiciary is where disputes are resolved between actors (Hyden, Court, and Mease, 2004:4).
USAID defines *governance* as the ability of government to develop an efficient, effective, and accountable public management process that is open to citizen participation and that strengthens rather than weakens a democratic system of government (USAID, 2013:4–6).	Democratic Governance involves building open, responsive, and accountable institutions and processes that serve the needs and preferences of the public. Participation—Ensuring that all have the opportunity to participate and have a voice in how they will be governed. Fair Competition—Promoting free, transparent, and fair political competition so that citizens' preferences are represented. Civil Society and Independent Media—Defending citizens' rights of association and expression, so that they can play a role in their country's future. Justice—Holding institutions and people responsible to the rule of law (USAID, 2020).

For IMF purposes, "governance" is generally understood to concern the various institutions, mechanisms, and established practices through which a country exercises governmental authority, discharges its responsibilities, and manages its public resources. This includes processes at the country level, including institution-level arrangements. Governance is an inherently neutral term, describing a framework—including the institutions, mechanisms, and practices through which a country exercises governmental authority and manages its public resources—but not its outcome (IMF, 1997:3; see also IMF, 2017:5).

The World Bank has identified three distinct aspects of governance: (i) the form of the political regime; (ii) the process by which authority is exercised in the management of a country's economic and social resources for development; and (iii) the capacity of governments to design, formulate, and implement policies and discharge functions (World Bank, 1994A:XIV).

"Good governance" recognizes that the quality of governance can impact its effectiveness. Despite this emphasis, there is no single agreed definition of the term but it has evolved over time to include economic issues (typically covering the management of public accounts, of public resources and the stability of the regulatory environment); social issues (typically covering strong institutions and an inclusive society); and political issues (typically covering the legitimacy of government through systems of public accountability, respect for human rights, and the rule of law) (IMF, 2017:7).

"Good governance" is the process through which state and non-state actors interact to design and implement policies within a given set of formal and informal rules that shape and are shaped by power. *Power* in this context of governance is defined as the ability of groups and individuals to make others act in the interest of those groups and individuals and to bring about specific outcomes. In addition, governance takes place at different levels, from international bodies, to national state institutions, to local government agencies, to community or business associations. These dimensions often overlap, creating a complex network of actors and interests (World Bank, 2017:3).

(Continued)

Table A.1 Compendium of Definitions of *Governance* and *Good Governance* (*Continued*)

What is Governance?	What is Good Governance?
	Good governance is offering the Americas a land of liberty and a favorable environment for the development of their personality and the realization of their just aspirations. This democratic sustainability does not only depend on clean elections; it depends, fundamentally on the conviction of every human being that this system leads to a better life through reinforcing democratic values and consolidating institutions; a dynamic exchange of ideas about democratic practices, not only among governments but also political parties, parliaments and congresses, academic institutions and civil society. Primary importance must also be given to states' development plans for the encouragement of education and culture, oriented toward the overall improvement of the individual, and as a foundation for democracy, social justice, and progress (OAS: 2006:1; see also OAS, 2020).
	A *quality democracy* is "a stable, institutional structure that enables citizens to achieve freedom and equality through the legitimate and correct operation of its institutions and mechanisms." In other words, a quality democracy provides three dimensions of quality: (1) it is a regime with broad legitimacy that fully satisfies its citizens (quality of outcomes); (2) it is a regime in which the citizens, associations, and communities that constitute it enjoy freedom and equality (quality of content); and (3) it is a regime in which citizens are able to verify and evaluate whether their government is pursuing the objectives of freedom and equality within the framework of the rule of law (quality of procedures) (IDEA, 2016:33).
	Good governance has eight major characteristics, namely (1) participation; (2) consensus oriented; (3) accountability; (4) transparency; (5) responsiveness; (6) effectiveness and efficiency; (7) equity and inclusiveness; and (8) rule of law (UNESCAP, 2013:2).

Source: Author's compilation.

Appendix II

Article XVII: Good Governance

The States shall adopt and implement all appropriate measures to ensure good governance which is just, open and accountable.[1]

The States recognize and affirm that the rule of law, the effective administration of justice and the maintenance of the independence and impartiality of the judiciary are essential to good governance.

The States, recognizing that integral to the concept of good governance are the complementary roles of government, the social partners and the citizenry, shall ensure that the rights and responsibilities of all are clearly established and that the appropriate environment for their exercise and discharge, as the case may be, is fostered.

The States, in order to ensure morality in public affairs, agree that holders of public office and all those who exercise power the exercise of which affects or may affect the public interest, shall so order their affairs in accordance with national law that such ordering gives no cause for conflict to arise or to appear to arise between their private interests and their duties to the public, or to otherwise compromise their integrity. To this end, the States agree to establish a Code governing the conduct of the holders of public office and all those who exercise power, the exercise of which affects or may affect the public interest.

The States shall undertake:

I. to foster continuously greater cost-effectiveness in their operations while being facilitative and supportive of the development process;
II. to ensure that all persons are treated fairly, humanely and equally by public authorities and holders of public office and all those who exercise power so as to affect the quality of life of our people;

III. to ensure responsiveness to the needs of the people as consumers in the delivery of goods and services.

The States undertake to preserve and respect the existence of an independent public service with attractive career opportunities open to all on the basis of merit and which is effective, efficient, responsive, adaptive and innovative in its conduct of public administration.

The States in order to further the participation of the people in the democratic process shall establish effective systems of ongoing consultations between the Government and the people.

The States shall undertake to ensure that in the process of governance, there is no victimization of any person.

NOTE

1. Source: CARICOM Secretariat, (1997). *The Charter of Civil Society.* Georgetown, Guyana: CARICOM Secretariat. Available at https://caricom.org/store/charter-of-civil-society.

References

6, P., (2010). When forethought and out-turn part: Types of unanticipated and unintended consequences. In Margetts, H., Hood, C., and 6, P., (Eds.) *The Paradoxes of Modernization. Unintended Consequences of Public Sector Reform.* Oxford: OUP.

Acemoglu, D., (2008). Interactions between governance and growth: What World Bank economists need to know. In North, D., Acemoglu, D., Fukuyama, F., and D. Rodrik (Eds.), *Governance, Growth and Development Decision-Making.* Washington, DC: The International Bank for Reconstruction and Development, The World Bank.

Acharya, A. Blackwell, M., and Sen, M., (2018). Explaining Preferences from Behaviour: A Cognitive Dissonance Approach. *The Journal of Politics* Vol. 80, No. 2. pp. 400–412.

Ackerman, J., (2004). Co-Governance for Accountability: Beyond 'Exit' and 'Voice. *World Development* Vol. 32, No. 3. pp. 447–463.

Addo, H., (2019). Crisis in development praxis: A global perspective. In Schuyler, G., and Veltmeyer, H., (Eds.). *Rethinking Caribbean Development.* Toronto, Canada: International Education Centre.

Agbude, G., and Etete, P., (2013). Ethical Leadership, Corruption and Irresponsible Governance: Rethinking the African Dilemma. *Mediterranean Journal of Social Sciences* Vol. 4, No. 6. pp. 481–488.

Agere, S., (2000). *Promoting Good Governance: Principles, Practices and Perspectives.* London: Commonwealth Secretariat.

Al-Aidro, A., Shamsudi, F., and Idris, K., (2013). Ethics and Ethical Theories from an Islamic Perspective. *International Journal of Islamic Thought* Vol. 4. pp. 1–13.

Alleyne, G., and Sealey, K., (1992). *Whither Caribbean Health.* Bridgetown: West Indian Commission Secretariat.

Alleyne, G., (2017a). Weekend Anxiety in Barbados. In *Caribbean Life News.* Available at https://www.caribbeanlifenews.com/weekend-anxiety-in-barbados.

Alleyne, G. (2017b). Barbados government may be yielding to marchers. In *Caribbean Life News*. Available at https://www.caribbeanlifenews.com/ barbados-govt-may-be-yielding-to-marchers.

Alleyne, G., (2018). Barbados Trade Union Blast Government. In *Caribbean Life News*. Available at https://www.caribbeanlifenews.com/ barbados-trade-union-blasts-government.

Alleyne, P., Cadogan-McClean, C., and Harper, A., (2013). Examining Personal Values and Ethical Behaviour: Perceptions between Accounting and Non-Accounting Students in the Caribbean. *The Accounting Educators' Journal* Vol. 23. pp. 47–70.

Aman, K., (Ed.) (1991). *Ethical Principles for Development: Needs, Capacities or Rights?* Upper Montclair, NJ: Institute for Critical Thinking.

Amin, A., (2010). Neighbourly bonds. In Citizen Ethics Network. *Citizen Ethics in a Time of Crisis*. London: Citizen Ethics Network/Barrow Cadbury Trust. Available at http://www.barrowcadbury.org.uk/wp-content/uploads/2012/07/Citizens-Ethics. pdf.

Amunsden, I., and Andrade, V., (2009). *Introduction to Public Sector Ethics*. Bergen, Norway: Chr. Michelsen Institute.

Anderson, L., (2009). The Myth of Relativism and the cult of Tolerance. *American Thinker*. Available at: https://www.americanthinker.com/articles/2009/03/the_my th_of_relativism_and_the.html.

Andrews, K., (1991). *Ethics in Practice: Managing the Moral Corporation*. Boston: Harvard Business School Press.

Anthony, K., (2015). "Delivered or Denied: The Dividends of Integration." Speech delivered at the Caribbean Lecture Series of the University of the West Indies St. Augustine Campus, Daaga Hall.

Antillean Media Group (AMG), (2014). Dame Louise removed as Antigua's Governor General. In Antillean Media Group. Available at https://www.antillean .org/antigua-barbuda-replaces-governor-general/.

Argandona, A., (1991). *Values, Institutions and Ethics*. Barcelona: IESE Business School University of Navarra, Working Paper No. 215.

Arrow, K., (1963). *Social Choice and Individual Values*. London: Yale University Press.

Astroulakis, N., (2013). Ethics and International Development: The Development Ethics Paradigm. *Journal of Economics and Business* Vol. 16, No.1. pp. 99–117.

Atkinson, A., (2007). Economics as a moral science. In Cowell, F., and Witztum, A., (Eds.) *Lionel Robbin's Essay on the Nature and Significance of Economic Science, 75th Anniversary Conference Proceedings*. London: London School of Economics and Political Science's Suntory and Toyota International Centres for Economics and Related Disciplines (SUNTORY). Available at http://darp.lse.ac.uk/papersdb/ LionelRobbinsConferenceProveedingsVolume.pdf.

Australian Public Service Commission (APSC) (2007). *Tackling Wicked Problems: A Public Policy Perspective*. Available at https://www.apsc.gov.au/tackling-wicked-problems-public-policy-perspective.

Baghramian, M., and Carter, J., (2017). Relativism. In Zalta, E. N., (Ed.) *The Stanford Encyclopedia of Philosophy* (Summer 2017 Edition), forthcoming URL. Available at https://plato.stanford.edu/archives/sum2017/entries/relativism/.

Balsamo, A., and Mitcham, C., (2010). Interdisciplinarity in ethics and the ethics of interdisciplinarity. In Frodeman, R., Klein, J., and Mitcham, C., (Eds.) *The Oxford Handbook of Inter-Disciplinarity*. Oxford: Oxford University Press.

Banuri, T., (1987). *Modernization and Its Discontents: A Perspective From the Sociology of Knowledge*. Helsinki: UNU-WIDER.

BBVA Foundation (2012). *Values and Ethics for the Twenty-First Century*. Available at https://www.bbvaopenmind.com/wp-content/uploads/2013/10/Values-and-Eth ics-for-the-21st-Century_BBVA.pdf.

Barbados Advocate (2018). "Editorial: Need for Reform?" *Online edition*. Available at www.barbadosadvocate.com/columns/editorial-need-reform.

Barbados Today (2017). Police Officer accused of two counts of fraud. *Barbados Today* Online Edition. Available at https://www.barbadostoday.bb/2017/05/05/ fraud-accused-released-on-5000-bail.

Bardhan, P., (2006). Institutions and development. In Clark, D., (Ed.) *The Elgar Companion to Development Studies*. Northampton: Edward Elgar.

Barnes, T., and Sheppard, E., (Eds.) (2000). *Companion to Economic Geography*. Oxford: Blackwell.

Bauman, Z., (1993). *Postmodern Ethics*. Oxford: Blackwell.

Bauman, Z., (2018). *Community*. Cambridge: Polity.

Beaton, K., Dowling, T., Kovtun, D., Loyola, F., Myrvoda, A., Chiedu Okwuokei, J., Ötker, I., and Turunen, J., (2017). *IMF Working Paper, Problem Loans in the Caribbean: Determinants, Impact and Strategies for Resolution*. Available at https ://www.imf.org/en/Publications/WP/Issues/2017/11/07/Problem-Loans-in-the-Ca ribbean-Determinants-Impact-and-Strategies-for-Resolution-45335.

Bebbington, A., and Foo, K., (2014). Social capital and development. In Desai, V., and Potter, R., (Eds.) *The Companion to Development Studies*. London: Routledge.

Bell, D., (2014). *Clashing Moral Civilisations: Why is Relativism a Threat to the Military?* Available at http://www.cgscfoundation.org/wp-content/uploads/2014/0 4/Bell-ChallengeRelativism.pdf.

Benn, S., (2010). Social Partnerships for Governance and Learning Towards Sustainability. *ARIES* working Paper No. 1. Available at http://aries.mq.edu.au/pu blications/aries/Working_Papers/Social_Partnerships_for_Gov_&_Learning.pdf.

Berger, P. L., (1974). *Pyramids of Sacrifice: Political Ethics and Social Change*. New-York: Basic Books.

Berger, C., (2013). Making Liberal Democracy Ethical: Aristotle on the Unity of Ethics and Politics. *The Agora: Political Science Undergraduate Journal* Vol. 3. pp. 73–90.

Best, J., (2007). The moral politics of IMF reforms, universal economics, particular ethics. In Day, R., and Masciulli, J., (Eds.) *Globalization and Political Ethics*. Leiden: Brill.

Bewaji, J., (2007) Ethics and morality: Critical exploration of western and African philosophical perspectives. In Cowell, N., Campbell, A., Chen, G., and Moore,

S., (Eds.) *Ethical Perspectives for Caribbean Business.* Kingston: Arawak Publications.

Bhide, A., and Stevenson, H., (1991). *Why Be Honest If Honesty Doesn't Pay?* Boston: Harvard Business School Press.

Biggar, N., (2010). The cult of freedom. In Citizen Ethics Network. *Citizen Ethics in a Time of Crisis.* London: Citizen Ethics Network/Barrow Cadbury Trust. Available at http://www.barrowcadbury.org.uk/wp-content/uploads/2012/07/Citizens-Ethics.pdf.

Bilhim, J., and Neves, B., (2005). *New Ethical Challenges in a Changing Public Administration.* Lisbon: Lisbon Technical University.

Bishop, M., (2016) State capacity and international politics. In Minto-Coy, I., and Berman, E., (Eds.). *Public Administration and Policy in the Caribbean.* Baton Rouge: CRC Press, Taylor and Francis Group.

Bissessar, A., (2016). Assessing public sector reform in the Anglophone Caribbean. In Minto-Coy, I., and Berman, E., (Eds.). *Public Administration and Policy in the Caribbean.* Baton Rouge: CRC Press, Taylor and Francis Group.

Blackburn, S., (2013). Relativism. In Lafollette, H., and Persson, I., (Eds.), *The Blackwell Guide to Ethical Theory.* Oxford: Wiley Blackwell.

Bloom, P., Miescher, S., and Manuh, T., (Eds.) (2014). *Modernization as Spectacle in Africa.* Bloomington: Indianna University Press.

Bluhm, W., (1978). *Theories of the Political System: Classics of Political Thought and Modern Political Analysis.* Englewoods Cliff, NJ: Prentice Hall.

Bluhm, W. T., and Heineman, R.A., (2007). *Ethics and Public Policy: Method and Cases.* Upper Saddle River, NJ: Pearson Prentice Hall.

Boas, M., (2014) Multilateral Institutions: Developing countries and emerging markets, stability or change. In Desai, V., and Potter, R., (Eds.) *The Companion to Development Studies.* London: Routledge.

Boddington, P., (2018). *Towards a Code of Ethics for Artificial Intelligence.* Switzerland: Springer.

Boghossian, P., (2011). *The Maze of Moral Relativism.* Available at http://opinionator.blogs.nytimes.com/2011/07/24/the-maze-of-moral-relativism/?scp=1&sq=boghossian&st=cse.

Bostock, D., (2000). *Aristotle's Ethics.* Oxford: Oxford University Press.

Boston, J., Bradstock, A., and Eng, D., (Eds.) (2011). *Ethics and Public Policy Contemporary Issues.* Victoria: Victoria University Press.

Boston, J., Bradstock, A., and Eng, D., (Eds.) (2010). *Public Policy, Why Ethics Matters.* Canberra: Australia National University Press.

Botton, de A., (2010). Questions of freedom. In Citizen Ethics Network. *Citizen Ethics in a Time of Crisis,* London: Citizen Ethics Network/Barrow Cadbury Trust. Available at http://www.barrowcadbury.org.uk/wp-content/uploads/2012/07/Citizens-Ethics.pdf.

Bouckaert, G., and Van de Walle, S., (2003). Quality of public service delivery and trust in government. In Salminen, A., (Ed.) *Governing Networks: EGPA Yearbook.* Amsterdam: IOS Press, pp. 299–318.

Boulding, K. E., (1990). *Three Faces of Power.* Newbury Park, CA: Sage Publications.

Bourdieu, P., (2011). The forms of capital. In Granovetter, M., and Swedberg, R., (Eds.) *The Sociology of Economic Life*. Colorado: Westview Press.

Boutros-Ghali, B., (2002). *The Interaction between Democracy and Development*. Paris: UNESCO.

Bowles, P., (2018). The developmental state and late industrialization: still feasible? And desirable? In Veltmeyer, H., and Bowles, P., (Eds.) *The Essential Guide to Critical Development Studies*. Routledge: New York.

Bowman, J. S., (1996). "Public service ethics: Prospects, problems, and promise in an age of reform", key-note address presented at the 'Public Sector Ethics – between past and future' Ethics in the Public Service 5th international conference, Brisbane, 5–9 August.

Bowman, J., and Elliston, F., (1988). *Ethics, Government and Public Policy, A Reference Guide*. Westport, CT: Greenwood Press.

Bracking, S., (Ed.) (2007). *Corruption and Development: The Anti-Corruption Campaigns*. Basingstoke: Palgrave Macmillan.

Braveboy-Wagner, J., and Gayle, D., (Eds.) (1998). *Caribbean Public Policy: Regional, Cultural and Socio-Economic Issues for the Twenty-First Century*. Oxford: Westview Press.

Brecht, A., (1959). *Political Theory*. Princeton, NJ: Princeton University Press.

Breckler, S., (2005). *The Importance of Disciplines*. Available at http://www.apa.org /science/about/psa/2005/10/ed-column.aspx.

Brennan, T., (1998). American democratic institutions and social values. In Carrow, M., Churchill, R., and Cordes, J., (Eds.). *Democracy, Social Values, and Public Policy*. Westport, CT: Praeger.

Bridglal, C., (2019). Breaking secrecy in the Caribbean. *Trinidad and Tobago Newsday* Online Edition. Available at https://newsday.co.tt/2019/12/22/breaking -secrecy-in-the-caribbean/.

Brinkman, K., (Ed.) (1999). *Ethics, Vol. 1 (The Proceedings of the Twentieth World Congress of Philosophy)*. Boston: Bowling Green State University.

British Broadcasting Corporation (BBC) (2019). *Venezuelan Pirates - The New Scourge of the Caribbean*. Available at https://www.bbc.com/news/stories-47003108.

Broome, P. A., (2003). *Information Technology and the Development Process: Caribbean Micro-States in the Global Economy*. Unpublished PhD. Dissertation. University of Cambridge.

Broome, P. A., Hinds-Harrison, K., et al (2013). *UWI/UNDP Statistical Report Democratic Governance Assessment Exercise in Small Island Developing States: The Case of Barbados and Antigua and Barbuda*. Bridgetown: UWI/UNDP.

Broome, P. A., and Adugu, E., (2014). Whither Social Media for Digital Activism: The Case of the Caribbean. *The British Journal of Education, Society and Behavioural Science* Vol. 10, No. 3. pp. 1–21.

Bromell, D., (2010). The public-servant as analyst, advisor and advocate. In Boston, J., Bradstock, A., and Eng, D., (Eds.). *Public Policy, Why Ethics Matters?* Canberra: Australia National University Press.

Brooks, L., (2010). The winner takes it all. In Citizen Ethics Network. *Citizen Ethics in a Time of Crisis*, London: Citizen Ethics Network/Barrow Cadbury

Trust. Available at http://www.barrowcadbury.org.uk/wp-content/uploads/2012/07/Citizens-Ethics.pdf.

Brown, P., (2008). *Ethics, Economics and International Relations.* Edinburgh: Edinburgh University Press.

Bunting, M., (2010). Fanning the flames of a vital debate. In Citizen Ethics Network. *Citizen Ethics in a Time of Crisis,* London: Citizen Ethics Network/Barrow Cadbury Trust. Available at http://www.barrowcadbury.org.uk/wp-content/uploads/2012/07/Citizens-Ethics.pdf.

Campbell, T., (2010). Justice, humanity and prudence. In Boston, J., Bradstock, A., and Eng, D., (Eds.). *Public Policy, Why Ethics Matters.* Canberra: Australia National University Press.

Caputo, J., (2013). The End of Ethics. In Lafollette, H., and Persson, I., (Eds). *The Blackwell Guide to Ethical Theory.* Oxford: Wiley Blackwell.

Cardoso, G., (2005). Societies in transition to the network society. In Castells, M., and Cardoso, G., (Eds.). *The Network Society from Knowledge to Policy.* Washington, D.C.: Johns Hopkins Centre for Transatlantic Relations.

Caribbean Development Bank (CDB) (2018a). *Country Economic Reviews from Antigua and Barbuda to Trinidad and Tobago.* Bridgetown: Caribbean Development Bank. Available at https://www.caribank.org/publications-and-resources.

Caribbean Development Bank (CDB) (2018b). *Regional Economic Summary, 2018.* Bridgetown: Caribbean Development Bank. Available at https://www.caribank.org/publications-and-resources.

Caribbean News Now (CNN) (2017). CARICOM to clampdown on returning ISIS fighters. *Caribbean News Now Online Edition.* Available at http://www.caribbeannewsnow.com/topstory-CARICOM-to-clampdown-on-returning-ISIS-fighters-34739.html.

Caribbean 360, (2017). *Brits Arrested in Barbados for Credit Card Fraud.* Available at http://www.caribbean360.com/news/brits-arrested-in-barbados-for-massive-credit-card-fraud.

Caribbean 360 (2018). *A New State of Emergency declared in Jamaica-This time in Parts of the Capital.* Available at http://www.caribbean360.com/news/a-new-state-of-emergency-declared-in-jamaica-this-time-in-parts-of-the-capital.

Carens, J., (2012). Immigration and citizenship. In BBVA Foundation. *Values and Ethics for the Twenty-First Century.* Available at https://www.bbvaopenmind.com/wp-content/uploads/2013/10/Values-and-Ethics-for-the-21st-Century_BBVA.pdf.

Caribbean Centre for Development Administration (CARICAD), (2015). *Implementation Guide: Charter for Caribbean Public Services (CCPS).* Bridgetown: CARICAD.

Carothers, T., and Brenchenmacher, S., (2014). *Accountability, Transparency, Participation and Inclusion. A New Development Consensus?* Washington, DC: Carnegie Endowment for International Peace.

Carrow, M., Churchill, R., and Cordes, J., (Eds.) (1998). *Democracy, Social Values, and Public Policy.* Westport, CT: Praeger.

Castells, M., (2010). *The Rise of the Network Society.* Oxford: Wiley-Blackwell.

Castells, M., (2005). The network society: From knowledge to policy. In Castells, M., and Cardoso, G., (Eds.) *The Network Society from Knowledge to Policy.* Washington, DC: Johns Hopkins Centre for Transatlantic Relations.

Castells, M., and Cardoso, G., (Eds.) (2005). *The Network Society from Knowledge to Policy.* Washington, D.C.: Johns Hopkins Centre for Transatlantic Relations.

Castells, M., (2014). *Rethinking Development in the Global Information Age.* Public lecture presented at Stellenbosch Institute for Advanced Study (STIAS). Available at https://stias.ac.za/ideas/projects/rethinking-development-in-the-global-informat ion-age-implications-for-africa.

Ceva, E., and Ferretti, M., (2019). The ethics of anti-corruption policies. In Lever, A., and Poama A., (Eds.) *The Routledge Handbook of Ethics and Public Policy.* Routledge: London.

Chaffee, J., (2012). *Thinking Critically.* Stamford: Cengage Learning.

Chakrabortty, A., (2010). The problem with transparent government. *The Guardian International* Online Edition. Available at https://www.theguardian.com/comment isfree/2010/jun/08/problem-transparent-government.

Chang, H. J., (2002). *Globalisation Economic Development and the Role of the State.* London: Zed Books Publishing.

Chang, H. J., (2003). *Kicking Away the Ladder: Development Strategy in Historical Perspective.* Wimbledon: Anthem Press.

Chang, H. J., and Grabel, I., (2004). *Reclaiming Development: An Alternative Economic Manual.* London: Zed Books.

Chang, H. J., (2010). *Bad Samaritans: The Myth of Free Trade and the Secret History of Capitalism.* London: Bloomsbury Publishing.

Chatterjee, D., and Krausz, M., (Eds.) (2007). *Globalization, Democracy, and Development: Philosophical Perspectives.* Lanham, MD: Rowman & Littlefield.

Chokr, N. N., (2007). *Relativism.* Available at http://web.stanford.edu/~allenw/web papers/Relativism.doc.

Christians, C., (2005). Ethics and politics in qualitative research. In Denzin, N., and Lincoln, Y., (Eds.) *The Handbook of Qualitative Research.* London: Sage.

Christie, I., and Astill, S., (2016). *Homo-Economicus* is dead! Long live Homo-Socialis!. In *Open Democracy Free Thinking for the World.* Available at https ://www.opendemocracy.net/neweconomics/homo-economicus-is-dead-long-live -homo-socialis.

Citizen Ethics Network (CEN) (2010). *Citizen Ethics in a Time of Crisis.* London: Citizen Ethics Network/Barrow Cadbury Trust. Available at http://www.barrowcad bury.org.uk/wp-content/uploads/2012/07/Citizens-Ethics.pdf.

Clark, D., (Ed.) (2006). *The Elgar Companion to Development Studies.* Northampton: Edward Elgar.

Clegg, S., (2011). Under reconstruction: Modern bureaucracies. In S. Clegg, M. Harris, & H. Hopfl (Eds.) *Managing Modernity: Beyond Bureaucracy.* Oxford, UK: Oxford University Press.

Clegg, S., Harris, M., and Hopfl, H., (Eds.) (2011). *Managing Modernity: Beyond Bureaucracy.* Oxford, UK: Oxford University Press.

Collier, M., (2005). *Political Corruption in the Caribbean Basin: Constructing a Theory to Combat Corruption.* London: Routledge.

Collingwood, V., (Ed.) (2001). *Good Governance and the World Bank.* University of Oxford: Nuffield College, mimeo 7. Available at http://www.ucl.ac.uk/dpu-proje cts/drivers_urb_change/urb_economy/pdf_glob_SAP/BWP_Governance_World %20Bank.pdf.

Committee on Standards in Public Life (CSPL) (2014). *Ethics in Practice: Promoting Ethical Conduct in Public Life.* Westminster. Available at https://www.gov.uk/g overnment/uploads/system/uploads/attachment_data/file/336976/2902536_CSPL _EthicsInPractice_acc.pdf.

Commonwealth Secretariat (1997). *A Future for Small States, Overcoming Vulnerability.* London: Commonwealth Secretariat.

Conway, D., (2014). Neo-Liberalism: Globalization's neo-conservative enforcers of austerity. In Desai, V., and Potter, R., (Eds.) *The Companion to Development Studies.* London: Routledge.

Conway, D., and Heynen, N., (2014). Dependency theories: From ECLA to Andre Gunder Frank and beyond. In Desai, V., and Potter, R., (Eds.) *The Companion to Development Studies.* London: Routledge.

Copp, D., (Ed.) (2006). *The Oxford Handbook of Ethical Theory.* Oxford: Oxford University Press.

Copson, A., (2010). Politics and humanism. In Citizen Ethics Network. *Citizen Ethics in a Time of Crisis.* London: Citizen Ethics Network/Barrow Cadbury Trust. Available at http://www.barrowcadbury.org.uk/wp-content/uploads/2012/07 /Citizens-Ethics.pdf.

Cowell, F., and Witztum, A., (Eds.) (2007). *Lionel Robbin's Essay on the Nature and Significance of Economic Science, 75th Anniversary Conference Proceedings.* London: London School of Economics and Political Science's Suntory and Toyota International Centres for Economics and Related Disciplines (SUNTORY). Available at http://darp.lse.ac.uk/papersdb/LionelRobbinsConferenceProveedings Volume.pdf.

Cowell, N., Campbell, A., Chen, G., and Moore, S., (Eds.) (2007). *Ethical Perspectives for Caribbean Business.* Kingston: Arawak Publications.

Crawford, N., (2004) *Argument and Change in World Politics.* Cambridge: Cambridge University Press.

Crocker, D., (2000). *International Development Ethics.* Boston: Boston University, The Paideia Project. Available at https://www.bu.edu/wcp/Papers/OApp/OAppC roc.htm.

Crocker, D., (2004). *Development Ethics: Sources, Agreements and Controversies.* Available at https://msu.edu/~phl/EandDWebsite/sources/Development_Ethics .pdf.

Crocker, D., (2008). *Ethics of Global Development: Agency Capability and Deliberative Democracy.* Cambridge: Cambridge University Press.

Crocker, D., (2014). Development and Global Ethics: Five Foci for the Future. *Journal of Global Ethics* Vol. 10, No. 3. pp. 245–253.

Crozier, M., Huntington, S., and Watanuki, J., (1975). *The Crisis of Democracy: Report on the Governability of Democracies to the Trilateral Commission.* New York: New York UP.

Crudas, J., and Rutherford, J., (2010). Politics must come from the people. In Citizen Ethics Network. *Citizen Ethics in a Time of Crisis.* London: Citizen Ethics Network/Barrow Cadbury Trust. Available at http://www.barrowcadbury.org.uk/wp-content/uploads/2012/07/Citizens-Ethics.pdf.

Dahl, R., (1983) *Dilemmas of Pluralist Democracy.* New Haven, CT: Yale University.

Dahl, R., Shapiro, I., and Cheibub, J. A., (2003). *The Democracy Sourcebook.* Cambridge, MA: MIT.

Dahl, R., (2006). *A Preface to Democratic Theory Expanded.* New Haven, CT: Yale University.

Dahl, R., (2015). *On Democracy.* New Haven, CT: Yale University.

Danes-Anyadike, M. et al (Ed.) (1995). *Business, Government and Society: Caribbean Writings on Caribbean Issues.* Bridgetown: Centre for Management Development Eastern Caribbean, University of the West Indies.

Daniel, J., (2016) Public administration in the French antilles: Historical trends and prospects. In Minto-Coy, I., and Berman, E., (Eds.). *Public Administration and Policy in the Caribbean.* Baton Rouge: CRC Press, Taylor and Francis Group.

Day, R., and Mascuilli, J., (Eds.) (2007). *Globalization and Political Ethics.* Leiden: Brill.

Demas, W., (1970). The New Caribbean Man. In Demas, W. *Change and renewal in the Caribbean* (1975). Bridgetown, Barbados: CCC Publishing.

Demas, W., (1973). The prospects for decolonisation in the Caribbean. In Demas, W. *Change and renewal in the Caribbean* (1975). Bridgetown, Barbados: CCC Publishing.

Demmke, C., and Moilanen, T., (2011). *Effectiveness of Good Governance and Ethics in Central Administration: Evaluating Reform Outcomes in the Context of the Financial Crisis.* Maastricht: European Institute of Public Administration/European Public Administration Network.

Denzin, N., and Lincoln, Y., (Eds.) (2005). *The Handbook of Qualitative Research.* London: Sage.

Department for International Development (2001). *Making Government Work for Poor People: Building State Capacity. Strategy Paper.* London: DFID.

Department for International Development (DFID), (2011) *Governance Portfolio Review Summary: Summary Review of DFID's Governance Portfolio 2009-2011.* London: DFID.

Desai,V., and Potter, R., (Eds.) (2014) *The Companion to Development Studies.* London: Routledge.

De Rosa, R., (2018). *Interdisciplinary Studies: A Connected Learning Approach.* Available at https://press.rebus.community/idsconnect/#main.

De Sousa Santos, B., (Ed.) (2005). *Democratizing Democracy: Beyond the Liberal Democratic Canon.* London: Verso.

De Sousa Santos, B., (Ed.) (2007). *Cognitive Justice in a Global World: Prudent Knowledges for a Decent Life.* London: Lexington Books.

Diescho, J., (2000). A Namibian perspective on good governance and ethics. In Namibia Institute for Democracy (NID) and Konrad-Adenauer-Stiftung (KAS) (Eds.) *Ethics and Good Governance in Namibia.* Windhoek: NID and KAS.

Dimaggio, P., (Ed.)., (2001). *The Twenty-first Century Firm: Changing Economic Organization in International Perspective.* Princeton, NJ: Princeton University Press.

Dorbeck-Jung, B., (1998). Towards Reflexive Responsibility New Ethics for Public Administration. In Hondeghem, A., (Ed.) *Ethics and Accountability in a Context of Governance and New Public Management.* Leuvan: EGPA/IOS Press.

Dower, N., (2006). *World Ethics: The New Agenda.* Edinburgh: Edinburgh University Press.

Dower, N., (2019). Global ethics. In Drydyk, J., and Keleher, L., (Eds.) *Routledge Handbook of Development Ethics.* London: Routledge.

Dreier, J., (2006). Moral relativism and moral nihilism. In Copp, D., (Ed.). *The Oxford Handbook of Ethical Theory.* Oxford: Oxford University Press.

Dror, Y., (2002). *The Capacity to Govern: A Report to the Club of Rome.* New York: Frank Cass Publishers.

Dror, Y., (2008). *When the Survival of the Jewish People is at Stake, There is No Place for Morals.* New York: Forward, The Jewish Daily. Available at https://forward.com/opinion/13388/when-survival-of-the-jewish-people-is-at-stake-th-01856.

Drydyk, J., and Keleher, L., (Eds.) (2019). *Routledge Handbook of Development Ethics.* Oxford: Routledge.

Dukor, M., (Ed.) (2003). *Philosophy and Politics: Discourse on values, Politics and Power in Africa.* Lagos: Malthouse Press Ltd.

Dworkin, R., (2008). *Is Democracy Possible Here? Principles for a New Political Debate.* Princeton, NJ: Princeton University Press.

Economic Commission for Latin America and the Caribbean (ECLAC) (2018). *The Caribbean Outlook 2018.* Santiago: United Nations.

The Economist Magazine (2008). A Caribbean Crime Wave: Crime Damages Society and Economy. *The Economist Magazine* online edition. Available at http://www.economist.com/node/10903343.

The Economist Intelligence Unit (2008). *The Economist Intelligence Unit's Index of Democracy.* London: The Economist.

Edmunds, J., (2015). Democracy and Good Governance in the Caribbean: A Retrospective Analysis. *Dominica Vibes* Online Edition. Available at https://www.dominicavibes.dm/readers-163376/.

Eisenstadt, S. N., (1966). *Modernization, Protest and Change.* Englewood Cliff: Prentice-Hall.

Eisenstadt, S. N., (1966). *Modernization, Protest and Change.* Englewood Cliffs, NJ: Prentice-Hall.

Eisenstadt, S. N., (Ed.) (1968). *The Protestant Ethic and Modernization.* London: Basic Books.

Eisenstadt, S., (2000). Multiple modernities. In Daedalus, Winter, No. 129. Vol. 1.

Eisenstadt, S. N., (2005). The basic characteristics of modernization. *Themenportal Europäische Geschichte*, 2006. Available at www.europa.clio-online.de/quelle/id/artikel-3283.

Eisenstadt, S., (2013). Latin America and the Problem Of Multiple Modernities. In Sznajder, M. Roniger, L., and C. Forment (Eds.). *Shifting Frontiers of Citizenship: The Latin American Experience*. Boston: Brill.

Ekbladh, D., (2010). *The Great American Mission: Modernization and the Construction of an American World Order*. Princeton, NJ: Princeton University Press.

Elster, J., (1989). *The Cement of Society*. Cambridge: Cambridge University Press.

Elsetain, J., Dallmayr, F., Merritt, M., and R. Vayrynen (Eds.) (1998). *New Wine and Old Bottles, International Politics and Ethical Discourse*. Indiana: University of Notre Dame.

English, W., (2013). *Institutional Corruption and the Crisis of Liberal Democracy*. In Edmond J. Safra Working Papers, No. 15, Cambridge, MA: Harvard University Edmond J Safra Centre for Ethics. Available at https://papers.ssrn.com/sol3/papers .cfm?abstract_id=2281305.

Escobar, A., (1995). *Encountering Development: The Making and Unmaking of the Third World*. Princeton, NJ: Princeton University Press.

Esquith, S., and Gifford, F., (Eds.) (2009). *Capabilities, Power and Institutions: Towards a More Critical Development Ethics*. University Park, PA: Pennsylvania State University Press.

Etzioni, A., (1958). *New Golden Rule: Community and Morality in a Democratic Society*. New York: Basic Books.

Etzioni, A., (2008). The unique methodology of policy research. In Goodin, R., Moran, M., and Rein, M., (Eds.) *The Oxford Handbook of Public Policy*. Oxford: Oxford University Press.

Etzioni, A., (2010). Is Transparency the Best Disinfectant. *Journal of Political Philosophy* Vol. 18, No. 4. pp. 389–404.

European Parliament (2017). The Impact of Schemes revealed by the Panama Papers on the economy and finances of a sample of Member States Working Paper PE 572.717 prepared by the Policy Department Directorate for Internal Policies of the Union - April 2017. Available at http://www.europarl.europa.eu/cmsdata/116947/ 20170412_panama_papers_study_final.pdf.

Fairbanks, M., (2000). Changing the mind of a nation: Elements in a process for creating prosperity. In Huntingdon, S., and Harrison, L., (Eds.) *Culture Matters: How Values Shape Human Progress*. New York: Basic Books.

Fenster, M., (2010). Seeing the State: Transparency as Metaphor. No. 62, Admin L. Rev 617 62 Admin L. Rev 617. Available at http://scholarship.law.ufl.edu/ facultypub/572.

Fleishman, J., Liebman, L., and Moore, M., (1981). *Public Duties: The Moral Obligations of Government Officials*. Cambridge: Harvard University Press.

Flynn N., and Strehl F., (Eds.), *Public Sector Management in Europe*. London, UK: Prentice Hall.

Fortner, R., and Fackler, P., (Eds.) (2011). *The Handbook of Global Communication and Media Ethics*, Vol. II. Sussex: Wiley and Blackwell.

Fortner, R., (2011). Modernization and its discontents: Ethics, development, and the diffusion of innovations. In Fortner, R., and Fackler, P., (Eds.). *The Handbook of Global Communication and Media Ethics*, Vol. II. Sussex: Wiley and Blackwell.

Foster, G., (2003). Ethics: Time to Revisit the Basics. *The Humanist.* Available at http://www.thefreelibrary.com/Ethics%3A+time+to+revisit+the+basics.-a098469 797.

Frederickson, H. G., (1997). *The Spirit of Public Administration.* San Francisco: Jossey-Bass.

Freire, P., (1970). *The Pedagogy of the Oppressed.* New York: Continuum.

Friedman, M., (1970). The social responsibility of business is to increase its profits. *The New York Times Magazine.* Available at http://umich.edu/~thecore/doc/Fried man.pdf.

Friedman, M., (1970). The social responsibility of business is to increase its profits. In White, J., (Ed.) *Contemporary Moral Problems.* London: Wadsworth.

Frey, B., (1997). A Constitution for Knaves Crowds Out Civic Virtues. *The Economic Journal* Vol. 107 (July). pp. 1043–1053.

Frodeman, R., Klein, J., and Mitcham, C., (Eds.) (2010). *The Oxford Handbook of Inter-disciplinarity.* Oxford: Oxford University Press.

Frost, M., (2012). Ethics and global governance. In BBVA Foundation. *Values and Ethics for the twenty-first Century.* Available at https://www.bbvaopenmind.com/ wp-content/uploads/2013/10/Values-and-Ethics-for-the-21st-Century_BBVA.pdf. Last accessed August 1, 2016.

Fukuyama, F., (2000). Social capital. In Huntingdon, S., and Harrison, L., (Eds.). *Culture Matters: How Values Shape Human Progress.* New York: Basic Books.

Fukuyama, F., (2008). What do we know about the relationship between the political and economic dimensions of development? In North, D., Acemoglu, D., Fukuyama, F., and D. Rodrik (Eds.). *Governance, Growth and Development Decision-Making.* Washington, DC: The International Bank for Reconstruction and Development/ The World Bank.

Fukuda-Parr, S., and Kumar, Shiva A. K., (Eds.) (2003) *Readings in Human Development.* Oxford: Oxford University Press.

Fund for Peace (FFP) (2016). *Fragile States Index 2016.* Washington, DC. Available at www.fundforpeace.org.

Gabay, C., (2012). The Millennium Development Goals and Ambitious Developmental Engineering. *Third World Quarterly* Vol. 33, No. 7. pp. 1249–1265.

Garner, J., (1907). Political Science and Ethics. *International Journal of Ethics* Vol. 17, No. 2. pp. 194–204.

Gaskin, D., (2020). Dominic Gaskin says he doesn't `buy' Mingo's figures. *Stabroek News* Online Edition. Available at https://www.stabroeknews.com/2020/03/20/ news/guyana/dominic-gaskin-says-doesnt-buy-mingos-figures/.

Gasper, D., (2004). *The Ethics of Development.* Edinburgh: Edinburgh University Press.

Gasper, D., (2006). What is the point of Development Ethics. *Ethics and Economics* Vol. 4, No. 2. http://ethics-economics.com/Volume-4Numero-2.html Selected papers from a 2006 International Development Ethics Association conference in Uganda.

Gasper, D., (2008). *Denis Goulet and the Project of Development Ethics. ISS Working Paper Series/General Series.* Vol. 456. International Institute of Social Studies of Erasmus University (ISS). Available at http://hdl.handle.net/1765/18738.

Gasper, D., (2009). *Development Ethics and Human Development*. Hague: Human Development Report.

Gasper, D., (2012). Development Ethics, What? Why? How? A formulation of the Field. *Journal of Global Ethics* Vol. 8, No. 1. pp. 117–135.

Gasper, D., (2014) Ethics and development. In Desai, V., and Potter, R., (Eds.) *The Companion to Development Studies*. London: Routledge.

Gasper, D., (2015). Ethics of development. In Haslam, P. Schafer, J., and Beaudet, P., (Eds.) *An Introduction to International Development*. Toronto: Oxford University Press.

Gaur, M., (2014). Good Governance: Promotion of Ethics and Moral Values. *Indian Journal of Applied Research* Vol. 4, No. 1. pp. 489–491.

Gaventa, J., (2006). *Triumph, Deficit or Contestation? Deepening the 'Deepening Democracy' Debate*. Sussex: Institute of Development Studies, University of Sussex.

Gearty, C., (2010). *An Heretical History: Rethinking the Foundations of Human Rights*. Available at Official URL: http://therightsfuture.com/.

Geingob, H., (2000). Introduction. In Namibia Institute for Democracy (NID) and Konrad-Adenauer-Stiftung (KAS) (Eds.). *Ethics and Good Governance in Namibia*. Windhoek: NID and KAS.

Gensler, H., (2018). Cultural relativism. In Landau, R., (Ed.) *The Ethical Life: Fundamental Readings in Ethics and Moral Problems*. New York: Oxford University Press.

Gerhardt, S., (2010). A labour of kindness. In Citizen Ethics Network. *Citizen Ethics in a Time of Crisis*. London: Citizen Ethics Network/Barrow Cadbury Trust. Available at http://www.barrowcadbury.org.uk/wp-content/uploads/2012/07/Citizens-Ethics.pdf.

Gilbert, A., (2014). The new international division of labour. In Desai, V., and Potter, R., (Eds.) *The Companion to Development Studies*. London: Routledge.

Gilbert-Roberts, T., (2011). CARICOM governance in crisis: Challenges of context and political traditions. *Trade Negotiations Insights* Vol. 10. No. 2. Available at http://www.ictsd.org/bridges-news/trade-negotiations-insights/overview.

Gill, S., (2012). *Global Crises, and the Crisis of Global Leadership*. Cambridge and New York: Cambridge University Press.

Gilman, S., (2005). *Ethics Codes and Codes of Conduct as Tools for Promoting and Ethical and Professional Public Service*. Washington, DC: World Bank.

Ginsberg, M., (1951). Ethical Relativity and Political Theory. *The British Journal of Sociology* Vol. 2, No. 1. pp. 1–11.

Girardin, B., (2012). *Ethics in Politics: Why it Matters More Than Ever and How It Can Make a Difference?* Geneva. Available at www.globalethics.net.

Girvan, N., (2011). *"Existential Threats in the Caribbean: Democratising Politics, Regionalising Governance"*. The CLR James Memorial lecture presented at the CLR James Lecture Theatre at the Cipriani Labour College, Valsayn. Available at http://www.caribbeanreview.org/2010/07/promises%e2%80%a6-promises%e2%80%a6-promises.

Girvan, N., (2015). Assessing Westminster in the Caribbean: Then and Now. *Commonwealth and Comparative Politics* Vol. 53, No. 1. pp. 95–107.

Glover, J., (2010). A conflict of values. In Citizen Ethics Network. *Citizen Ethics in a Time of Crisis*. London: Citizen Ethics Network/Barrow Cadbury Trust. Available at http://www.barrowcadbury.org.uk/wp-content/uploads/2012/07/Citizens-Ethics. pdf.

Goede, M., (2016). The history of public administration in the Dutch Caribbean. In Minto-Coy, I., and Berman, E., (Eds.) *Public Administration and Policy in the Caribbean*. Baton Rouge: CRC Press, Taylor and Francis Group.

Goodin, R. E., (1988). Review: Political Ethics and Public Office by Dennis Thompson. *Political Theory* Vol. 16, No. 4. pp. 663–666.

Goodin, R. E., (1995). *Utilitarianism as a Public Philosophy*. Cambridge: Cambridge University Press.

Goodin, R., Moran, M., and Rein, M., (2008). *The Oxford Handbook of Public Policy*. Oxford: Oxford University Press.

Gotz, N., and Marklund, C., (Eds.) (2014). *The Paradox of Openness: Transparency and Participation in Nordic Cultures of Consensus*. Lieden: Brill.

Goulet, D., (1971). *The Cruel Choice*. New York: Atheneum.

Goulet, D., (1988). Tasks and Methods in Development Ethics. *Cross Currents* Vol. 38, No. 2. pp. 146–163.

Goulet, D., (1995). *Development Ethics: A Guide to Theory and Practise*. New York: Apex Press.

Goulet, D., (1996). *A New Discipline: Development Ethics*. The Helen Kellog Institute for International Studies, University of Notre Dame. Available at https://kellogg.nd.edu/publications/workingpapers/WPS/231.pdf.

Goulet, D., (2000). Changing Development Debates under Globalization. Working Paper No. 276, delivered at The Helen Kellogg Institute for International Studies. Available at https://kellogg.nd.edu/publications/workingpapers/WPS/276.pdf.

Goulet, D., (2005a). *Lebret, a Pioneer, Pt I*. Available at http://www.lebret-irfed.org /spip.php?article403.

Goulet, D., (2005b). *Lebret, a Pioneer, Pt II*. Available at http://www.lebret-irfed.o rg/spip.php?article403.

Goulet, D., (2006). *Development Ethics at Work: Explorations 1960-2002*. New York: Routledge.

Graig, E.J., (2005). *Meeting the Ethical Challenges of Leadership*. New Delhi: Sage Publications.

Graham, M., and Haarstad, H., (2011). Transparency and Development: Ethical Consumption and Economic Development Through Web 2.0 and the Internet of Things. *Information Technologies and International Development* Vol. 7, No. 1. pp. 1–18.

Granovetter, M., and Swedberg, R., (Eds.) (2011). *The Sociology of Economic Life*. Colorado: Westview Press.

Granovetter, M., (2017). *Society and Economy: Framework and Principles*. Cambridge: The Belknap Press of Harvard University Press.

Granvorka, C., (2016) Poverty in the Caribbean. In Minto-Coy, I., and Berman, E., (Eds.) *Public Administration and Policy in the Caribbean*. Baton Rouge: CRC Press, Taylor and Francis Group.

Grew, R., (1977). Modernization and Its Discontents. *American Behavioural Scientist*, Vol. 21, No. 2. pp. 289–312.

Grindle, M., (2004). Good Enough Governance: Poverty Reduction and Reform in Developing Countries. In *Governance: An International Journal of Policy, Administration and Institutions* Vol. 17. pp. 525–548. Also available at http://cit eseerx.ist.psu.edu/viewdoc/download?doi=10.1.1.614.7940&rep=rep1&type=pdf.

Grindle, M., (2010). *Good Governance: The Inflation of an Idea*. Harvard Kennedy School Faculty Research Working Paper Series, RWP10-023, John F. Kennedy School of Government, Harvard University. Also available at https://dash.harvard .edu/bitstream/handle/1/4448993/grindle_goodgovernance.pdf?sequence=1.

Grindle, M., (2011). Good enough Governance Revisited. *Development Policy Review* Vol. 29. pp. 199–221.

Gunatilleke, G., Tiruchelvam, N., Coomaraswamy, R., (Eds.) (1983). *Ethical Dilemmas of Development in Asia*. London: Lexington Books.

Gutmann, A., and Thompson, D., (2006). *Ethics and Politics: Cases and Comments* (4th edition). Chicago, IL: Nelson-Hall.

Guyana Chronicle (2009). Editorial: The Need to Arrest Lawlessness. *The Guyana Chronicle*. Available at https://guyanachronicle.com/2009/04/02/the-need-to-arre st-lawlessness.

Habermas, J., (1990). *Moral Consciousness and Communicative Action*. Cambridge, MA: MIT Press.

Hall, K., and Benn, D., (Eds.) (2001). *The Caribbean Community: Beyond Survival*. Kinston: Ian Randle Publishers.

Hall, K., (Ed.) (2003). *Integrate or Perish: Perspectives of Heads of Government of the Caribbean Community and Commonwealth Caribbean Countries 1963-2002*. Kingston: Ian Randle Publishers.

Hall, K., and Benn, D., (Eds.) (2004). *Governance in the Age of Globalization*. Kingston: Ian Randle Publishers.

Hall, K., and Benn, D., (2005). *Caribbean Imperatives: Regional Governance and Integrated Development*. Kingston: Ian Randle Press.

Hall, K., and Chuck-A-Sang, M., (2007). *The Caribbean Integration Process: A People-Centred Approach*. Kingston: Ian Randle Publishers.

Hamelink, C., (1997). Making moral choices in development co-operation: The agenda for ethics. In Hamelink, C., (Ed.) *Ethics and Development - On Making Moral Choices in Development Co-operation*. Kampen, The Netherlands: Uitgeverij Kok.

Hampshire, S., (Ed.) (1978). *Public and Private Morality*. Cambridge: Cambridge University Press.

Hampshire, S., (2010). *Justice is Conflict*. Cambridge MA: Princeton University Press.

Hanna, N., (2010). *Transforming Government and Building the Information Society: Challenges and Opportunities for the Developing World*. New York: Springer.

Harris, J., and Freeman, R., (2008). The impossibility of the separation thesis. *Business Ethics Quarterly* Vol. 18, No. 4. pp. 541–548.

Hausman, D., and Mcpherson, M., (2006). *Economic Analysis, Moral Philosophy, and Public Policy*. New York: Cambridge University Press.

Hartnell, N., (2016). Political parties lack big ideas. *The Tribune 242*, Online Edition. Available at http://www.tribune242.com/news/2016/apr/25/political-parties-lack-big-ideas/.

Harrison, L., (2000). Promoting progressive cultural change. In Huntingdon, S., and Harrison, L., (Eds.) *Culture Matters: How Values Shape Human Progress*. New York: Basic Books.

Hay, C., (Ed.) (2010). *New Directions in Political Science*. Hampshire: Palgrave Macmillan.

Head, B., (2008). Wicked Problems in Public Policy. *Public Policy* Vol. 3, No. 2. pp. 101–118.

Heckscher, C., and Donnellon, A., (Eds.) (1994). *The Post-Bureaucratic Organization: New Perspectives on Organizational Change*. London: Sage.

Heckscher, C., (1994). Introduction. In Heckscher, C., and Donnellon, A., (Eds.) *The Post-Bureaucratic Organization: New Perspectives on Organizational Change*. London: Sage.

Helleiner, G. K., (2001). Markets, Politics, and Globalization: Can the Global Economy Be Civilized? *Journal of Human Development* Vol. 2, No. 1. pp. 27–46.

Hellsten, S., (2019). Corruption. In Drydyk, J., and Keleher, L., (Eds.) *The Routledge Handbook of Development Ethics*. London: Routledge.

Henke, H., and Reno, F., (Eds.) (2003). *Modern Political Culture in the Caribbean*. Kingston: University of the West Indies Press.

Henry, C. M., (1987). Economic Growth and Economic Development: A distinction without a difference. *Social and Economic Studies* Vol. 36, No. 4. pp. 67–85.

Hewitt de Alcántara, C., (1998). Uses and Abuses of the Concept of Governance. *International Social Science Journal* Vol. 50, No. 155. pp. 105–113.

Hickel, J., (2012). The World Bank and the development delusion. *Opinion Piece*. Available at http://www.aljazeera.com/indepth/opinion/2012/09/201292673233 720461.html.

Hicks, C., (2007). A Case for Public Sector Ethics. *Policy Quarterly*. Institute of Policy Studies, Vol. 3, No. 3. pp. 11–15.

Hicks, S., (2008). Ethics and economics. In *The Concise Encyclopedia of Economics*. Available at http://www.econlib.org/library/Enc/EthicsandEconomics.html.

Hinds, D., (2008). Beyond Formal Democracy: The Discourse on Democracy and Governance in the Anglophone Caribbean. *Commonwealth and Caribbean Politics* Vol. 46, No. 3. pp. 388–406.

Hintzen, P., (2014). After modernization, globalization and the African Dilemma. In Bloom, P., Miescher, S., and Manuh, T., (Eds.) *Modernization as Spectacle in Africa*. Bloomington: Indianna University Press.

Hirschman, D., (2016). Stylised facts in the Social Sciences. In *Sociological Science*, Vol. 3. pp. 604–626.

Hofmeister, W., and Grabow, K., (2011). *Political Parties: Functions and Organization in Democratic Societies*. Singapore: Konrad Adenauer Stiftung.

Hofstede, G., (2012). National cultures, organizational culture and the role of management. In BBVA Foundation. *Values and Ethics for the Twenty-First Century*. Available at https://www.bbvaopenmind.com/wp-content/uploads/2013/10/Values -and-Ethics-for-the-21st-Century_BBVA.pdf.

Hodgkinson, C., (1996). *Administrative Philosophy: Values and Motivations in Administrative Life*. Oxford: Elsevier Science Ltd.

Hodgson, G., (1988). *Economics and Institutions*. Cambridge: Polity Press.

Hondeghem, A., (1998). *Ethics and Accountability in a Context of Governance and New Public Management*. Leuvan: EGPA/IOS Press.

Hood, C., Margetts, H., and 6, P., (2010). The drive to modernize: A world of surprises? In Margetts, H., Hood, C., and 6, P., (Eds.) *The Paradoxes of Modernization. Unintended Consequences of Public Sector Reform*. Oxford: OUP.

Hood, C., (1998). Remedies for misgovernment: Changing the mix, but not the ingredients?. In Hondeghem, A., (Ed.). *Ethics and Accountability in a Context of Governance and New Public Management*. Leuvan: EGPA/IOS Press.

Howard, A., (2010). Perspective on Practice: A New Global Ethic. *Journal of Management Development* Vol. 29, No. 5. pp. 506–517.

Howard, J., (2019). The public role of ethics and public policy. In Lever, A., and Poama A., (Eds.) *The Routledge Handbook of Ethics and Public Policy*. Routledge: London.

Hurley, G., (2013). The Caribbean's Silent Debt Crisis. Sheffield Political Economy Research Institute. Available at http://speri.dept.shef.ac.uk/2013/10/28/caribbeans -silent-debt-crisis/.

Huntingdon, S., (1971). The Change to Change: Modernization Development and Politics. *Comparative Politics* Vol. 3, No. 3. pp. 283–322.

Huntingdon, S., and Harrison, L., (Eds.) (2000). *Culture Matters: How Values Shape Human Progress*. New York: Basic Books.

Hutton, W., (2010). Self-serving half-truths trick us. In Citizen Ethics Network. *Citizen Ethics in a Time of Crisis*. London: Citizen Ethics Network/Barrow Cadbury Trust. Available at http://www.barrowcadbury.org.uk/wp-content/up loads/2012/07/Citizens-Ethics.pdf.

Hyden, G., Court, J., and Mease, K., (2004). *Making Sense of Governance: Empirical Evidence from Sixteen Developing Countries*. Boulder, CO and London: Lynne Rienner Publishers.

IFEX-ALC (2012). *Annual Report on Impunity 2012: Faces and Traces of Freedom of Expression in Latin America and the Caribbean*. Toronto: IFEXALC. Available at https://ifex.org/alc/es/impunidad2012/en/sobre.html.

Indiviglio, D., (2011). Do economists need a Code of Ethics. *The Atlantic Daily*. Available athttps://www.theatlantic.com/business/archive/2011/01/do-economists -need-a-code-of-ethics/68807.

Inglehart, R., (1997). *Modernization and Post-Modernization: Cultural, Economic and Political Change in Forty-Three Societies*. Princeton, NJ: Princeton University Press.

Inglehart, R., and Baker, W., (2000). Modernization Cultural Change and the Persistence of Calues. *American Sociological Review* Vol. 65, No. 1. pp. 19–51.

Inglehart, R., and Welzel C., (2005). *Modernization, Cultural Change and Democracy: The Human Development Sequence.* Cambridge: Cambridge University Press.

Inglehart, R., and Welzel C., (2009). Development and Democracy: What We Know About Modernization Today. *Foreign Affairs* March/April, pp. 33–41.

International Institute for Democracy and Electoral Assistance (IDEA) (2016). *The Quality of Democracies in Latin America.* Stromsborg, Sweden: IDEA.

International Monetary Fund (1997–2020). *Good Governance: The IMF's Role: 1997-2020* Washington, DC: International Monetary Fund.

International Monetary Fund (IMF) (2015). *IMF Data Mapper.* Available at http://www.imf.org/external/datamapper/DEBT1/OEMDC/SDVEC/WEOWORLD/ATG/BRB/BHS/BLZ/DMA/GRD/GUY/HTI/JAM/TTO/SUR/VCT/LCA/KNA.

Institute for Global Ethics (2016). *The Foundation of an Ethical Culture.* Available at https://www.globalethics.org/documents/the_foundation_of_an_ethical_culture.pdf.

Institute for the Integration of Latin America and the Caribbean (INTAL Connection) (2017). *High-Level Dialogue on International Financial Architecture: Ethics and Economics.* Available at http://conexionintal.iadb.org/2017/01/31/etica-y-economia-un-dialogo-de-alto-nivel-camino-al-g20-2018/?lang=en#_ftnref1.

Issa, A., and David, A. K., (2012). The Challenges of Leadership and Governance in Africa. In *International Journal of Academic Research in Business and Social Sciences* Vol. 2, No. 9. pp. 142–157.

Jackal, R., (1991). *Moral Mazes: Bureaucracy and Managerial Work.* Boston: Harvard Business School Press.

Jagan, C., (1988) The role of the state in development. In Schuyler, G., and Veltmeyer, H., (Eds.) *Rethinking Caribbean Development.* Canada: International Education Centre.

James, O., (2010). A missed opportunity. In Citizen Ethics Network. *Citizen Ethics in a Time of Crisis.* London: Citizen Ethics Network/Barrow Cadbury Trust. Available at http://www.barrowcadbury.org.uk/wp-content/uploads/2012/07/Citizens-Ethics.pdf.

Jamaica Observer (2018). Ethics is in an Organization's highest interest. *Jamaica Observer* Online Edition available at http://www.jamaicaobserver.com/business-observer/ethics-is-in-an-organisation-8217-s-highest-interest_132568.

Jessop, D., (2009). *Caribbean Regionalism.* Available at http://www.bbc.co.uk/caribbean/news/story/2009/06/090602_jessop_caribbean_regionalism.shtml.

Jessop, D., (2012). Banks, fraud and Caribbean exposure. *The Jamaica Gleaner* Online Edition. Available at http://jamaica-gleaner.com/gleaner/20120701/business/business73.html.

Johnson, A., (2007). Bridging the gap: Ethics, social capital and economic accumulation in Jamaica. In Cowell, N. Campbell, A., Chen, G., and Moore, S., (Eds.) *Ethical Perspectives for Caribbean Business.* Kingston: Arawak Publications.

Jones, C., (2009). "Interdisciplinary Approach: Advantages, Disadvantages, and the Future Benefits of Interdisciplinary Studies". *ESSAI*, Vol. 7, No. 26. Available at: http://dc.cod.edu/essai/vol7/iss1/26.

Jones, E., (2003). Institutional design for sub-national governance. In Hall, K., and Benn, D., (Eds.) *Governance in the Age of Globalization* (2004). Kingston: Ian Randle Publishers.

Jones, E., Walcott, A., and Grey-Alvaranga, S., (2016). Contending with Caribbean public sector leadership in the twenty-first century. In Minto-Coy, I., and Berman, E., (Eds.) *Public Administration and Policy in the Caribbean*. Baton Rouge: CRC Press, Taylor and Francis Group.

Kaufmann, D., and Kraay, A., (2007). *Governance Indicators: Where Are We, Where Should We Be Going?* Policy Research Working Paper. The World Bank.

Keefer, P., and Vlaicu, R., (2017). *Vote Buying and Campaign Promises*. Available at SSRN https://ssrn.com.

Keen, A., (2007). *The Cult of the Amateur. How Today's Internet is Killing our culture*. New York: Doubleday.

Keen, A., (2012). *Digital Vertigo: How Today's Social Revolution is Dividing, Diminishing and Disorienting Us*. New York: St. Martin's Press.

Kelsen, H., (1948). Absolutism and Relativism in Philosophy and Politics. *The American Political Science Review* Vol. XLII, No. 6. pp. 906–914.

Keohane, R. O., and Nye, J., (2000). Globalization: What's New? What's Not? (And So What?). *Foreign Policy*, no. 118, pp. 104–119.

Khan, J., (1982). *Public Management: The Eastern Caribbean Experience*. The Hague: Smits.

Kiely, R., (2006). Modernization theory. In Clark, D., (Ed.) *The Elgar Companion to Development Studies*. Northampton: Edward Elgar.

Kiely, R., (2014). Global shift: Industrialisation and development. In Desai, V., and Potter, R., (Eds.) *The Companion to Development Studies*. London: Routledge.

Kille, K., (2007). *The United Nations Secretary-General and Moral Authority: Ethics and Religion in International Leadership*. Washington DC: Georgetown University Press.

Kim, Y., (1999). *A Common Framework for Ethics in the Twenty-First Century*. Paris: UNESCO.

Klak, T., (2014) World-systems theory: Core, semi-peripheral, and peripheral regions. In Desai, V., and Potter, R., (Eds.) *The Companion to Development Studies*. London: Routledge.

Kliest, C., (2019). Global ethics: Capabilities approach. *Internet Encyclopedia of Philosophy: A Peer-Reviewed Academic Resource*. Available at https://www.iep.utm.edu/ge-capab/.

Kliksberg, B., (1999). Social Capital and Culture: Master Keys to Development. *CEPAL Review* No. 69, pp. 83–102. Santiago: Chile. Available at http://www.cepal.org/publicaciones/xml/6/20116/kliksberg.pdf.

Kliksberg, B., (2012). Re-examining the relationship between ethics and the economy. In BBVA Foundation. *Values and Ethics for the Twenty-First Century*. Available at https://www.bbvaopenmind.com/wp-content/uploads/2013/10/Values-and-Ethics-for-the-21st-Century_BBVA.pdf.

Knight, F., and Palmer, C., (Eds.) (1989). *The Modern Caribbean*. London: The University of North Carolina Press.

Knights, D., and Willmot, H., (Eds.) (2007). *Introducing Organizational Behaviour Management*. Hampshire: Cengage Learning.

Kolthoff, E., Huberts, L., and Heuvel, H., (2007). The Ethics of New Public Management: Is integrity at stake?. *Public Administration Quarterly* Vol. 30, No. 4. pp. 399–439.

Kooiman J., (2003). *Governing as Governance*. London: Sage.

Kraft, M., and Furlong, S., (2015). *Public Policy: Politics, Analysis and Alternatives*. London: Sage.

Knill, C., and Tosun, J., (2012). *Public Policy a New Introduction*. New-York: Palgrave MacMillan.

Kragelund, P., (2018). International cooperation for development. In Veltmeyer, H., and Bowles, P., (Eds.) *The Essential Guide to Critical Development Studies*. Routledge: New York.

Küng, H., (1997). *A Global Ethic for Global Politics and Economics*. London: SCM Press.

Küng, H., (2009). *A Declaration towards Global Ethics*. Geneva: Global Ethics.

Kung, H., (2012). The Global Economic Crisis requires a global ethic. In BBVA Foundation. *Values and Ethics for the Twenty-First Century*. Available at https://www.bbvaopenmind.com/wp-content/uploads/2013/10/Values-and-Ethics-for-the-21st-Century_BBVA.pdf.

Lafollette, H., (1991). The Truth in Ethical Relativism. *Journal of Social Philosophy*, Vol. 22, No. 1. pp. 146–154.

Lafollette, H., (Ed.) (2013). Pragmatic ethics. In Lafollette, H., and Persson, I., (Eds.) *The Blackwell Guide to Ethical Theory*. Oxford: Wiley Blackwell.

Lafollette, H., (Ed.) (2013). *International Encyclopedia of Ethics*. Oxford: Wiley-Blackwell.

Lafollette, H., and Persson, I., (2013). *The Blackwell Guide to Ethical Theory*. Oxford: Wiley Blackwell.

Laguerre, J., and Bissessar, A., (2009). The Role of Leadership in Public Management: The Case of Trinidad and Tobago and Guyana. *Social and Economic Studies: Special Issue in honour of Edwin Jones* Vol. 58, No. 1. pp. 125–139.

Landau, R. S., (Ed.) (2013). *Ethical Theory: An Anthology*. West-Sussex: Wiley-Blackwell Publishing.

Landau, R., (Ed.) (2018). *The Ethical Life: Fundamental Readings in Ethics and Moral Problems*. New York: Oxford University Press.

Landes, D., (2000). Culture makes almost all the difference. In Huntingdon, S., and Harrison, L., (Eds.) *Culture Matters: How Values Shape Human Progress*. New York: Basic Books.

Lapeyre, F., (2004). *Globalization and Structural Adjustment as a Development Tool*. Geneva: ILO.

Lasch, C., (1979). *The Culture of Narcissism: American Life in the Age of Diminishing Expectations*. London: W.W. Norton.

Laszlo, E., Baker, R., and Eisenberg, E., (1978). *The Objectives of the New International Economic Order*. New York: Pergamon Press.

Lasswell, H. D., (1951). *The Political Writings of Harold D. Lasswell*. Glencoe, IL: Glencoe Press.

Lasswell, H., Lerner, D., and Montgomery, J., (Eds.) (1976). *Values and Development: Appraising Asian Experience.* Cambridge: MIT Press.

Lederach, J., (1997). *Building Peace: Sustainable Reconciliation in Divided Societies.* Washington, DC: United States Institute of Peace.

Lerner, D., (1958). *The Passing of Traditional Society.* New York: Free Press.

Lent, A., (2010). The ethical is political. In Citizen Ethics Network. *Citizen Ethics in a Time of Crisis.* London: Citizen Ethics Network/Barrow Cadbury Trust. Available at http://www.barrowcadbury.org.uk/wp-content/uploads/2012/07/Citizens-Ethics.pdf.

Lepenies, P., (2014). New institutional economics and development. In Desai, V., and Potter, R., (Eds.) *The Companion to Development Studies.* London: Routledge.

Lessig, L., (2009). Against transparency: The perils of openess in government. *The New Republic.* Available at https://newrepublic.com/article/70097/against-transparency.

Lever, A., and Poama A., (Eds.) (2019). *The Routledge Handbook of Ethics and Public Policy.* Routledge: London.

Levitt, K., (2018). History from a critical development perspective. In Veltmeyer, H., and Bowles, P., (Eds.) *The Essential Guide to Critical Development Studies.* Routledge: New York.

Levitt, K., (2005). *Reclaiming Development: Independent Thought and Caribbean Community.* Kingston: Ian Randle Publishers.

Levy, B., (2014). *Working With the Grain: Integrating Governance and Growth in Development Strategies.* Oxford: Oxford University Press.

Lewis, G. K., (1968). *The Growth of the Modern West Indies.* London: Monthly Review Press.

Lewis, V. A., (2010). The long transition: thinking ourselves through change of our circumstances. In Meeks, B., and Girvan, N., (Eds.) *Caribbean Reasonings: The Thought of New World: The Quest for Decolonisation.* Jamaica: Ian Randle Publishers.

Lewis, W.A., (1950). The industrialisation of the British West Indies. In *Caribbean Economic Review*, Vol. 12. Mona: University of the West Indies Mona Campus.

Lewis, W.A., (1965). *Theory of Economic Growth.* London: George Allen & Unwin.

Lewis, W. A., (1977) *The Evolution of the International Economic Order.* Princeton, NJ: Princeton University Press.

Lewis, L., (2006). Re-regulating the State in the celebration of the Market and the crisis of civil society in the Commonwealth Caribbean. *Ca0ribbean Quarterly*, June-September.

Lewis, L., (Ed.) (2013). *Caribbean Sovereignty Development and Democracy in an Age of Globalisation.* Oxford: Taylor and Francis.

Lindsay, S., (2000). Culture, mental models, and national prosperity. In Huntingdon, S., and Harrison, L., (Eds.) *Culture Matters: How Values Shape Human Progress.* New York: Basic Books.

Lipset, S. M., (1959). Some Social Requisites of Democracy: Economic Development and Political Legitimacy. *The American Political Science Review* Vol. 53, No. 1. pp. 69–105.

Lipset, S. M., (1960). *Political Man: The Social Bases of Politics.* New York: Doubleday.

Lomborg, B., (Ed.) (2013). *Global Crisis, Global Solutions.* Cambridge: Cambridge University Press.

Longstaff, S., (1998). *The Ethical Dimension of Corporate Governance.* Available at http://www.ethics.org.au/on-ethics/blog/december-1998/the-ethical-dimension-of -corporate-governance.

Lovin, R. W., (2014). *Ethics and Politics: Restoring a Moral Vocabulary.* The Maguire Lecture, delivered at the Kluge Center-The Library of Congress.

Lukes, S., (1990). Marxism and Morality: Reflections on the Revolutions of 1989. *Ethics and International Affairs* Vol. 4. pp. 19–31.

Madden, F., (2011). *It's not Sbout Me: Working with Communities: Processes and Challenges, The Grace and Staff Community Development Foundation Experience.* Kingston: Phoenix Publishing.

Mackie, J. L., (2013). The Subjectivity of Values. In Shafer-Landau, R., (Ed.) *Ethical Theory: An Anthology.* Oxford: Wiley-Blackwell.

Maclean, D., (1998). The ethics of cost-benefit analysis: Incommensurable, Incompatible and incomparable values. In Carrow, M., Churchill, R., and Cordes, J., (Eds.). *Democracy, Social Values, and Public Policy.* Westport, CT: Praeger.

Maguire, M., (1998). Ethics in the public service - Current issues and practice. In Hondeghem, A., (Ed.) *Ethics and Accountability in a Context of Governance and New Public Management.* Leuven: EGPA/IOS Press.

Malavisi, A., (2014). The Need for an Effective Development Ethics. *Journal of Global Ethics* Vol. 10. No. 3. pp. 297–303.

Malavisi, A., (2019) Epistemology. In Drydyk, J., and Keleher, L., (Eds.) *The Routledge Handbook of Development Ethics.* London: Routledge.

Manley, M., (1988). Caribbean development in historical perspective. In Schuyler, G., and Veltmeyer, H., (Eds.) *Rethinking Caribbean Development.* Canada: International Education Centre.

Marczak, J., Engelke, P., Bohl, D., Saldarriaga, J., (2016). *Latin America and the Caribbean 2030: Future Scenarios.* Washington, DC: Atlantic Council and Inter-American Development Bank.

Margetts, H., (2010). Modernization dreams and public policy reform. In Margetts, H., Hood, C., and 6, P., (Eds.). *The Paradoxes of Modernization. Unintended Consequences of Public Sector Reform.* Oxford: OUP.

Margetts, H., Hood, C., and 6, P., (Eds.) (2010). *The Paradoxes of Modernization. Unintended Consequences of Public Sector Reform.* Oxford: OUP.

Marshall, D., (2014). The new world group of dependency scholars: Reflections of a Caribbean avant-garde movement. In Desai, V., and Potter, R., (eds.) *The Companion to Development Studies.* London: Routledge.

Martin, R. L., (2000). Institutional approaches to economic geography. In Barnes, T., and Sheppard, E., (Eds.). *Companion to Economic Geography.* Oxford: Blackwell.

Martin, R. L., (2001). Geography and Public Policy: The Case of the Missing Agenda. *Progress in Human Geography* Vol. 25, No. 2. pp. 189–210.

Massy, A., and Bovens, M., (1998). Report of the working group on responsibility. In Hondeghem, A., (Ed.) *Ethics and Accountability in a Context of Governance and New Public Management.* Leuvan: EGPA/IOS Press.

Mayanja, E., (2013). *Strengthening Ethical Political Leadership for Sustainable Peace and Social Justice in Africa: Uganda as a Case Study.* African Centre for the Constructive Resolution of Disputes. Available at http://www.accord.org.za/ ajcr-issues/%EF%BF%BCstrengthening-ethical-political-leadership-for-sustain able-peace-and-social-justice-in-africa/.

Mazrui, A., (2004). *The Ethics of Africa's Governance: Rights, Rules and Relativism.* Accra, Ghana: Africa Legal Aid.

McCloskey, D., (2007). *The Bourgeois Virtues, Ethics for an Age of Commerce.* Chicago: University of Chicago Press.

McIntyre, L., (2018). *Post-Truth.* Cambridge, MA: MIT.

McKoy, D., (2012). *Corruption: Law, Governance and Ethics in the Commonwealth Caribbean.* Hertfordshire: Hansib Publications.

Meeks, B., and Lindahl, F., (Eds.) (2001). *New Caribbean Thought.* Kingston, Jamaica: UWI Press.

Meeks, B., and Girvan, N., (Eds.) (2010). *Caribbean Reasonings: The Thought of New World: The Quest for Decolonisation.* Jamaica: Ian Randle Publishers.

Mendes, M., (2013). Overview of Corruption in the Media in developing countries. *Transparency International.* Available at https://www.u4.no/publications/over view-of-corruption-in-the-media-in-developing-countries/.

Milbank, J., (2010). A free market is a moral market. In Citizen Ethics Network. *Citizen Ethics in a Time of Crisis.* London: Citizen Ethics Network/Barrow Cadbury Trust. Available at http://www.barrowcadbury.org.uk/wp-content/up loads/2012/07/Citizens-Ethics.pdf.

Miller, D., (2011). *Neo-Liberalism Politics and Institutional Corruption: Against the Institutional Malaise Hypothesis.* Available at http://www.academia.edu/128150 67/Neoliberalism_Politics_and_Institutional_Corruption_Against_the_Institutio nal_Malaise_Hypothesis.

Mills, G. E., (1970). Public Administration in the Commonwealth Caribbean: Evolution, Conflicts and Challenges. *Social and Economic Studies* Vol. 19, No. 1. pp. 8–20.

Mills, G. E., (1997). *Westminster Style Democracy: The Jamaica Experience.* Jamaica: The Grace, Kennedy Foundation.

Mills, O., (2014). Our Caribbean: The political party and the elected government. In *Caribbean News Now!* Online Edition. Available at http://www.caribbeannewsn ow.com/headline-Commentary%3A-Our-Caribbean%3A-The-party-and-the-elect ed-government-21011.html.

Minority Rights Group International (MRGI) (2007). *The State of the World's Minorities.* London: MRGI.

Minto-Coy, I., and Berman, E., (Eds.) (2016). *Public Administration and Policy in the Caribbean.* Baton Rouge: CRC Press, Taylor and Francis Group.

Minto-Coy, I., (2016). The History of public administration in the Commonwealth Caribbean. In Minto-Coy, I., and Berman, E., (Eds.) *Public Administration and Policy in the Caribbean.* Baton Rouge: CRC Press, Taylor and Francis Group.

Mintrom, M., (2010). Doing ethical policy analysis. In Boston, J., Bradstock, A., and Eng, D., (Eds.) *Public Policy, Why Ethics Matters.* Canberra: Australia National University Press.

Mishcon de Reya (2017). *Fraud Insights: Corruption in Latin America and the Caribbean.* Available at https://www.mishcon.com/news/articles/fraud-insights-co rruption-in-latin-america-and-the-caribbean.

Montgomery, J., (1976). Toward a value theory of modernization. In Lasswell, H., Lerner, D., and Montgomery, J., (Eds.) *Values and Development: Appraising Asian Experience.* Cambridge: MIT Press.

Moore, G. E., (2013). The subject matter of Ethics. In Shafer-Landau, R., (Ed.) *Ethical Theory: An Anthology.* Oxford: Wiley-Blackwell.

Mullins, G., (2002). "Ethics, Reformation and Development in the Caribbean". The Second, Annual Ethics Lecture of the Jamaica Theological Seminary and Caribbean Graduate School of Theology Public Lecture Series. Available at http://www.glob ethics.net/gel/10215865/ethics-reformation-and-development-in-the-caribbean.

Munck, R., (2018a). Critical development theory: Results and prospects. In Veltmeyer, H., and Bowles, P., (Eds.) *The Essential Guide to Critical Development Studies.* Routledge: New York.

Munck, R., (2018b). Rethinking Latin America: Towards new development para-digms. In Veltmeyer, H., and Bowles, P., (Eds.) *The Essential Guide to Critical Development Studies.* Routledge: New York.

Munroe, T., (1999). *Renewing Democracy into the Millennium.* Kingston: The Press, University of the West Indies.

Murray, W. E., and Overton, J., (2014). *Geographies of Globalization.* London and New York: Routledge.

Nwagboso, J., (2008). *Professional Ethics, Skill and Standards* (Maiden Edition). Jos, Nigeria: Inspirationz Media Konsult.

Namibia Institute for Democracy (NID) and Konrad-Adenauer-Stiftung (KAS) (Eds.) (2000). *Ethics and Good Governance in Namibia.* Windhoek: NID and KAS.

Nation Newspaper (2016). In the Public's Interest House slacking with drop in meet-ings. *Nationnews.* Available at http://www.nationnews.com/nationnews/news/881 89/public-house-slacking-drop-meetings.

Nation Newspaper (2016). Not a Bad Thing. *Nationnews* online. Available at http://www.nationnews.com/nationnews/news/88461/bad.

Nation Newspaper (2017). *Region's Sovereigns All Rated as Junk.* Bridgetown, Barbados: Nation News Publishing Company.

Narveson, J., (2013). Libertarianism. In Lafollette, H., and Persson, I., (Eds.) *The Blackwell Guide to Ethical Theory.* Oxford: Wiley Blackwell.

Neilsen, R., and Massa, F., (2013). Reintegrating Ethics and Institutional Theories. *Journal of Business Ethics* Vol. 115. pp. 135–147.

Neo, B., and Chen, G., (Eds.) (2007). *Dynamic Governance: Embedding Culture Capabilities and Change in Singapore.* Singapore: World Scientific.

Nhema, A., and Zinyama T., (2016). Modernization, Dependency, and Structural Adjustment Development Theories and Africa: A Critical Appraisal. *International Journal of Social Science Research* Vol. 4, No. 1. pp. 151–163.

Nohria N., and Berkley, J., (1994). The virtual organization: Bureaucracy, technology and the implosion of control. In Heckscher, C., and Donnellon, A., (Eds.) *The Post-Bureaucratic Organization: New Perspectives on Organizational Change.* London: Sage.

Norman, J., (2010). The ethical core of conservatism. In Citizen Ethics Network. *Citizen Ethics in a Time of Crisis.* London: Citizen Ethics Network/Barrow Cadbury Trust. Available at http://www.barrowcadbury.org.uk/wp-content/up loads/2012/07/Citizens-Ethics.pdf.

North, D., Acemoglu, D., Fukuyama, F., and D. Rodrik (Eds.) (2008). *Governance, Growth and Development Decision-Making.* Washington, DC: The International Bank for Reconstruction and Development/The World Bank.

North, D.C., Wallis, J., and Weingast, B., (2009). *Violence and Social Orders: A Conceptual Framework for Interpreting Recorded Human History.* Cambridge: Cambridge University Press.

Northouse, P. G., (2004). *Leadership Theory and Practice* (3rd edition). London: Sage Publications.

Nussbaum, M., (2000). *Women and Human Development: The Capabilities Approach.* Cambridge, MA: Cambridge University Press.

Nussbaum, M., (2004). Beyond the Social Contract: Capabilities and Global Justice. *The Journal of Oxford Development Studies* Vol. 32. No. 1. pp. 3–18.

Nussbaum, M., (2011). *Creating Capabilities: The Human Development Approach.* Cambridge: Harvard University Press.

Nunes, F. E., (1976). The Nonsense of Neutrality. *Social and Economic Studies* Vol. 25, No. 4. pp. 347–366.

Nunez, G. G., (2016). Public policy and management in Cuba. In Minto-Coy, I., and Berman, E., (Eds.) *Public Administration and Policy in the Caribbean.* Baton Rouge: CRC Press, Taylor and Francis Group.

Obrien, D., (2013). Fundamental Human Rights and the Community Law of CARICOM. *Oxford Human Rights Hub.* Available at http://ohrh.law.ox.ac.uk/ fundamental-human-rights-and-the-community-law-of-caricom/.

Obrien, D., (2015). Westminster in the Caribbean: The problem with Prime Ministerial Patronage. *International Constitutional Law Blog.* Available at http: //www.iconnectblog.com/2015/06/westminster-in-the-caribbean-the-problem-of-prime-ministerial-patronage/.

Odugbemi, S., and Lee, T., (2011). *Accountability through Public Opinion: From Inertia to Public Action.* Washington, DC: World Bank.

Oppenheim, C., (2010). Ethical policymaking. In Citizen Ethics Network. *Citizen Ethics in a Time of Crisis.* London: Citizen Ethics Network/Barrow Cadbury Trust. Available at http://www.barrowcadbury.org.uk/wp-content/uploads/2012/07 /Citizens-Ethics.pdf.

Organization of American States (OAS) (2002). *Constitutional Reform in the Caribbean.* Washington, DC: OAS. Available at http://www.oas.org/sap/publica

tions/2002/constitutional_reform_caribbean/doc/pbl_constitutional_reform_02 _eng.pdf.

Organization of American States (OAS) (2006) *Declaration of Santo Domingo: Good Governance and Development in the Knowledge-Based Society.* Available at https ://www.oas.org/docs/declarations/AG-DEC-46-Declaration-of-Santo-Domingo -ENG.pdf.

Organisation for Economic Cooperation and Development (OECD) and Brookings Institution (2002). *Public Sector Transparency and Accountability: Making it Happen.* Paris: OECD.

Organisation for Economic Cooperation and Development (OECD) (2005). *Fighting Corruption and Promoting Integrity in Public Procurement.* Paris: OECD.

Orr, S., and Johnson, J., (2019). Models, mechanisms, metrics: The entanglement of methods of policy inquiry with democratic possibilities. In Lever, A., and Poama A., (Eds.) *The Routledge Handbook of Ethics and Public Policy.* Routledge: London.

Osborne, D., and Gaebler T., (1992). *Reinventing Government: How the Entrepreneurial Spirit is Transforming the Public Sector.* London: Penguin.

Ostrom, E., (2003). *Governing the Commons: The Evolution of Institutions for Collective Action.* Cambridge: Cambridge University Press.

Pantin, D., (Ed.) (2005). *The Caribbean Economy: A Reader.* Kingston: Ian Randle Publishers.

Paris, R., (2015). Global Governance and Power Politics: Back to Basics. *Ethics and International Affairs* Vol. 29, No. 4. pp. 407–418.

Parker, M., (Ed.) (1998). *Ethics and Organizations.* London: Sage.

Parker, M., (2003). Introduction: Ethics, Politics and Organizing. *Organization* Vol. 10, No. 2. pp. 187–203.

Parsons, W., (1998). Fuzzy in Theory and Getting Fuzzier in Practice: Post-modern reflections on Responsibility in Public-Administration and Management. In Hondeghem, A., (Ed.) *Ethics and Accountability in a Context of Governance and New Public Management.* Leuven: EGPA/IOS Press.

Parrish, J. M., (2007). *Paradoxes of Political Ethics: From Dirty Hands to the Invisible Hand.* Cambridge: Cambridge University Press.

Patrick, M., (2016). British Virgin Islands find it tough to remove Panama Papers Stain. *Wall Street Journal* Online Edition. Available at https://www.wsj.com/artic les/british-virgin-islands-finds-it-tough-to-remove-panama-papers-stain-14792210 27.

Patterson, M., and Macintyre, M., (2011). *Managing Modernity in the Western Pacific.* Queensland: University of Queensland Press.

Patton, M. Q., (2015). *Qualitative Research and Evaluation Methods.* London: Sage.

Payne, A., and Bishop, M., (2010). *Caribbean Regional Governance and the Sovereignty/Statehood Problem.* In Caribbean Paper No. 8. Waterloo, Ontario: The Centre for International Governance Innovation. Available at www.cigionline .org.

Peacock, J., (1998). The wellsprings of social values. In Carrow, M., Churchill, R., and Cordes, J., (Eds.). *Democracy, Social Values, and Public Policy.* Westport, CT: Praeger.

Perkins, A., (2013). *Moral Disease Making Jamaica Ill: Re-Engaging the Conversation on Morality.* Kingston: Grace Kennedy Foundation.

Perry, C., (1937). The Relation between Ethics and Political Science. *International Journal of Ethics* Vol. 47, No. 2. pp. 163-179.

Petras, J., and Veltmeyer, H., (2018) Imperialism, capitalism and development. In Veltmeyer, H., and Bowles, P., (Eds.). *The Essential Guide to Critical Development Studies.* Routledge: New York.

Phillips, L., (Ed.) (1998). *The Third Wave of Modernization in Latin America: Cultural Perspectives on Neo-Liberalism.* Wilmington, NC: Scholarly Resources Inc.

Polyani, K., (2011). The economy as instituted process. In Granovetter, M., and Swedberg, R., (Eds.). *The Sociology of Economic Life.* Boulder, CO: Westview Press.

Porter, M., (2000). Attitudes, values, beliefs and the microeconomics of prosperity. In Huntingdon, S., and Harrison, L., (Eds.) *Culture Matters: How Values Shape Human Progress.* New York: Basic Books.

Potter, R., Barker, D., Conway, D., and Klak, T., (Eds.) (2004). *The Contemporary Caribbean.* Edinburgh: Pearson Education Limited.

Potter, R., (2014a). Measuring development: From GDP to the HDI and wider approaches. In Desai, V., and Potter, R., (Eds.) *The Companion to Development Studies.* London: Routledge.

Potter, R., (2014b). Theories, strategies and ideologies of development: An overview. In Desai, V., and Potter, R., (Eds.) *The Companion to Development Studies.* London: Routledge.

Potter, R., Binns, T., Elliott, J., Etienne, N., and Smith, D., (2019). *Geographies of Development: An Introduction to Development Studies.* London: Routledge.

Posner, R., (2010). *The Crisis of Capitalist Democracy.* Cambridge, MA: Harvard University Press.

Power, M., (2014). Enlightenment and the era of modernity. In Desai, V., and Potter, R., (Eds.) *The Companion to Development Studies.* London: Routledge.

Pracher, C., (1996). New models of guidance and steering in public administration. In Flynn, N., and Strehl, F., (Eds.) *Public Sector Management in Europe.* London, UK: Prentice Hall.

Prince, R., (2012). Allen Stanford: From King of the Caribbean to penniless in prison. *The Telegraph* Online Edition. Available at http://www.telegraph.co.uk/finance/financetopics/sir-allen-stanford/9321282/Allen-Stanford-From-king-of-the-Caribbean-to-penniless-in-prison.html.

Przeworski, A., (1995). *Sustainable Democracy.* Cambridge: Cambridge University Press.

Pulman, P., (2010). Foreword. In Citizen Ethics Network. *Citizen Ethics in a Time of Crisis.* London: Citizen Ethics Network/Barrow Cadbury Trust. Available at http://www.barrowcadbury.org.uk/wp-content/uploads/2012/07/Citizens-Ethics.pdf.

Putnam, R. D., (1993). *Making Democracy Work: Civic Traditions in Modern Italy.* Princeton, NJ: Princeton University Press.

Quah, J., (2010). *Public Administration Singapore-Style.* Bingley, UK: Emerald Publishing.

Quinn, K., (2015). Introduction: Revisiting Westminster in the Caribbean. *Commonwealth and Comparative Politics* Vol. 53, No. 1. pp. 1–7.

Rabidas, U., (2016). *Are 'Tax Havens' the latest Threats in Row to the Caribbean SIDS: The Panama Papers in Question.* Available at http://hispanicindia.com/are-t ax-havens-the-latest-threats-caribbean-sids-the-panama-papers-in-question.

Rabinow, P., and Sullivan, W., (Eds.) (1979). *Interpretive Social Science: A Reader.* Berkeley: University of California Press.

Ramphal, S., (1991). *To be a Canoe.* Bridgetown: West Indian Commission.

Ramsarran, R., (1988). Industrialization and development: The commonwealth Caribbean experience. In Schuyler, G., and Veltmeyer, H., (Eds.) *Rethinking Caribbean Development.* Canada: International Education Centre.

Ramsaran, R., (Ed.) (2001). *Caribbean Survival and Global Challenge.* Kingston: Ian Randle Publishers.

Raes, K., (1998). Moral powerlessness in relations of subordination moral responsibility and organisational culture. In Hondeghem, A., (Ed.) *Ethics and Accountability in a Context of Governance and New Public Management.* Leuvan: EGPA/IOS Press.

Ratter, B., (2018). *Geography of Small Islands: Outposts of Globalisation.* Hamburg: Elsevier.

Rawls, J., (2001). *Justice as Fairness: A Restatement.* Cambridge MA: Belknap Press.

Rego, S., and Palacios, M., (2016). Ethics and Democracy in Times of Crisis. *Rio de Janeiro* Vol. 40, pp. 63–72.

Reeves, R., (2010). Liberalism: The key to moral renewal. In Citizen Ethics Network. *Citizen Ethics in a Time of Crisis.* London: Citizen Ethics Network/Barrow Cadbury Trust. Available at http://www.barrowcadbury.org.uk/wp-content/up loads/2012/07/Citizens-Ethics.pdf.

Reno, W., (2000). Clandestine Economies, Violence and States in Africa. In *Journal of International Affairs*, Vol. 53. No. 2, pp. 433–59.

Rhodes, R. A. W., (1996). The New Governance: Governance without Government. *Political Studies* Vol. 44. pp. 652–657.

Richards, K., (2017). CSME's struggling status up for discussion at CARICOM Summit in Grenada. *Caribbean News Now Online Edition.* Available at http://www.caribbeannewsnow.com/headline-CSME%27s-struggling-status-up-for-discussion-at-CARICOM-summit-in-Grenada-34945.html.

Ricœur, P., (1991). Ethics and politics. In Ricœur, P. *From Text to Action: Essays in Hermeneutics II.* Evanston: Northwestern University Press.

Rittel, H., and Webber, M., (1973). Dilemmas in a general theory of planning. In *Working Papers from the Urban and Regional Development,* University of California Berkeley, pp. 155–169, reproduced in *Policy Sciences* Vol. 4. pp. 155–169.

Robben, K., (1998). The recent debate on curbing political corruption. In Hondeghem, A. *Ethics and Accountability in a context of governance and New Public Management.* Leuvan: EGPA/IOS Press.

Roberts, N. C., (2002). Keeping Public Officials Accountable Through Dialogue: Resolving the Accountability Paradox. *Public Administration Review* Vol. 62, No. 6, (November/December). pp. 658–669.

Roberts, W., (1941). *The Problem of Choice: An Introduction to Ethics.* Boston: Ginn and Company.

Roberts, T., (2011). CARICOM Governance in Crisis: Challenges of Context and Political Traditions. *Trade Negotiations Insights* Vol. 10. No. 2. Available at www .ictsd.org.

Robbins, L., (1935). An *Essay on the Nature and Significance of Economic Science.* London: Macmillan.

Rodrik, D., (2008). Thinking about governance. In North, D., Acemoglu, D., Fukuyama, F., and D. Rodrik (Eds.) *Governance, Growth and Development Decision-Making.* Washington, DC: The International Bank for Reconstruction and Development/The World Bank.

Rosado, C., (1996). *Towards a Definition of Multiculturalism.* Available at http://ros ado.net/pdf/Def_of_Multiculturalism.pdf.

Rose-Ackerman, S., (2014). Corruption and development. In Desai, V., and Potter, R., (Eds.) *The Companion to Development Studies.* London: Routledge.

Rose-Ackerman, S., and Truex, R., (2013). Corruption and policy reform. In Lomborg, B., (Ed.) *Global Crisis, Global Solutions.* Cambridge: Cambridge University Press.

Rosen, M., (2000). The Marxist critique of morality and the theory of ideology. In Harcourt, E., (Ed.) *Morality, Reflection and Ideology* (2001). Oxford: Clarendon Press

Rosenau, J. N., and Singh, J. P., (Eds.) (2002). *Information Technologies and Global Politics: The Changing Scope of Power and Governance.* Albany, NY: State University of New York Press.

Roser, M., (2019). *Global Inequality of Opportunity.* Available at https://ourworl dindata.org/global-inequality-of-opportunity.

Rossouw, D., and Stuckelberger, C., (Eds.) (2012). *Global Survey of Business Ethics in Teaching Training and Research.* Geneva: Global ethics.net.

Rostow, W.W., (1962) *The Stages of Economic Growth: A Non-Communist Manifesto.* London: Cambridge University Press.

Russell, B., (1947). *Philosophy and Politics.* Cambridge: Cambridge University Press.

Rustomjee, C., (2017). *Pathways through the Silent Crisis: Innovations to Resolve Unsustainable Caribbean Public Debt.* CIGI Papers No 125. Available at https ://www.cigionline.org/publications/pathways-through-silent-crisis-innovations-re solve-unsustainable-caribbean-public-debt.

Ryan, S., (1999). *Winner Takes All: The Experience of Westminster in the Caribbean.* St. Augustine, Trinidad and Tobago: ISER.

Ryan, S., (2001). Democratic governance in the anglophone Caribbean. In Meeks, B., and Lindahl, F., (Eds.) *New Caribbean Thought,* Kingston, Jamaica: UWI Press.

Ryan, S., and Bissessar, A., (2002). *Governance in the Caribbean*. St. Augustine, Trinidad and Tobago: ISER.

Sachs, J., (2000). Notes on a new sociology of economic development. In Huntingdon, S., and Harrison, L., (Eds.) *Culture Matters: How Values Shape Human Progress*. New York: Basic Books.

Sandel, M., (1984). *Liberalism and Its Critics: Readings in Social and Political Theory*. New York: NYU Press.

Sandel, M., (1996). *Democracy's Discontent: America in Search of a Public Philosophy*. Cambridge, MA: Harvard University Press.

Sandel, M., (2006). *Public Philosophy: Essays on Morality in Politics*. Cambridge: Harvard University Press.

Sandel, M., (2010). We need a public life with purpose. In Citizen Ethics Network. *Citizen Ethics in a Time of Crisis*. London: Citizen Ethics Network/Barrow Cadbury Trust. Available at http://www.barrowcadbury.org.uk/wp-content/up loads/2012/07/Citizens-Ethics.pdf.

Satz, D., (2010). *Why Some Things Should Not Be for Sale: The Moral Limits of Markets*. Oxford: Oxford University Press.

Schumann, S., (2015). *How the Internet Shapes Collective Actions*. Oxford: Palgrave Macmillan.

Schwenke, C., (2008). *Reclaiming Value in International Development: The Moral Dimensions of Development Policy and Practice in Poor Countries*. Westport, CT: Greenwood Press.

Schwenke, C., (2019). Development practitioners: Absent in the deliberative discourse on development ethics. In Drydyk, J., and Keleher, L., (Eds.) *Routledge Handbook of Development Ethics*. London: Routledge.

Scott, D., (2004). Modernity that predated the Modern: Sidney Mintz's Caribbean. *History Workshop Journal* Vol. 58 (Autumn) pp. 191–210.

Schlick, M., (1939). *Problems of Ethics*. New York: Prentice Hall.

Schuyler, G., and Veltmeyer, H., (Eds.) (1988) *Rethinking Caribbean Development*. Canada: International Education Centre.

Shuler, D., (2008). An ethical dilemma: The imposition of values on other cultures. In Reid, L,. (2008). *Global Mormonism in the 21st Century*. Brigham Young University: Religious Studies Centre. Also available at https://rsc.byu.edu/archived /global-mormonism-21st-century/part-v-international-challenges-facing-church/18 -ethical.

Sen, A., (1987). *On Ethics and Economics*. Oxford: Blackwell.

Sen, A., (1999a). Democracy as a Universal Value. *Journal of Democracy* Vol. 10. pp. 3–17.

Sen, A., (1999b). *Development as Freedom*. New York: A knopf.

Sen, A., (2000). *"What Difference Can Ethics Make?"* Available at http://sadc-reep .org.za/MESA%20Toolkit/4)%20Module%202/Values%20and%20Ethics/Ethics- %20Sen.pdf.

Sen, A., (2003). "Ethical Challenges: Old and New". Paper presented at the International Congress on "The Ethical Dimensions of Development: The New

Ethical Challenges of State, Business and Civil Society". Available at www.iadb .org/etica/ingles/index-i.cfm.

Sen, A., (2003). Development as capability expansion. In Fukuda-Parr, S., and Kumar, Shiva A. K., (Eds.) *Readings in Human Development*. Oxford: Oxford University Press.

Sen, A., (2009). *The Idea of Justice*. Cambridge, MA: Belknap.

Serageldin, I., and Martin-Brown, J., (Eds.) (1997). *Ethics and Global Values*. Washington, DC: The World Bank.

Shafer-Landau, R., (Ed.) (2013). *Ethical Theory: An Anthology*. Oxford: Wiley-Blackwell.

Shah, R., (2014). Politics and Ethics Only Rhyme. *Trinidadandtobagonews.com*, online edition. Available at https://www.trinidadandtobagonews.com/blog/?p=8391.

Shue, H., (2008). The ethical dimensions of public policy. In Goodin, R., Moran, M., and Rein, M., (Eds.) *The Oxford Handbook of Public Policy*. Oxford: Oxford University Press.

Singer, P., (2012). Ethics and poverty. In BBVA Foundation. *Values and Ethics for the twenty-first Century*. Available at https://www.bbvaopenmind.com/wp-content/ uploads/2013/10/Values-and-Ethics-for-the-21st-Century_BBVA.pdf.

Singh, R., (2012). CARICOM's Challenge of Declining Moral Values. *The Jamaica Observer Newspaper*, online edition. Available at http://www.jamaicaobserver .com/columns/Caricom-s-challenge-of-declining-moral-values_12340078.

Singh, R., (2016). Our Caribbean: Painful Truth about CARICOM. *The Nation News Paper*, online edition. Available at http://www.nationnews.com/nationnews/news /85230/caribbean-painful-truth-about-caricom.

Snellen, I., and Donk, V.W., (1998). Report of the study group on informatization in public administration. In Hondeghem, A., (Ed.) *Ethics and Accountability in a Context of Governance and New Public Management*. Leuven: EGPA/IOS Press.

Smith, M., (2013). Moral Realism. In Lafollette, H., and Persson, I., (2013). *The Blackwell Guide to Ethical Theory*. Oxford: Wiley Blackwell.

Smith, A. D., (2016). Samoa's Prime Minister defends country's role as Offshore Tax Haven. *The Guardian Online Edition*. Available at https://www.theguardian.com/ global-development/2016/jul/01/samoa-prime-minister-defends-offshore-tax-have n-panama-papers-mossack-fonseca-tuilaepa-aiono-sailele-malielegaoi.

Smith, L., (2014). The Flaws of Westminster- The Winner Takes All. *The Cayman Reporter* Online Edition. Available at http://www.caymanreporter.com/2014/06/13 /the-flaws-of-westminster-the-winner-takes-all/.

Sookram, R., (2016). Corporate Governance in the Emerging Economics of the Caribbean: Peculiarities, Challenges and a Future Pathway. *The Journal of Values-Based Leadership* Vol. 9, No. 1, Article 9. pp. 1–20. Available at http://scholar. valpo.edu/jvbl/vol.9/iss1/9.

Souffrant, E., (2019). *Global Development Ethics: A Critique of Global Capitalism*. London: Rowman and Littlefield.

Soverall, W., (2016). Civil service performance in the Caribbean. In Minto-Coy, I., and Berman, E., (Eds.) *Public Administration and Policy in the Caribbean*. Baton Rouge: CRC Press, Taylor and Francis Group.

Spragens, T., (1973). *The Dilemma of Contemporary Political Theory: Toward a Post Behavioural Science of Politics*. New York: Dunellen.

Srebrnik, H., (2004). Small Island nations and Democratic Values. *World Development* Vol. 32, No. 2. pp. 329–341.

Staples, K., (2004). *The Norms and Ethics of Deliberative Democracy Beyond Liberalism*. Working paper, Manchester: University of Manchester.

Stark, A., (2003). *Conflict of Interest in American Public Life*. Cambridge: Harvard University Press.

Stiglitz, J., (2000). *Ethics, Economic Advice and Economic Policy*. A publication of Carnegie Council. Available at http://www.policyinnovations.org/ideas/policy_libr ary/data/01216.

Stiglitz, J., (2003). Towards a new paradigm of development. In Dunning, J., (Ed.) *Making Globalization Good: The Moral Challenges of Global Capitalism*. Oxford: Oxford University Press.

Stiglitz, J., Sen, A., and Fitoussi, J.P., (2010). *Mis-measuring our Lives: Why GDP Doesn't Add Up*. New York: The New Press.

Sterba, J., (2013). Toward reconciliation in Ethics. In Lafollette, H., and Persson, I., (Eds.) *The Blackwell Guide to Ethical Theory*. Oxford: Wiley Blackwell.

Stolle, D. Stoker, L., (1992). Interests and Ethics in Politics. In *The American Political Science Review* Vol. 86, No. 2, June, pp. 369–380.

Stolle, D., (2007). Social capital. In Dalton, R. J., and Klingemann, H. D., (Eds.) *Oxford Handbook of Political Behaviour*. Oxford: Oxford University Press.

Stone, D., (2012). *Policy Paradox: The Art of Political Decision Making*. New-York: W.W. Norton and Company Publishers.

Strang, J., (1999). Ethics as politics: On Aristotelian ethics and its context. In Brinkman, K., (Ed.) *Ethics, Vol. 1 (The Proceedings of the Twentieth World Congress of Philosophy)*. Boston: Bowling Green State University.

Strange, J., (1999). *Ethics as Politics: On Aristotelian Ethics and Its Context*. Boston: Boston University, The Paidiea Project. Available at https://www.bu.edu/wcp/Pa pers/Anci/AnciStra.htm.

Sumner, L. W., (2013). Rights. In Lafollette, H., and Persson, I., (Eds.) *The Blackwell Guide to Ethical Theory*. Oxford: Wiley Blackwell.

Sutton, P., (1999). Democracy in the Commonwealth Caribbean. *Democratization* Vol. 6, No. 1. pp. 67–86.

Sutton P., and Bissessar, A., (2006). *Modernizing the state, public-sector reform in the Caribbean*. Kingston, Jamaica: Ian Randle Press.

Sutton, P., (2008). Public Sector Reform in the Commonwealth Caribbean: A Review of Recent Experiences. *Caribbean Paper* No. 6. Available at cigionline.org.

Sutton, H., and Ruprah, I., (Eds.) (2017). *Restoring Paradise in the Caribbean: Combatting Violence with Numbers*. Washington, DC: Inter-American Development Bank.

Sznajder, M., Roniger, L., and Forment, C., (Eds.) (2013). *Shifting Frontiers of Citizenship: The Latin American Experience*. Boston: Brill.

Taylor, C., (1979) Interpretation and the Sciences of Man. In Rabinow, P., and Sullivan, W., (Eds.) *Interpretive Social Science: A Reader*. Berkeley: University of California Press.

Taylor, C., (2012). Secularism and Multiculturalism. In BBVA Foundation. *Values and Ethics for the Twenty-First Century*. Available at https://www.bbvaopen mind.com/wp-content/uploads/2013/10/Values-and-Ethics-for-the-21st-Century_BBVA.pdf.

The Jamaica Gleaner (2015). Grace Kennedy: Cable Operators and Unashamedly Ethical. *The Jamaica Gleaner* Online Edition. Available at http://jamaica-glean er.com/article/commentary/20150507/grace-kennedy-cable-operators-and-unasha medly-ethical.

Thompson, D. F., (1987). *Political Ethics and Public Office*. Cambridge, MA: Harvard University Press.

Thompson, D., (1991). *The Paradoxes of Political Ethics*. Speech given to Office of Government Ethics, United States of America. Available at http://www.cityethics .org/harvard-lab/oge-speech.

Thompson, D., (2017). Designing responsibility: The problem of many hands in complex organisations. In Van den Hoven, J., Miller, S., and Pogge, T., (Eds.) *Designing in Ethics*. Cambridge University Press.

Thompson, D., (2018). Political ethics. In Lafollette, H., (Ed.) *International Encyclopedia of Ethics*. Oxford: Wiley-Blackwell.

Thompson, D., (2019). The political ethics of political campaigns. In Lever, A., and Poama A., (Eds.) *The Routledge Handbook of Ethics and Public Policy*. Routledge: London.

Tirole, J., (2018). *Morality and the Market*. J.M Keynes Lecture delivered at The University of Cambridge. Available at www.econ.cam.ac.uk.

Toonen, T., and Doorn, N., (2017). Good Governance for the Commons: Design for Legitimacy. In Van den Hoven, J., Miller, S., and Pogge,T., (Eds.) *Designing in Ethics*. Cambridge University Press.

The South Commission (1990). *The Challenge to the South: The Report of the South Commission*. Oxford: Oxford University Press.

Transparency International (TI) (2000). *Confronting Corruption: the Elements of a National Integrity System*, TI Source Book 2000. Available at www.transparency .org/publications/sourcebook.

Transparency International (TI) (2005). *National Integrity Systems Caribbean Composite Study 2004*, Berlin, Germany: Transparency International.

Transparency International (TI) (2017). *Corruption Perception Index 2016*. Available at https://www.transparency%20international2016_CPIReport_EN.pdf.

Trusted, J., (1998). The origin of social values. In Carrow, M., Churchill, R., and Cordes, J., (Eds.) *Democracy, Social Values, and Public Policy*. Westport, CT: Praeger.

Tutu, D., (2000). *No Future Without Forgiveness* (1st Image Books edition). New York: Doubleday.

Twiss, S., (2011). Global Ethics and Human Rights: A reflection. *Journal of Religious Ethics* Vol. 2, No. 39. pp. 204–222.

Uhr, J., (2010). Be careful what you wish for. In Boston, J., Bradstock, A., and Eng, D., (Eds.) *Public Policy, Why Ethics Matters*. Canberra: Australia National University Press.

United Nations General Assembly (UNGA) (1974). *The Declaration on the Establishment of a New International Economic Order*. New York: UNGA.

United Nations International Children's Emergency Fund (UNICEF) (2005). *Voices of Caribbean Youth: A Report on the Youth Forum and on the Caribbean Regional Consultation on the UN Secretary General Study on Violence Against Children.* Available at https://sustainabledevelopment.un.org/sids2014/samoapathway.

United Nations Department of Economic and Social Affairs (UNDESA) (2005). *Toward Participatory and Transparent Governance: Report on the Sixth Global Forum on Reinventing Government.* New York: United Nations.

United Nations Educational Scientific and Cultural Organisation (UNESCO) (2000). *A Report from the Expert Meeting on Ethics for the Twenty-First Century.* Paris: UNESCO.

United Nations Development Programme (UNDP) (1997). *Governance and Sustainable Human Development.* New York: UNDP.

United Nations Development Programme (UNDP) (1998). *UNDP and Governance: Experience and Lessons Learned. Management Development and Governance Division, Lessons-Learned Series No. 1.* New York: UNDP.

United Nations Development Programme (UNDP) (2006). *Governance for the Future: Democracy and Development in the Least Developed Countries Report.* New York: UNDP.

United Nations Development Programme (UNDP) (2012). *Caribbean Human Development Report (2012) Caribbean Human Development Report 2012: Human Development and the Shift to Better Citizen Security.* New York: United Nations.

United Nations Development Programme (UNDP) (2016). *Caribbean Human Development Report: Multidimensional Progress: Well-Being Beyond Income.* New York: UNDP.

United Nations General Assembly (UNGA) (2014). *SIDS Accelerated Modalities of Action (SAMOA) Pathway.* New York: UNGA also available at https://sustainabled evelopment.un.org/sids2014/samoapathway.

United Sates Agency for International Development (USAID) (2005–2020). *USAID Anti-Corruption Strategy.* Washington, DC: USAID.

Ujomo, P., and Olatunji, F., (2015). Morality and the Sustenance of Social Order in Africa. *Law and Politics* Vol. 13, No. 2. pp. 169–186.

Van den Hoven, J., Miller, S., and Pogge, T., (Eds.) (2017). *Designing in Ethics.* Cambridge University Press.

Van der Linden, H., (1984). Marx and Morality: An Impossible Synthesis? *Theory and Society* Vol. 13, No. 1. pp. 119–135. Available at https://digitalcommons.bu tler.edu/facsch_papers/132.

Veenendaal, W., and Corbett, J., (2015). Why Small States offer Important Answers to Large Questions. *Comparative Political Studies* Vol. 48, No. 4. pp. 527–549.

Veltmeyer, H., and Bowles, P., (Eds.) (2018). *The Essential Guide to Critical Development Studies.* Routledge: New York.

Verineulen, P., (1998). The Civil Servant, Society and the Citizen in Quest of Good Ethical Behaviour. In Hondeghem, A., (Ed.) *Ethics and Accountability in a Context of Governance and New Public Management.* Leuvan: EGPA/IOS Press.

Vernon, M., (2010). Ethics with a little help from friends. In Citizen Ethics Network. *Citizen Ethics in a Time of Crisis.* London: Citizen Ethics Network/Barrow

Cadbury Trust. Available at http://www.barrowcadbury.org.uk/wp-content/up loads/2012/07/Citizens-Ethics.pdf.

VOX (2016) *Against Transparency Government Officials' Emails Should Be Private Just Like Their Phone Calls.* Available at https://www.vox.com/2016/9/6/127322 52/against-transparency.

Waeyenberge, E., (2018). The post-Washington consensus. In Veltmeyer, H., and Bowles, P., (Eds.). *The Essential Guide to Critical Development Studies.* Routledge: New York.

Walzer, M., (1983). *Spheres of Justice. A Defense of Pluralism and Equality.* New York: Basic Books.

Walzer, M., (1973). Political Action: The Problem of Dirty Hands. *Philosophy and Public Affairs* Vol. 2. pp. 160–180.

Weale, A., (2019). Public policy and normative methods. In Lever, A., and Poama A., (Eds.). *The Routledge Handbook of Ethics and Public Policy.* Routledge: London.

West Indian Commission (WIC) (1992). *Time for Action: Report of the West Indian Commission.* Barbados: West Indian Commission.

Wildavsky, A., (2018). *Speaking Truth to Power: The Art and Craft of Policy Analysis.* New-York: Palgrave MacMillan.

Williams, R., (2010). How to live as if we were human. In Citizen Ethics Network. *Citizen Ethics in a Time of Crisis.* London: Citizen Ethics Network/Barrow Cadbury Trust. Available at http://www.barrowcadbury.org.uk/wp-content/up loads/2012/07/Citizens-Ethics.pdf.

Williamson, R. D. V., (1947). The Challenge of Political Relativism. *The Journal of Politics* Vol. IX, No. 2. pp. 147–177.

Winston, K., (2015) *Ethics in Public Life: Good Practitioners in a Rising Asia.* New York: Palgrave Macmillan.

Witztum, A., (2007). Ethics and the science of economics: Robbin's enduring fallacy. In Cowell, F., and Witztum, A., (Eds.) *Lionel Robbin's Essay on the Nature and Significance of Economic Science, 75th Anniversary Conference Proceedings.* London: London School of Economics and Political Science's Suntory and Toyota International Centres for Economics and Related Disciplines (SUNTORY). Available at http://darp.lse.ac.uk/papersdb/LionelRobbinsConferenceProveedings Volume.pdf.

Woolcock, M., (2010). The RISE and Routinization of Social Capital, 1988–2008. *Annual Review of Political Science* Vol. 13. pp. 469–487.

Wood, A., (2004). *Relativism.* Available at http://web.stanford.edu/~allenw/web papers/ and https://web.stanford.edu/~allenw/webpapers/Relativism.doc.

The World Bank (1991). *The Challenge of Development: World Development Report, 1991.* New York: Oxford University Press.

The World Bank (1994a). *Development in Practice: Governance. The World Bank's Experience.* Washington, DC: World Bank.

The World Bank (1994b). *Governance: The World Bank's Experience.* Washington, DC: World Bank.

The World Bank (1997). The State in a Changing World. *World Development Report.* Washington, DC: World Bank.

The World Bank (2000). *Entering the 21st century: World Development Report 2000.* Washington, DC: Oxford University Press.

The World Bank (2001). *Building Institutions for Markets: World Development Report 2001.* Washington, DC: Oxford University Press.

The World Bank (2017). Governance and the Law. In *World Development Report.* Washington, DC: World Bank.

World Tribune (2017a). Unrest roils Dominica after reports reveal government's collusion with China, Iran. *World Tribune* Online Edition. Available at http://www.worldtribune.com/unrest-roils-dominica-after-reports-reveal-governments-collusion-with-china-iran.

World Tribune (2017b). Dominica crisis update: Prime Minister Skerrit struggling for political survival. *World Tribune* Online Edition. Available at http://www.worldtribune.com/dominica-crisis-update-prime-minister-skerrit-struggling-for-political-survival.

Wray-Bliss, E., (2007). Ethics at work. In Knights, D., and Willmot, H., (Eds.) *Introducing Organizational Behaviour Management.* Hampshire: Cengage Learning.

Wray-Bliss, E., (2013). A Crisis of Leadership: Towards an Anti-Sovereign Ethics of Organization. *Business Ethics: A European View* Vol. 22, No. 1. pp. 86–101.

Wucherpfennig, J., and Deutch, J., (2009). *Modernization and Democracy: Theories and Evidence revisited,* published by Living reviews of Democracy. Available at https://www.ethz.ch/content/dam/ethz/special-interest/gess/cis/cis-dam/CIS_DAM_2 015/WorkingPapers/Living_Reviews_Democracy/Wucherpfennig%20Deutsch.pdf.

Yeh, S., (1989). *Understanding Development: Modernization and cultural values in Asia and the Pacific Region.* Hawaii: UNESCO.

Young, I., (2000). *Inclusion and Democracy.* Oxford: Oxford University Press.

Yung, B., and Yu, K., (Eds.) (2016). *Ethical Dilemmas in Public Policy: The Dynamics of Social Values in the East-West Context of Hong Kong.* Hong Kong: Springer.

Index

Note: *Italicized* pages refer to tables

Protestantism, 70
psychic empathy, 105
public debt. *See* debt/GDP ratio
public opinion, 173–77
public policy, 23, 58, 215–17;
    challenges of, 11–14; national,
    216; "nonspatial," 215–16; path
    dependency in, 219; societal values
    and, 70; spatial biases, 216; wicked,
    96–97n1
public–private partnerships, 192
public sector, 62–63; responsibilities
    of, 63
public sector reform, 12, 103
public work, 213
Putnam, R. D., 135

quality of life, 203
quantification of government, 125–27
quantitative *versus* qualitative methods,
    31–34

Rabinow, P., 42n10
rational choice theory, 72, 97n3
rationalities, 28
Rawls, John, 47
Rawlsians, 84
realpolitik, 65
reason, 204, 209; contemplative, 221n4;
    practical, 221n4
reciprocity, 47
*Reconstruction and Interpretation in the
    Social Sciences* (Habermas), 42n10
redistributive justice, 83–84. *See also*
    distributive justice
regional network, 3
regulatory-based systems, 68
relativism, 150, 203–18; absolutism
    versus, 204, 206; appeal to, 204;
    cultural, 204–7; dealing with, 210;
    defenders of, 203; objective reality,
    210; as a philosophical construct,
    210; philosophical subdisciplines,
    204; principled, 208, 210; problem
    with, 209; social values, 212–14;

subjective reality, 210; time and,
    211; universalist pretentions, 205
religion, 209
religious beliefs, 47
religious freedom, 128
remittances, 10–11
rent seeking, 182
Reporters Without Borders (RSF) Press
    Freedom Index, 166
representative democracy, 2, 108, 128,
    200
representative government, 122–23,
    127–30, 134, 145, 147
The Republic (Plato), 48
responsibility: changing dimension of,
    122–25; civil servants with, 123;
    politicians with, 123
Revised Treaty of Chaguaramas, 139
revolving doors, 182, 192
rights: conflict of, 131–33; rhetoric, 131;
    as safeguards, 131
Roberts, Alasdair, 170
Rodrik, Dani, 211–12
root cause analysis, 24
Rose-Ackerman, S., 184–85
*The Routledge Handbook of
    Development Ethics* (Drydyk and
    Keleher), 97n4
rugged individualism, 111

scapegoating, 182
Schumpeter, Joseph, 197
science, 27, 42n10; economic, 72;
    ethics, 50, 55, 60n2; innovations in,
    115; management, 75–79; modern
    natural, 60n2; monopoly on reason
    and truth, 209; value-free, 72
scientific discoveries, 26
scientific knowledge, 64
scientific method/turn, 60n2
secession of the successful, 137
secular asceticism, 111
secularization of culture, 110–11
separation thesis, 27
service and knowledge workers, 110

About the Author

Pearson A. Broome received his BA (Hons.) Double Major in History and Political Science from the University of the West Indies Cave Hill Campus; his MSc. (Econ.) Development Studies/International Relations from the London School of Economics and Political Science; and his PhD. Information Technology and Economic Development from the University of Cambridge, England; a Diploma in Diplomatic training from the San Andreas Bello Diplomatic Academy, Santiago Chile and a Post-Graduate Certificate in Teaching and Learning (Distinction) University of the West Indies, Cave-Hill Campus. He has worked in the Barbados Foreign Service and the CARICOM Secretariat in Georgetown Guyana.

He joined the Department of Government, Sociology and Social Work at the University of the West Indies, Cave Hill Campus, Bridgetown, Barbados where he lives currently and is a lecturer in Political Science and the Program Coordinator for the Post-Graduate Diploma in Public Sector Management and the MSc. e-Governance for Small Island Developing Countries.

He also has diverse working experience in the Caribbean and served as a Consultant for the UNDP, the Commonwealth Secretariat, Caricom Single Market and Economy Unit, CARICAD, and CARICOM Secretariat. His research interests include:

- E-governance/e-government/e-commerce/e-democracy with particular emphasis on the theoretical approaches and the institutionalization of ICTs.
- Digital activism and civic engagement.
- ICTs and the globalization process focusing on outsourcing, trade, investment, and technology transfer flows; the evaluation of national

ICT Policies and national systems of innovation and Science and Technology Policy.
- Restructuring of state bureaucracies and the developmental state.
- Industry 4.0 and the future of work in developing countries.
- Public policy and the ethics of governance in developing countries.